DATE DUE

DEMCO, INC. 38-2931

THE
State
OF THE
Animals
2001

edited by **Deborah J. Salem**
and **Andrew N. Rowan**

Humane Society Press
an affiliate of

**THE HUMANE SOCIETY
OF THE UNITED STATES.**

Deborah J. Salem is director and editor in chief
of Humane Society Press.

Andrew N. Rowan is senior vice president for research,
education, and international issues for The Humane
Society of the United States.

First edition
ISBN 9658942-3-l
Library of Congress Control Number 2001131096

Printed in the United States of America

Humane Society Press
An affiliate of The Humane Society of the United States
2100 L Street, NW
Washington, D.C. 20037

Contents

Preface v

Overview
   Paul G. Irwin 1

1. A Social History of Postwar Animal Protection
   Bernard Unti and Andrew N. Rowan 21

2. Cruelty to Animals: Changing Psychological, Social, and Legislative Perspectives
   Frank R. Ascione and Randall Lockwood 39

3. Social Attitudes and Animals
   Harold Herzog, Andrew N. Rowan, and Daniel Kossow 55

4. From Pets to Companion Animals
   Researched by Martha C. Armstrong, Susan Tomasello,
   and Christyna Hunter 71

5. Farm Animals and Their Welfare in 2000
   David Fraser, Joy Mench, and Suzanne Millman 87

6. Progress in Livestock Handling and Slaughter Techniques in the United States, 1970–2000
   Temple Grandin. 101

7. Animal Research: A Review of Developments, 1950–2000
   Andrew N. Rowan and Franklin M. Loew. 111

8. The First Forty Years of the Alternatives Approach: Refining, Reducing, and Replacing the Use of Laboratory Animals
   Martin L. Stephens, Alan M. Goldberg, and Andrew N. Rowan 121

9. Is There a Place in the World for Zoos?

David Hancocks 137

Another View of Zoos

Richard Farinato 145

10. Animal Protection in a World Dominated by the World Trade Organization

Leesteffy Jenkins and Bob Stumberg 149

11. Urban Wildlife

John Hadidian and Sydney Smith 165

12. Fertility Control in Animals

Jay F. Kirkpatrick and Allen T. Rutberg 183

List of Contributors 199

Index 201

Preface

The Humane Society of the United States (HSUS) envisions a world in which people meet the physical and emotional needs of domestic animals; protect wild animals and their environments; and change their interaction with other animals, evolving from exploitation and harm to respect and compassion. Since this vision, and its supporting mission, have been the guiding principles underlying The HSUS's far-flung activities, we wished to make a data-based assessment of our progress (or lack of progress) toward achieving them. This volume is the result of our goal of developing an analytical framework for evaluating progress. While it is not comprehensive, we hope that you will find it to be a creditable beginning.

We chose the authors of the contributed chapters for their knowledge and expertise in a particular area of animal protection. As far as possible, we paired an HSUS staff person with an "outside" expert to provide a broad perspective on each issue. The authors were asked to review the ways in which their fields have changed in the past fifty years—from 1950 to 2000. As a result, we have chapters reviewing the care and welfare of companion animals, laboratory animals, farm animals, and wild animals. In addition, there is a chapter reviewing developments in the animal protection community itself and another addressing public attitudes to animal welfare. An overview chapter by the HSUS President Paul G. Irwin offers a broad summary of changes and progress in each field.

This volume is envisioned as the first in a series reviewing the state of animal protection in North America and worldwide. This series will form the cornerstone of the Public Policy Series of our newly-formed Humane Society Press (HSP). HSP's Public Policy Series is planned as a source of information and informed opinion for policymakers, the academic community, animal advocates, and the media.

The editors wish to thank Lester Brown and the Worldwatch Institute for providing an excellent model for this volume, and we especially wish to express our appreciation to all the contributors for their commitment to the project. In addition, we wish to thank Paul G. Irwin for his encouragement and support and all the HSUS staff who helped make the volume what it is, most notably Creative Director Paula Jaworski and copyeditor Kristin Zimmer. All these individuals have put in time and effort to produce what we hope you, the reader, will view as a valuable publication, *The State of the Animals: 2001*.

Overview: The State of Animals in 2001

Paul G. Irwin

The blizzard of commentary marking the turn of the millennium is slowly coming to an end. Assessments of the past century (and, more ambitiously, the past millennium) have ranged from the self-congratulatory to the condemnatory. Written from political, technological, cultural, environmental, and other perspectives, some of these commentaries have provided the public with thoughtful, uplifting analyses. At least one commentary has concluded that a major issue facing the United States and the world is the place and plight of animals in the twenty-first century, positing that the last few decades of the twentieth century saw unprecedented and unsustainable destruction of the natural world. This was taking place even as the concepts of animal rights and human obligations gained currency in modern life for the first time (Irwin 2000).

My own conclusions aside, it seems highly appropriate for scholars, researchers, and opinion makers in the animal protection and animal research fields to evaluate the position of animals in society at the dawn of the twenty-first century. Many contributors to this volume are members of the staff of The Humane Society of the United States (HSUS) and, as such, share an overarching commitment to creating a more humane society. Others are scholars from higher education. All of the contribu-

tors have taken part in a fascinating, sometimes frustrating, dialogue that seeks to balance the needs of the natural world with those of the world's most dominant species—and in the process create a truly humane society.

The strains created by unrestrained development and accelerating harm to the natural world make it imperative that the new century's understanding of the word "humane" incorporate the insight that our human fate is linked inextricably to that of all nonhuman animals and that we all have a duty to promote active, steady, thorough notions of justice and fair treatment to animals and nonhuman nature.

A humane society is compassionate, sustainable, and just. It counts on a hopeful worldview that calls on the better qualities of all people. It is driven by the moral imperative that every creature deserves (1) our concern, by which we mean a caring heart, (2) our respect, by which we mean a mindful attitude, and (3) our consideration, by which we mean intellectual engagement with the threats and diminutions to that animal's well-being. It is perhaps obvious why The HSUS believes it has as its mission the creation of a humane society. Indeed our vision statement envisions a world in which people meet the physical and emotional needs of domestic animals; protect wild animals and their

environments; and change their interactions with other animals, evolving from exploitation and harm to respect and compassion.

Based upon that mission, The HSUS almost fifty years after its founding in 1954, "has sought to respond creatively and realistically to new challenges and opportunities to protect animals" (HSUS 1991), primarily through legislative, investigative, and educational means.

It is only coincidentally that the choice has been made to view the animal condition through thoughtful analysis of the past half century—the life span of The HSUS—rather than of the past hundred years. It is in the last half-century that the role of animals in modern life has changed in unprecedented ways. Only in the last half century, for example, have domestic animals in the developed world been freed from lives as beasts of burden or have nonhuman primates been granted recognition, by some thinkers, as so cognitively similar to their human relatives that they merit inclusion in the human social framework of protection and justice (Cavalieri and Singer 1993).

From the animals' perspective, the past half-century has not been one of uninterrupted progress, however. Indeed, as some conditions have improved, others have remained frustratingly unchanged, and still others have undoubtedly deteriorated.

Table 1
Shelter Euthanasia of Owned Animals

Year	Total Owned Dogs and Cats	Euthanized	Approximate % of Owned Animals Euthanized
1973	65 million	13.5 million	21.0
1982	92 million	8–10 million	10.0
1992	110 million	5–6 million	5.5
2000	120 million	4–6 million	4.5

How then to assess progress and failure? In the absence of a universally accepted, consistently applied set of standards for data collection and analysis, any attempt to answer the question, What is the state of animals in 2001?, must be based on a series of snapshots, an accumulation of statistics from which we can draw conclusions.

How Has the State of the Animals Improved?

Dogs and Cats: No Longer Expendable Property

In 1950 in the United States, by and large, dogs and cats were termed "pets" and typically roamed and reproduced at will. If they made nuisances of themselves, they were relegated to the "pound," where they received an unmourned, often inhumane, death. If they wandered off or were hit by cars, their human families—if they had one—might view the loss regretfully, but fatalistically. Leash laws, spay/neuter contracts, animal-care facilities, and companion animals were alien concepts. By 2000 most "pounds" had given way to "animal shelters" and "animal-care-and-control facilities" and spaying and neutering had become part of the concept of "responsible pet own-

ership." The term "pet" itself had begun to be replaced by the more dignified and evocative "companion animal," which was being applied to animals who carried with them more than minimal monetary value.

There are few good data on owned animal populations in the United States from 1950 to 1972. From 1970 onwards, however, we have relatively reliable trend information as a result of surveys by a variety of organizations. The surveys do not all agree in terms of the total number of owned dogs and cats, but the trend data are the same. In summary, the number of owned dogs and cats has increased from around 60 million in 1970 to around 115–120 million in 2000. While total numbers of owned dogs and cats have steadily increased (because the total number of households in the United States almost doubled, from around 60 to 100 million, over this time period), the actual rate of ownership of dogs (i.e., the number per household) began to decline in the mid- to late-1980s while the rate of ownership of cats stabilized in the mid- to late-1990s (Patronek and Rowan 1995; Rowan and Williams 1987). Currently, approximately 32 percent of households own at least one dog and 28 percent own at least one cat (Rowan 1992a; AVMA 1997). Over the same time frame, the number of stray or feral dogs appears to have declined substantially. The same cannot be said of stray and feral cats. There are no reliable estimates of the stray and feral cat population in the United States, but it could range from 25 to 50 million individuals.

From 1973 to the present, the demographics of dogs and cats in shelters has changed dramatically. Table 1 presents summary estimates of what has happened in the nation's approximately 3,000 shelters (data from Rowan and Williams 1987; Rowan 1992b; HSUS 2000).

As one can see, shelters have made tremendous strides in reducing both the absolute and the relative number of animals euthanized because they are not wanted. Other evidence indicates that the rates of sterilization of owned animals are already high and continue to rise slowly and that there are parts of the country where it is difficult to find puppies available for adoption in shelters. Shelters are now addressing the challenges represented by the stray and feral cat populations by reaching out to cat colony feeders and are also looking at the challenges posed by harder-to-adopt groups of dogs (e.g., those with behavior problems and older animals).

A number of trends can be cited as proof of improving conditions for dogs and cats. The most enlightened shelters have invested in better facilities, better training of shelter personnel, and broad-based public education campaigns extolling the benefits of pet sterilization; they have developed more innovative adoption policies, better forms of euthanasia and sterilization, and a more sophisticated interaction with local governing bodies. Other shelters have struggled to improve their efforts in these areas as expectations in their communities rose. Dialogue on the validity of euthanasia as a means of pet population control and on the intrinsic value of companion animals above and beyond their "market" value has added a moral dimension to the previously unexplored relationship between "guardian" and "companion animal." An expanding recognition of the link between cruelty to animals and other forms of human violence has legitimized concerns about pet abuse. Such concerns have goaded law enforcement officials into pursuing abusers more vigorously and judges into sentencing offenders to more than a slap on the wrist. Knee-jerk, simplistic responses, such as dog-breed-specific bans, to community companion animal problems have prompted serious discussions of responsible pet ownership, discussions that would have been impossible to hold in 1950. The need for data on pet population demographics spawned the creation of the National Council on Pet Population Study and Policy in 1993.

The decline in pound seizures and the widening disapproval of puppy mills reflected the rejection of the concept of dogs and cats as commodities. That rejection was nowhere more evident than in the revulsion generated nationwide in 1998 by the revelation that foreign-made clothing and novelties using dog and cat fur were being sold in the United States (HSUS 1998). Federal legislation to ban the items (which are produced under inhumane conditions) was introduced in the U.S. Congress and by mid-2000 had thirteen cosponsors.

The Decline in Sport Hunting

The number of hunters as a percentage of the population has been declining in the United States for nearly thirty years (see Table 2). A number of factors are thought to be contributing to the decline, including lack of discretionary recreational time; difficulty in gaining access to acreage on which hunting is permitted; decreasing acreage on which hunting is permitted (and the resultant crowded conditions experienced therein); and most important, changes in the social support system that once encouraged hunting as a recreational pastime, but that now discourages it.

State wildlife agencies, most of which rely heavily on sales of hunting and fishing licenses and disbursement of hunting-related federal dollars for their funding, are concerned by the decline (see Table 3). In recent years they have developed programs aimed at retaining current hunters and recruiting new ones, focusing on under-

Table 2
Hunters, by Census Division, 1955–1985

Year	Number of Hunters (Millions)	Total U.S. Population (Millions)*	Percent
1955	11.8	118.4	10.0
1960	14.6	131.2	11.2
1965	13.6	142.0	9.6
1970	14.3	155.2	9.2
1975	17.1	171.9	9.9
1980	16.7	184.7	9.1
1985	16.3	195.7	8.4

*U.S. population twelve years and older

Note: 1955 was the first year that the survey was conducted. The information is based on data from seven surveys conducted every five years, from 1955 to 1985.

Source: 1991 National Survey of Fishing, Hunting, and Wildlife-associated Recreation, U.S. Fish and Wildlife Service

Table 3
Paid Hunting License Holders, 1989–1999

Year	Number of Paid License Holders (Millions)*	National Population Estimate (Millions)**	Percentage of Population that Hunts
1999	15.1	273.8	5.5
1998	14.9	270.3	5.5
1997	14.9	267.8	5.6
1996	15.2	265.2	5.7
1995	15.2	262.8	5.8
1994	15.3	260.3	5.9
1993	15.6	257.8	6.1
1992	15.8	255.0	6.2
1991	15.7	252.2	6.2
1990	15.8	249.5	6.3
1989	15.9	246.8	6.4

*A paid license holder is one individual regardless of the number of licenses purchased.

Source: Fiscal Year Reports of U.S. Fish and Wildlife Service, Office of Federal Aid

**Source: Historical National Population Estimates, Population Estimates Program, Population Division, U.S. Census Bureau

Table 4
Public Opinion on Wearing Fur

Question	Year	% Accepting Fur	% Opposing Fur
Is it okay to wear (ranch) fur coats? (Sieber 1986)*	1986	45	47
Thinking about specific ways that humans assert their dominance over animals, please tell me if you think each of the following practices is wrong and should be prohibited by law, if you personally disapprove but don't feel it should be illegal, or if it is acceptable to you: Killing animals to use their skins for fur coats. (Roper Center 1989a)	1989	13	85
Do you think there are some circumstances where it's perfectly okay to kill an animal for its fur or do you think it's wrong to kill an animal for its fur? (Roper Center 1989b)	1989	50**	46***
Do you generally favor or oppose the wearing of clothes made of animal furs? (Balzar 1993)	1993	35	50
The use of animal fur in clothing should be banned in the United States. (Survey Research Center, University of Maryland, College Park 1999)	1999	43.8	51.4

*Survey of 802 Toronto adults
**Responding that under some circumstances it would be all right to kill an animal for its fur.
***Responding that it would always be wrong to kill an animal for its fur.

represented constituencies such as women and children. How long one remains an active hunter is strongly associated with the age at which one first begins to hunt, so state agencies are recruiting very young hunters through special licenses and special children's days. Most state wildlife agencies sponsor "outdoors woman" workshops that focus on developing skills associated with sport hunting. Sport hunting continues an overall decline that began in 1975, both in overall numbers and in percent of the

population taking part in the activity.

The best news for animals may be that the decline in hunting has more to do with changes in society—a growing rejection of the idea of killing for fun—than with any logistical problems that make hunting more difficult. In the late 1970s, 64 percent of 2,500 Americans surveyed approved of recreational hunting provided that the hunter used the meat (Kellert 1979). A 1993 poll by the *Los Angeles Times* found that 54 percent of the polled sample opposed hunting

for sport—a reversal in attitudes in twenty years (Balzar 1993). A 1995 Associated Press poll revealed similar attitudes (Foster 1995).

The decline of hunting in the United States is likely to continue.

The Decline in Trapping and Fur Sales

Since the 1980s, the fur fashion industry also has declined significantly. Once a widely desired symbol of

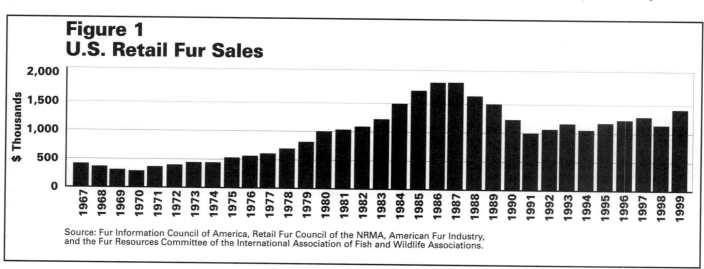

Figure 1
U.S. Retail Fur Sales

Source: Fur Information Council of America, Retail Fur Council of the NRMA, American Fur Industry, and the Fur Resources Committee of the International Association of Fish and Wildlife Associations.

success and beauty, fur fashion has become controversial because of its link to questionable practices such as trapping and fur ranching, publicized by animal protection and animal rights groups. Surveys from 1986 to 1999 on public attitudes toward fur reported a range of attitudes. Acceptance of fur varied from a high of 50 percent ("under some circumstances") to a low of 13 percent (see Table 4). Despite the "fur is back" hype spread by the fur industry at the end of the decade, U.S. retail fur sales—a statistic created by the fur industry itself—remain flat (see Figure 1). Even with zero inflation, low unemployment, a booming stock market, and increased spending by consumers, fur apparel is not selling. Imports of all types of fur apparel continue to decline as retailers fail to empty their showrooms by winter's end. Fur-apparel imports, which make up at least 60 percent of the U.S. fur market, are considered to be a reliable indicator of the health of the U.S. fur industry (see Figure 2). The number of wild animals trapped for their fur in the United States has declined from 17 million in the mid-1980s to 3 million in 1999–2000. The United States is one of only three nations in the world that allows the use of devices such as the steel-jawed leghold trap, and the fashion industry has tried its best to distance itself from the cruelties of trapping. Fur from wild-caught animals has lost favor in the United States, and Russia, which traditionally has been a top consumer of wild-caught fur, has suffered an economic downturn that has hit the fur industry hard.

U.S. caged (or ranched) mink facilities have decreased by more than 50 percent since the mid-1980s (see Figure 3). The decline is attributed by the fur industry and anti-fur activists alike to low profits and an uncertain market future. Some fur farms have closed down completely; others have consolidated. Farmers face selling mink pelts at prices lower than the costs associated with breeding and raising the animals. As a result, the number of mink killed annually in the

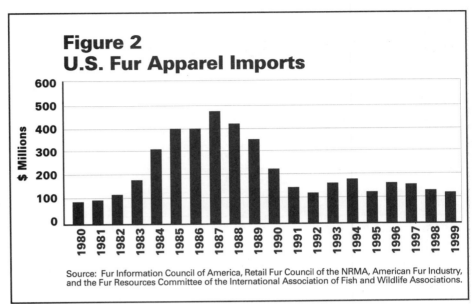

**Figure 2
U.S. Fur Apparel Imports**

Source: Fur Information Council of America, Retail Fur Council of the NRMA, American Fur Industry, and the Fur Resources Committee of the International Association of Fish and Wildlife Associations.

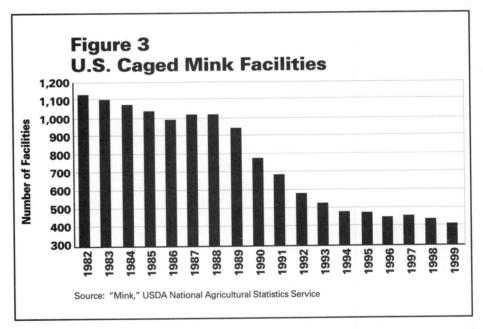

**Figure 3
U.S. Caged Mink Facilities**

Source: "Mink," USDA National Agricultural Statistics Service

United States has fallen from 4.6 million in 1989 to 2.8 million in 1999 (see Table 5). The number of cage-raised foxes has declined from 100,000 to 20,000 annually over the decade from 1990 to 2000. Items of clothing made primarily from fur comprise only 20 percent of the fur-apparel market; the rest is made up of fur-lined garments (50–60 percent) and fur-trimmed items (20 percent), a reflection of the trend to "hide" fur in linings or accents to avoid controversy.

In Europe and elsewhere, the story is the same. The number of cage-raised mink killed worldwide declined from 41.8 million in 1988 to 26 million in 1999. Farmed foxes fell from 5.6 million killed in 1988 to approximately 3 million killed in 1999. The Netherlands and Sweden have outlawed fox farming, and Austria has effectively banned fur farming altogether.

However, the fur industry is now turning its attention to Asia as a primary market for fur apparel. New-found wealth has allowed many Asians to adopt traditional Western lifestyles, including luxury goods such as fur coats.

Table 5
U.S. Caged-Fur Statistics

Year	Pelts Produced (Millions)	Pelt Value (Millions)	Average $/pelt	No. of Females Bred	No. of U.S. Mink Facilities	No. of Farms with Fox
1975	3.07	$74.0	$24.10		1,084	
1976	3.03	$87.8	$29.00		1,015	
1977	3.08	$87.1	$28.30		1,040	
1978	3.36	$132.0	$39.30		1,095	
1979	3.39	$139.5	$41.10		1,105	
1980	3.5	$123.6	$35.30		1,122	
1981			$32.20			
1982	4.09	$118.1	$28.90		1,116	
1983	4.14	$123.7	$29.90		1,098	
1984	4.22	$130.0	$30.80	1,115,000	1,084	
1985	4.17	$116.8	$28.00	1,115,000	1,042	
1986	4.1	$170.0	$41.30	1,073,000	989	
1987	4.12	$177.2	$43.00	1,077,000	1,027	
1988	4.45	$143.8	$32.30	1,198,000	1,027	
1989	4.60	$93.9	$20.40	1,202,000	940	
1990	3.37	$85.8	$25.50	922,200	771	
1991	3.27	$71.6	$21.90	874,000	683	
1992	2.89	$71.8	$24.80	782,000	571	
1993	2.53	$86.2	$34.10	712,800	523	58
1994	2.53	$82.6	$33.00	708,300	484	47
1995	2.69	$142.8	$53.10	678,200	478	49
1996	2.65	$93.5	$35.30	714,900	449	40
1997	2.99	$99.1	$33.10	705,200	452	31
1998	2.94	$72.9	$24.80	659,900	438	31
1999	2.81	$94.8	$33.70	660,400	404	27

Source: "Mink" USDA National Agricultural Statistics Service

An Increased Presence in Federal and State Legislation

Many animal protection issues are handled exclusively at the state level. Mandatory spay/neuter legislation, animal control laws, and general anticruelty laws, for example, must be passed state by state. Although in 1950 every state had an anticruelty law, a multitude of new and important laws have been passed since then. The period between 1980 and 2000 was particularly active. Although Massachusetts made cruelty to animals a felony offense in 1804, only three other states (Oklahoma, Rhode Island, and Michigan) had joined it by 1950. By 2000 twenty-seven other states had made cruelty to animals a felony offense—all since 1986 (see Figure 4). Sixteen states have mandated psychological counseling as part of their anticruelty provisions. A requirement that a bond be posted to cover costs associated with holding animals prior to court disposition has been passed in six states. This brings to thirteen the number of states that ease the financial burden on animal shelters, which may have to house seized animals for months until a cruelty case comes to trial. Forty-five state laws making dogfighting a felony offense have been passed since 1975. Cockfighting is illegal in forty-seven states and a felony offense in twenty. Thirteen states now have vanity-license plate programs that support spay/neuter efforts and six states have pet overpopulation funds to help increase the number of spayed or neutered pets in the community. Twenty-seven states have laws mandating that animals adopted from shelters be spayed or neutered, and sixteen states now have consumer protection laws covering the purchase of animals from pet stores. Eight states prohibit tripping horses for the purposes of sport or entertainment. Nine states have passed laws prohibiting the sale of items made from the fur of dogs and cats. As of 2000 six states had enacted laws that give vet-

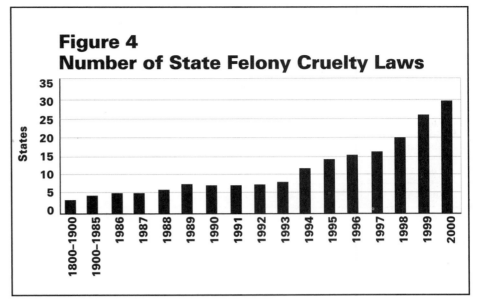

Figure 4
Number of State Felony Cruelty Laws

erinarians reporting suspected animal cruelty immunity from civil and/or criminal liability.

In 1950 there were three significant pieces of federal legislation protecting animals from suffering: the so-called Twenty-Eight Hour Law, which requires that animals be unloaded and provided with food, water, and rest for five hours when transported across state lines for more than twenty-eight hours; the Lacey Act (1900), which prohibits commerce in animals protected by law; and the Bald Eagle Protection Act (1940). (The Smoot-Hawley Tariff Act, passed in 1930, and the Migratory Bird Treaty Act, passed in 1918, might also be included as animal protection legislation.) By 2000 there were ten pieces of federal legislation, including the Humane Slaughter Act (1958); the Endangered Species Act (1966); the Laboratory Animal Welfare Act (1966) and its subsequent amendments, in 1970—when the name was changed to the Animal Welfare Act—1976, 1985, and 1990; the Wild Free-Roaming Horse and Burro Act (1971); the Horse Protection Act and Fur Seal Act (1976); the Marine Mammal Protection Act (1982); and the Humane Transport of Equines to Slaughter Act (1998).

One factor behind the increased success at the federal level was the tremendous expansion of national

animal protection, animal welfare, and animal rights organizations over last fifty years. In the United States prior to 1950, only the American Humane Association had an overtly national focus on *all* aspects of animal protection. Three anti-vivisection organizations had claimed national audiences for many decades. Several prestigious and influential state-oriented organizations, including the American Society for the Prevention of Cruelty to Animals (ASPCA), the Massachusetts Society for the Prevention of Cruelty to Animals, and the Women's SPCA of Pennsylvania, had set agendas within their jurisdictions that served as models and inspirations for groups across the country, but, by and large, had not lobbied Congress. The 1950s saw the creation of the Animal Welfare Institute, the Society for Animal Protective Legislation, Friends of Animals, the Catholic Society for Animal Welfare (later the International Society for Animal Rights), and The HSUS. The 1960s gave birth to the Fund for Animals, United Action for Animals, the Animal Protection Institute, and the International Fund for Animal Welfare. Greenpeace, the Animal Legal Defense Fund, People for the Ethical Treatment of Animals, and a number of single-issue national groups followed in the 1970s and 1980s. By the 1990s these groups had solidified

Table 6
Number of Horses and Participants by Industry, 1999

Activity	No. of Horses	No. of Participants
Racing	725,000	941,400
Showing	1,974,000	3,607,900
Recreation	2,970,000	4,346,100
Other*	1,262,000	1,607,900
Total	**6,931,000**	**7,062,500****

*Includes farm and ranch work, police work, rodeo, and polo.

**The sum of participants by activity does not equal the total number of participants because individuals could be counted in more than one activity.

Source: American Horse Council

their bases of support and had invested resources in lobbying members of Congress. They could point to several significant successes at formal coalition building among themselves, but the majority of their efforts were undertaken in informal alliances, particularly at the federal level. Alliances with environmental and conservation, social-justice, health advocacy, and consumer groups were less frequent but had occurred in pushing successfully for favorable action on shared agendas. Such cooperation reflected a level of political sophistication unheard of on the national scene prior to 1950.

The Evolution of the Horse from Commodity to Companion

After centuries of exploitation as a means of transport in war and peace, the horse was fast becoming obsolete in the United States by 1950. The domestic horse and mule population had peaked in 1915, at approximately 26 million, in response to increased demands from farming, particularly in hauling large tilling equipment. After 1915 tractors and other mechanized vehicles quickly began replacing horses for farm work and for conveying men and artillery into battle. Through the 1920s horses disappeared at the rate of 500,000 a year. Most were sold to meatpackers to be processed into dog food, bonemeal, leather, and glue. The price of horses reached an all-time low in 1950, and the horse population continued its steady decline until only about 3 million horses could be found in the United States in 1960, according to the U.S. Department of Commerce. Then, a generally expanding economy and an emerging middle class located in the new suburbs (surrounded by open land) led to an increase in participation in equestrian sports. A 1964 Cornell University study concluded that "The horse has become a status symbol for...entire families" (Howard 1965). Previously, only the Thoroughbred's role in racing, long acknowledged as the sport of kings, had given horses a patina of glamour.

For many newly minted equestrians, the horse evolved from a status symbol to a member of the family. Early television series like "My Friend Flicka," "Mr. Ed," "The Roy Rogers Show," and "Fury" featured horse heroes interacting with their human families much as did the canine stars of "Lassie" and "Rin Tin Tin." Nowhere was the evolving perception of horses in the American conscious-

ness more apparent than in the remarkable transformation of wild horse from vermin to symbol of American freedom. Since the 1920s, thousands of wild horses had been systematically slaughtered each year by Western ranchers, who viewed the horses as competition for their cattle-grazing public range land. By the early 1950s, hundreds of thousands of wild horses had been rounded up and sent to slaughter. Galvanized by Velma B. "Wild Horse Annie" Johnson of Nevada, an early opponent of such roundups, schoolchildren nationwide undertook a letter-writing campaign that resulted in passage of the federal Wild Free-Roaming Horse and Burro Act of 1971. This law prohibited the capture, branding, harassment, and slaughter of wild horses and delegated their oversight, removal, and adoption into private hands to the U.S. Department of Interior's Bureau of Land Management (BLM). Although the BLM has been strongly criticized for its management of wild horses, their protection was a major achievement and demonstrated the depth of the affection of the American public for the horse.

The horse-racing industry expanded under the influence of increased pari-mutuel wagering until the mid-1980s. The number of registered Thoroughbreds (the vast majority of which have always been bred for the racetrack) rose from 9,095 in 1950 to 24,361 in 1970 and peaked in 1986 at 51,296 before a change in tax laws made it less attractive to be involved in horse-related businesses. Competition from heavily televised sports led to an overall decline in racetrack attendance and betting handle, although annual Thoroughbred foal registrations rebounded somewhat in the 1990s to stabilize at approximately 36,000.

Racehorses did not all live the life of Secretariat, the 1973 Triple Crown winner who was named Athlete of the Year by *Sports Illustrated* (against human competition), as well as the Eclipse Award winner of Horse of the Year. Indeed, many thousands of former and failed racehorses went to slaughter for human consumption in Europe, along with thousands of long-suffering veterans of riding academies, summer camps, and backyard horse-keeping experiments, particularly in the 1980s, when prices for horsemeat were higher than those for nondescript but serviceable riding animals. In response to inhumane conditions at horse auctions and slaughterhouses in the 1980s and 1990s, documented by animal protection advocates, federal legislation was passed in 1998 to address some of the most serious problems with horse transport and slaughter. As of mid-2000 more than seventy horse rescue organizations and/or equine sanctuaries were on the Internet (*www. equinerescueleague.org*). (That number did not include facilities associated with or operated by animal shelters.) These groups rescued slaughter-bound horses (sometimes through outright purchase at auctions) and rehabilitated horses seized from private parties.

There was also a public outcry over horses used in the production of the estrogen-replacement product Premarin®, commonly prescribed to ease the symptoms of menopausal women and to treat osteoporosis. Manufactured from the urine of pregnant mares who are tethered for six months at a time in narrow stalls to facilitate urine collection, Premarin was the most prescribed drug in the United States in 2000, with more than 47 million prescriptions dispensed (Noonan 2000). Animal protection groups have publicized their welfare concerns about the treatment of the 35,000-plus horses involved in Premarin production and have intensified their efforts to make information on plant-based alternatives to the drug more widely available.

As of 1999, according to a survey commissioned by the American Horse Council Foundation, 1.9 million people owned 6.9 million horses in the United States. Of that number, 725,000 were involved in racing and race horse breeding, 2 million were involved in horse showing, 3 million were involved in recreational activities, and 1.25 million were used in

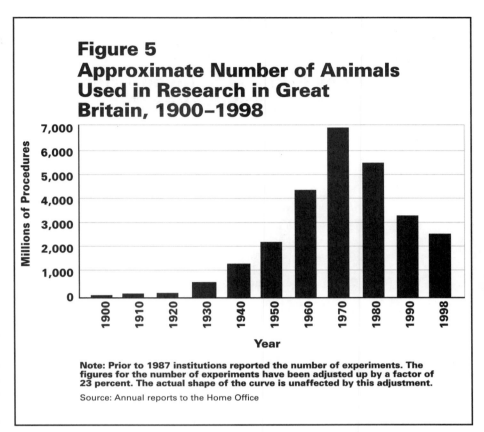

Figure 5
Approximate Number of Animals Used in Research in Great Britain, 1900–1998

Note: Prior to 1987 institutions reported the number of experiments. The figures for the number of experiments have been adjusted up by a factor of 23 percent. The actual shape of the curve is unaffected by this adjustment.

Source: Annual reports to the Home Office

other activities, such as farm and ranch work, rodeo, polo, and police work (American Horse Council 2000) (see Table 6). In each of these environments, individual horses were vulnerable to exploitation and abuse (the decades-long practice of "soring" Tennessee Walking Horses—altering their gait through painful means to gain advantage in the show ring—is a prime example). Nonetheless, it can be persuasively argued that the status of horses in the United States is higher than in 1950 and that their welfare has improved.

A Decline in the Use of Animals as Research Subjects

After World War II, the U.S. government began to fund scientific research, including biomedical research, at levels previously unseen. The discoveries of a polio vaccine (in 1955) and of antibiotics such as penicillin fueled an intense interest in research as the clear and shining pathway to curing—literally—the ills of the world.

The demand for laboratory animals to support such research increased as well. One survey conducted in the late 1950s found that 17 million animals were being used in laboratories in the United States. Laboratory animal use reached its peak in the 1970s and then began a steady downward trend, as evidenced by figures from Great Britain (see Figure 5). It is probable that the same pattern of laboratory animal use occurred in the United States (Rowan, Loew, and Weer 1995), although the data from the United States are not as reliable. By the early 1990s, laboratory animal use was estimated to have declined by 50 percent from its peak in the early 1970s. Alternative scientific techniques, such as Russell and Burch's (1959) Three Rs (reduction, replacement, and refinement of animal use in biomedical experimentation), had gained wide acceptance in all but the most conservative of scientific circles.

Public attitudes toward animal research have also changed over the last half century. A survey conducted in 1948 by the Gallup organization

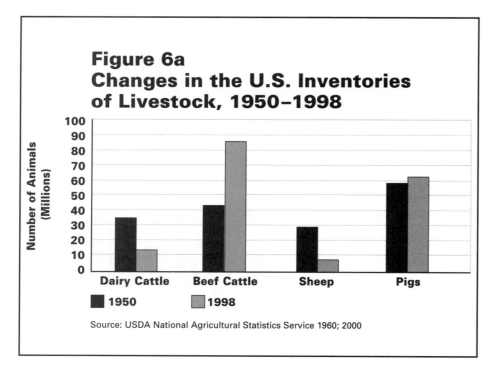

Figure 6a
Changes in the U.S. Inventories of Livestock, 1950–1998

Source: USDA National Agricultural Statistics Service 1960; 2000

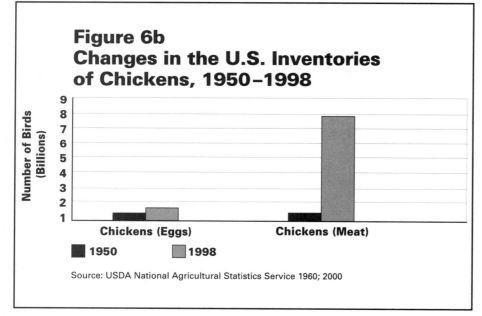

Figure 6b
Changes in the U.S. Inventories of Chickens, 1950–1998

Source: USDA National Agricultural Statistics Service 1960; 2000

available from commercial suppliers. Nevertheless, government centers devoted to the validation and regulatory acceptance of alternative methods established during the 1990s seemed to signal that alternatives "had arrived" and that animal research was poised to enter a new and promising era from an animal protection perspective.

How Has the State of the Animals Worsened?

More Animals Raised for Food More Intensively

Although conditions for some animals have improved significantly in the United States during the past fifty years, the story of farm animals is much more depressing. Humans are raising many more animals for food and fiber production (and the demand for food animals is far greater than for any other human use of animals). Increases in human population and meat consumption indicate that problems associated with animal agriculture are likely to intensify in the future. In the United States, the number of cattle raised for meat doubled during the past fifty years (see Figure 6a). More dramatic is the one-thousand-fold increase in chickens raised for meat (see Figure 6b); almost 8 billion chickens are now raised for meat each year in the United States alone.

The face of agriculture in the United States is changing at an alarming rate. Traditionally, animals formed an integral part of sustainable farming systems; they were fed from crops and forages grown on the farm, and their manure was returned to the land as fertilizer. With demands on animal agriculture increasing, however, family farms are being replaced by large "factory farms." Factory farms have grown out of our ability to keep ani-

for the American Medical Association found that 85 percent of those polled favored the use of live animals in medical teaching and research. By 1985 that number had dropped to 58.5 percent in a poll undertaken by the Baylor University Center for Community Research and Development (see "Social Attitudes and Animals" in this volume). Spurred by public pressure, the alternatives approach (as the Three Rs came to be called) was incorporated into national legislation

throughout the developed world and embraced by industry in Europe and the United States. In the meantime, procurement of disease-free animals became more expensive, as did virtually all aspects of research. These factors contributed to a reduction in the number of animals being used in experiments, although the declines in mouse use were reversed somewhat in the 1990s as researchers began to maintain breeding colonies of genetically engineered strains of mice not

mals alive and growing in intensive confinement. Advances in feed formulation and dietary supplements have permitted farmers to raise animals almost entirely indoors, where the animals are mechanically supplied with carefully formulated feed that maximizes their growth rates. In such intensive environments, however, the animals have virtually no chance to express their normal behaviors. The waste from all these confined animals (farm animals in the United States produce more than one hundred times as much waste as humans) has to be managed. In sum, factory farms are associated with problems of environmental degradation, poor animal welfare, human illness and health risks, and damage to rural communities.

Changes in the U.S. pork industry illustrate the problems of factory farm systems. The 1980s and 1990s saw a dramatic decrease in the number of hog farms, with a corresponding increase in farm size. By 2000 more than 80 percent of pigs were raised on farms housing one thousand or more animals (see Figure 7). Furthermore, vertical integration in the pork industry has increased, and single companies now control all elements of the production system, from breeding and growing the pigs, to slaughtering the animals and processing their meat. Smithfields Foods, the largest hog producer and processor in the world (see Figure 8), swallowed its competitors through company mergers and acquisitions throughout the 1990s and, as of 2000, had substantial hog operations in the United States, Poland, Mexico, and Brazil (Miller 2000). The same multinational company names, such as ConAgra, Continental Grain, and Cargill, dominate production of beef, pork, and poultry meat, as well as grain production, and they export their farming systems throughout the world (Heffernan 1999). In China, where demand for pork has skyrocketed (see Figure 9), hog factories are replacing traditional backyard production systems. Without the supporting infrastructure of abundant water supply, well-maintained transportation systems,

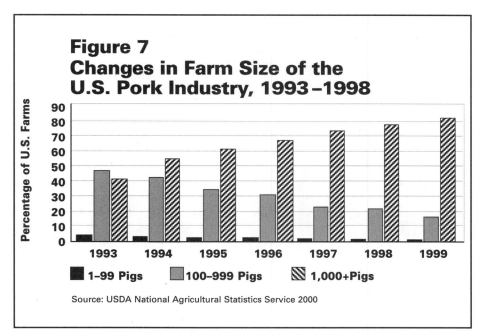

Figure 7
Changes in Farm Size of the U.S. Pork Industry, 1993–1998

Source: USDA National Agricultural Statistics Service 2000

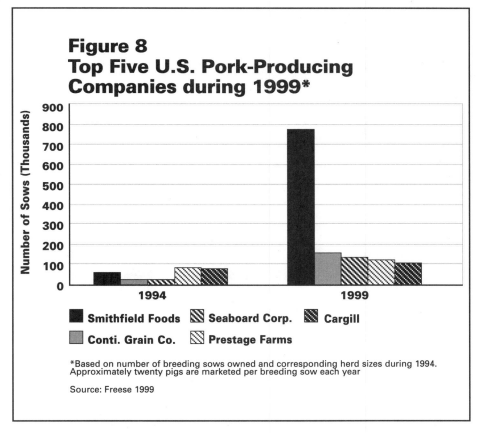

Figure 8
Top Five U.S. Pork-Producing Companies during 1999*

*Based on number of breeding sows owned and corresponding herd sizes during 1994. Approximately twenty pigs are marketed per breeding sow each year

Source: Freese 1999

and reliable energy sources, adoption of factory farm systems is likely to cause a plethora of environmental, health, and socioeconomic problems. In the United States—and elsewhere—it is increasingly difficult for family farmers to compete with agribusiness due to their limited access to high-

volume markets to sell animals and higher input costs for feed, breeding stock, and veterinary care.

Animal production has also become concentrated in particular regions within the United States. Sixty-five percent of U.S. pigs are raised in just five states (see Figure 10), 15 million

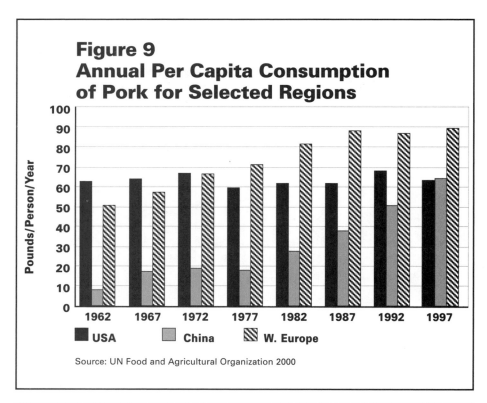

Figure 9
Annual Per Capita Consumption of Pork for Selected Regions

Pounds/Person/Year

| | 1962 | 1967 | 1972 | 1977 | 1982 | 1987 | 1992 | 1997 |

■ USA   ▦ China   ▨ W. Europe

Source: UN Food and Agricultural Organization 2000

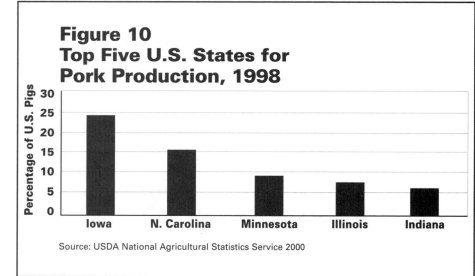

Figure 10
Top Five U.S. States for Pork Production, 1998

Percentage of U.S. Pigs

| Iowa | N. Carolina | Minnesota | Illinois | Indiana |

Source: USDA National Agricultural Statistics Service 2000

mals indoors. Research into mechanisms of growth facilitated the use of hormones and synthetic compounds to boost productivity. Building design focused on minimizing labor and maximizing numbers of animals housed rather than on improving the quality of the environment for workers and animals.

Consequently, animals on factory farms are raised in crowded, barren environments that do not correspond with the habitats in which their anatomy, physiology, and behavior evolved. Dairy and beef cattle often live in groups with ten thousand or more animals in outdoor yards, where there is no pasture for grazing or resting and no shelter from wind and sun. Pigs are raised in buildings with several thousand animals, where providing bedding material such as straw would interfere with the manure handling systems required on such large farms. Laying hens are housed in cages, without opportunity to perch, dust-bathe, or even flap their wings. The vast majority of breeding sows and veal calves in the United States are housed individually in crates, where there is insufficient space to walk or even to turn around, and where there is little opportunity to interact with social companions. This level of animal husbandry is unacceptable.

There is ample evidence to suggest that farm animals suffer in these factory farm systems. Painful procedures such as castration and tail-docking are standard management practices in the cattle, sheep, and pig industries, but unlike their companion animal counterparts, farm animals do not receive anesthesia or analgesia. Lameness, resulting from rapid growth and poor resting surfaces, is a painful and persistent problem in cattle, hog, and broiler chicken operations. Feeding high-grain diets results in rapid growth rates, but also causes ulcers in pigs and digestive problems such as bloat in cattle. Sores, injuries, and feather- and hair-loss are common due to chronic irritation with pen and cage surfaces. Injuries and bruising often result when animals are handled, loaded, and transported. Where these

in Iowa alone (USDA National Agricultural Statistics Service 2000). Similar trends exist in the raising and processing of beef, poultry meat, milk, and eggs. Regional concentration of animal production places an enormous strain on local ecosystems and results in environmental degradation. Poor handling, storage, and application of manure contaminates rural drinking water resources, destroys wetland areas, and kills fish and aquatic wildlife downstream (Clean Water

Network and the Izaak Walton League of America 1999). It is particularly distressing to observe the negative impact that changes in agriculture have had on the well-being of farm animals. In 2000 the welfare of farm animals in the United States was shameful, despite the much-publicized gains in farm animal productivity. Availability of antibiotics allowed management of subclinical levels of disease and thus facilitated the housing of large numbers of ani-

problems have economic impacts, companies are motivated to make improvements. However, there are few financial incentives for addressing problems that affect animals of low economic value, such as non-productive dairy cows or laying hens.

Currently, farm animals receive almost no protection from U.S. legislation (Wolfson 1999). The Animal Welfare Act, designed to protect animals used in research or exhibition, specifically exempts animals that are kept for food or fiber production. Farm animals are specifically exempt from anticruelty laws in most states. The two federal laws affecting the care of farm animals are limited in scope and poorly enforced. The Humane Slaughter Act requires that livestock be rendered unconscious prior to slaughter; however, poultry are excluded from this law. The Twenty-Eight Hour Law was discussed previously (see p. 7).

Until recently, farm animals have received surprisingly little sympathy from U.S. citizens, compared to the attention they have received in the European Union (EU), Canada, Australia, and New Zealand. Recent public opinion polls, however, indicate that concerns regarding agricultural practices are increasing. In telephone surveys, 93 percent of U.S. citizens polled agreed that animal pain and suffering should be reduced as much as possible, even though the animals were going to be slaughtered (Caravan Opinion Research Center 1995). Seventy-seven percent expressed concern for abuse and inhumane treatment of animals on factory farms (Lake Snell Perry and Associates 1999). More significantly, citizens have showed a willingness to take farm animal issues to the ballot box and are demanding more from their elected officials. Several states, including Colorado and North Carolina, have passed moratoriums blocking the development of factory hog farms. Consumers are becoming critical of their food purchases, with increased sales of organic products and increased involvement in community-supported agriculture projects. Some

animal scientists are also addressing farm animal welfare by designing equipment that addresses farm animal behavior and by using behavior to understand suffering and pleasure experienced by farm animals. Although the welfare of farm animals has diminished during the past fifty years, improvements are possible if citizens, government officials, and farmers address the issue.

The Environment: A Bumper Crop of Extinctions

There is a growing consensus that the wild animal kingdom is under the greatest threat in 65 million years—when the reign of the dinosaurs was ended by an asteroid that collided with earth. Every day an estimated one hundred species of animals are being pushed into extinction.

Scientists are not certain about the exact rate of extinction because no global effort has ever been funded to find out how many species share the planet. This deficiency can be explained by human beings' lack of appreciation for the interdependence of all living things and for the importance of other life-forms to human survival. That said, estimates of the total number range from 10 million to 30 million species, the vast majority of them invertebrate.

There is a wide consensus that believes that the increasing human population is making escalating demands on the resources of the planet. Animal habitats are routinely modified, degraded, and eventually destroyed. Those attempts that are being made to preserve species typically concentrate on the biggest, the most beautiful, and the most charismatic species (using human criteria) such as Asian elephants, snow leopards, Bengal tigers, Javan rhinoceros, orangutans, marine mammals, giant pandas, cheetahs, gorillas, eagles, cranes, and sea turtles. These species all require large areas of relatively unspoiled habitat, and, as a result, existing small populations of such "keystone" species require human

decision makers to protect areas where large numbers of other species have a chance to survive.

In December 1999 government scientists reported that in the mid-1970s average global surface temperatures had begun increasing at a rate of 3.5 degrees Fahrenheit per century and would continue to rise by 2–6 degrees over the next one hundred years. While that rate might appear moderate, in reality it is very rapid, given that the earth has warmed only 5–9 degrees over the last 18,000–20,000 years (Irwin 2000). Global warming will affect the earth in ways currently unknown. The melting of the polar icecaps and resulting rise in ocean levels—so that entire islands and large areas along coastlines are submerged and populations are displaced—is one possible, if alarming, scenario (Irwin 2000). Since the mid-1970s scientists have known that the earth's ozone layer has been affected by industrial chemicals introduced into the earth's atmosphere, causing it to thin and thereby reducing its ability to protect nature from the sun's ultraviolet radiation. Such findings are slowly finding an audience beyond scientific circles.

The outlook for wild animals is rather bleak. While many organizations and individuals struggle to save wild species threatened with extinction, rising human populations and human consumption continue to erode our efforts. The animal protection community is concerned not only about the threats to animal populations, but also about the animal suffering that is caused by human encroachment on and depredations in wild habitat.

Where Are Gains under Threat?

Marine Mammals: Hanging On

For marine mammals, the significant gains of the last twenty-five years are now being threatened.

Whales

In 1950 tens of thousands of whales were being killed every year by whaling nations (most notably the United States, Japan, Norway, Iceland, and the USSR). The International Whaling Commission (IWC), which had been established in 1946, set species quotas based mainly on assumptions grounded in human economic interests—not on whale biology. Unsustainable quotas set by the IWC were frequently exceeded. As a result, several species (such as grey whales and right whales) were pushed to the brink of extinction. Other species (such as blue whales, fin whales, and humpbacks) continued to be hunted in very large numbers until the 1960s, when some species received a degree of protection from whalers. Public sentiment in favor of whale protection continued to grow through the 1970s. In 1986 a world-wide moratorium on whaling was established. By 2000 this moratorium on all commercial whaling had allowed some species (eastern grey whales, northern right whales) to begin to recover. Other species, however, such as western gray whales and southern right whales, showed no signs of recovery. Japan (via a "scientific" whaling exemption) and Norway (which had continued to conduct domestic commercial whaling) were killing 1,200–1,400 minke whales annually despite the ban. In the 2000 whaling season Japan also began killing Brydes' and sperm whales, and the IWC appeared to be poised to lift the moratorium.

Dolphins

Beginning in 1959 and continuing through the 1960s, as many as 300,000 spinner and spotted dolphins were killed annually as a consequence of purse-seine operations in the tuna fishery of the eastern tropical Pacific Ocean (ETP). By the 1980s these stocks had been reduced to 15–20 percent of their original numbers and were declared depleted under the U.S. Marine Mammal Protection Act, passed in 1972. From 1990 to 2000 the mortality rate of dolphins in the ETP fishery had been reduced by 97 percent, due to the insistence by consumers that the "dolphin-safe" label, introduced in 1994 as a means of identifying product caught without harming dolphins, be applied to include the chasing and encircling of dolphins—not just to outright killing. So-called dolphin-deadly tuna was embargoed in the United States from 1994 until 2000. Due to pressure from Mexico (under the threat of a World Trade Organization challenge), however, the United States seemed to be on the verge of accepting fishing practices that would kill more dolphin as "dolphin-safe" for labeling purposes. This is doubly troubling since there is no evidence that dolphin stocks made an appreciable recovery in the decade 1990–2000. This is probably because the stress and trauma created by chasing and encircling the dolphins adversely affects reproductive success.

Seals

In the 1950s hundreds of thousands of harp seals, including upwards of 300,000 white-coat pups, were killed in Canada each year for their fur. The population declined significantly as a result, and the seals were brutally slaughtered using inhumane methods such as clubs and *hakapiks*. This slaughter was documented on film in the 1960s and 1970s by animal protection organizations and broadcast across the United States. The intense hue and cry that followed influenced the Canadian government to outlaw the killing of white-coat pups in the early 1980s and decrease the annual quota of harp seals that could be killed to 60,000. As few as 25,000 harp seals were actually killed in any one year as the public shunned products made of seal fur and the EU threatened a complete embargo on seal products.

By 1995 the quota had been increased to 200,000 harp seals, both to address fishermen's concerns about depleted cod stocks (seals were suspected of taking cod as their populations increased) and to give jobs to unemployed Newfoundlanders. Seals were being killed for their meat as much as for their fur. Killing the white-coat pups remained illegal, but several thousand were being poached every year. In 2000 the quota for harp seals stood at 275,000. The future of the harp seal looks threatening.

Captive Cetaceans

Captive cetaceans were almost unknown in the 1950s (although a few bottlenose dolphins were kept in aquariums) but, in the 1960s, a boom in marine parks, circuses, and dolphinaria was sparked by the successful television series "Flipper" and the saga of Namu, the killer whale who lived a year in captivity after being rescued from a fishing net. By the 1970s hundreds of dolphins and whales were being captured and maintained in marine parks and aquariums. By 2000 the situation worldwide was mixed. Captive populations and captures themselves were on the increase in Asia, particularly in China, Japan, and Indochina. Captive populations/captures were stable in eastern Europe and the Caribbean. In western Europe and Canada, captive populations were decreasing and there had been no known recent captures. Captive populations were stable or increasing in Africa, with captures proposed. Captive populations were stable or possibly increasing with no known recent captures in South America.

In the United States the captive population was stable or decreasing and there had been no known recent captures. The phenomenal success of the "Free Willy" movies in the 1990s focused the attention of millions on the dark side of captivity for cetaceans. It would be ironic indeed if the publicity generated by "Free Willy" served as an impetus for the release of cetaceans kept in bondage as a result of enthusiasm generated by "Flipper" decades earlier.

Polar Bears

In the mid-twentieth century, polar bears were hunted indiscriminately. This was a major cause of population declines throughout their ranges. By the time the decline was addressed—in the 1973 International Agreement on the Conservation of Polar Bears—several populations worldwide were severely depleted. All five signatories (USSR/Russia, the United States, Denmark/Greenland, Norway, and Canada) later disagreed on the interpretation of the agreement's provisions on sport hunting. Gains made during twenty-five years of strong protection were undercut by the 1994 amendments to the Marine Mammal Protection Act, which lifted the prohibition against importing sport-hunted polar bear trophies into the United States. Since then, hundreds of trophies have been imported from Canada, including many that had been warehoused from earlier hunts. Environmental degradation of polar bear habitats was the biggest threat to polar bear populations in 2000 and the future is guarded at best.

Where Is the State of Animals Unknown?

The Plight of Zoo Animals

The state of the approximately 900,000 to 1 million zoo animals around the world is, unfortunately, largely unknown. Although great strides may have been made in the

standards of care—both physical and behavioral—in the last fifty years, only a minority of zoo animals living in a handful of progressive institutions (fewer than 20 percent of the whole) can be said to benefit from them. The vast majority languish unpublicized in barren, unsafe, and/or inhumane conditions, their only advocates the occasional shocked zoo visitor who attempts to interest local authorities or zoo management in mitigating the general misery of the animals. The larger zoos are now devoting more time and attention to in situ conservation and to conservation education. However, in the majority of institutions, public education is abysmal.

The Way Ahead

Fifty years ago, problems with urban wildlife (with the exception of humankind's centuries-long battle with rodents), the link between cruelty to animals and other forms of human violence, and the potential of immunocontraception for species population control were unheard of. Now these issues are at the forefront of some of the most promising work being done in animal protection.

Wild Neighbors: Moving Ever Closer

Although cities occupy no more than 2 percent of the world's habitable land mass, human urban populations now outnumber the rural population. Soon the majority of all humans on earth will live in urban environments. Those environments will be created through land development—clearing, grading, soil compression, wetlands draining, and infilling—all of which have a major impact on native species of mammals, amphibians, invertebrates, and reptiles. Those species that can withstand the drastic change in habitat—and those that can flourish within it—will ensure that the human tenants of these most human of environments will not be alone.

Although human beings have interacted with urban wildlife, particularly

rodents, since the beginning of recorded time, their relationships with many other species are relatively new. Urbanization is associated with a relatively small number of species in the environment, but in higher concentrations than are found in "wild" nature. These species interact with people in a variety of ways, and although many people enjoy their relationships with urban wildlife, particularly songbirds, it is the conflicts with wildlife that garner the attention of community leaders. These conflicts can involve individual animals, local groups, or regional populations.

Squirrels, white-tailed deer, raccoons, skunks, or Canada geese can, by their very existence, create tension and anger in communities that are intolerant of droppings on walkways or the consumption of ornamental plants. Species involved in actively changing the environment (such as beavers) or that are seen as threats to human well-being (such as bats) may be actively pursued by state and local officials either independently or in response to public pressure. Virtually all species interacting with human urban populations run the risk of being termed "nuisance" or "pest" species in specific situations and are dealt with via a variety of methods, ranging from the benign to the lethal. A consensus is needed among private nuisance wildlife control operators, wildlife rehabilitators, animal protection organizations, and state and local government agencies, in the absence of state regulatory and statutory oversight, to address growing public demand for solutions to wildlife problems that include nonlethal options before lethal options are considered. (In this context, problems are defined as human perceptions of the results of urban wildlife doing what it can to survive and compete for resources.) Tolerance must be accepted as a primary response, and solutions that are "environmentally sound, lasting, and humane" must continually be sought and developed.

The Tangled Web of Animal Abuse

Although cruelty to animals has been acknowledged in the cultural and religious traditions of most societies, only in the past few decades has systematic attention focused on the link between cruelty to animals and other forms of human violence. Patterns of behavior of serial killers, spousal abusers, and juvenile murderers became the subject of active investigation in the 1980s and 1990s, but insightful observers had sounded warnings earlier. In 1963 anthropologist Margaret Mead wrote, "It would . . . seem wise to include a more carefully planned handling of behavior toward living creatures in our school curriculum…and alert all child therapists to watch for any record of killing or torturing a living thing. It may well be that this could prove a diagnostic sign and that such children, diagnosed early, could be helped instead of being allowed to embark on a long career of episodic violence and murder" (Lockwood and Ascione 1998).

Lockwood and Hodge brought the link between cruelty to animals and other forms of human abuse, particularly serial murder, to the attention of the animal protection community in 1986 through a review of work of Hellman and Blackman in 1966, Tapia in the early 1970s, and Felthous and Kellert in the early 1980s (Lockwood and Hodge 1986). Interest from the law-enforcement community came later, after FBI profiling of serial killers incorporated cruelty to animals as a predictor of violence (HSUS 1996). In the period 1995–2000, interest in the topic increased incrementally, as evidence of links between cruelty to animals and domestic abuse, youth violence, and other forms of criminal activity began to mount and was disseminated by the media. Ascione and Lockwood have identified five areas in need of attention in the coming decades: the "ecology" of violence against animals; the developmental dynamics of cruelty to animals and other forms of human violence; the relationship between animal abuse and domestic violence; the social service response to cruelty to animals; and the dynamics of prevention and intervention/treatment. These assume greater urgency as American communities grapple with highly publicized incidents of seemingly random violence (such as the murders at Colorado's Columbine High School in 1999) that implicate perpetrators with a history of animal abuse. Such incidents strike at the heart of a community's feeling of safety and well-being and increase the urgency felt by society as a whole for diagnosis and intervention.

Wildlife Contraception

The history of wildlife contraception is wholly contained in the period from 1950 to 2000. Technologically, nonhormonal chemicals, steroid hormones, nonsteroidal hormones, barrier methods, and immunocontraceptives have all been explored with varying degrees of success. This exploration has taken place against a backdrop of considerable resistance from traditional state wildlife agencies, grounded in the "hunt/shoot/trap" school of wildlife population control.

Immunocontraceptive vaccines show considerable promise, particularly in light of significant success with the porcine zona pellucida (PZP) vaccine. Kirkpatrick and Turner (1991) created a standard by which wildlife immunocontraception could be evaluated, which included contraceptive effectiveness of at least 90 percent; the capacity for remote delivery; the reversibility of effects; safety for use in pregnant animals; absence of significant health side effects; isolation of the contraceptive agent from the food chain; minimal effects on individual and social behaviors; and low cost. By these criteria the PZP vaccine has scored well and has shown exciting results in field use in wild horses, white-tailed and black-tailed deer, African elephants, water buffalo, Tule elk, and more than ninety species of zoo animals. Work continues on refining and developing a one-shot vaccine (as opposed to the current two-shot regimen) and on expanding the vaccine's potential for use in domestic animals such as dogs and cats. The development of a permanent, one-shot, cost-effective vaccine would undoubtedly be a major weapon in the struggle against companion animal overpopulation. It could alleviate the effects of the painful and divisive debates over euthanasia, animal shelter spaying/neutering policies, and stray animal control and potentially unite many people of good will in their efforts to improve the lives of companion animals here and abroad.

The Next Fifty Years

This chapter provides only a brief snapshot of the progress achieved and the setbacks that have occurred in animal protection from 1950 to 2000. Doubtless other people would select a different set of topics and view the situation slightly differently. Nonetheless, the animal protection movement can, I believe, be reasonably pleased with the progress made. Public opinion polls and academic treatises support the idea that concern for animals has increased and that this has led to gains in animal welfare in a range of areas.

On the other hand, there have also been significant setbacks. The threats to wild populations from habitat destruction, human encroachment, and human consumption are on the increase and the plight of farm animals in modern intensive systems (from birth to slaughter) can only be described as dreadful. The number of farm animals affected by such intensive systems has increased steadily through the last half of the twentieth century and looks as though it will continue to increase in the coming century.

Therefore, any plans and strategic suggestions for the next century must include some ideas to address the welfare of farm animals and the survival of wildlife. Such plans must come to grips with a range of strategic challenges that will confront any nonprofit advocacy group. These challenges include human population growth, increased human consumption (leading humans to walk a little less "softly" on the earth with each passing decade), threats to the security of human societies and the natural areas that they occupy, technological changes and innovations (e.g., the Internet), and questions relating to different cultural, theological, and political views on a wide variety of issues around the world (e.g., differences among Islam, Christianity, Judaism, and Buddhism on a variety of topics). These strategic challenges can appear overwhelming and beyond the grasp of even a relatively large and influential sector of human society (such as a major religious denomination), let alone groups that enjoy less influence in the corridors of geopolitical power, such as the environmental movement or the animal protection movement. Nonetheless, any of these movements (a term used loosely since there are many shades of opinion—and even internecine conflicts—within such movements) must continue monitoring the larger strategic issues and develop its own strategies for progress that take into account larger geopolitical forces.

For example, the World Trade Organization (WTO) has the potential to have a major impact on animal protection. Its decisions or influence have already had an adverse impact on dolphin protection programs. The WTO is likely to continue to slow animal protection progress. Countries defer setting standards for animal welfare that may result in sanctions by the WTO, which could interpret such standards as unfair non-tariff trade barriers. Attempts to reverse or to ameliorate some of the worst practices in intensive animal husbandry are bound to run up against WTO problems (as Europe has already discovered with its attempts to limit the importation of hormone-free beef or fur from animals caught in leghold traps).

Despite the problems and the larg-er threats to animal protection progress mentioned above, there are also grounds for optimism that we can move ahead to create a more humane society in the United States, the EU, and even worldwide.

Nonetheless, more needs to be done. Some cultural traditions, for example, are perceived to be less sympathetic to animal welfare than others. The Roman Catholic Church has generally been viewed as less supportive of animal welfare than have been some Protestant denominations. Such stereotyping, however, is based on the observation that animal welfare legislation and activity is more advanced in Northern European and American communities than in the Mediterranean countries and in Central and South America. Such differences may be more a matter of economic than theological disparities. In the end, we do not know how attitudes to animal protection are influenced by different cultural traditions as opposed to economic or political constraints.

Our ignorance of the influence of important cultural, religious, and political traditions on animal welfare thinking must be addressed. We need to understand whether Islamic societies are less supportive of animal welfare as a result of their theology or if their lack of attention to such issues is due to political and economic constraints. If the latter, we can devise strategies to address and to eliminate such constraints and develop programs that will advance animal welfare in traditional Islamic cultures. The HSUS plans to develop institutions and projects that will address some of the broader cultural issues and to devise plans to promote animal welfare more effectively in both the developed and the developing world. It may be possible to extend our First Strike initiative, which focuses on the close links between human violence to animals and human violence to humans, and argue that societies (and countries) that pay more attention to animal welfare are likely to be more civil and more secure for their human inhabitants than societies that ignore this issue.

In moving forward with plans to promote a more humane society, we perceive a number of elements and strategies to be critical components of such a goal. First, we need to be more inclusive in developing partners and alliances. Many nonprofit organizations view the corporate sector with suspicion and thus cut themselves off from opportunities to make a considerable impact on how society views animals. Arguably, the most powerful influence on the decline in hunting in the United States is the Walt Disney film "Bambi" (urbanization, another candidate, has not increased in the past thirty years). If one can work with a corporation like Disney to produce such a product (or products), the impact on animal protection is likely to be far greater than if we rely simply on our own channels of outreach. Thus, we need to look for partners in the corporate community and persuade them that they, too, have short- and long-term interests in promoting animal welfare.

Second, we need to work more closely and effectively with academe. From 1950 to 2000, the most common interaction between animal protection and academe involved a conflict over the use of animals in research. Thus, both communities have a tendency to view the other with suspicion. Nonetheless, an increasing number of academics are paying attention to the place of animals in society (the American Sociological Association recently gave permission for a group to try to establish an "animals and society" section) and their writings and studies influence the way society views animals and animal welfare. In the wake of the civil rights and women's rights movements, centers for African-American and Women's Studies sprang up at a variety of campuses across the United States. These centers have kept both movements vigorous and refreshed with new ideas and new findings. Several centers for animal welfare or the human-animal bond have been established in the last decade at a few North American universities. The animal protection movement needs to support and work more closely with such centers and to help expand their number and influence.

Third, we need to develop a new approach to our interactions with wildlife. Immunocontraception, mentioned earlier, is a major new technology because it begins to give us an alternative to killing animals when conflicts between animals and humans occur. Thus, it allows us to change our mindset from lethal control to potentially gentler solutions. There are many ways in which we can arrange our human communities to lessen human-wildlife conflicts and increase our enjoyment at sharing our lives with wild creatures. Close interaction between a human and an animal can be (and has been in many cases) a transforming experience for the human involved. Such interactions need to be safe, enjoyable, and common for both animals and humans.

Fourth, for many people, a family is not a true family unless it includes at least one companion animal. Approximately 95 percent of Americans grow up experiencing such a relationship, but it is not always as satisfying for the humans and animals as it could be. We need to develop programs that increasingly celebrate the positive aspects of this human-animal interaction—including improved physical and mental health for the human partners (Wilson and Turner 1997)—and prevent the negative aspects. Shelters could become the focus of such a celebration in communities across the United States and thereby shed the image of being places that only handle failed human-animal bonds.

Fifth, there are three categories of verbal abuse in many languages: profanities, obscenities, and animal terms (Leach 1989). It is easy for us to understand why terms dealing with God and sex should have the power to shock us or to help us express vehemence and passion. It is less understandable why animal terms should have the same potency. We should understand that our relationships with animals (and with nature and wilderness) are not a simple matter of exaggerated sentiment or displaced human empathy. They are fundamental to our being and to our long-term survival as a species and a self-sustaining society. We discount such relationships at our peril. As Gandhi is reputed to have said, "One can judge the civilization of a society by the way it treats its animals and its prisoners." When we reach 2050, let us hope that we can say that societies across the globe are more civilized—and more humane—in the broadest sense.

Literature Cited

American Horse Council. 2000. *The economic impact of the horse industry in the United States.* Washington, D.C.: American Horse Council.

American Veterinary Medical Association (AVMA). 1997. *U.S. pet ownership and demographics sourcebook.* Schaumburg, Ill.: Center for Information Management, AVMA.

Balzar, J. 1993. Creatures great and—equal? *Los Angeles Times.* 23 December: A–1.

Caravan Opinion Research Center. 1995. *Attitudes toward protecting farm animals from cruelty.* Princeton, N.J.: Opinion Research Corporation.

Cavalieri, P., and P. Singer, eds. 1993. *The great ape project: Equality beyond humanity.* New York: St. Martin's Press/Griffin.

Clean Water Network and the Izaak Walton League of America. 1999. *Spilling swill: A survey of factory farm water pollution in 1999.* Washington, D.C.: Clean Water Network.

Food and Agricultural Organization of the United Nations. 2000. Statistical database. Available at *www. faostat.org/default.htm.*

Foster, D. 1995. Animal rights pleas heard. Associated Press, 2 December.

Freese, B. 1999. Pork powerhouses. Successful farming on-line. Available at *http:// www.agriculture.com/sfonline/archives/sf/porkpwr/pp.html.* Accessed December 1999.

Heffernan, W. 1999. Consolidation in the food and agriculture system. Report to the National Farmers Union, 5 February.

Howard, R.W. 1965. *The horse in America.* Chicago: Follett Publishing Company.

Humane Society of the United States (HSUS). 1991. *Statements of policy.* Washington, D.C.: HSUS.

—————. 1996. Deadly serious: An FBI perspective on animal cruelty. *HSUS News.* Fall.

—————. 1998. What is that they're wearing? Washington, D.C.: HSUS.

—————. 2000. *HSUS Pet Overpopulation Estimates.* Available at *http://hsus.org/programs/companion/overpopulation/opfaq.html.*

Irwin, P. 2000. *Losing paradise.* Garden City Park, N.Y.: Square One Publishers.

Kellert, S. 1979. *Public attitudes toward critical wildlife and natural habitat issues.* Phase I of U.S. Fish and Wildlife survey: American attitudes, knowledge, and behaviors toward wildlife and natural habitats. Washington, D.C.: U.S. Fish and Wildlife Service.

Kirkpatrick, J., and J.W. Turner Jr. 1991. Reversible fertility control in nondomestic animals. *Journal of Zoo and Wildlife Medicine* 22: 392–408.

Lake Snell Perry and Associates. 1999. *A nationwide survey of 1,000 registered voters about factory farms.* Washington, D.C.: Lake Snell Perry and Associates, Inc.

Leach, E.R. 1989. Anthropological aspects of language: Animal categories and verbal abuse. *Anthrozoös* 2: 151–165. First published in *New directions in the study of language* Cambridge, Mass: MIT Press, 1964, 23–63. (See also the companion articles in *Anthrozoös* 2: 166–174 and 3: 214–233.)

Lockwood, R., and F. Ascione, eds. 1998. *Cruelty to animals and interpersonal violence.* West Lafayette, Ind.: Purdue University Press.

Lockwood, R., and G. Hodge. 1986. The tangled web of animal abuse. *HSUS News.* Summer.

Miller, D. 2000. Straight talk from Smithfield's Joe Luter. *National Hog Farmer,* 15 May, 12–16.

Noonan, D. 2000. Why drugs cost so much. *Newsweek,* 25 September.

Patronek, G., and A.N. Rowan. 1995. Determining dog and cat numbers and population dynamics. *Anthrozoös* 8: 199–205.

Roper Center for Public Opinion. 1989a. Question USKANE. 89PM10. ROZ2. *Parents* magazine. September 22.

——————. 1989b. Question USABC. 89. R10. ABC Newspoll.

Rowan A.N. 1992a. Companion animal demographics and unwanted animals in the United States. *Anthrozoös* 5: 222–225.

Rowan, A.N. 1992b. Shelters and pet overpopulation: A statistical black hole. *Anthrozoös* 5: 140–143.

Rowan, A.N., F.M. Loew, and J.C. Weer. 1995. *The animal research controversy: Protest, process and public policy—An analysis of strategic issues.* Grafton, Mass.: Tufts University School of Veterinary Medicine.

Rowan, A.N., and J. Williams. 1987. The success of companion animal management programs: A review. *Anthrozoös* 1: 110–122.

Russell, W.M.S., and R.L. Burch. 1959. *The principles of humane experimental technique.* London: Methuen.

Sieber, J. 1986. Students and scientists' attitudes on animal research. *The American Biology Teacher* 48, 2.

Survey Research Center. 1999. National Omnibus 1999 Questionaire Project #1367. College Park, Md.: University of Maryland.

USDA National Agricultural Statistics Service. 1960. *Agricultural statistics 1960.* Washington, D.C.: USDA.

——————. 2000. *Agricultural statistics 2000.* Washington, D.C.: USDA.

Wilson, C.C., and D.C. Turner, eds. 1997. *Companion animals in human health.* Thousand Oaks, Cal.: Sage Publications.

Wolfson, D.J. 1999. *Beyond the law: Agribusiness and the systematic abuse of animals raised for food or food production.* Watkins Glen, N.Y. and Orland, Cal.: Farm Sanctuary, Inc.

A Social History of Postwar Animal Protection

Bernard Unti and Andrew N. Rowan

Introduction

The rise of concern for animals during the post–World War II period was an unanticipated result of convergent trends in demographics, animal utilization, science, technology, moral philosophy, and popular culture. Together, these factors brought certain forms of animal use under greater scrutiny and created the structures of opportunity necessary to challenge and transform those uses. These trends also spurred the revitalization and extension of a movement that, in the nineteenth century, had been robust. Alongside older notions about the humane treatment of animals, modern animal protection introduced new and different premises that both reflected and shaped emerging attitudes about the relationship between humans and nonhuman animals.

Organized animal protection in America dates from the 1860s, when like-minded citizens launched independent, nonprofit societies for the protection of cruelty to animals (SPCAs) in one city after another and pursued their goals of kind treatment on a range of fronts. After a period of considerable vitality, however, the movement lost ground after World War I and its concerns dropped from the public view. Several generations of leaders failed to match the vision, energy, or executive abilities of the humane movement's founding figures. The period between World War I

and World War II proved to be an infertile social context for the consideration of animal issues, and the American humane movement became quiescent and ineffectual. This decline in movement strength coincided with the beginning of an expansion of animal use in such major segments of the twentieth-century economy as agriculture, biomedical research, and product testing. Humane advocates were either unaware of trends in animal husbandry and animal research or were unable to effect reforms in practices that were increasingly hidden from view and often exempted from extant anticruelty statutes and regulations. By 1950 animal protection, once a vibrant reform, stood mired in a phase of insularity, lack of vision, and irrelevance.

During the first decades of the century, the anticruelty societies had shifted their energy and resources away from the promotion of a coherent humane ideology and a broad-based approach to the prevention of cruelty. They focused their attention on the management of horse, dog, and cat welfare problems and to educational activities tied to pet keeping. The assumption of urban animal control duties by humane societies throughout the country made it difficult to sustain broader educational campaigns addressing the cruel treatment of animals in other contexts. Animal control was largely thankless

work, undersubsidized by municipal governments, and it usually overtaxed the staff and financial resources of the local SPCAs. The American Humane Association (AHA), the movement's umbrella association during that period, catered mainly to the interests of its constituent local societies, which were increasingly absorbed with urban animal control issues.

After World War II, the animal protection movement enjoyed the revival that we discuss in this chapter. Contemporary scholarship suggests that social movements are more or less continuous, shifting from periods of peak activity to those of relative decline. The renaissance of animal protection during the past half century involved several distinct phases of evolution. Such divisions are discretionary, but they can clarify important trends. This analysis relies on a three-stage chronology in considering the progress of postwar animal protection, one that emphasizes revival, mobilization and transformation, and consolidation of gains.

1950–1975: Revival

A specific grievance, the issue of "pound seizure," rooted in existing animal shelter principles and policies, precipitated the transformation and revitalization of organized animal protection in the early 1950s. At the time, both the AHA and the wealthier local and regional humane societies had narrowed their focus, for the most part, to companion animal issues. The postwar boom in expenditures on biomedical research greatly increased the demand for laboratory animals, and in the mid-1940s, scientific institutions began to turn to municipal shelters as a cheap source of research dogs and cats. Animal procurement laws were developed and usually passed without much difficulty.

Responding to the situation, leaders within the AHA attempted to negotiate with the biomedical research community. This antagonized some supporters, who attacked the propriety of such negotiations. As a result the AHA backed away altogether from the issue. This decision also generated discord, and several important breakaway factions emerged from the resulting intraorganizational dispute within the AHA. Before long, there were two new national organizations in the field (Rowan 1984).

As it turned out, the same people who parted ways with the AHA over its pound release policy quickly found other reasons to chart a new course for the work of animal protection. Renewal began in earnest with the formation, in 1951, of the Animal Welfare Institute and, in 1954, of The Humane Society of the United States (HSUS), both of which were founded by individuals formerly associated with the AHA. The new groups explicitly distinguished themselves from extant organizations and their approaches. Although they were in sympathy with the problems and challenges that local SPCAs faced, they did not become directly involved with the management of animal shelters or municipal animal control work. Instead, they focused on areas of animal use that their predecessors had either failed to address or had neglected for some time. Among other accomplishments they revived and revitalized early twentieth-century campaigns devoted to humane slaughter, the regulation of laboratory animal use, and the abolition of the steel-jawed leghold trap. However, they also identified and campaigned against emerging animal welfare issues that their predecessors had never faced.

The revitalization of humane work took place during the peak years of the Cold War, a period in which some protest movements faced serious repression, and the boundaries of acceptable protest were generally circumscribed. While animal issues were rarely deemed politically partisan in nature, they were largely pursued with tactical moderation and rhetorical restraint during this era. Thus, it is no surprise that the new advocates avoided absolutism, embracing pragmatic and gradualist approaches. They directed much of their energy toward the objectives of federal legislation, regulatory reform, and the amelioration of cruel practices through humane innovation and policy evolution. They developed in-depth critiques and proposals for reform of the major areas of animal exploitation. Cruelty investigations at both the national and local levels played an occasional role in advancing the work, and helped to place different issues onto the public agenda. In the meantime, the movement slowly expanded.

During the 1950s humane groups squared off with the meat industry to secure the enactment of the Humane Slaughter Act (1958). In the following decade, humane groups confronted widespread opposition from the biomedical research community to win passage of the Animal Welfare Act (AWA) (1966). To a great extent, the earliest federal legislative victories of the humane movement were the result of elite politics in which well-connected advocates conscripted influential congressional sponsors (such as Hubert Humphrey) who were ready and able to push heavily contested bills through to passage. The support of key members of Congress made it possible for animal protection interests to overcome the natural advantages that the animal-using groups had—namely, that they were part of large institutional, governmental, or economic interests with substantial resources or excellent administrative ties that allowed them to secure and defend their positions. With the legislative achievements on slaughter and animal research, animal protection gained a place on the American political landscape. In 1966 the humane treatment of animals even inspired a five-cent postal-service stamp.

Opposition to hunting, and the protection of wildlife in general, had not been a high priority for humane organizations in the pre–World War II period. However, wildlife concerns became prominent platforms for several of the groups that joined the field in the late 1950s and 1960s. The most notable were Friends of Animals (1957), the Catholic Society for Animal Welfare (1959, later to become the International Society for Animal Rights), and the Fund for Animals (1967). Other groups focusing on wildlife issues continued to emerge throughout the 1960s and early 1970s. During this same era—one of exploding human population levels, rapid land and resource development, and an unheard-of destruction of habitat—the somewhat different question of global species survival joined the goal of better treatment on the humane agenda. Rising public sympathy for wildlife protection also led environmental organizations to emphasize the protection of animal species, especially endangered ones, in their work and fund raising. Animals became increasingly iconic in campaigns for the protection of the natural environment, and their compelling appeal as fund-raising symbols was heavily exploited. Certain animals, especially seals, dolphins, whales, and pandas, entered the public consciousness as never before.

During the postwar period, the rise of ecology as both a science and a social movement underpinned calls for an expanded moral community that would include both animate and inanimate nature, including animals. In the late 1960s, a number of academic philosophers and ethicists resurrected the debate over animals' status, which to a limited degree had engaged their predecessors in both classical (before A.D. 200) and early modern times (1600–1900). The advent of serious philosophical and academic debate concerning the treatment of animals changed not only the movement's own frame of reference, but also the way in which it was perceived by outsiders. If animal protection had suffered from the stigma of being perceived as based largely in emotion and sentiment, the addition of rational argument and debate was a crucial factor in its move toward wider legitimacy.

Renewed attention to animal cognition bolstered these reinvigorated ethical arguments concerning human obligation to animals (Griffin 1976). In the latter half of the nineteenth century, Darwin's theory of evolution spurred a strong interest in animal cognition that led some to argue that animals deserved better treatment. By the early 1900s, however, the rise of behaviorism as a scientific paradigm reduced the study of animal mind to an investigation of physiological facts rather than an exploration of consciousness, and the argument that animals deserved greater consideration, based on higher mental faculties, waned. From the early 1950s onward, another cycle of intense interest in animal consciousness commenced, as scientists and others established and explored the cognitive, psychological, and social capacities of animals. This new generation of scientists, including Konrad Lorenz and Niko Tinbergen, combined field observations with scientific methods, and the result was a new discipline—ethology—the naturalistic study of animal behavior. Importantly, the pioneering ethologists discussed their works with explicit reference to the mental and emotional states of animals. A subsequent generation of field scientists extended the discipline by showing that non-human animals possessed many of the abilities previously assumed to be singularly human. Researchers working with primates in the laboratory cast

doubt even on the uniqueness of the human ability to communicate through language. These various inquiries set the stage for a renewal of arguments over the moral status of animals.

The dissemination of such research to a broad public audience through the mass media was another crucial stimulus. Television nature programs and relevant books and articles have catered to and encouraged a virtually limitless popular taste for information and insight concerning whales, dolphins, chimpanzees, and other highly valued species. During the same period, the television series "Lassie," Walt Disney productions, and other animal-related programming that drew heavily upon anthropomorphism attracted mass audiences and shaped public attitudes toward animals (Cartmill 1993; Payne 1995; Mitman 1999).

The steady expansion of pet keeping during the postwar period also heightened popular interest in animal capacities. It has been suggested that this continuing fascination with the intelligence and emotional faculties of companion animals also led more people to question the mistreatment or misuse of animals in numerous other contexts (Serpell 1986).

The principal areas of concern for humane groups in the late 1960s and early 1970s included general wildlife protection, anti-hunting, anti-fur and anti-trapping, animal research, endangered species, wild horse and burro round-ups, and companion animal overpopulation. Other issues, like those of intensive farming, cruelty to performing animals, and zoo practices, were largely neglected. Few humane organizations had either the resources or the assurances of public and membership support for sustained exploration of these concerns.

The two major legislative benchmarks of the postwar period, the Humane Slaughter Act and the AWA, depended less on coalition-building with other interest groups than on securing the agreement of the regulated parties under pressure from elite politicians. Subsequent legisla-

tive accomplishments in the 1960s and 1970s drew more on grassroots mobilization and direct-mail contact with supporters to generate the necessary support for positive legislation. Animal protection groups began to explore tentative and situational alliances with interest groups working in related areas, especially those connected with environmental protection. Thus, humane groups joined environmentalists in successful legislative campaigns that resulted in the passage of the Endangered Species Act (1967), the Wild Free-Roaming Horse and Burro Act (1971), and the Marine Mammal Protection Act (1972). Gradually animal protection became a pressure group movement with a realizable legislative agenda and the capacity for national mobilization.

Even so, a collective consciousness among those sharing in the work was slow to coalesce. Humanitarians did not contest their public characterization as an armchair army, composed of "little old ladies in tennis shoes," although they took pride in the fact that their efforts were beginning to bring results. While steady gains were being made in protective legislation and public awareness, for the most part, congressional offices still assigned animal issues to junior aides or temporary interns. Notwithstanding the substantial progress that had been achieved from 1950 to 1975, animal protection had yet to become a "household" issue, and it rarely featured in the media or in popular culture. Few advocates thought of themselves as participants in a movement. By 1975, however, this would change, as a sense of collective identity began to emerge, and new issues and actors came into the field.

1975–1990: Mobilization and Transformation

Some animal organizations working in the 1960s and 1970s were already beginning to rely on more extensive research and planning, more perceptive political strategies, and the language of rights and liberation. A number of the people who emerged as key figures in post-1975 activism began their careers in the established organizations. There was considerable continuity and cooperation between the older and the newer animal advocates. Many longtime adherents, including some of those who had been part of the 1954 breakaway faction and subsequent minor schisms, continued to make important contributions (Taylor 1989).

These precedents notwithstanding, it is still clear that the publication of Peter Singer's *Animal Liberation* in 1975 and the formation of Animal Rights International by Henry Spira in 1976 inaugurated a new phase of the work. In his book Singer recast the cause as a justice-based movement that underscored human obligation to animals, while challenging traditional justifications for their exclusion from ethical consideration. *Animal Liberation* also gave the animal protection movement a unifying ideology (based more on reason than emotion)—whose elements included anti-speciesism, equal consideration of interests, and the notion that animal liberation is human liberation—around which most of its factions could mobilize.

Spira had interacted directly with other advocates of this new ethical sensibility concerning animals, notably Singer himself. More importantly, he brought a lifetime of experience in the labor, civil rights, peace, and women's movements to bear on the problem of animal suffering. Spira was one of the first activists to apply the methods and tactics of other postwar movements in the animal protection arena. For movement loyalists who had suffered through decades of meager media attention and few tangible successes, as well as for newcomers primed by the public discussion of *Animal Liberation*, such innovation was inspiring. His work had dramatic results, including an elevation of the general standard of campaigning throughout the humane movement as others began to emulate and extend his approach. Another important outcome of the Spira-led campaigns was the formation of channels of dialog among government, industry, and the humane community. Spira proved especially skillful at mediating between the traditional humane societies, insurgent factions, and the animal-use constituencies in the interest of reform (Singer 1998).

In the early 1980s, an important wave of group formation and movement expansion commenced. Several key conferences gave rise to new organizations and generated considerable momentum toward the development of a national grassroots movement. The animal rights ideology that Tom Regan and other contemporary philosophers popularized expressed itself powerfully in the rhetoric and platforms of these new organizations. They challenged the arbitrariness of moral boundaries that subordinated animals to human interests. Some began to conceive and articulate broad demands that the traditional movement had either abandoned or never formulated. The groups that adopted progressive campaign styles gained members at a rapid rate during the mid-1980s, as their confrontational and more militant approaches appealed to both the media (which "discovered" animal rights after 1980) and to a public ready for protest drama and direct action. A number of single-issue groups also emerged, sharpening the focus of attack on relatively neglected problems of animal use in entertainment, food production, and so-called sport.

The decade also saw an unparalleled expression of grassroots-level activism in support of animal protection, as local and regional organizations formed in both large and small communities in every state. Their monthly meetings sometimes resembled the consciousness-raising sessions of the early feminist movement, incorporating personal testimony, guest speakers, the distribution of literature, the circulation of petitions, the planning of actions and events, and the viewing of videos detailing animal abuse in various contexts. Incoming activists were not encouraged simply to send money to the national groups; instead, they were conscripted into campaigns that targeted animal exploitation in their own locales. The movement also showed increasing reticulation, as local organizations knit themselves together as part of larger state or regional coalitions.

The new generation of animal advocates brought the message to the public through high-profile tactics, such as demonstrations outside the institutions where animals were used, including factory farms, stockyards, restaurants, laboratories, fur salons, circuses, zoos, and bird shoots. About 1984 activists began to employ civil disobedience measures, and the movement's reliance on sit-ins, site blockage, and similar tactics expanded steadily through the rest of the decade. National days of action focusing on such high-priority issues as veal production, animal experimentation, pigeon shooting, and fur took on "high holiday" status, as activists honored their commitment by participation in mass rallies and protests on these calendar dates. Some American campaigners borrowed the tactic of hunt sabotage from England, entering the woods to challenge hunters and the constitutionality of the "harassment" laws passed to protect them. They also took to the airwaves, challenging a wide range of animal uses in mass media debates. This expanded repertoire of protest kept the issue before the public and drew new participants into the work.

In the age of twenty-four-hour mass media and the hand-held video camera, the growing reliance of animal groups on casework and investigation also proved to be very important. People for the Ethical Treatment of Animals (1981) set the standard for such work. When other groups began to adopt the investigative approach as well, it had an energizing effect. The credibility of both individuals and organizations mounted in the wake of exposés that substantiated longstanding allegations concerning abusive treatment of animals in a number of realms, and provided crucial momentum to the cause as a whole. A highly publicized case involving the so-called Silver Spring monkeys (1981 et seq.), which focused on allegations of neglect in the laboratory of a Maryland researcher, made it apparent that neglect and improper care of animals could and did occur in American research facilities. Three years later a scandal involving the treatment of baboons at the head-injury laboratory of the University of Pennsylvania made it clear that the Silver Spring case had not been an anomaly. In the wake of these and subsequent episodes, advocates working in support of the Dole/Brown amendments to the AWA found it far easier to demonstrate the value of the proposed legislation. Investigative exposés of stockyards, cosmetics testing laboratories, and other targets spurred legislative and public awareness campaigns designed to restrict or suppress animal suffering in these and other social locations.

Professionalization within the ranks of animal protection groups began in the 1970s at both the national and local levels, as humane organizations attracted knowledgeable staff members who enhanced both the organizations' daily operations and their ability to serve the cause. For many of the newly recruited professionals, the rationality that Regan, Singer, and other philosophers introduced to the debate made participation in the movement possible. By 1985 The HSUS employed a large number of staff members with professional and academic credentials in a broad range of disciplines related to animals and their well-being.

Outside of the established organi-zations, a different form of professional recruitment aided the movement's growth. Animal-interest caucuses began to form among attorneys, biologists, medical doctors, nurses, veterinarians, and psychologists, to name the most visible. These new groups were especially influential in the pursuit and implementation of innovative ideas and tactics. They also made it possible for the humane movement to present stronger evidence in support of its positions in legislatures, courts, and professional arenas and to the public.

All of the foregoing developments contributed to the emergence of a science of animal welfare that has slowly penetrated discussions of animals' treatment in many fields of agricultural, industrial, and scientific endeavor, as well as in other contexts. In the wake of rising social concern about animals, animal welfare science began to develop into an established scientific discipline drawing on ethology, veterinary medicine, and psychology. A growing number of scientists are applying their energies to the reduction of animal suffering and similar objectives. The science of animal welfare has thus opened the way for innovations and refinements touching on animal use in a wide range of areas and established itself as an influence in policy debates on the use and treatment of nonhuman animals.

If the decade of the 1980s saw intense and widespread protest against animal exploitation, it was also one of considerable media visibility for animal protection and great change within the movement itself. The entry of new groups into the competition for resources via direct mail not only flooded the mailboxes of potential supporters, but it also led established organizations to reinvent themselves in light of new pressures and opportunities. Many of these groups lagged in providing either leadership or resources for advancing the cause. The advent of dynamic competition and the heightened expectations of an increasingly mobilized constituency spurred consider-able change. The movement as a whole developed greater consistency and adopted more progressive positions on a range of issues. Even in the case of groups whose political ideology remained moderate, tactical radicalization brought both practical gains and new supporters. Finally, greater informal interaction between the staff members of various organizations ensured better coordination of effort and approach.

Adherents of the animal movement have often compared their cause to other postwar movements for change, especially the African American freedom struggle and that of women's liberation. In a sense, the claim has been mainly putative. A few people graduated from the civil rights and feminist movements into the struggle for animals' rights, but the evidence for overlap of personnel and constituencies remains largely anecdotal. In any case, it is more important that the 1960s-era rights-based movements generated a "master frame" ("the interpretive medium through which collective actors associated with different movements" in a given cycle of activity define and comprehend their goals and targets), and a belief in agency that proved helpful to the formation of an animal rights movement (Snow and Benford 1992). The appropriation by animal advocates of the strategic thinking and mobilization methods characteristic of established justice-based movements was significant and lay at the core of many of the dramatic victories accomplished by animal rights groups throughout the decade.

The policies and ideology of the Reagan administration also catalyzed animal protection, just as it affected a number of other movements that appeared or reappeared during the 1980s. The presence of an apparently hostile administration led to the resurgence of feminism, environmentalism, antimilitarism, and the nuclear freeze movement, as well as animal protection. The proposed executive branch budgets provided no support for the AWA during all eight years of President Ronald Reagan's tenure. At the same time, federal agencies under the president's authority took a number of other steps that animal protectionists perceived as threatening to the well-being of both domestic and wild animals.

One measure of the movement's success during this phase of its development was the launching of counteroffensive tactics and campaigns by its adversaries. Furriers, agribusiness interests, product testing companies, hunting and trapping groups, and biomedical research concerns collectively spent tens of millions of dollars for public awareness campaigns and other activities aimed at squelching the animal movement. Their pressure sparked a political backlash, too, as congressional representatives introduced legislation to shield animal use from the scrutiny and challenge of animal protectionists. Old stereotypes were also revised—the dismissive symbolism of the "little old lady in tennis shoes" was deemed no longer adequate to the task. Targeted institutions and individuals promoted instead the more threatening image of animal-rights terrorist in their efforts to thwart the growth of public sympathy with animal advocates.

Sidney Tarrow's observation that movement cycles are activated by tactical innovation applies well to the transformation and impressive growth of organized animal protection during the period 1975–1990 (Tarrow 1998). The emergence of a unifying ideology and new organizational actors committed to new strategies of protest and mobilization further reinvigorated the field of humane work after the renaissance of the 1950s and 1960s. Institutions that had long gone unchallenged now faced a strong and tactically resourceful movement with a strong base of grassroots volunteers. Animal protectionists registered a series of successes as the targeted interests struggled to reestablish their accustomed dominance. A new generation of activists came into the groups most closely associated with tactical innovation and campaign success. However, all groups enjoyed increasing membership during the

period. By the end of the 1980s, the animal protection movement had set a number of reforms into play, and the argument that animals were deserving of greater moral consideration had penetrated public consciousness. By then, too, however, government, industrial, institutional, and entrepreneurial interests with a stake in animal use had mobilized with sufficient authority to slow the movement's momentum and influence. The field of contest, the relevant parties, and the issues themselves were all in evolution.

Understanding Animal Protection

Concern for animals has sparked a considerable body of literary, historical, philosophical, legal, scientific, and cultural studies that focus on the human-animal relationship. However, in the late 1980s, the animal protection movement itself, and its popular reception, began to attract the attention of scholarly analysts. This accumulated scholarship focuses on the movement's social composition, its recruitment and mobilization methods, its overall accomplishments, and general attitudinal surveys about the treatment of animals in American society.

The body of relevant scholarship concerning the social composition of the humane movement and its activities is limited. Nevertheless, a few conclusions are common to virtually all of the extant studies. The most striking is that women are more likely to be participants in animal protection work than are men. Indeed, levels of female participation in humane work appear to be as high as in any other social movement not explicitly tied to feminist objectives. Women have played a significant role in the formation of most of the newer organizations, and a 1976 survey using a national sample of 3,000 persons reported that 2 percent of women had supported an animal organization

while only 0.6 percent of men had (Kellert and Berry 1981).

In the light of such findings, it is worth noting that the rise of animal protection in the nineteenth century coincided with a period of sustained vitality within American feminism. Thus, one might plausibly speculate that the post–World War II campaigns for sexual equality have helped to place issues tied to care, concern, and nurture on the public and political agenda. While the principal organs and agents of modern feminism have largely failed to embrace the issue of animal suffering and exploitation, many feminists have found the cause on their own. A number of authors have argued that nurturing and caregiving values are higher priorities for women, and still more have attempted to draw explicit links between feminism and animal protection. In fact, by the early 1990s, the feminist ethic of caring emerged as an alternative to the liberation- and rights-oriented perspectives of Singer and Regan (Adams 1990; Donovan and Adams 1996).

Extant research also indicates that the majority of active animal advocates are white, with middle- and upper-class backgrounds. They appear to be more highly educated than most Americans, and tend to live in communities with populations of 10,000 or more. A high percentage of animal advocates have companion animals in the home and they are generally not affiliated with traditional religious institutions. Many consider themselves atheists or agnostics (Plous 1991; Richards and Krannich 1991; Jamison and Lunch 1992; Herzog 1993; Shapiro 1994).

A 1990 survey based on controlled sampling was typical. The researchers found their sample to be 97 percent white, 78 percent female, while 57 percent were in the 30–49-year age group (compared to 21 percent for the United States overall). Animal advocates proved to be highly educated in comparison with the general population (33 percent had higher degrees compared with 7.6 percent of all Americans), and financially well off (39 percent had incomes of $50,000 or more, compared with 5 percent of the national population, although it should be noted that educational and income levels are strongly correlated). Seven out of ten respondents reported having no living children, while nine out of ten had companion animals (compared with about four out of ten in a national sample). In fact, respondents had an average of 4.7 animals each, about five times the national average (Richards and Krannich 1991).

How and why do people come to the cause? Here, too, academic studies have begun to provide some insights into the recruitment of adherents. Resource mobilization has been a dominant theory of social movement development. As its name implies, resource mobilization theory posits that movements emerge when an adversely affected or dissatisfied population gains enough momentum to attract or combine the resources necessary to advance its own interests through organization and protest (McAdam 1982). Such explanations of movement dynamics usually rely on the study of recruitment networks: in the civil rights era, for example, churches were the earliest and most significant sites of conscription and engagement.

Resource mobilization theory has been judged inadequate for the study of the so-called "new social movements," which pursue quality-of-life or lifestyle objectives as distinct from the material or class-based goals of more traditional social movements. Resource mobilization, its critics charge, overlooks the cultural components of social movement formation, and its inattention to identity, culture, and meaning as factors in leading people to join movements has led scholars to the new social movement framework (Morris and Mueller 1992). New social movements draw supporters whose own basic rights are secure and who are typically well integrated into their society. Examples include the anti–nuclear power, environmental, disarmament, and alternative medicine movements. It is proposed that animal protection falls

among them. These causes tend to link people who share certain views about reforms needed to improve modern life. Their movements aim for changes in the political system as well as in the systems of cultural production within the society. In other words, they seek fundamental changes in social consciousness (Melucci 1985). However, delineating the character of such movements does not answer a key question about their emergence and expansion. If the new social movements do not recruit and mobilize from within preexisting networks, then how and why do people enter and participate?

Why do some people seem to care more about animals than do others? Indeed, why do they care enough to join campaigns for animal rights and well-being? Considerable progress toward comprehension and assessment of the animal protection movement has come with the emergence of studies that combine research on the social psychology of attitudes toward animal use with theories about mobilization and organization. Childhood experience, social conditioning, the manifestation of an empathic style, and identification with the oppressed have all been considered as factors in the development of regard for animals (Shapiro 1994).

One of the few sociologists to write extensively about the animal protection movement, James Jasper, proposes that greater attention be paid to the social-psychological identity formation of activists. In the model he proposes, one or more greater or smaller "moral shocks" (discrete events, experiences, or realizations) raise a sense of outrage or responsibility within individuals. These shocks spur them to seek out or form organizations (Jasper 1997). The animal protection movement, then, does not bring new supporters into the work by exposure through a preexisting social network like a church, women's rights group, or union. More typically, it "collects" them from a pool of citizens within whom some critical experience or insight has sparked a sense of empathy with animals.

There is no apparent self-interest for those involved in the work, yet animal protection, like other new social movements, also appears to confer psychological benefits. Many animal activists experience alienation from a wider society that does not value animals as much as they do. For such people the emergence and rapid mobilization of a movement that unites like-minded individuals, that investigates and challenges the abuse and suffering of animals, and that attempts to enculturate the principles of animal protection within society has considerable allure (Shapiro 1994).

Some believe that attitudes acquired in childhood can account for individuals' disposition toward animals and their protection; accordingly, animal protectionists have laid a great emphasis on humane education of children. A 1984 survey stressed the significance of childhood experience on distinguishing individuals' attitudes toward animals, and the developmental origin of concern for animals has begun to attract attention (Kellert 1985; Myers 1988). Despite a growing number of studies that focus on humane education, however, we know very little about its effectiveness and impact.

While underutilized, the community study approach has also helped to shed light upon the social composition of the humane movement. Just as importantly, however, community studies have made it possible to explore the outcomes of animal protection campaigns in a number of cases. These studies frame the efforts of activists and their opposition interactively, taking into account the evolutionary character of specific campaigns and of humane work as a whole. For instance, Einwohner's study of a statewide organization suggests that the importance of cultural assumptions about protesters, as well as the targeted practices and behaviors, are as vital to the assessment of the movement's outcomes as is a study of its tactics, organizational strategy, and structures of opportunity. Grove's study of confrontations over animal experimentation in a North Carolina university town explores how stakeholders on either side acted to redress certain perceived deficits in their approach to the issue. For example, the animal activists emphasized more rational and dispassionate lines of argument, while researchers drew on emotional appeals in their defense of the status quo (Einwohner 1997; Grove 1997).

Both Einwohner's and Grove's studies confirm the potential of studies of local and regional contexts to produce insight into the dynamics of contention over animal use. In shorter case studies of community-level challenges to biomedical research, Jasper and Poulsen suggest that the animal movement can quickly lose its advantage when targeted institutions decide to fight back with equal tenacity. Jasper and Sanders conclude that, where both sides avoid strongly polarized disagreement over basic principles, compromises can be achieved (Jasper and Poulsen 1993; Sanders and Jasper 1994). A full appraisal of animal protection and its accomplishments during the past half-century will require many more such investigations. Not just the recent history, but the future of animal protection work, may be clarified by careful attention to the substance and legacy of such case studies.

It seems clear that the 1960s legacy of critical skepticism and cultural radicalism created a favorable context for the growth and spread of new social movements such as animal protection. Disaffection with American foreign policy and with racial and sexual discrimination at home led many Americans to question the authority and honesty of government and institutional actors, a tendency that infused most of the post-1960s movements. While animal protectionists have rarely adopted wholesale critiques of the American political economic order, the movement has often relied on rhetoric and assumptions that identify animals as victims of rampant commercialism, greed, vanity, and the coercive power of big institutions. Like other post-industrial,

post-citizenship causes (environmentalism and anti-nuclear activism, for example), animal protection carries with it an implicit ambivalence about science and technology and frequently has drawn on the potent and popular stereotype of the uncaring, cold, and dispassionate scientist.

However, this attitude, commonly called anti-instrumentalist, does not in itself define the movement. In fact, humane advocates have often counterpoised their skepticism of science with enthusiasm about the possibilities of technology to ameliorate the circumstances of animals. For example, advocates have relied on the development of knowledge through science to advance arguments concerning the replacement of animals in research, testing, and education; to critique the reliance on hunting as a wildlife management policy; to reduce animal overpopulation; and to promote alternative food-animal husbandry systems.

1990–2000: Consolidation

By 1990 national media coverage of animal rights protests had apparently peaked, leading to speculation that the movement was losing the public's attention and waning in influence (Herzog 1995). Certainly, the novelty of the movement's provocative challenges to the use and mistreatment of animals wore off, undoubtedly leading media decision makers to the conclusion that the cause, no longer "new," was less deserving of special coverage. The high level of local grassroots activism that had characterized the 1980s subsided, and several national activist organizations, tied to the movement's growth in the previous decade, dissolved or waned in influence. Some participants in the work, accustomed to seeing large numbers of people at events and extensive media coverage, worried about the health of the animal protection movement. Others asserted that the animal rights movement was in ideological retreat (Francione 1996).

Such judgments overlook the fact that movements cannot perpetually be novel or operate at constantly high levels of protest activity. Even the most enthusiastic adherents tire and may curtail their levels of participation due to fatigue, and it is difficult to hold the interest of the public and the media over the long term. Intense interest, and the commitment to seeing an issue resolved, usually recede as the complexity of certain issues, and their imperviousness to quick and easy resolution, become more obvious. The philosophy of animal rights, an ideology largely defined in terms of moral absolutes, did not make evolution of the animal movement from a novel protest force to a mature contestant in the political marketplace any easier. Animal advocates have begun to develop other descriptive rhetorics that are more pragmatic and inclusive.

As a result, in the 1990s the animal protection movement shifted into other, less dramatic, and less obviously newsworthy channels of activity. For example, some of the battles between animal users and animal defenders moved into the political, legislative, and regulatory arenas. These confrontations called for new kinds of knowledge and action, often more subtle and nuanced than street-level protests and less likely to attract the notice of the mass media. For instance, humane advocates have succeeded in the establishment of basic frameworks for regulating the use of animals in certain contexts and in some of their campaigns to strengthen earlier "foothold" legislation such as the AWA, obtaining incremental advances in a steady pattern. As the issues and the arenas of debate and action evolved, they drew new and different players into animal protection work.

Among recent accomplishments, attorneys representing various humane organizations scored victories in cases relating to wildlife management, species preservation initiatives, wildlife import-permit challenges, standing to sue, and open-government/public-participation laws. Legal advocacy showed increasing promise as a strategy for helping animals. In 1999 discussion of the merits of extending rights to animals within the American legal system spilled into the national media, as Harvard University's law school announced that it would offer a course in animal law for the first time (Glaberson 1999).

In a trend that began in the early 1990s, The HSUS and the Fund for Animals pioneered the use of state-wide public referenda to curb certain kinds of animal use and abuse. These initiatives, while costly, enjoyed a high rate of success. It is worth noting that the determination of public opinion through scientific polling and attention to demographic changes in the targeted states were vital to the development and prosecution of these campaigns. They also relied on the more democratic political channel of the popular referendum, forcing special interests to face the judgments of the voting public. This approach sidestepped the usual domination of public policy networks by opposition groups through the lobbying of elected representatives, large campaign contributions, or other means.

In some cases, too, the introduction of a bill in the federal legislature signaled a particular issue's "arrival" or helped to frame a debate that was ultimately resolved through administrative or other channels. In 1989, for instance, the Veal Calf Protection Act gained a hearing in Congress, the first farm animal welfare bill to do so in a decade, more or less. The bill came in the wake of considerable negative publicity about the way in which calves were raised for market. Observers credit another bill, the Research Modernization Act, introduced annually since 1979, for highlighting the issue of duplication in experiments and the need to search for alternatives. Ultimately, both of these goals were pursued through nonlegislative means.

In recent years there has been some evidence of greater federal commitment to enforcement action. In the mid-1990s the U.S. Depart-

ment of Agriculture (USDA) eliminated the face branding of cattle because of animal welfare concerns. In 1999 the USDA took the virtually unprecedented step of forcing a consent agreement upon a controversial private laboratory, resulting in the promised relinquishment of chimpanzees to other facilities after a number of serious animal welfare violations had been reported (Spira 1995; Brownlee 1999).

In general, the movement has enjoyed greater success in reshaping cultural attitudes than in securing laws. Every movement produces culture, and the animal protection cause has done especially well in the broad diffusion of its values. While it might be the case that straight news coverage of animal issues has declined, these issues are more likely to be mentioned in popular cultural forms such as television entertainment or magazine features than was the case twenty years ago. Concern for animals has been increasingly represented within a variety of cultural forms, including literature, television, music, and art. During the past twenty years, it has become strongly associated with successive generations of youth culture. Through this sequence of acculturation, the movement has helped to normalize a number of practices and beliefs that support the animal protection agenda.

The embrace of humane lifestyle choices has been one significant result of this process. Animal advocates have taken the pursuit of principles embodied in the 1960s slogan "the personal is political" to considerable lengths. The embrace of humane products, ones that involve no (or less) harm to animals and the environment, has been a core principle for animal protectionists during the past fifteen years. Over time, exposure to humane ideology typically prompts its adherents to become highly conscious of the ethical implications of their wardrobe, diet, entertainment, household, and other lifestyle choices. Humane advocates, as purchasers of vegetarian, "cruelty-free," and environmentally safe products, have come

to constitute an increasingly important market segment. The "green consumerism" of the 1990s both encouraged and relied upon marketplace expressions of affinity with animals. Such patterns of consumption have caught on outside the animal protection movement itself, as other Americans, exposed to relevant information and sensitized to humane values, changed their lifestyles. The success of supermarkets and other retailers attuned to these values reflects the longer-term influence of campaigns waged in the 1970s and 1980s.

Similar choices outside the realm of food and household product purchases have also become more popular. Those who object to the presence of animals in circuses can now patronize troupes that eschew their use. Students who wish to choose nonanimal alternatives, whether in the high school cafeteria or the veterinary school classroom, now find it easier to do so. Even *haute couture* has condescended to meet the demand for elegant but cruelty-free fur.

Judging the success of a social movement is a notoriously difficult exercise. A simple verdict of success or failure in any specific category of effort is usually inadequate for the assessment of animal protection as an ongoing social and political endeavor. There are different forms of success: political success, mobilization success, campaign success, economic success, and success in the realm of public opinion. Beyond this, dichotomous assessments of "success" and "failure" are often inappropriate in the assessment of a complex and ongoing process of struggle and debate (Einwohner 1997). A broad evaluation of animal protection's relative accomplishments must include an understanding of the ever-changing terrain wrought by shifts in public taste and opinion. Other factors that must also be considered include

- the relative embeddedness of the practices under scrutiny,
- countermeasures undertaken by the targeted interests,
- negative publicity wrought by

misguided activism,
- changes in the political economy,
- technical advances that change opportunities and threats, and
- many other advances and reversals that occur over the long term.

Goals must necessarily change as conditions and opportunities change and issues are disputed, negotiated, and transformed by subsequent debate and action.

With these considerations in mind, one should not overstate the effectiveness and sophistication of animal protectionists' tactics or the general caliber of their leadership. The movement's history provides compelling examples of expenditure of funds and effort on strategically pointless gestures and/or campaigns with little attention to long-term strategy or follow-up campaigns. In the early 1980s, for example, Mobilization for Animals (MfA) organized a year-long campaign against the nation's seven primate centers and conducted major protests outside four of the seven facilities. Yet MfA and its collaborators never developed a follow-up strategy; ironically, the major outcome of the protest was an increase in funding for the primate centers in the wake of the demonstrations. The 1990 March for Animals drew 25,000 people to Washington for a protest, but there was no larger strategy developed beyond holding the event itself. A last-minute legislative agenda, which produced little or no follow-up, was a failure. In the end, groups opposed to the animal activist agenda exploited the event to get their story out and the media coverage was mostly negative. Six years later, many of the same groups staged a follow-up event that drew only several thousand supporters. While some argued that the turnout was low because the event was badly organized, the 1996 gathering effectively ended attempts to convert animal activism into some sort of mass movement.

It is also important to note that optimistic predictions about the demise of certain forms of animal use during the past two decades have usu-ally not been borne out. Although the movement made significant progress toward the goal of deglamorizing fur in the 1980s, the fur industry has survived and continues to attract consumers. Its ability to cut prices in the short term, shift production to cheaper overseas facilities, and deploy advertising resources to promote its product as an affirmative choice have allowed the industry to survive during even the worst of times. Veal consumption may be down, but it is not out. Americans eat a little less red meat than they used to, but poultry consumption has risen dramatically, resulting in more animal suffering overall. Internationally, intensive animal agriculture and meat consumption have been increasing fast. Not even in the field of animal testing, which drew so much attention in the 1980s and where evidence indicates that animal use has declined substantially, can continuing progress be taken for granted. In 1999 animal organizations had to fight off a product-safety initiative launched by environmental groups and sponsored by the federal government that would have led to an expansion of animal testing. After two decades of work on alternatives, it was still necessary for humane advocates to persuade other stakeholders that different and better testing, not more animal testing, was the appropriate course for the program to chart.

Current Context

The animal protection movement may have growing popular appeal, but this has not necessarily been translated into commensurate political success. In the political arena, the power of interests tied to animal exploitation has prevented the passage and implementation of many initiatives. Frequent tensions between federal and state authority have limited the chances of success for some proposals, especially those relating to wildlife issues. Only a small percentage of the many bills to halt or curb animal suffering introduced during the past half century in the U.S. Congress have actually passed. Many have not even gained a hearing, let alone a vote. Despite the frequent complaints of the regulated parties, the legislative and regulatory restraints on animal use remain modest. The quality of enforcement is at times questionable, and funding for administration of animal protection programs is also limited. For instance, at the time of this writing, federal Wildlife Services, (known until 1997 as the Animal Damage Control program), which underwrites the extermination of predators, enjoyed a budget of $40 million, while the AWA, designed to protect laboratory animals, got just one-fourth of that amount.

Efforts to translate substantial popular concern for animals into legislative and regulatory progress have been stymied by the fact that political success in animal protection depends not on the breadth of public support but on the movement's influence within the networks responsible for policy-making about animals. As it happens, movement access to these networks is relatively poor. In general, the proponents and beneficiaries of animal use dominate such networks, while animal advocates and organizations struggle to improve their access (Garner 1998).

It also remains the case that, despite humanitarians' efforts to place concern for animals in its own right into public discourse, a number of the most successful initiatives have relied on secondary and tertiary arguments tied to human interest or to civil liberties. The campaign against youthful acts of cruelty has emphasized the potential for escalating sociopathic behavior and interpersonal violence on the part of the perpetrators. The campaign against dissection has underscored the right to conscientious objection on the part of students coerced to participate in the practice. Campaigns against the factory farming and animal research industries have emphasized the potential harm to humans of the products that may result from those institutions and their activities. The need to place emphasis and priority on considerations unrelated to the integrity and well-being of animals themselves appears to be an essential feature of many successful campaigns.

One of the most serious obstacles faced by animal protection has been its difficulty in forging viable and enduring alliances with other movements. This deficiency has been most evident in the pursuit of legislative objectives, but it has manifested itself in other arenas as well. Public health organizations, for example, have generally resisted overtures from animal organizations when it comes to the reform of product testing requirements. Relations with the veterinary community, which could provide considerable technical expertise as well as substantial moral support for the movement's goals, are often strained. Animal protectionists have also neglected to cultivate ties with universities, which could be a source of potentially useful scholarship, expertise, and societal credibility. Finally, it has proved difficult for humane groups to establish reliable cooperation with environmental and wildlife conservation organizations. Admittedly, coalition building is a two-way street, and it is not clear that animal protectionists can readily overcome the dismissive attitude of other interest groups, whose concern for animal protection issues is not deep enough to underpin a strong alliance solely on the basis of animal welfare interests.

The Next Ten Years

The engagement of animal protection with environmentalism looms especially important, as environmentalism has emerged as the pivotal foundation of new social movements worldwide. Other movements' prospects for general success rest to a significant degree on their ability to include the language of environmentalism in their own rhetoric. Among all new social movements, environmentalism elicits the most support and the greatest degree of consensus (Martig 1995). Movements grow and increase

their political power by forging alliances with one another and developing broader societal networks (Zald and McCarthy 1987). Among other implications, the broad public base of support for both environmentalism and animal protection suggests that the reconciliation of differences between the animal and environmental movements should be a high priority for both. One potential conflict pits environmentalism's focus on animals as populations that need conserving (or preserving) from extinction against animal protection's interest in animals as individuals that need protection from suffering. Another potential conflict arises from the tendency for environmental groups to seek solutions in appropriate human intervention (they are still ready to trust human ingenuity). Animal advocates usually offer some variation of a call for humans to leave Nature alone to her own devices (they distrust what humans do in the name of preservation).

In the coming decade, the farm animal issue would seem to pose the most interesting and challenging test of the animal movement's capacity for alliance building. Until the last few years, humane organizations have been virtually alone in attempts to challenge factory-farming practices in the political arena. Unfortunately, the movement has been unable to penetrate the relevant political decision-making networks, which are dominated by industry-based groups with substantial power and influence (Garner 1998). However, the mainstream environmental movement, traditionally indifferent to the suffering of animals on factory farms, has begun to address intensive animal agriculture from the perspective of concern over environmental despoliation resulting from increased quantities of animal waste. The practices of industrialized agriculture are also drawing increased attention from legislative and regulatory bodies. It remains to be seen whether these convergent interests can lead to long-term cooperation aimed at the reform of the agricultural sector, where more

than 90 percent of all animal abuse and suffering occurs.

Some models of movement development suggest that, at a critical stage, some adherents who believe that little or no progress is being made or that change is not occurring fast enough, may turn to extralegal and/or to violent tactics. In recent years there has been an apparent increase in the number of illegal actions directed against those who make their living through the use of animals. Most amount to property damage, cast by its perpetrators as a form of economic warfare against those who exploit animals. On some occasions, however, the targeted individuals and institutions have been the subject of threats to life and limb. Such threats undermine the moral basis of the modern animal movement, which holds that all sentient beings (presumably including humans) should not be subject to abuse or threat. In a democratic and pluralistic society, the boundaries of acceptable protest, direct action, and civil disobedience may be difficult to determine. Nevertheless, the animal protection movement cannot countenance violence towards either animals or humans. As a matter of historical fact, threats of bodily harm and acts of destruction intended merely or mainly to intimidate or harm others are nearly always counterproductive in the long term and will always undermine efforts to build a humane society (as both Gandhi and Martin Luther King Jr. understood).

Conclusion

During the first phase of revitalization (1950–1975) that followed World War II, animal protectionists sought to reinstate the broad question of the proper treatment for animals on the national agenda. New and compelling philosophies of human responsibility toward animals entered into public discourse. In the middle period, between 1975 and 1990, the movement gained popular support, and triggered changes in attitudes and behavior (buying patterns, for example) that continue to register broadly within American society.

The evidence of concern for animals within popular American culture strongly suggests that the humane impulse has made significant inroads into popular consciousness at the beginning of the new millennium. During the last quarter of the twentieth century, millions of Americans came to view the mistreatment of animals, in various contexts, as a social evil that merits attention. Grassroots action and targeted campaign work generated unprecedented pressure for reform within most areas of animal use. Animal protectionists tried to capitalize on public interest and concern by pushing for legislative gains. This effort to realize legislative objectives continued during the consolidation phase of 1990–2000. Animal organizations and their supporters have established themselves as an interest faction in political debates that affect the well-being and future of nonhuman animals and have penetrated some of the institutions where relevant policy decisions are made.

At the same time, cruelty to animals remains peculiarly subject to social definition. Some of the humane movement's greatest challenges involve the regulation or suppression of socially sanctioned cruelties, many of which remain largely outside the scope of anticruelty laws and administrative standards. Animal advocates cannot likely succeed in bringing sweeping reform on their own. The future development of the animal protection movement will depend on the ability of its leaders to identify and take advantage of social trends and to build appropriate alliances with other movements whose goals converge with the objective of a humane society, one that is compassionate, sustainable, and just toward all of its inhabitants.

Literature Cited

Adams, C.J. 1990. *The sexual politics of meat.* New York: Continuum Press.

Brownlee, S. 1999. Foundation gives up 300 research chimps. *New York Times.* 14 September.

Cartmill, M. 1993. *A view to a death in the morning: Hunting and nature through history.* Cambridge: Harvard University Press.

Donovan, J., and C.J. Adams. 1996. *Beyond animal rights: A feminist caring ethic for the treatment of animals.* New York: Continuum.

Einwohner, R.L. 1997. The efficacy of protest: Meaning and social movement outcomes. Doctoral dissertation, University of Washington.

Francione, G.L. 1996. *Rain without thunder: The ideology of the animal rights movement.* Philadelphia: Temple University Press.

Garner, R. 1998. *Political animals: Animal protection politics in Britain and the United States.* Manchester: Manchester University Press.

Glaberson, W. 1999. Legal pioneers seek to raise lowly status of animals. *New York Times,* 18 August, A–1.

Griffin, D. 1976. *The question of animal awareness.* New York: Rockefeller University Press.

Grove, J.M. 1997. *Hearts and minds: The controversy over lab animals.* Philadelphia: Temple University Press.

Herzog, H.A. 1993. "The movement is my life": The psychology of animal rights activism. *Journal of Social Issues* 49: 103–119.

—————. 1995. Has public interest in animal rights peaked? *American Psychologist* (November): 945–947.

Jamison, W., and W. Lunch. 1992. Rights of animals, perceptions of science, and political activism: Profile of animal rights activists. *Science, Technology, and Human Values* 17 (1992): 438–458.

Jasper, J. 1997. *The art of moral protest: Culture, biography, and creativity in social movements.* Chicago: University of Chicago Press.

Jasper, J.S., and J. Poulsen. 1993. Fighting back: Vulnerabilities, blunders, and countermobilization by the targets in three animal rights campaigns. *Sociological Forum* 8: 639–57.

Kellert, S.R. 1985. Attitudes toward animals: Age related development among children. *Journal of Environmental Education* 16: 29–39.

Kellert, S.R., and J. Berry. 1981. *Knowledge, affection and basic attitudes towards animals in American society.* Washington, D.C.: Government Printing Office.

Martig, A. 1995. Public support for the goals of new social movements: A cross-national study. Doctoral dissertation, Washington State University.

McAdam, D. 1982. *Political process and the development of black insurgency.* Chicago: University of Chicago Press.

Melucci, A. 1985. The symbolic challenge of contemporary movements. *Social Research* 52: 789–816.

Mitman, G. 1999. *Reel nature: America's romance with wildlife on film.* Cambridge: Harvard University Press.

Morris, A.D. and C. M. Mueller. 1992. *Frontiers in social movement theory.* New Haven: Yale University Press.

Myers, E. 1998. *Children and animals: Social development and our connection to other species.* Boulder, Colo.: Westview Press.

Payne, D. 1995. Bambi. In *From mouse to mermaid: The politics of film, gender, and culture,* eds. E. Bell, L. Haas, and L. Sells. Bloomington: Indiana University Press.

Plous, S. 1991. An attitude survey of animal rights activists. *Psychological Science* 2 (1991): 194–196.

Richards, R.T., and R.S. Krannich. 1991. The ideology of the animal rights movement and activists' attitudes toward wildlife. In Transactions of the Fifty-Sixth North American Wildlife and Natural Resources Conference. Washington, D.C.: Wildlife Management Institute.

Rowan, A.N. 1984. *Of mice, models, and men: A critical evaluation of animal research.* Albany: State University of New York Press.

Sanders, S., and J. Jasper. 1994. Civil politics in the animal rights conflict: God terms versus casuistry in Cambridge, Massachusetts. *Science, Technology, and Human Values* 19(2): 169–88.

Serpell, J. 1986. *In the company of animals: A study of human-animal relationships*. Oxford: Basil Blackwell.

Shapiro, K. 1994. The caring sleuth: Portrait of an animal rights activist. *Society and Animals* 2: 145–166.

Singer, P. 1998. *Ethics into action: Henry Spira and the animal rights movement*. New York: Rowman and Littlefield.

Snow, D.A., and R.D. Benford. 1992. Master frames and cycles of protest. In *Frontiers in social movement theory,* eds. A.D. Morris and C.M. Mueller. New Haven: Yale University Press.

Spira, H. 1995. *Coordinator's report of the Coalition for Non-Violent Food*. New York: Animal Rights International.

Tarrow, S. 1998. *Power in movement*. New York: Cambridge University Press.

Taylor, V. 1989. Social movement continuity: The women's movement in abeyance. *American Sociological Review* 54: 761–75.

Zald, M., and J.M. McCarthy, eds. 1987. *Social movements in an organizational society*. New Brunswick: Transaction Books.

Appendix
Milestones in Postwar Animal Protection

	ORGANIZATIONS FOUNDED	LEGISLATION PASSED/AMENDED	OTHER
1951	Animal Welfare Institute		
1954	Humane Society of the U.S.		
1955	Society for Animal Protective Legislation		
1957	Friends of Animals		
1958		Humane Slaughter Act (HSA)	
1959	Catholic Society for Animal Welfare (now ISAR) Beauty Without Cruelty	Wild Horses Act	*The Principles of Humane Experimental Technique* published
1962		Bald and Golden Eagle Act	
1966		Endangered Species Act (ESA) Laboratory Animal Welfare Act (LAWA)	
1967	Fund for Animals United Action for Animals		
1968	Animal Protection Institute	Canadian Council on Animal Care	
1969	International Fund for Animal Welfare		
1970		Animal Welfare Act (AWA) amendments	
1971	Greenpeace	Wild Free-Roaming Horse and Burro Act	*Diet for a Small Planet* published
1972		Decompression chamber banned for euthanasia in California Marine Mammal Protection Act (MMPA)	
1973	International Primate Protection League (IPPL)	ESA amendments	Convention on International Trade in Endangered Species (CITES) Air Force beagles campaign
1974	North American Vegetarian Society (NAVS)		*Mankind?* published
1975			*Animal Liberation* published
1976	Animal Rights International (ARI) Committee to Abolish Sport Hunting (CASH)	AWA amendments Horse Protection Act Fur Seal Act	American Museum of Natural History protests *The Question of Animal Awareness* published
1977	Sea Shepherd Conservation Society Scientists Center for Animal Welfare formed American Fund for Alternatives to Animal Research		"Undersea Railroad" releases porpoises in Hawaii
1978	Animal Legal Defense Fund (ALDF) Medical Research Modernization Committee	HSA amendments	Indian government bans rhesus monkey exports

continued from previous page

Appendix
Milestones in Postwar Animal Protection

	ORGANIZATIONS FOUNDED	LEGISLATION PASSED/AMENDED	OTHER
1979	Committee to End Animal Suffering in Experiments (CEASE)	Metcalf-Hatch Act (authorizing pound seizure) repealed in New York State	Coalition to Abolish the Draize Test launched
		Packwood-Magnuson Amendment to the International Fishery Conservation Act	*The Animals' Agenda* launched
			Research Modernization Act introduced in Congress
			Animal Liberation Front (ALF) raid, first in the United States, at New York Univ. Medical Center
			Vegetarianism: A Way of Life published
1980	People for the Ethical Treatment of Animals (PETA)		Action for Life conference launched
	Psychologists for the Ethical Treatment of Animals (PsyETA)		*Animal Factories* published
	Student Action Corps for Animals (SACA)		
1981	Farm Animal Reform Movement (FARM)		Silver Spring Monkeys confiscated from IBR
	Trans-Species Unlimited (TSU)		
	Mobilization for Animals (MfA)		
	Association of Veterinarians for Animal Rights (AVAR)		
	Johns Hopkins Center for Alternatives to Animal Testing (CAAT)		
	Primarily Primates sanctuary		
1982	Food Animal Concerns Trust (FACT)	MMPA reauthorized	Veal ban campaign launched
	Vegetarian Resource Group (VRG)		
	National Alliance for Animal Legislation (NAA)		
	Feminists for Animal Rights (FAR)		
1983	In Defense of Animals (IDA)		*The Case for Animal Rights* published
			A Vegetarian Sourcebook published
1984	Humane Farming Association (HFA)	Pound seizure in Massachusetts repealed	ALF raid at Head Injury Clinical Research Center, Univ. of Pennsylvania
	Performing Animal Welfare Society (PAWS)		*Modern Meat*, focusing on antibiotics in meat production, published

continued from previous page

Appendix
Milestones in Postwar Animal Protection

	ORGANIZATIONS FOUNDED	LEGISLATION PASSED/AMENDED	OTHER
1985	Physicians Committee for Responsible Medicine (PCRM) Last Chance for Animals (LCA) Culture and Animals Foundation (CAF) Tufts Center for Animals and Public Policy	AWA amended to include focus on alternatives and control of pain and distress	ProPets Coalition launched Hegins pigeon shoot campaign launched Campaign for a Fur Free America and Fur Free Friday launched Great American MeatOut launched Federal funding for Head Injury Clinical Research Center suspended
1986	Farm Sanctuary Animal Welfare Information Center (AWIC)		Cambridge Committee for Responsible Research (CCRR) initiative
1987			*The Animals' Voice* launched *Diet for a New America* published Jenifer Graham case filed
1988	Doris Day Animal League (DDAL)		
1989			Avon Corporation ends its animal testing Veal Calf Protection Bill hearings, U.S. Congress
1990	United Poultry Concerns	AWA amended California referendum bans mountain-lion hunting San Mateo County spay/neuter ordinance passed	March for the Animals
1991	Ark Trust	Cambridge, Mass., bans LD50 and Draize tests	Stockyard "downer" campaign launched
1992		Wild Bird Conservation Act International Dolphin Conservation Act Driftnet Fishery Conservation Act Colorado referendum bans spring, bait, and hound bear hunting	Student Right Not to Dissect approved in Pennsylvania
1993		NIH Revitalization [Reauthorization] Act mandates development of research methods using no animals	Marie Moore Chair in Humane Studies and Veterinary Ethics endowed at Univ. of Pennsylvania First World Congress on Alternatives and Animals in the Life Sciences
1994		Arizona banned trapping on public lands (public initiative) Oregon referendum bans bear baiting, bear and cougar hounding	

continued from previous page

Appendix
Milestones in Postwar Animal Protection

	ORGANIZATIONS FOUNDED	LEGISLATION PASSED/AMENDED	OTHER
1995			USDA ends face branding under pressure
			Spay Day USA launched
1996		Colorado referendum bans body-gripping traps	
		Massachusetts referendum bans bear baiting, hound hunting, body-gripping traps, and reforms Fisheries and Wildlife Commission	
		Washington referendum bans bear baiting and hound hunting bears, cougars, and bobcats	
1998		Arizona referendum bans cockfighting	
		Missouri referendum bans cockfighting	
		California referendum bans body-gripping traps	
1999			Harvard Univ. announces launch of animal rights law course
2000			Hegins pigeon shoot terminated

Cruelty to Animals: Changing Psychological, Social, and Legislative Perspectives

CHAPTER 2

Frank R. Ascione and Randall Lockwood

Introduction

During the last half of the twentieth century, many of society's concerns were focused on the quality of our physical environment and the threats to the integrity and health of that environment. As we enter the new millennium, it is becoming clear that societal concerns about the proliferation of violence will constitute another environmental movement, one dealing with the problems that Garbarino (1995) has termed "social toxicity." Research, debate, and discussion about the causes and cures of violence in American society are already part of the discourse of nearly every discipline, from philosophy to criminology to evolutionary biology.

Society is looking for new tools and resources to employ in the efforts to combat violence, identify real or potential perpetrators at an early stage, and define actions that might predict or prevent violent behavior. Closer examination of cruelty to animals within the framework of family and societal violence offers an opportunity to explore violence outside of the traditional nature–nurture debate over the origins of aggression. Cruelty to animals represents an objectively definable behavior that occurs within a societal context. It also represents a good measure of the interaction between the behavior of which an individual is intrinsically capable and the behavior his or her environment has allowed or encouraged. The fact that the definition of cruelty to animals is so strongly influenced by cultures and subcultures need not be a complication but rather an opportunity to unravel the many influences that can shape violent behavior. Closer analysis of the connections between cruelty to animals and other forms of violence offers new opportunities for the study of violence and the hope for new insights and solutions.

Concern about cruelty to animals has been part of the cultural, ethical, and religious traditions of most societies (Regenstein 1991). Serpell (1999) observes that many historical accounts of the rise of the animal protection movement link the growth of this concern to other social reform movements of the eighteenth and nineteenth centuries. These include abolition of slavery, women's suffrage, and the protection of children, the disabled, and the severely mentally ill (*see* e.g., Turner 1980; Ritvo 1987; Ryder 1989). However, Serpell argues that the exclusion of animals from moral consideration in pre–eighteenth-century Europe was the exception, rather than the rule. Hunter-gatherer and early agrarian societies tended to view animals as fully rational, sentient beings with whom humans were to maintain correct and respectful relationships. Even cultures that made use of domesticated animals for food (Greece, Egypt, Mesopotamia, Assyria, India) looked upon killing of animals in a nonsacrificial way as the moral equivalent of manslaughter.

As the sacred elements of animal use changed with the expansion of utilization of domestic animals, so did Western views of animal maltreatment. Key to this transformation were the reinterpretations of Biblical statements on animals by Saint Augustine (A.D. 354–430) and Thomas Aquinas (1225–1274). These denied that animals had the capacity for reason and immortality and advanced the concept that maltreatment of animals was wrong only in the context of its connection to the development of violence against people. In *Summa Contra Gentiles*, Aquinas follows his defense of the exploitation of animals with this observation:

> If any passages of Holy Writ seem to forbid us to be cruel to dumb animals, for instance to kill a bird with its young, this is "to remove man's thoughts from being cruel to other men, and lest through being cruel to other animals one becomes cruel to human beings" (Regan and Singer 1976, 59).

Immanuel Kant echoed these same sentiments five hundred years later in his essay "Metaphysical Principles of the Doctrine of Virtue":

> Cruelty to animals is contrary to man's duty to himself, because it

deadens in him the feeling of sympathy for their sufferings, and thus a natural tendency that is very useful to morality in relation to other human beings is weakened. (Regan and Singer 1976, 125)

Ironically this view recognizes that cruelty to animals can have serious effects on the perpetrator, effects that can shape how he or she interacts with other people, but at the same time it dismisses as immaterial the direct impact of such maltreatment on the nonhuman victim. We at last seem to be moving toward recognition that cruelty to animals can result in great harm to the victim, the perpetrator, and society as a whole. As Serpell (1999) notes, we are arriving at the realization that the roots of cruelty do not lie in some primitive nature that is to be transcended through enhanced civility, as the Victorians believed, but in the complex consequences of personal experiences within the context of cultures and subcultures.

The Renewal of a Research Emphasis

Most of the attention given to the topic of cruelty to animals within scientific and academic communities during the last two hundred years is contained within a relatively small number of reports (Lockwood and Ascione 1998). A sign of the growing maturity of scholarly attention to theory and research on animal abuse is the recent blossoming of conceptual and review papers on this topic. In developmental psychology Ascione (1993) reviewed the literature on animal abuse from the perspective of developmental psychopathology. He noted the early historical interest in animal abuse in the psychoanalytic and child psychology literatures at the beginning of the twentieth century but also noted the failure of developmental psychologists to attend to the role of pets and other animals in the lives of children. Beirne (1999) has examined the literature on ani-

mal abuse and urged the field of criminology to pay greater attention to this phenomenon both as an object of study in its own right and as a factor related to human violence and crime. This theme also runs through a recent South African article published by Schiff et al. (1999). In an earlier paper, Beirne (1997) highlighted the sexual abuse of animals (bestiality) as a topic virtually ignored in the sociological and criminological fields. Agnew (1998) has provided a thoughtful analysis of the need to integrate animal abuse into criminological theories of crime and deviance. Robin (1999) and Flynn (2000a,b) have contributed valuable conceptual papers encouraging the fields of public health and family relations, respectively, to broaden their research domains to include animal maltreatment as a significant form of violence. Arluke and Lockwood (1997), Lockwood and Ascione (1998), and Ascione et al. (2000) have also called for greater collaborative work among animal welfare, domestic violence, child welfare, and child clinical fields both in terms of research efforts and program (preventive and treatment) development.

These reviews have set the stage for implementing a revitalized research agenda on animal abuse issues for this new century. Rather than simply documenting that animal abuse is a significant problem in its own right and a problem related to human victimization, we can now begin to ask the more difficult questions about factors related to the ontogeny, prevention, and treatment of animal maltreatment and its relation to other mental health problems.

Developmental Aspects of Animal Abuse

The relationship between cruelty to animals and stages of human development can be characterized in at least five ways: maintenance, emergence, desistence, escalation, and absence.

First, animal abuse may be present at both an early and a later stage, a relation we could call maintenance. Second, animal abuse may be absent during an early stage but appear at a later stage, a relation called emergence. Third, animal abuse may be present early but may cease to occur later, a relation labeled desistence (though this can be supplanted by escalation, discussed below). Finally, animal abuse may be absent at all developmental stages.

In each of the first four relations, animal abuse is present in some form at some developmental period. These relations are further complicated, however, when we consider that animal abuse may be just one form of antisocial behavior displayed during childhood and adolescence.

In the case of maintenance, animal abuse may be accompanied by other antisocial symptomatology (e.g., fire setting, vandalism) at any developmental periods. In the case of emergence, other antisocial behavior (e.g., bullying children) may precede animal abuse. And in the case of desistence, although animal abuse ceases, it may be supplanted by other antisocial behavior (e.g., the five-year-old who sexually abuses animals becomes a fifteen-year-old who sexually assaults humans). This last condition, in which animal abuse precedes other forms of violence toward people, has sometimes been referred to as the graduation or escalation hypothesis.

The escalation hypothesis suggests that the presence of cruelty to animals at one developmental period predicts interpersonal violence at a later developmental period. According to this hypothesis, the five-year-old who abuses animals is on the way to becoming an elementary-school bully, aggressive adolescent, and adult violent offender. This type of progression fails to consider the complex associations between childhood and adolescent antisocial behavior and adult violence and criminality. In the following sections, we outline relevant material from the area of developmental psychopathology that suggests the escalation hypothesis may be more the exception than the rule.

A more general form of the escalation hypothesis is actually codified in the *Diagnostic and Statistical Manual of Mental Disorders*, fourth edition (DSM-IV) (American Psychiatric Association [APA] 1994). The adult personality disorder most closely related to violent behavior is antisocial personality disorder (APD) (code 301.7) and its diagnosis has, as a prerequisite, the presence of conduct disorder (CD) (code 312.8) prior to age fifteen years. The first area of concern listed under the APD diagnostic criteria is "failure to conform to social norms with respect to lawful behaviors as indicated by repeatedly performing acts that are grounds for arrest" (APA 1994, 649). Although aggressiveness is also listed as a symptom of APD, there is no specific mention of animal abuse. This contrasts with the diagnostic symptoms for CD, which include cases where a child or adolescent "has been physically cruel to animals" (APA 1994, 90). Physical cruelty to animals, however, is only one of fifteen distinct symptoms listed under the CD classification. To receive a diagnosis of CD, the child or adolescent must display at least three of the fifteen symptoms within the previous twelve months. Therefore, cruelty to animals, alone, is neither necessary nor sufficient for a diagnosis of CD.

Unfortunately, we are not aware of any research that ties the presence of cruelty to animals as a CD symptom to the probability of APD in adults. If a strong form of the escalation hypothesis were viable (i.e., early cruelty to animals always leads to later interpersonal violence) and we located a sufficient sample of APD clients, we would expect many of the clients to have displayed cruelty to animals as part of their CD symptomatology. Furthermore, a prospective study could determine whether children identified as conduct disordered who display cruelty toward animals as part of their symptomatology are more likely to display interpersonally violent behavior in adulthood and are more likely to be classified as APD than are children who do not abuse animals.

However, a few caveats accompany this expectation. First, cruelty to animals has been listed as a CD symptom only since the 1987 version of the DSM. Clinical research and practice prior to 1987 may not include questions about animal abuse. A thirty-year-old with APD who was abusive to animals as a fourteen-year-old might not show up as a positive instance of the escalation hypothesis.

Second, covert cruelty to animals may not come to the attention of parents, who are usually the respondents to symptom checklists/questionnaires about their children's current behavior and history. Teachers, who may also be asked to complete such checklists and questionnaires, may be unaware of a child's abuse of animals, since this behavior is unlikely to occur in school environments. In addition, since cruelty to animals has until very recently been classified as a "minor" crime in most jurisdictions, even when discovered it has often been dismissed as trivial or irrelevant. Behaviors that are more overt, such as vandalism, theft, fire setting, and truancy, may be more likely to come to the attention of parents and authorities and to be reported.

Third, there is some evidence that cruelty to animals is one of the earliest CD symptoms to emerge, but its significance may not be noted until additional symptoms (e.g., fire setting, vandalism) begin to accumulate. Frick et al. (1993, 330) noted that parental reports on the emergence of CD symptoms mark 6.5 years as the median age of onset for "hurting animals." Other potentially criminal behaviors emerge later (e.g., stealing, 7.5 years; setting fires, 8.0 years). Note that these data are based on retrospective parental reports. Frick et al. recommend soliciting information, both retrospective and contemporary, directly from children (that is, self-reports), especially for covert behaviors. We may discover that children's self-reports regarding the age of onset of cruelty to animals may be earlier than parental reports indicate. Offord et al. (1991) interviewed a large sample (N=1,232) of

nonclinic twelve- to fourteen-year-olds and their parents. The prevalence of cruelty to animals based on parental reports was 1.2 percent for girls, and 2.7 percent for boys, but the rates based on children's self reports were 9.1 percent and 10.2 percent, respectively. It is also unclear from Frick et al. (1) how long hurting animals persists over childhood and adolescence, (2) whether hurting animals is displaced by other forms of destructiveness and antisocial behavior, and (3) how often cruelty to animals, given that opportunities for its commission are available, is absent in both CD and APD.

The Prevalence of Cruelty to Animals

The occurence of cruelty to animals in children referred to mental health services and in nonreferred children has been estimated in two studies by Achenbach and Edelbrock (1981) and Achenbach et al. (1991). Although these were cross-sectional, not longitudinal, studies, both suggest that cruelty to animals is most prevalent among preschoolers and then decreases over childhood to mid-adolescence (age sixteen). This could represent a real developmental decrease but could also be due to overt cruelty becoming covert and, thus, less likely to be captured in parental reports. These studies do suggest that cruelty to animals is more common for boys than for girls and for referred than for nonreferred children (cruelty to animals ranges from 10–30 percent for referred children in contrast to 0–5 percent for nonreferred children). Larzelere et al. (1989) found that cruelty to animals in a nonclinic sample of children from infants to toddlers, according to parental reports, appeared to increase over this developmental period. Cruelty to animals was "sometimes" or "frequently" present for 4 percent of one-year-olds and 8 percent of four-year-olds. It is unclear what anchor, or definition of "cruelty to animals," is being used by respondents reporting on these very young children. What these studies also cannot tell us is whether a five-year-old who is cruel to animals will display this behavior at later ages.

Comparing Cruelty to Animals with Other Symptoms of CD

Since cruelty to animals is only one of the fifteen symptoms of CD, it is appropriate to ask how it compares with the other symptoms on its diagnostic value. Spitzer, Davies, and Barkley (1990), as part of a larger study, examined the diagnostic utility of individual CD symptoms using data gathered from psychological and psychiatric facilities at ten different geographic sites. One of the measures of symptom utility they computed was an odds ratio. The odds ratio is calculated by taking the probability of a symptom in children diagnosed with CD and dividing it by the probability of the same symptom in children without CD. For physical cruelty to animals, Spitzer et al. found an odds ratio of 5.07. That is, if we take 5 percent as the prevalence of cruelty in a sample of non-CD children, the prevalence in a sample of CD-diagnosed children would be 25 percent (5.07 [odds ratio]=.25/.05). (The odds ratio for two other symptoms, for comparison, are 11.34 for stealing without confrontation of a victim and 3.14 for physical cruelty to people.) This odds ratio was sufficiently high for Spitzer et al. to recommend that the symptom be retained in future revisions of the DSM. However, if the estimates above are correct, the odds ratio suggests that only one in four (25 percent) CD-diagnosed children might engage in animal abuse. The critical question that remains is what

percentage of this 25 percent persists in displaying cruelty to animals into adolescence and adulthood.

A recent paper published in Australia and New Zealand suggests that this analysis may not be far off the mark. Luk et al. (1999) reanalyzed case data from a sample of children (N=141) referred to mental health services with "symptoms suggestive of oppositional defiant/conduct disorder" (p. 30) and a sample of community children (N=37). The clinic-referred group was subdivided into two groups. Children in the "no–cruelty–to-animals" ("no CTA") group (N=101) were *not* reported to have been cruel to animals on the Child Behavior Checklist (CBCL). In contrast, children in the cruelty–to–animals (CTA) group (N=40) were reported to be sometimes or often cruel to animals. Thus, 40 of 141, or 28.4 percent, of the clinic-referred children displayed the symptom of animal abuse.

Luk et al. also demonstrated that differentiating the clinic-referred subgroups on the basis of presence of reported animal abuse was related to another measure of childhood problem behaviors which, unlike the CBCL, does not include an item assessing cruelty to animals. Using the Eyberg Child Behavior Inventory, they found that the mean problem and problem severity scores of children in the CTA clinical group significantly (p<.001) exceeded the means for the "No CTA" clinical group and the community control group.

The issue of CD symptom utility was also addressed in a study by Frick et al. (1994). Using data gathered from 440 clinic-referred children and adolescents, they examined the utility of proposed DSM-IV CD symptoms in predicting the presence or absence of the disorder. They computed the positive predictive power (PPP) and the negative predictive power (NPP) of each symptom. PPP can be expressed as the proportion of children who display the symptom and who are also diagnosed with the disorder. NPP is the proportion of children who do not display the symptom and are not diagnosed with the disorder. Frick et al.

also computed base rates for each CD symptom, allowing comparison of symptom prevalence in their sample (for example, the following symptoms and the percentage of subjects displaying them were cruel to animals, 12 percent; setting fires, 3 percent; cruel to people, 5 percent; stealing, 34 percent; fighting, 27 percent; lying, 31 percent). The PPP for cruelty to animals was .82, indicating that 82 percent of the children displaying cruelty to animals received a CD diagnosis (the comparable PPPs were 1.0 for setting fires, .83 for cruelty to people, .65 for stealing, .64 for fighting, and .54 for lying). The NPP for cruelty to animals was .22, indicating that 22 percent of the children not displaying the symptom did not receive a CD diagnosis. As the authors note, "although the presence of the symptom was highly indicative of the disorder, the disorder was often present without the symptom" (ibid., 533).

Usually CD is diagnosed only if symptoms have been present within the previous twelve months. One child may have had one severe episode of animal abuse within the previous twelve months but no previous episodes. Another child may have been severely abusive toward animals in the five years prior to and including the year he or she was evaluated. Current diagnostic criteria would not be sensitive to the quantitative, as well as qualitative, differences likely to exist between these two children's behavioral history. This is a critical issue, since Loeber et al. (1993), for example, found that cruelty to animals only differentiated a sample of children with oppositional defiant disorder from CD children when information about cruelty to animals was aggregated over a three-year period. Assessing whether animal abuse is a chronic or acute problem thus appears essential in making predictions about future behavior.

Checklist Assessments of Animal Abuse

While the rather lengthy and time-consuming psychiatric assessments of child psychopathology based on the DSM-IV are useful (e.g., the Diagnostic Interview Scale for Children, the Diagnostic Interview Scale for Adolescents), questionnaires and checklists are more often used to assess childhood behavior and psychological problems. One of the most common is the previously cited CBCL, developed by Achenbach et al. (1991). Cruelty to animals is assessed through parental responses to one item (out of 112 items related to behaviors ranging from "acts too young for his/her age" to "worries"). Using a time frame of the previous six months, the respondent rates his or her child as "cruel to animals" using the following choices: "not true (as far as you know)," "somewhat or sometimes true," or "very true or often true." For the specific study of animal abuse, this instrument leaves much to be desired. First, "cruel to animals" is undefined, and different parents may use different definitions of cruelty when rating their children. Second, the response format suggests that parents may use either frequency of cruelty, severity of cruelty, or both in rating their child. Third, the "not true" choice acknowledges that parents may not be aware of such cruelty and suggests that obtaining children's self-reports may be critical for potentially covert behaviors like animal abuse (the youth self-report form of the CBCL, unfortunately, does not include an item on cruelty to animals). Fourth, the time period of six months precludes assessing cruelty to animals that may have occurred prior to this time. In defense of the CBCL, it must be stated that a focus on assessing animal abuse was never one of the purposes for which it was designed. The CBCL's value lies in its economical assessment of a broad range of internalizing and externalizing problems.

The Interview for Antisocial Behavior (IAB) developed by Kazdin and Esveldt-Dawson (1986) assesses primarily externalizing problems and also includes "being cruel to animals" among a total of thirty items reflective of antisocial behavior, a number of which are reflective of current CD symptomatology. The IAB can be administered as a parental report or as a self-report. The response format includes ratings of the severity of each problem (1=none at all, 5=very much) as well as its duration or chronicity (1=present six months or less, 3=always present). The IAB thus provides more detail about cruelty to animals but respondents' interpretations of "cruel" may still vary. It should be noted that Kazdin and Esveldt-Dawson found that the "cruel to animals" item correlated .46 (p<.001) with the total IAB score and differentiated a sample of CD and non-CD children F(1,256)=8.44, (p<.01).

This excursion into the symptomatology of CD reinforces the point that cruelty to animals is but one piece of the puzzle relating childhood antisocial behavior to adult violence and criminality. Since this piece has not received extensive research attention, it is understandable that animal welfare organizations have emphasized high-profile cases where animal abuse appears related to interpersonal violence. For example, in interviews with executed serial killer Arthur Gary Bishop, Mike Carter (personal communication, March 23, 1998) discovered that Bishop was so distressed by the abduction, torture, and murder of his first child victim that he was pursuing ways of "de-escalating." Bishop's "solution" was to acquire nearly fifty puppies from animal shelters and pet shops, take them home, and torture and kill them. Instead of reducing his need for violence, Bishop found that he so enjoyed the tortured cries of the animals, that the animal abuse helped motivate him to abduct, torture, and kill more children. Cases such as these, where animal abuse seems directly tied to interpersonal violence, abound in the literature on serial homicide (Ressler and Schact-

man 1992). Animal abuse may desensitize a perpetrator. It may represent a form of rehearsal for the abuse of humans and, if undetected, embolden the perpetrator to believe he can escape both the authorities and the consequences of his acts. Most, if not all, serial killers very likely were conduct-disordered as children and adolescents, but thankfully, only a minuscule proportion of conduct disordered children are likely to develop into such offenders. As noted by a colleague who works with juvenile fire setters (Marcel Chappuis, personal communication, March 23, 1998), every adult arsonist he has encountered has had a childhood history of fire setting, yet very few fire setting children progress to adult arson.

We know of only one recent study that has attempted to address directly the relationships among a history of animal abuse, physical punitiveness by parents, and adult criminality, differentiating violent and nonviolent offending. Miller and Knutson (1997) referred to research by Widom (1989), based on archival data, showing positive associations between experiences of child maltreatment and adult criminality and violent offending. But Miller and Knutson raised concerns about the failure of archival records to capture actual histories of abuse (due to under-reporting and the fact that only a minority of incidents may come to the attention of authorities). Using self-reports, Miller and Knutson reportedly failed to find a substantial association between past experiences of animal abuse and physical punitiveness (r=.13, p<.05) and noted that past experiences of animal abuse did not differentiate among the four groups of offenders they had classified (homicide, violent, sex, and other offense). They did find that the violent offender group scored higher on the physical punitiveness measure than did the other three groups.

Miller and Knutson's incarcerated sample (N=314) was predominantly male (84 percent). After 15 participants were dropped due to incomplete data, 71 percent of the remaining 299 participants reported some experience with cruelty to animals. However, "cruelty to animals" needs to be elaborated upon. Miller and Knutson used an adaptation of Boat's (1999) Animal-related Trauma Inventory to assess experiences with cruelty to animals. Seven types of cruelty to animals listed in this qualitative inventory were used to create a composite measure yielding a quantitative summary score. A major problem with this composite measure is that some of the items may reflect a respondent's antagonism toward animals while others may be neutral or suggest a strong affectional attachment to animals. According to the seven types of cruelty to animals, the respondent (1) saw an animal killed, (2) killed a pet, (3) killed a stray, (4) was forced to hurt an animal, (5) hurt an animal, (6) saw others hurt an animal, or (7) was controlled by a threat to hurt or kill an animal.

Composite scores could range from 0 to 46, but it is apparent that this quantitative rating masks the complexity of "exposure to animal abuse." The methodology makes no clear distinction between the perpetration of cruelty to animals and exposure to such acts performed by others, either incidentally or as a specific threat to coerce the subject. For example, an individual could receive a high score for responding positively only to items 1, 4, 6, and 7, which involve either witnessing others' cruelty to animals, being forced to abuse animals, or being coerced by threatened animal abuse. Another individual might receive a similarly high score by responding positively only to items 2, 3, and 5, which involve participant animal abuse or killing. Assessing the internal consistency of this composite scale would have been useful. Low internal consistency might suggest that single items or groups of items may be measuring different constructs. High internal consistency would substantiate that witnessing and perpetrating animal abuse form a single construct. In other qualitative research, Ascione et al. (1997) specifically separated observation of animal abuse performed by others

from respondents' own cruelty toward animals. Such a separation would have been useful in the Miller and Knutson research.

Although Miller and Knutson conclude that their data were "not consistent with the hypothesis that exposure to cruelty to animals is importantly related to antisocial behavior or child maltreatment" (1997, 59), they themselves urge caution about interpretation of their findings. First, they note that base rates of some exposure to cruelty to animals were quite high in this incarcerated sample (i.e., 71 percent reported some exposure). This was also the case in a second study they conducted with 308 undergraduates in which 68.9 percent of males and 33 percent of females reported some exposure to cruelty to animals (this gender difference was statistically significant). Second, Miller and Knutson note that the distribution of scores on the composite measure of exposure to cruelty to animals was positively skewed (i.e., most respondents scored in the low range) and leptokurtic (i.e., more sharply peaked than bell shaped). Since these characteristics indicate a restricted range of scores, correlational analyses were less likely to yield significant results.

Although there are methodological difficulties with the Miller and Knutson study, the study does suggest the value of using more than a single-item assessment of experience with animal abuse. It would be valuable to have an assessment instrument that was both efficient (e.g., checklist or structured questionnaire) and targeted at both performing acts of animal abuse and witnessing such acts performed by others. Although Ascione et al. (1997) assessed both performing and witnessing animal abuse, the instrument they developed is a lengthy interview protocol that may diminish its attractiveness in nonresearch applications.

One model that could be used to develop an animal abuse assessment instrument is the approach that has been taken to assess juvenile fire setting. Fire setting shares many features with animal abuse: both are CD

symptoms; both may show developmental changes and display the relations of maintenance, emergence, and desistence; both may share etiological factors; both are often performed covertly; and both may be early sentinels for later psychological problems.

The U.S. Department of Justice funded the production of the Salt Lake Area Juvenile Firesetter/Arson Control and Prevention Program (1992). The program is based on a typology of juvenile fire setters that may be relevant to developing a typology of children who abuse animals (Marcel Chappuis, personal communication, March 23, 1998). The typology of juvenile fire setters is as follows:

Normal curiosity fire setters: These children have a mean age of five years (range three to seven years) and often share the characteristics of poor parental supervision, a lack of fire education, and no fear of fire.

"Plea-for-help" fire setters: These children have a mean age of nine years (range seven to thirteen years); their fire setting is often symptomatic of more deep-seated psychological disturbance. These individuals usually have had adequate fire education.

Delinquent fire setters: These individuals have a mean age of fourteen years (range thirteen years to adulthood); their fire setting may be one of a host of adolescent-onset antisocial behaviors, including gang-related activities.

The Salt Lake program has developed a series of assessment scales that are geared to each age group of fire setters and that can be administered to the child's parent/guardian and to the child. In addition to questions about fire education and the fire setting incident(s), questions about general behavior problems (similar to those on the CBCL) are included. It is noteworthy that among these questions is an item about cruelty to animals (there is also a direct question about whether the fire setting incident involved the burning of an animal). Responses to these assessments are then used to direct the selection of an intervention strategy. Children who fall into the normal curiosity group are often enrolled in a fire education program, and attempts may also be made to educate parents about fire safety and the need for supervising young children. Children who fall into the other two groups are referred to mental health services, since fire departments are not prepared to deal with the psychological problems these young people may present.

It might be possible to develop a similar typology for children who present with the problem of animal abuse. Although there is not a great deal of empirical information to rely on, the study by Ascione et al. (1997) suggests the varied motivations that may underlie child and adolescent animal abuse. Together with the extensive experience of animal control and animal welfare professionals, one could develop a typology mirroring that for juvenile fire setters. A sketch of such a typology might approximate the following:

Exploratory/curiousity-based animal abuse: Children in this category would likely be of preschool or early elementary school age, poorly supervised, and lacking training on the physical care and humane treatment of a variety of animals, especially family pets and/or stray animals and wildlife in the neighborhood. Humane education interventions are likely to be sufficient to produce desistence of animal abuse in these children. It should be noted that age alone should not be the determining factor in including children in this category. For example, CD symptoms may have an early developmental onset and, as noted earlier, cruelty to animals is one of the earliest CD symptoms to be noted by caretakers.

Pathognomonic animal abuse: Children in this category are more likely to be older (though, as noted above, not necessarily) than children in the exploratory/curious group. Rather than a lack of education about the humane treatment of animals, psychological malfunction varying in severity may be the root of these children's animal abuse. For example, childhood animal abuse may be abuse-reactive behavior tied to childhood histories of physical abuse, sexual abuse,

and exposure to domestic violence.

Delinquent animal abuse: Youth in this category are most likely to be adolescents whose animal abuse may be but one of a number of antisocial activities. In some cases, the animal abuse may be a component of gang/cult-related activities (e.g., initiation rites) or less formal group violence and destructiveness. The associated use of alcohol and other substances may be implicated with these youth.

A study by Arluke et al. (1999) makes clear the connection between animal abuse and a variety of criminal activities that affect human welfare. Using records from the MSPCA, they located 153 individuals who had been prosecuted for cruelty to animals (abusers) and a comparison group of 153 individuals, residing in the same neighborhoods, with no record of animal abuse (nonabusers). They then checked the state's criminal records for all of these individuals, noting four categories of criminal offense. Abusers were more likely to have been arrested for violent (37 percent), property-related (44 percent), drug-related (37 percent), and public disorder (37 percent) offenses than were nonabusers (7 percent, 11 percent, 11 percent, and 12 percent, respectively). The difference between abusers' and nonabusers' percentages was significant ($p < .0001$) for all four types of offenses.

Information in a recent U.S. Department of Justice report (Office of Justice Programs 1998) ties animal abuse to other criminal activity. Sampling 625 women and 168 men who were victims of stalking, the results of the survey noted that 9 percent of the women and 6 percent of the men reported that stalkers had killed or threatened to kill family pets (ibid., 13). These estimates of pet abuse should be viewed as lower limits since it can be assumed that not all participants were pet owners. This provides another example of animals endangered by human interpersonal threats and violence.

Clearly, more detailed research is needed to understand how exposure to or perpetration of cruelty to animals may interact with other physio-

logical, developmental, and social forces to influence the potential for antisocial and/or violent juvenile and adult behaviors. Athens (1992) provides one holistic approach to understanding this process that may help clarify some of the dynamics in extreme cases. He divides the process of development of violent dangerous criminal behavior into several stages. The first of these, which Athens terms "brutalization," is the result of a combination of experiences, including being the victim of physical or sexual abuse, being a witness to extreme violence against others, and "violent coaching" (i.e., being encouraged to respond violently to real or perceived threats). This process then engenders the later stages, which are characterized by the routine use of violence and acceptance of one's violent notoriety. Although Athens does not specifically focus on cruelty to animals as part of this process, it is often a potential feature of the process at several stages, especially in the initial "brutalization" stage.

Research with Nonclinical, Noncriminal Samples

Research on the relation between animal abuse and forms of human victimization in nonclinical samples is also beginning to emerge. Flynn (1999a) surveyed 267 university students (68.4 percent were women) about their personal history of abusing animals and then asked them if they endorsed the use of corporal punishment in child rearing and if they condoned a husband slapping his wife. Of the men, 34.5 percent admitted to at least one incident of animal abuse perpetrated during childhood; for the women that figure was 9.3 percent. Flynn found that participants who had abused animals had more favorable attitudes toward the use of corporal punishment in child rearing. Those abusing animals were more likely to approve of a husband slapping his wife (15.6 percent) than were those who did not report abusing animals in childhood (5.4 percent).

In a parallel study, Flynn (1999b) examined the relation between perpetrating animal abuse and being a victim of parental corporal punishment. Participants were those studied in Flynn (1999a). He found that the frequency of being spanked by fathers was positively related to the participants' perpetrating animal abuse, but this relation only held for men in the sample. As noted by Flynn, "Nearly 60 percent of male respondents who were physically punished as teens by their fathers perpetrated animal abuse, compared with 23 percent who were not hit as teens by their fathers" (977).

These two studies by Flynn clearly bring the issue of animal abuse into the sociological research realm of family violence. The studies also illustrate that animal abuse–family violence associations are not limited to clinical samples or samples of adjudicated animal abuse–family violence offenders.

Animal Abuse and Domestic Violence

The last three decades of the twentieth century also witnessed a dramatic refocusing of attention on the problem of domestic violence. The publication of books, monographs, articles, and government studies provided needed depth to our understanding of intimate violence in families. Once again companion animals did not escape the terror present in some homes. Most of the information available about pet abuse in families experiencing domestic violence took the form of anecdotal reports, often used to illustrate the callous violence perpetrated by some batterers. In addition, Ascione et al. (1997) found that the majority of domestic violence shelters may not ask women about their experiences with pet abuse. However, it was not until 1998 that

the first empirical study appeared whose specific aim was to assess the prevalence and forms of animal abuse in the context of human domestic violence.

Ascione (1998) enlisted the aid of a domestic violence shelter to interview thirty-eight women who had recently entered the shelter to escape violence. The women were asked about pet ownership, whether their pets had been threatened or harmed by the batterer, and the possible effects of pet abuse on women's decision making about leaving batterers. Twenty-two of the 38 women had children, and the women were asked if their children had abused animals.

Parallel to national data on pet ownership in American families with children, 74 percent of the women interviewed by Ascione reported owning a pet or having owned one in the past twelve months. Threats or actual harm to pets was reported by 71 percent of these women, and 57 percent reported that their pets had been hurt or killed by their adult partner. Thirty-two percent of women with children reported that one of their children had hurt or killed pets.

One of the other disturbing findings of this study was that 18 percent of women reported that they had delayed entering the shelter out of concern for their pets' welfare. The level of animal abuse in these homes was unexpected, as was the discovery that pet welfare was a significant issue for some women in their decision to leave batterers.

That these findings were not idiosyncratic to the particular sample of women studied was confirmed in a replication conducted by Flynn (2000b). He interviewed forty-three women, all of whom owned pets, who had entered a shelter in South Carolina for battered women. Flynn found that 46.5 percent of these women reported that their pets had been threatened or harmed. Although only two women reported that their children had also abused pets, women whose pets had been abused were more than twice as likely to report that their children had also been

abused (33.3 percent) than women whose pets had not been abused (15.8 percent).

Flynn also found that 40 percent of women whose pets had been abused had delayed seeking shelter out of concern for their pets' welfare and safety. In five of these eight cases, the delays exceeded two months. These findings support those of Ascione (1998) and confirm that worrying about their pets is a significant obstacle for women who are trying to leave batterers. It is encouraging that programs designed to remove this obstacle, by sheltering pets for women who are battered, are becoming more common (Ascione et al. 2000). These programs represent an innovative form of collaboration among domestic violence, animal welfare, and veterinary medical professionals, as well as members of the lay community, to address a human and animal safety and health problem.

Assessing animal abuse in the context of domestic violence is likely to become more systematic as other forms of overlap (e.g., that between child abuse and domestic violence) are more carefully examined. Flynn's study (2000a) hints that the time is ripe for a larger-scale study examining the confluence of animal abuse, child maltreatment, and domestic violence.

Cruelty to Animals and Elder Abuse and Neglect

In the last decade, reports of cruelty to animals within the context of elder abuse and neglect have also begun to emerge (Rosen 1995; National Committee for Prevention of Elder Abuse 1997; Cooke-Daniels 1999). Such connections can parallel those seen in domestic violence. They can also take the form of economic exploitation of the elderly through threats of harm to or denial of care for pets of the elderly. All forms of elder abuse tend to be under-reported, and very little empirical data have been gathered on cruelty to animals in this context, but professionals in both adult protective services and animal protection have begun to address this connection through training and community collaboration. Growing attention also is being given to the suffering of animals and people that can result from the hoarding of large numbers of animals by individuals, often older women (Lockwood 1994; Patronek 1999). This form of cruelty to animals has received little attention in the psychiatric literature but is increasingly being recognized as a serious concern for both human and animal welfare agencies (Frost 2000).

Societal Concerns and Responses to Cruelty to Animals

In addition to an increase in attention to cruelty to animals from the scientific community in the last decade, the general public has expressed growing concern about the issue, both for its effects on animals and its implications for human safety. A December 1996 survey of 1,008 American households conducted by Penn and Schoen for The Humane Society of the United States (HSUS) found that 42 percent of respondents believed cruelty to animals to be moderately to extremely serious as a problem in this country, compared with 61 percent responding in this way to environmental issues and 78 percent to child abuse. Of those surveyed, 71 percent supported making animal abuse a felony, and 81 percent felt that the enforcement of cruelty-to-animals laws should be strengthened. Respondents were equally divided about the primary reason for their concern. About one-third said the main reason to take cruelty to animals seriously was that intentional harm to animals was simply wrong, while an equal number said that their main concern was that such cruelty was predictive or indicative of other forms of violence against people.

Another measure of the widespread interest in and concern about cruelty to animals is the growing media attention devoted to high-profile cases. The March 2000 killing of a woman's dog by an individual who pulled the dog, Leo, from the woman's car and threw him into traffic attracted international coverage and offers of rewards that exceeded $110,000 (Kalfrin 2000). The story of the killing of more than a dozen cats in an Iowa animal shelter by three teenagers drew more mail to *People* magazine that any other story except the death of the Princess of Wales (Jewel and Sandler 1997). Similarly, the 1998 torture/ killing of a dog by four teenagers served as the centerpiece of an hour-long British Broadcast Corporation/ Arts and Entertainment Network documentary, *The Cruelty Connection,* which aired in the United Kingdom, the United States, and Australia.

Legislative and Law Enforcement Responses to Cruelty to Animals

Society's response to cruelty to animals is also reflected in the laws that are enacted to respond to the problem and in the level of enforcement of those laws. As of July 2000, thirty-one states had enacted felony–level provisions within their cruelty to animals codes, a dramatic rise from less than a decade ago (see Figure 1). This is in addition to the forty-three states that treat dogfighting as a felony offense and thirteen in which cockfighting is a felony. Such provisions reflect both societal pressure to respond to cruelty to animals and legislative willingness to accommodate this demand. While animal neglect continues to be a misdemeanor crime, most of these laws recognize extreme forms of malicious animal abuse or torture as crimes that transcend the simple destruction of property and fall in the ranks of violent crimes whose perpetrators need special attention.

Severe, intentional animal abuse has increasingly been viewed as symptomatic of mental disorder. State laws have reflected this viewpoint in requiring or recommending psychological assessment and treatment for those convicted under these laws. Since 1998 California has required such assessment in all cruelty-to-animals convictions. Colorado law requires assessment and recommends treatment; New Mexico mandates counseling in cases of animal abuse by juve-

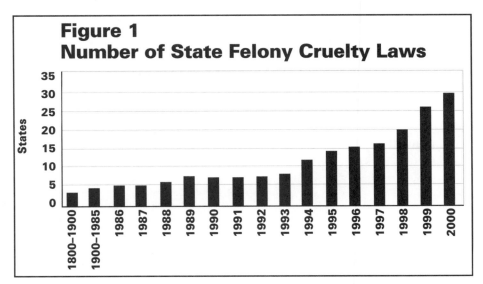

Figure 1
Number of State Felony Cruelty Laws

niles and recommends it for adult offenders. In the last decade, more than a dozen other states have added counseling and treatment as a sentencing option within their cruelty-to-animals codes.

Although the need for assessment and treatment for cruelty-to-animals offenders is increasingly recognized, the small number of such referrals in the past has prevented the development and evaluation of appropriate assessment and treatment protocols. Several assessment tools and treatment approaches have been suggested (Boat 1999; Jory and Randour 1999; Lewchanin and Zimmerman 2000; Zimmerman and Lewchanin 2000). Existing mandated treatment protocols for juvenile or adult sex offenders or batterers may be appropriate for only a small segment of animal abusers and are clearly not appropriate for convicted offenders in cases involving extreme neglect or hoarding.

In states where assessment and/ or treatment of cruelty-to-animals offenders is mandated, particularly California, judges and prosecutors have begun to seek out mental-health-care providers who have knowledge of the dynamics of cruelty to animals. To meet this need, in 1999 the Mental Research Institute (MRI) and The HSUS began providing training in this area for such professionals and made lists of professionals with an interest in taking on such cases available to the appropriate court authorities (Loar 2000).

As laws dealing with animal abuse have been strengthened over the last decade, law enforcement officials have given greater attention to such cases. There is, as yet, no established national system for tracking the incidence of and law enforcement response to crimes against animals, so we can offer no quantitative assessment of the number of cruelty-to-animals cases being charged. However, there are several indicators of growing interest in the connections between cruelty to animals and its association with other forms of violence. This link has been addressed in several recent law review articles and texts (Davidson 1998; LaCroix 1998; Lockwood 1999; Frasch et al. 2000). It has also been reviewed in material provided to all chiefs of police (Lockwood 1989) as well as material used in the training of newly appointed juvenile prosecutors (American Prosecutors Research Institute 1999).

Recent trends in the juvenile justice system resonate well with growing recognition of cruelty to animals as an early warning sign of the potential for criminal or antisocial behavior. The model increasingly applied in the case of young or first-time offenders is that of "balanced and restorative justice," or BARJ (Office of Juvenile Justice and Delinquency Prevention 1998). The BARJ model attempts to steer away from conventional interventions that are purely punitive. Programs based on this model seek simultaneously to address the needs of the victim, hold perpetrators accountable for their actions, and address the gaps in the competencies of the perpetrator that may have contributed to the offense. The model also emphasizes making use of a variety of community resources to respond to each of these requirements. This approach is consistent with the growing use of animal-oriented programs targeting youthful offenders or those at risk of becoming violent perpetrators. Structured experiences with animals, such as learning humane dog-training techniques, are being incorporated into a variety of programs designed to enhance empathy and build nonviolent competencies (Duel 2000). Such programs have not, as yet, been evaluated for their long-term effectiveness compared with other traditional approaches (e.g., "boot camp"), but they provide unique opportunities to incorporate humane values into broader programs for violence prevention.

Cruelty to Animals and Human Violence: Future Needs and Directions

There are many unanswered and unasked questions in the study of cruelty to animals and other violence, as well as obstacles that need to be overcome in the search for answers. We hope that the coming years will see increased attention in the following five areas.

1. The Ecology of Violence against Animals

Because cruelty to animals has traditionally been seen as a minor crime, basic quantitative information as to the nature and extent of serious cruelty to animals has been limited. Good criminological analysis can begin with a solid "victimology," or reporting of exactly what has been done to animals and by whom. Vermeulen and Odendaal (1993) and Arluke et al. (1999) have provided important first steps in remedying this gap. Further progress will depend on standardized reporting and tracking of cruelty-to-animals cases around the country. Many key questions remain.

What is the true incidence and prevalence of various forms of animal abuse and neglect?

How does this victimology vary for different kinds of animals (e.g., by species, as well as other factors, such as owned versus stray, wild versus tame versus domestic)?

What are the demographic attributes of the offenders and the frequency and severity of their acts?

How do these demographics (age, sex, culture, residence, family size and structure, and criminal history) interact with victimology? For example, how closely do the actions of female offenders resemble those of the far more prevalent male offenders?

How does the victimology and

offender profile of intentional abuse differ from that of neglect or passive abuse or abandonment or hoarding? Are these differences relevant in predicting the likelihood of future involvement in violence?

What are the trends in cruelty-to-animals cases (frequency, severity, chronicity, offender demographics) within specific reporting areas? Are such cases becoming more frequent, more severe, or more likely to involve younger perpetrators?

What is the extent of overlap with records of other known violent offenses, particularly interpersonal violence, including child abuse, domestic violence and elder abuse?

What is the outcome of animal-abuse and -neglect cases that are reported and enter the criminal justice system? What proportion are dealt with through education, diversion, or other alternative mechanisms? Are cases handled differently by the juvenile court system and by the adult courts? Does the inaccessibility of juvenile court records prevent the effective assessment of the predictive value of tracking cruelty to animals?

2. The Developmental Dynamics of Cruelty to Animals and Human Violence

If we are to use the connections between cruelty to animals and other forms of violence in a meaningful way to predict and/or intervene in the progression of violence, we need a much clearer picture of the place of animal abuse in the patterns and progression of violence. Most of our understanding of this connection has come from retrospective analysis of individuals or families in which serious human violence has already taken place. Far more attention is needed to identify normal versus pathological pathways involving participation in or witnessing the mistreatment of animals. Future study may address a range of questions.

What are the underlying dynamics of the victimology? The killing of a dog may have different significance if it is

the killer's own dog, a parent's or sibling's dog, a stray dog, a newborn puppy, or an aggressive animal that has bitten the perpetrator. The incident may have different significance if the offender is alone or in a group; is a six-year-old, a twelve-year-old, or an adult; or if it is the first, third, or twentieth such incident.

What critical incidents may be related to the earliest expressions of violence? What is the influence of the response of parents, peers, and siblings to these events?

What is the trajectory of the development of interpersonal violence that incorporates cruelty to animals? How often is animal abuse truly predictive of escalation? If violence has already progressed to serious or lethal levels, how often do offenders "regress" to violence against animals?

How important are frequency, severity, and persistence of cruelty to animals as indicators of cruelty that represent a true potential for progression rather than a stage of experimentation with power and control?

What factors are present when cruelty to animals stops altogether or does not escalate to other forms of violence? If we recognize that many individuals might engage in some acts of intentional animal abuse without progressing to other antisocial acts, it becomes essential to identify the sources of stability and resilience (internal, familial, or societal) that have prevented such a progression. These sources include parental response to early cruelty; intervention by school, social service, or law enforcement authorities; and mental-health interventions.

What physiological, neuropsychological correlates of cruelty to animals might exist that relate to other possible correlates of antisocial behavior (such as thrill-seeking or low responsiveness to stressful situations)?

What is the role of external influences (drugs, alcohol) in the initiation of violent incidents against animals and others?

What is the role of exposure to media and video-game violence against animals and others in promoting imitation

of or desensitization to such violence?

How does the real or symbolic sexual role of animals influence the form of abuse that might be perpetrated? How prevalent is the direct sexual abuse of animals among violent offenders?

3. Animal Abuse and Domestic Violence

Animal abuse that takes place in the context of domestic violence presents several compelling opportunities for research. One would evaluate the animal sheltering programs being developed for women who have left their homes to seek shelter. Another would replicate research on battered women's experiences with animal abuse but would include assessment of the batterers' reports. A third would assess the animal-abuse experiences of women who are battered but who have not decided or been able to leave their batterer.

Programs are proliferating to shelter the pets of battered women who have left home to seek safety elsewhere. In the limited experience with such programs, little attention seems to be given to collecting data on their implementation, use, and evaluation. A standard protocol would not only be useful for the programs already established but could also assist in the planning and development of new programs.

Such a protocol should include basic questions:

What types and numbers of animals are being boarded?

What is the condition of animals brought to the shelter? Was the animal directly threatened? Was the animal actually abused? If so, how and by whom?

Was the purpose of boarding the animal explained to the children (if applicable)? Did the woman leave home in order to live with others (friends, relatives), was she entering a shelter for battered women, or was she remaining at home but obtaining a protective order against her partner?

What was the length of time the animal was boarded? What was the disposition of the case?

Did the batterer make contact with

the animal shelter while the animal was boarded? If so, what was the nature of the contact? Did the batterer try to retrieve the animal while it was at the shelter? If so, how was this handled?

Did the woman ask to visit the animal while it was being sheltered? If so, how was this arranged? How often did it occur?

Research on domestic violence has begun to focus on characteristics of batterers, especially as a method for developing typologies of batterers. These efforts are often directed at matching "types" of batterers with "types" of interventions. Most of our information about animal abuse in domestic violence situations has been derived from victims' (women's) reports. It is important to assess the batterers' perceptions of animal abuse as well. One approach would replicate two studies of women who are battered (Ascione 1998 and Flynn 2000b) with the addition of interviews with the batterers. Another study would interview both partners to assess, for example, the concordance (or lack thereof) of their reports on incidents (frequency, severity) of animal abuse. Questions about motivations for and judgments of seriousness of animal abuse could be included. If the animal abuse occurred in the presence of children, the batterer could be asked about his perception of the effects of such witnessing on his children's welfare.

Most of the research on domestic violence has studied women in shelters for battered women. Less is known, however, about women who remain with their batterer and women who are in the process of deciding whether to stay or leave. This latter group would be a logical audience for information campaigns about animal sheltering options and information about the significance of animal abuse as an indicator of danger (and as a potential symptom of children's psychological disturbance). The following issues need to be assessed:

How many and what types of pets are involved currently and in the past?

Were these pets the woman's, the partner's, mainly the children's, or truly family pets?

What factors have influenced the woman's decision to stay or leave (e.g., personal welfare, children's welfare, economic issues, religious reasons, animal welfare)?

Has the woman ever told her partner she was thinking of leaving? His reaction? Has she ever made an attempt to leave that was aborted? Why? Has she ever called a women's shelter or domestic violence (DV) crisis line? Why?

Has she, the children, or others ever called police to report a DV incident? What was the outcome?

Have the children ever tried to protect her? A sibling? A pet?

If she did leave (but did not enter a shelter) what factor(s) prompted this?

What is her knowledge of the partner's history (as child, adolescent, and adult prior to this relationship) of animal abuse?

Have other adults (e.g., partner's friends) ever been involved in her abuse?

4. Social-Service Responses to Cruelty to Animals

Humane organizations have made significant inroads in alerting social-service agencies to regard cruelty to animals as a form of family violence that can be both indicative and predictive of other violence. Although only California formally includes animal control officers and state humane officers among mandated reporters of child abuse, many other communities are providing for the cross-training of animal-abuse and child-abuse investigators or are including humane society representatives in local coalitions against violence. To maximize the effectiveness of these bridges between animal- and human-welfare advocates, we need more information about these cooperative efforts.

How frequently are child-, elder-, or domestic-abuse reports filed by humane officers? What proportion are validated, and how does this compare

with frequency of filing by other mandated reporters?

If few reports are being made by well-trained reporters, what are the obstacles to such reporting?

5. Prevention and Intervention/Treatment

The core assumption of many of the efforts against violence is that earlier detection of predispositions for violence will give the best opportunity for meaningful intervention. However, the lack of any standardized programs for assessment and intervention has left this concept untested.

What types of cruelty-to-animals offenses constitute the most significant warnings that intervention is needed?

Is it more cost-effective or productive to target at-risk groups at a young age rather than active offenders?

Which interventions are most effective in deterring violent behavior (e.g., pairing offenders or high-risk individuals with nonviolent or humane mentors, formal instruction in nonviolent skills or humane attitudes)?

How important are opportunities for undoing harm or being confronted by victims in structuring effective interventions?

How important is it for animals to be involved in prevention and intervention programs? Can nurturing and other prosocial skills be taught in other ways (such as gardening projects) (Rathmann 1999)?

When is the use of animals in therapy inadvisable? Are there patterns of violent history that should not be addressed through animal-assisted therapy or animal-assisted activities?

What are the best short- and long-term attitudinal and behavioral measures of successful intervention in dealing with animal-abusing populations?

Looking Out for Our Future

Answers to these questions will require the cooperation of individuals and agencies from many different disciplines. They will also require a truly prospective approach, identifying individuals who are involved in cruelty to animals at the earliest possible age or stage and tracking the influences that prevent or promote the escalation to other forms of violent behavior. Cruelty to animals must be taken seriously as a problem in its own right, independent of what it may tell us about the potential for human harm.

Violence makes victims of us all. All segments of the community that deal with health and safety, kindness and cruelty, people and animals, must constantly find ways to build the connections that will make it possible to end this victimization.

Understanding our complex relationships with animals is already starting to provide us with an impressive range of new resources that aid our efforts against violence, cruelty, and victimization. The programs and policies being put into action are already saving animal and human lives. Incorporating our understanding of these relationships into our understanding of violence in a sense unites our concerns for the damage to our physical and psychological environment. By seeing ourselves as a part of nature and not apart from it, we can gain personal strength and satisfaction. By seeing ourselves as connected to families and communities and not controlled by them, we can reduce the need for violence.

Literature Cited

Achenbach, T.M., and C.S. Edelbrock. 1981. Behavioral problems and competencies reported by parents of normal and disturbed children aged four through sixteen. *Monographs of the Society for Research in Child Development* 46: 188.

Achenbach, T.M., C.T. Howell, H.C. Quay, and K. Conners. 1991. *National survey of problems and competencies among four to sixteen-year-olds.* Monographs of the Society for Research in Child Development 56, Serial No. 225.

Agnew, R. 1998. The causes of animal abuse: A social-psychological analysis. *Theoretical Criminology* 2: 177–209.

American Prosecutors Research Institute (APRI). 1999. *Jumpstart: Resource Manual for Newly Assigned Juvenile Prosecutors.* Alexandria, Va.: APRI.

American Psychiatric Association (APA). 1994. *Diagnostic and Statistical Manual of Mental Disorders* (fourth ed.). Washington, D.C.: APA.

Arluke, A., and R. Lockwood. 1997. Understanding cruelty to animals. *Society and Animals* 5(3): 183–93.

Arluke, A., J. Levin, C. Luke, and F. Ascione. 1999. The relationship of animal abuse to violence and other forms of antisocial behavior. *Journal of Interpersonal Violence* 14: 963–75.

Ascione, F.R. 1993. Children who are cruel to animals: A review of research and implications for developmental psychopathology. *Anthrozoös* 6: 226–47.

————. 1998. Battered women's reports of their partners' and their children's cruelty to animals. *Journal of Emotional Abuse* 1: 119–33.

Ascione, F.R., and P. Arkow, eds. 1999. *Child abuse, domestic violence, and animal abuse: Linking the circles of compassion for prevention and intervention.* West Lafayette: Purdue University Press

Ascione, F.R., M.E. Kaufmann, and S.M. Brooks. 2000. Animal abuse and developmental psychopathology: Recent research, programmatic, and therapeutic issues and challenges for the future. In *Handbook on animal-assisted therapy: Theoretical foundations and guidelines for practice*, ed. A. Fine, New York: Academic Press.

Ascione, F.R., T.M. Thompson, and T. Black. 1997. Childhood cruelty to animals: Assessing cruelty dimensions and motivations. *Anthrozoös* 10: 170–77.

Ascione, F.R., and C.V. Weber. 1997. *Battered partner shelter survey.* Logan, Utah: Utah State University.

Ascione, F.R., C.V. Weber, and D.S. Wood. 1997. The abuse of animals and domestic violence: A national survey of shelters for women who are battered. *Society and Animals* 5: 205–18.

Athens, L. 1992. *The creation of dangerous violent criminals.* Urbana, Ill.: University of Illinois Press.

Beirne, P. 1997. Rethinking bestiality: Towards a sociology of interspecies sexual assault. *Theoretical Criminology* 1: 317–40.

————. 1999. For a non-speciesist criminology: Animal abuse as an object of study. *Criminology* 37: 117–47.

Boat, B.W. 1999. Animal-related trauma inventory. In *Child abuse, domestic violence, and animal abuse: Linking the circles of compassion for prevention and intervention*, eds. F.R. Ascione and P. Arkow. West Lafayette, Ind.: Purdue University Press.

Cooke-Daniels, L. 1999. The connection between animals and elder abuse. *Victimization of the Elderly and Disabled* 2(3): 37, 46–47.

Davidson, H. 1998. What lawyers and judges should know about the link between child abuse and cruelty to animals. *American Bar Association Child Law Practice* 17: 60–63.

Duel, D. 2000. *Violence prevention and intervention: A directory of animal-related programs.* Washington, D.C.: The Humane Society of the United States.

Flynn, C.P. 1999a. Animal abuse in childhood and later support for interpersonal violence in families. *Society and Animals* 7: 161–71.

————. 1999b. Exploring the link between corporal punishment and children's cruelty to animals. *Journal of Marriage and the Family* 61: 971–81.

————. 2000a. Why family professionals can no longer ignore violence toward animals. *Family Relations* 49: 87–95.

————. 2000b. Woman's best friend: Pet abuse and the role of companion animals in the lives of battered women. *Violence Against Women* 6: 162–77.

Frasch, P., S. Waisman, B. Wagman, and S. Beckstead. 2000. *Animal law*. Durham, N.C.: Carolina Academic Press.

Frick, P.J., B.B. Lahey, B. Applegate, L. Kerdyck, T. Ollendick, G.W. Hynd, B. Garfinkel, L. Greenhill, J. Biederman, R.A. Barkley, K. McBurnett, J. Newcorn, and I. Waldman. 1994. DSM-IV field trials for the disruptive behavior disorders: Symptom utility estimates. *Journal of the American Academy of Child and Adolescent Psychiatry* 33: 529–539.

Frick, P.J., Y. Van Horn, B.B. Lahey, M.A.G. Christ, R. Loeber, E.A. Hart, L. Tannenbaum, and K. Hanson. 1993. Oppositional defiant disorder and conduct disorder: A meta-analytic review of factor analyses and cross-validation in a clinical sample. *Clinical Psychology Review* 13: 319–40.

Frost, R. 2000. People who hoard animals. *Psychiatric Times* 14(4): 1–7.

Garbarino, J. 1995. *Raising children in a socially toxic environment*. San Francisco: Jossey-Bass.

Jewel, D., and B. Sandler. 1997. Mischief or murder? *People*, November 24.

Jory, B. and M.L. Randour. 1999. *The AniCare model of treatment for animal abuse*. Washington Grove, Md.: Psychologists for the Ethical Treatment of Animals.

Kalfrin, V. 2000. Leads pour in from sketch of dog's killer. *APB News*, March 23.

Kazdin, A.E., and K. Esveldt-Dawson. 1986. The interview for antisocial behavior: Psychometric characteristics and concurrent validity with child psychiatric inpatients. *Journal of Psychopathology and Behavioral Assessment* 8: 289–303.

LaCroix, C.A. 1998. Another weapon for combating family violence: Prevention of animal abuse. *Animal Law* 4: 1–32.

Larzelere, R.E., J.A. Martin, and T.G. Amberson. 1989. The toddler behavior checklist: A parent-completed assessment of social-emotional characteristics of young preschoolers. *Family Relations* 38: 418–25.

Lewchanin, S., and E. Zimmerman. 2000. *Clinical assessment of juvenile cruelty to animals*. Brunswick, Me.: Biddle Publishing.

Loar, L. 2000. Treatment for people who hurt animals . . . It's the law. *C.H.A.I.N. (Collective Humane Action and Information Network) Letter* 13(1): 10, 18.

Lockwood, R. 1989. Cruelty to animals and human violence. *Training key No. 392*. Arlington, Va.: International Association of Chiefs of Police.

———. 1994. The psychology of animal collectors. *American Animal Hospital Association Trends* 9: 18–21.

———. 1999. Cruelty to animals and violence against humans: Making the connection. *Animal Law* 5: 81–87.

Lockwood, R., and F.R. Ascione, eds. 1998. *Cruelty to animals and interpersonal violence: Readings in research and application*. West Lafayette, Ind.: Purdue University Press.

Loeber, R., K. Keenan, B. Lahey, S. Green, and C. Thomas. 1993. Evidence for developmentally based diagnoses of oppositional defiant disorder and conduct disorder. *Journal of Abnormal Child Psychology* 21: 377–410.

Luk, E.S.L., P.K. Staiger, L. Wong, J. Mathai. 1999. Children who are cruel to animals: A revisit. *Australia and New Zealand Journal of Psychiatry* 33: 29–36.

Miller, K.S. and J.F. Knutson. 1997. Reports of severe physical punishment and exposure to cruelty to animals by inmates convicted of felonies and by university students. *Child Abuse and Neglect* 21: 59–82.

National Committee for the Prevention of Elder Abuse. 1997. Elder abuse and cruelty to animals: Is there a link? *Nexus* 3(3): 1, 4–6.

Office of Juvenile Justice and Delinquency Prevention. 1998. *Guide for implementing the balanced and restorative justice model*. Washington, D.C.: U.S. Department of Justice.

Office of Justice Programs. 1998. *Stalking and domestic violence*. Washington, D.C.: U.S. Department of Justice.

Offord, D.R., M.H. Boyle, and Y.A. Racine. 1991. The epidemiology of antisocial behavior in childhood and adolescence. In *The development and treatment of childhood aggression*, eds. D.J. Pepler and K.H. Rubin. Hillsdale, N.J.: Lawrence Erlbaum Associates.

Patronek, G. 1999. Hoarding of animals: An under-recognized public health problem in a difficult-to-study population. *Public Health Reports* 144: 81–87.

Randour, M.L. 1999. Battering the wife, kicking the dog, and slapping the kids: The link between domestic violence and animal abuse. *Voice* 2: 7–9.

Rathmann, C. 1999. Forget Me Not Farm: Teaching gentleness with gardens and animals to children from violent homes and communities. In *Child abuse, domestic violence, and animal abuse*, eds. F.R. Ascione and P. Arkow. W. Lafayette, Ind.: Purdue University Press.

Regan, T., and P. Singer. eds. 1976. *Animal rights and human obligations*. Princeton: Prentice-Hall.

Regenstein, L. 1991. *Replenish the earth*. New York: Crossroad Publishing.

Ressler, R.K., and T. Shachtman. 1992. *Whoever fights monsters*. New York: St. Martin's Press.

Ritvo, H. 1987. *The animal estate*. Cambridge, Mass.: Harvard University Press.

Robin, M. 1999. Innocent victims: The connection between animal abuse and violence toward humans. *Public Health Reports* 82: 42–44.

Rosen, B. 1995. Watch for pet abuse—It might save your client's life. *Shepard's Elder Care/Law Newsletter* 5: 1–9.

Ryder, R. 1989. *Animal revolution: Changing attitudes toward speciesism*. Oxford: Basil Blackwell.

Schiff, K.G., D.A. Louw, and F.R. Ascione. 1999. The link between cruelty to animals and later violent behaviour against humans: A theoretical foundation. *Acta Criminologica* 12: 25–33.

Serpell, J. 1999. Working out the beast. In *Child abuse, domestic violence, and animal abuse: Linking the circles of compassion for prevention and intervention,* eds. F.R. Ascione and P. Arkow. West Lafayette, Ind.: Purdue University Press.

Spitzer, R.L., M. Davies, and R.A. Barkley. 1990. The DSM-III-R field trial of disruptive behavior disorders. *Journal of the American Academy of Child and Adolescent Psychiatry* 29: 690–97.

Turner, J. 1980. *Reckoning with the beast: Animals, pain, and humanity in the Victorian mind.* Baltimore: Johns Hopkins University Press.

Vermeulen, H., and J.S.J. Odendaal. 1993. Proposed typology of animal abuse. *Anthrozoös* 6: 248–57.

Widom, C.S. 1989. Does violence beget violence? A critical examination of the literature. *Psychological Bulletin* 106: 3–28.

Zimmerman, E., and S. Lewchanin. 2000. *Community intervention in juvenile cruelty to animals.* Brunswick, Me.: Biddle Publishing.

Social Attitudes and Animals

CHAPTER **3**

Harold Herzog, Andrew Rowan, and Daniel Kossow

Introduction

Under the headline "Concentration Camp for Dogs," *Life* magazine published in 1966 a dramatic photograph of an emaciated dog (Wayman 1966). The accompanying article, a harrowing depiction of the lives of research animals, provoked a public outcry over the use of pound animals in research. The result was a deluge of mail to Congress, which subsequently passed the Laboratory Animal Welfare Act, the first federal legislation directed at improving the lot of animals used in research.

As we enter the new millennium, our collective views on the treatment of animals continue to influence public policy. In the United States, however, public opinion regarding the status of nonhuman animals is divided. Animal activists aggressively argue that activities such as the use of animals in scientific research and the consumption of animal flesh involve considerable animal suffering and are unethical. A substantial number of Americans are just as adamant in opposing those views. While there does not yet seem to be a society-wide consensus regarding the moral status of animals, it is clear that significant shifts in public opinion have taken place during the last twenty-five years. Changing attitudes in favor of greater protection for animals have resulted in the enactment of legislation such as the Animal Welfare Act,

decreased reliance on animal testing of consumer products, a decline in acceptance of the fur trade, and a dramatic increase in the number of Americans who are members of animal protection organizations.

This chapter is an overview of the attitudes of Americans toward the treatment and moral status of nonhuman animals. We discuss problems of attitude assessment, the social psychology of attitudes toward animals, and the complex relationship between attitudes and behavior. We also review changes in attitudes toward animals over the past fifty years and current public opinion regarding a variety of issues related to animal welfare.

Measuring Attitudes

The assessment of attitudes is complex. Any attempt at assessment must deal with two fundamental issues: what to ask and whom to ask.

The Questions Asked

One of the biggest problems faced by social scientists interested in assessing public opinion on controversial issues is how to word the questions.

Ideally, questions should be phrased to minimize bias. For example, in a 1992 survey sponsored by *Reader's Digest*, more than a thousand adults were asked how they felt about the statement, "It is wrong to use animals in laboratory experiments for medical research." The results indicated that 31 percent of the respondents opposed animal research to some degree (Roper Center 1992a). A similar survey commissioned by *Parents* magazine, however, produced quite different results (Roper Center 1989a). It asked one thousand adults, "If the only way we could find a cure for AIDS would be by using animals as research subjects, would you favor or oppose this kind of research." When the animal research question was phrased this way, the proportion opposing the use of animals for this research dropped to 15 percent.

In some cases, particularly when a survey is commissioned by an advocacy group, questions are apparently designed to skew the responses in favor of the position held by the organization. A 1990 survey commissioned by the National Shooting Sports Foundation, a pro-hunting group, asked, "Certain animal rights groups want a total ban on all types of hunting. Do you strongly support this goal, somewhat support the goal, somewhat oppose this goal, or strongly oppose this goal." Only 21 percent of the one thousand respondents were either strongly or somewhat opposed to hunting; 57 percent said they approved of hunting (Roper Center 1990). In contrast, when asked in a 1991 poll by the position-neutral Princeton Survey Research Associates, "Do you think that hunting animals as a sport is morally right or wrong," a minority (33 percent) felt hunting was morally right; 56 percent felt it was morally wrong (Princeton Survey Research 1991).

The Sample Surveyed

Much of the research on attitudes toward animal welfare has been conducted using the most convenient subjects available to social scientists—college students. Many of these studies have focused on the relationship between attitudes toward animal welfare and other variables such as gender, personality, and social/political dispositions. Typically, attitudes toward animals in these studies are assessed by multi-item questionnaires such as the Animal Research Survey (Takooshian 1988), the Animal Attitudes Scale (Herzog et al. 1991) and the Scale of Attitudes toward the Treatment of Animals (Bowd 1984).

An example of this type of research is a study by Broida et al. (1993). They gave approximately a thousand college students Takooshian's 1991 Animal Research Survey, along with a personality test (the Myers-Briggs Personality Type Inventory), the Bem Sex Role Inventory, and other instruments designed to measure various social attitudes. The attitudes measured included political and religious ideologies, faith in science, assertiveness, and beliefs about abortion. The results indicated that pro-animal research attitudes were associated with conservative political ideology, religious fundamentalism, and less empathy for animals. Attitudes toward animal research were related to personality type; "intuitive" and "feeling" types were more likely to oppose animal research than were "sensing"

and "thinking" types. While these results were statistically significant, all the variables combined accounted for less than 10 percent of the total variation in views about animal welfare. The authors concluded that their study actually demonstrated that attitudes toward animal research are generally not highly related to other variables.

Some researchers have focused their attention on the attitudes of specific interest groups rather than on those of college students. They have studied hunters and birders (Kellert 1996), animal activists (Plous 1991; Richards and Krannich 1991; Jamison and Lunch 1992; Galvin and Herzog 1998) and psychologists (Plous 1996a). Plous's survey is a good example of this type of research. Plous randomly sampled five thousand members of the American Psychological Association. Eighty percent of the 3,982 psychologists who responded supported animal research; only 14 percent opposed it, but the level of support depended strongly on the type of research in question. There was, for example, greater support for research involving rats or pigeons than for that involving primates or dogs. The margin of support declined substantially if the research involved pain or death and/or the use of primates. Only 10 percent of the psychologists claimed that they used the findings of animal research in their own work frequently, whereas about 60 percent indicated that they rarely or never used the results of anmal research. Male psychologists were more likely to support animal research than were female psychologists, and recently graduated Ph.D.s were less supportive of animal research than were older respondents.

Ironically, perhaps the best information on American public opinion concerning attitudes toward animal welfare is the least known—it is found in polls conducted by professional polling organizations. In many cases a trade group (e.g., the American Medical Association or the National Shooting Sports Foundation) or a magazine or news organization will

commission an organization such as ICR Survey Research Group, the Gallup Organization, or Louis Harris and Associates to conduct a public opinion survey. These polls are typically conducted by telephone and have the advantage of being based on large probability samples of adult Americans (usually about a thousand) rather than on potentially biased groups such as college students or hunters. On the other hand, the level of assessment of specific issues may be superficial, because items related to the treatment of animals are often limited to only a few questions imbedded in a host of political and demographic questions.

One problem with data gathered by professional polling organizations is that they are often difficult to locate or are not made available to researchers. Brief summaries usually lacking essential background information may appear in daily newspapers or trade publications, or the results may not be published at all. Fortunately, a good deal of this information is available (for a fee) via the Internet through the Roper Center for Public Opinion Research at the University of Connecticut. The Roper Center is a nonprofit, nonpartisan organization that provides access to more than ten thousand survey files covering more than 275,000 questions dating back to the 1930s. Dozens of these items deal with animal welfare issues ranging from the transplantation of anmal organs into humans to the concerns of fur-coat owners about harassment by animal activists (Herzog and Dorr, in press).

Another valuable and easily accessible source of information about public opinion concerning animals is the General Social Survey (GSS). The GSS is based on a probability sample of adults in the United States and is conducted on a regular basis by the National Opinion Research Center. The GSS contains hundreds of questions assessing demography and social/political attitudes. Statistical techniques such as multiple regression can be used to analyze clusters of attitudes. In 1993 and 1994, several animal-related questions were included in the GSS. One of these dealt with attitudes toward animal rights and another with the use of animals for medical testing. These two items have been used by researchers to examine the relationships between attitudes about animal welfare and variables such as gender, education, religiosity, and attitudes about science (Peek et al. 1996; Kruse 1999).

Consistency of Attitudes

One reason that attitudes toward animals are important is they are related to action (Eagly and Chaiken 1993). For example, Nickell and Herzog (1996) asked a sample of college students to evaluate the effectiveness of propaganda that either supported or opposed animal research. At the end of the experimental session, the students were offered the opportunity to sign postcards addressed to their federal legislators that either supported or opposed the use of public funds for animal research. The students' views of the effectiveness of the materials significantly predicted which of the postcards they would sign.

The relationships between attitudes and behavior are complex. Certainly some aspects of the behavior of the American public have changed as a result of increased awareness of anmal welfare issues. Nearly half of adult supermarket shoppers in two thousand households surveyed by the Food Marketing Institute in 1994 said they had refused to buy products in which the ethical treatment of animals had been called into question (Roper Center 1994a).

However, we must be careful with generalizations about animals, attitudes, and social behavior. Polls show that Americans as a group are more sensitive toward the ethical issues raised by sport hunting than they were in the past. (This is evidenced by a steep drop in the number of sport hunters in the United States between 1965 and 1995. When asked in 1995 to list their favorite leisure activities,

fewer than 5 percent of Americans listed hunting.) But not all demographic groups have shown a decline of interest in the sport. Women, for example, are joining the ranks of hunters in surprising numbers. Indeed, women make up the fastest growing segment of the hunting community.

Perhaps the most common paradigm for understanding the dynamics of attitudes is referred to by social psychologists as the A-B-C model. It posits that attitudes are the result of three types of psychological processes: affective (or emotional), behavioral, and cognitive. These three often work together, as they do in animal activism. Ethnographic studies (Sperling 1988; Herzog 1993) have found that animal activists often go to great lengths to bring their emotions, behavior, and thoughts into a coherent package.

Take the hypothetical case of Bill. His life is proceeding quite conventionally until a friend passed him a used copy of Peter Singer's *Animal Liberation*, often referred to as the Bible of the animal rights movement. Bill reads the book and for the first time begins to think about issues related to the treatment of other species (the cognitive component). He also has a visceral reaction to some of Singer's descriptions of the treatment of animals on factory farms (the emotional component)—so much so that he sends $50 to an animal rights organization (the behavioral component). Now that he is on that organization's mailing list, Bill is deluged with brochures and solicitations from all sorts of animal protection groups. Through them, he learns more about the treatment of animals on factory farms and in research labs (at least from an animal activist's perspective). His behavior changes further; he puts an animal rights bumper sticker on his car, changes his diet, and begins showing up at demonstrations. As one activist put it, "The more my ideas changed, the more my behavior changed. And the more my behavior changed, the more my ideas changed."

Bill's case nicely illustrates the A-B-

C model. Emotion, behavior, and cognition work together in a consistent fashion. In reality, however, things are rarely so neat. Take our collective beliefs about the moral status of animals. A 1995 poll sponsored by the Associated Press found that two-thirds of Americans agreed with the statement, "An animal's right to live free of suffering should be just as important as a person's right to live free of suffering" (Roper Center 1995a). A Princeton Survey Research Associates survey conducted in 1994 with thirty-four hundred adults found that 65 percent of respondents had very favorable or mostly favorable views of the animal rights movement (Roper Center 1994c).

One might think that the United States is a nation of animal lovers—but how strong are these beliefs? Americans consume animal flesh in ever larger quantities per capita. While the consumption of red meat is down, having dropped roughly 8 percent between 1975 and 1995, the average American still eats an average of 170 pounds of beef and pork per year. The modest drop in red meat consumption has been more than made up for by a dramatic increase in the consumption of chicken—now between seven and eight billion chickens are killed each year. Only about 2 percent of Americans are "true" vegetarians (Rowan and Shapiro 1996), and many of these say that their diet is the product of their health concerns rather than a reflection of a moral stance (Amato and Partridge 1989; Rozin et al. 1997). (When asked in a 1995 Louis Harris poll what they intended to eat as a main course for Christmas dinner, only 1 percent of adults indicated a vegetarian dish—Roper Center 1995b).

A question in a 1993 poll commissioned by the *Los Angeles Times* exemplifies the contradictions characteristic of public opinion surveys about animals and ethics (Balzar 1993). When asked, 47 percent of respondents indicated that they agreed with the statement "animals are just like people in all important ways." The sample was almost exactly evenly split, and very few people were unde-cided. Herzog (unpublished) recently used this question to examine consis-tency in beliefs about the use of ani-mals in research among college students. One hundred and two stu-dents were given a survey that includ-ed the question, along with ten other questions related to the ethics of ani-mal research taken from national public opinion polls. Just as in the *Los Angeles Times* sample, 47 percent agreed with the "just like humans" statement. However, half of the stu-dents who said that animals were "just like humans in all important ways" were in favor of animal re-search, 40 percent supported the use of animal organs to replace diseased human body parts, and half favored experimentation on pound animals. Ninety percent of all the students indicated that they regularly ate the beings that they claimed were "just like humans."

What are we to make of these con-tradictions? How is it that in a nation where the overwhelming majority of individuals eat meat daily, more than two-thirds of the people claim to support the agenda of the animal rights movement?

Attitudes have several dimensions, including direction, complexity, and strength. Strong attitudes are central to who we are. They are the focus of thought and emotion. They are typi-cally embedded in a matrix of beliefs and emotions and may be associated with profound behavior changes. In the extreme, these attitudes form a coherent package that coalesces into ideology. This coalescence can be seen in animal activists whose lives come to revolve around issues related to the treatment of other species.

In contrast, many individuals have attitudes about animals that are peripheral and superficial. These beliefs are variously called "non-atti-tudes" or "vacuous attitudes" (Eagly and Chaikan 1993). They typically have little coherence and emotional resonance and may be simply a col-lection of preferences and isolated opinions. While non-attitudes may have little real salience in a person's

life, they can affect responses on opinion polls. Public opinion polls about the use of animals in research largely reflect these "non-attitudes."

Take the hypothetical case of Sally who loves her cat, Millie, but who gen-erally spends very little time actually thinking about animal welfare, moral philosophy, and public policy. One evening she is called by a telephone pollster. The pollster asks if she strongly agrees, agrees, disagrees, or strongly disagrees with the statement "animals and people should have the same basic rights." She glances at Millie and replies, "Strongly agree." As the pollster records her answer on his tally sheet, Sally goes back to what she was doing before the telephone rang, dismembering a chicken car-cass for her family's dinner. What allows Sally to believe in fundamental rights of animals at the same time that she eats them?

Just as Sally can profess a respect for animals even as she prepares one for dinner, the public can demon-strate an inconsistency in its opinion on animal research. We believe there are several reasons why. First, the moral status of animals is a complex issue, and many people are ambiva-lent about it or simply do not care. This is supported by data from the 1994 GSS. When asked how they felt about medical testing on ani-mals, only 20 percent of the respon-dents had strong opinions on the issue (that is, they either strongly agreed or strongly disagreed with the item). The majority had less strong feelings (they simply agreed or dis-agreed) and about 15 percent had no opinion at all (Roper Center 1994b). In contrast, 80 percent of a sample of approximately two hun-dred animals rights demonstrators surveyed by Galvin and Herzog (unpublished) at the 1996 March for the Animals in Washington, D.C., expressed strong feelings about this issue. (In nearly all cases, they strong-ly opposed animal testing).

The fact is that the treatment of animals is not an issue of high priori-ty to most people. A 1989 poll con-ducted by the American Medical Asso-

ciation asked fourteen hundred re-spondents to rank the importance of twelve issues facing the country. Edu-cation was at the top of the list and finding cures for fatal diseases was ranked third. The treatment of ani-mals came in last (American Medical Association 1989). A 1987 poll com-missioned by *Rolling Stone* magazine asked 816 randomly selected Ameri-cans between the ages of eighteen and forty four to name two or three causes that they would like to work for. Only 7 percent mentioned animal rights—about the same number that indicated that they would like to work for the mandatory teaching of cre-ationism in public schools (Roper Center 1987).

We are not arguing that the animal rights movement has not had an effect on our culture. When an opin-ion poll on animal research was con-ducted by the National Opinion Research Center in 1948, only 37 per-cent of approximately two thousand adults sampled had ever heard of groups opposing the use of animals in research (Roper Center 1948a). By now, everyone is familiar with the ani-mal protection movement, and refer-ences to the animal movement are much more common in the media than they were thirty years ago. When Yale University social scientist Stephen Kellert polled American atti-tudes toward wildlife in 1976, he found that about 1.2 percent of Amer-ican adults (2 percent of female respondents and 0.6 percent of male respondents) were members of ani-mal protection groups. When a major consumer corporation asked a similar question in 1990, it found that 6 per-cent of American adults claimed to be members of animal protection groups and more than 20 percent said they had contributed money to ani-mal protection.

It is clear that there have been changes in public opinion on animal welfare issues in the last fifty years. Perhaps the best example is provided by an analysis of public attitudes toward the use of animals in biomed-ical research.

Table 1
Public Opinion on Using Nonhuman Animals in Research

Question	Year	% Supporting	% Opposing
In general, do you favor or oppose the use of live animals in medical teaching and research? (Roper Center 1948b)	1948	85	8
Do you agree with the use of animals in experiments? (Baylor University, Center for Community Research and Development 1985)	1985	58.8	41.2
In general, do you support or oppose the use of animals in biomedical research? And do you feel strongly about that? (Roper Center 1989c)	1989	64	29
Should we continue to conduct tests on animals to aid medical research? (The University of North Carolina of Chapel Hill 1991)	1991	63	37
In general, do you support or oppose the use of animals in biomedical research? (If you support or oppose) Do you feel strongly about that? (Roper Center 1992b)	1992	63	33
In general, do you support or oppose the use of animals in biomedical research? Do you feel strongly about that? (Roper Center 1993)	1993	65	31
It is okay to perform medical tests on animals? (Survey Research Center of Maryland, College Park 1999)	1999	61.4	36.5

Table 2
Public Opinion on Using Nonhuman Animals in Painful and Injurious Research

Survey Statement: Scientists should be allowed to do research that causes pain and injury to animals like dogs and chimpanzees if it produces new information about human health problems.

Year	Supporting plus Strongly Supporting Animal Research (%)	Opposing plus Strongly Opposing Animal Research (%)
1985	63	30
1988	53	42
1990	50	45
1993	53	42
1996	50	45

National Science Board 1985–1998

Table 3
Public Opinion on Using Nonhuman Animals in Research for Specific Illnesses

Question	Year	% Supporting	% Opposing
As you may know, many medical findings have been made using animal experiments. But some people question the need for animal experiments in some cases. Do you think it is necessary to use animals for			
allergy testing? (Roper Center 1985a)	1985	61	27
some medical research, such as cancer, heart diseases, and diabetes? (Roper Center 1985b)	1985	81	12
There has been some controversy recently about the use of animals in medical research. If the only way we could find a cure for AIDS (Acquired Immune Deficiency Syndrome) would be by using animals as research subjects, would you favor or oppose this kind of research? (Roper Center 1989a)	1989	78	15
Do you favor or oppose animal testing on medical products used to combat serious illness? (Ward 1990)	1990	76	20

Attitudes toward Animal Research

In the late 1940s, respondents were asked, "In general, do you favor or oppose the use of live animals in medical teaching and research." Eighty-four percent of the respondents approved of and 8 percent opposed animal research (Roper Center 1948b). A poll conducted one year later by the National Society for Medical Research found that 85 percent of the respondents approved and 8 percent opposed the use of animals in medical research. As these polls show, fifty years ago, public opposition to using nonhuman animals in both medical teaching and research was extremely low. More recently, there has been a significant negative shift in attitudes toward the use of animals in research and testing (see Table 1).

Table 1 indicates that compared with 1948 there is a significant minority of the public opposing animal use in research and testing. The variation in results probably reflects differences in the wording of the question and the context of the question, both known to affect public responses. In the last ten to fifteen years, it appears as though public opinion of nonhuman animal research has been relatively constant, with approximately 60 to 65 percent of the public approving or accepting the practice and 30 to 40 percent opposing it.

However, since 1985 the National Science Board (NSB) "Science Indicator" surveys have included the following statement: "Scientists should be allowed to do research that causes pain and injury to animals like dogs and chimpanzees if it produces new information about human health problems." The statement pointedly identifies the use of dogs and chimpanzees (very high-profile animals) in research that causes pain or injury (a high "cost") but is offset by benefits (information that can cure human health problems).

The results (Table 2) give us a clear indication of public attitude trends of the last fifteen years. Public support of animal research has declined—and it appears to have declined markedly since the late 1940s, when questions asking about the use of dogs in medical research garnered support from 80 percent or more of the public. In the last decade, which coincides with a much more active campaign by bio-medical interests to promote the importance of animal research and to characterize all animal activists as, at best, emotional Luddites, support for animal research has remained stable. It could have declined further without such vigorous pro-research PR. In the United Kingdom in 1988, only 35 percent of the public supported the NSB statement, and most Europeans have a more negative attitude about the use of animals in research and testing than do Americans (see Pifer et al. 1994).

While Tables 1 and 2 show the decline in support for using nonhuman animals in general, other surveys have explored how particular variations in the question might affect the responses. Table 3 indicates that public concern appears to depend on the perceived importance of the illness being studied. For example, within the context of using nonhuman animals in biomedical research, there is about a 20-percent difference in approval ratings between research on illnesses perceived to be "life threatening" (such as cancer) and those perceived to be "non–life threatening" (such as allergies).

As Table 4 demonstrates, the public's concern over the use of animals varies depending on the type of animal. In the first poll, responses to a general question on animal welfare show an evolutionary hierarchy of concern. Respondents were more than four times as concerned about dogs as they were about snakes. In the second poll, which specifically addressed the use of animals in research, dogs were the most favored, while mice and rats were regarded as the most expendable. Table 5 also shows this hierarchy of concern for mice and monkeys.

The results in Tables 4 and 5 are consistent with findings that the public weighs benefits and costs when determining whether nonhuman animals should be used in research. The more benefits perceived (in terms of the importance of the disease and the magnitude of the human suffering caused by it), the more tolerant the public is of animal research. The greater the perceived costs (in terms of animal suffering or the use of favored or familiar animals), the less tolerant the public is of animal research (Aldhous et al. 1999).

Table 5 provides direct evidence of this weighing of costs and benefits, albeit from a survey of British atti-

Table 4
Animal-Related Hierarchy of Concern

Poll #1: General Welfare of Particular Animals

Type of Animal	% Expressing Concern
Dogs	89
Seals	85
Whales/dolphins/porpoises	84
Horses	78
Birds	76
Cats	71
Farm animals	70
Rabbits	67
Fish	64
Hamsters/guinea pigs/mice	34
Frogs	33
Snakes	21

Doyle, Dane, and Bernbach, Inc. 1983

Poll #2: Use of Particular Animals

Type of Animal	% Supporting	% Opposing
Monkeys	59.5	34.5
Dogs	51.3	43.1
Cats	53.3	41.5
Rats/Mice	76.1	18.5

The University of North Carolina of Chapel Hill 1989

Table 5
Public Opinion (United Kingdom) on Using Monkeys and Mice in Specific Research

Type of Research	Monkeys are not subjected to pain, illness, or surgery (% approving)	Monkeys are subjected to pain, illness, or surgery (% approving)	Mice are not subjected to pain, illness, or surgery (% approving)	Mice are subjected to pain, illness, or surgery (% approving)
To ensure that a new drug to cure leukemia in children is safe and effective	75	52	83	65
To develop a new vaccine against the virus that causes AIDS	69	44	77	57
To ensure that a new painkilling drug is safe and effective	65	35	74	47
To enable scientists to study how the sense of hearing works	56	21	70	36
To test whether an ingredient for use in cosmetics will be harmful to people	30	6	38	12

Aldhous et al. 1999

Table 6
Opinions of American Psychological Association Members and Psychology Students Concerning Use of Animals for Specific Research Procedures

Type of Research		APA Members % Supporting	Psychology Students % Supporting
Observational studies	Primates	96.0	94.8
	Dogs	89.4	91.0
	Pigeons	86.1	89.4
	Rats	87.3	91.2
Research involving caging or confinement	Primates	63.0	57.7
	Dogs	63.4	57.7
	Pigeons	73.8	71.3
	Rats	77.2	79.6
Research involving pain and death	Primates	17.7	10.3
	Dogs	18.8	9.4
	Pigeons	29.6	21.6
	Rats	34.0	29.1

Plous 1996a,b

tudes to animal research. (Note: British attitudes to animal research are more negative than American attitudes.) The public is more supportive of painful research on mice than on monkeys. The British journal *New Scientist* published on May 22, 1999, the results of a poll that looked at how the public views certain types of animal research when different costs are involved. The poll focused exclusively on studies using either monkeys or mice and included a specific variable: the amount of harm done to the animal. It also tested the level of support for animal research when the question was weighted with specific benefits accruing from the research.

The poll asked half of a sample of 2,009 adults simply whether they agreed or disagreed that scientists should be allowed to experiment on animals (the "cold-start" version). The other half of the sample was

Table 7
Public Opinion on the Humane Treatment of Laboratory Animals

Question	Year	% Agreeing (Yes)	% Opposing (No)
When medical schools have animals that they are using in research, do you think they take as good care of them as individual owners would? (National Opinion Research Center 1949)	1948	79	9
In general, when doctors use animals in their work do you think they really try to keep from hurting the animals? (National Opinion Research Center 1949)	1948	75	11
Do medical schools take as good care of animals as individual owners would? (National Society for Medical Research 1949)	1948	75	11
Generally, do you think researchers who use animals in experiments treat them humanely, or not? (Roper Center 1985c)	1985	46	30
As far as you know, are the animals used in medical and pharmaceutical research treated humanely, or not? (Animal Industry Foundation 1989b)	1989	33	40
Are animals treated humanely? (Schaefer Center for Public Policy: University of Baltimore 1992)	1992	46.9	35.8

Table 8
Public Behavior Regarding Cosmetics Testing

Question	Year	% Refusing to Buy	% Who Do Not Refuse to Buy
I'd like to know if you personally have already done any of the following...	1991	58	38
refuse to buy products where ethical treatment of animals may be called into question.	1992	48	46
(Food Marketing Institute 1991–94)	1993	51	42
	1994	51	43

asked the same question but were first told, "Some scientists are developing and testing new drugs to reduce pain or developing new treatments for life-threatening diseases such as leukemia and AIDS. By conducting experiments on live animals, scientists believe they can make more rapid progress than would otherwise have been possible" (the "warm-start" version). Sixty-four percent of those presented with the cold-start version opposed the use of animals in research, compared with 41 percent of those given the warm-start version. This result shows a significant shift in attitudes and illustrates the impact a question's wording can have on the replies received.

When the hypothetical situation indicated that the animal would be subjected to pain, illness, or surgery (factors associated with suffering), the approval percentage decreased by 16 to 35 percent for both mice and monkeys. The percentage of the public objecting to the research did not increase, however, when the research involved the likely death of some of the mice or monkeys. As the perceived importance of the research increases, public support rises but as the costs increase, public support declines.

Scott Plous, of Wesleyan University, found similar results in two surveys of selected American populations (Table 6). The first survey (mentioned previously) involved five thousand randomly selected members of the American Psychological Association (APA). The parallel survey questioned 2,022 psy-

chology students randomly sampled from fifty colleges and universities within the United States (Plous 1996 a,b). Plous presented both sample groups with twelve different types of psychological research and asked them to indicate which types of research are justified and which are unjustified, assuming "all research has been institutionally approved and deemed of scientific merit." The results from both surveys were similar to those found by the *New Scientist*. As Table 6 shows, the majority of respondents from both surveys expressed much greater concern for animal research when it caused pain or death (even though the population surveyed was broadly supportive of animal research in theory).

Similar attitude trends are evident when the public is questioned about whether laboratory animals are treated humanely in research settings. In 1947 the public's view of the research community was one of trust and respect. By 1985 that trust had been sharply eroded, and there was evidence of much more public concern about the treatment of laboratory animals (Table 7). This increase in concern occurred despite the improvement in standards of care, husbandry, and use that had occurred in the intervening thirty-eight years.

One research-related issue has been particularly contentious, especially during the past decade (Table 8). In 1989 *Parents* magazine found that 58 percent of the respondents felt that testing of cosmetics on animals was wrong and should be illegal.

Another 23 percent felt it was wrong but should not be illegal; only 13 percent felt that the practice was acceptable. In 1991 *Self* magazine polled the public and found that 72 percent agreed to the statement, "If the cosmetics are the same quality, I would prefer to buy cosmetics that aren't tested on animals" (Significance, Inc. 1991). However, when the public was asked in 1990 by the Gallup Organization, "Would you purchase cosmetics that had not been tested on animals?" 89 percent of the public said "no." In 1990 the National Consumer's League asked the public, "If a health and beauty-aid product indicates that it has not been tested on animals, how does this affect your decision to buy it?" (Ward 1990). In direct contrast with the Gallup results, 39 percent of the subjects said the lack of animal testing would have no effect on their buying the product; 29 percent said it would make them more likely to buy the product.

Wearing Fur

The wearing of garments made from animal fur has long been a particular target of animal protection organizations. Table 9 provides data from a number of polls about public attitudes toward wearing fur. The wording of the questions in Table 9 is so variable that it is not really possible to make any reliable trend analysis. However, it is generally believed that public opposition to the wearing of animal fur has increased over the past fifty years. The fur industry in the United States has been struggling for

Table 9
Public Opinion on Wearing Fur

Question	Year	% Accepting Fur	% Opposing Fur
Is it okay to wear (ranch) fur coats? (Sieber 1986)*	1986	45	47
Thinking about specific ways that humans assert their dominance over animals, please tell me if you think each of the following practices is wrong and should be prohibited by law, if you personally disapprove but don't feel it should be illegal, or if it is acceptable to you: Killing animals to use their skins for fur coats. (Roper Center 1989b)	1989	13	85
Do you think there are some circumstances where it's perfectly okay to kill an animal for its fur or do you think it's wrong to kill an animal for its fur? (Roper Center 1989d)	1989	50**	46***
Do you generally favor or oppose the wearing of clothes made of animal furs? (Balzar 1993)	1993	35	50
The use of animal fur in clothing should be banned in the United States. (Survey Research Center, University of Maryland, College Park 1999)	1999	43.8	51.4

*Survey of 802 Toronto adults
**Responding that under some circumstances it would be all right to kill an animal for its fur.
***Responding that it would always be wrong to kill an animal for its fur.

the past decade, and retail fur sales, after peaking in the late 1980s, are lower (in inflation adjusted dollars) than they have been in the past thirty years. In 1999, when respondents were asked whether they believe the use of animal fur in clothing should be banned, the results revealed that the public is slightly more opposed (51.4 percent) to the practice than supportive (43.8 percent). This is significant because the public is, in general, reluctant to proscribe activities that do not directly affect the health or safety of other humans.

Hunting

Hunting is another controversial issue that has been looked at closely. Surveys have mainly consisted of asking for opinions on hunting or asking about the degree to which respondents participate in hunting.

The National Opinion Research Center conducted GSS surveys from 1972 to 1994 on the prevalence of hunting. The percentage of people who reported that they, their spouse, or both hunt decreased from 26.8 percent in 1972 to 20.3 percent in

1994. However, it must be noted that because hunting is predominantly a male sport and because past surveys have focused on married males, most of the information on hunting practices comes from married males. In 1975 33 percent of married males had participated in hunting, compared to 20 percent in 1995. Other surveys have produced similar results. On October 26, 1999, the *Wall Street Journal* reported that, according to Mediamark Research, the number of adults who hunt had fallen 17 percent from 1990 to 1998 (O'Connell and Barrett 1999).

One of the most telling signs of the decrease in hunting is the drop in the number of hunting licenses issued, a measure of actual behavior as opposed to attitudes. As reported in the same *Wall Street Journal* piece, the U.S. Fish and Wildlife Service revealed that the number of hunting-license holders had dropped to 14.9 million people, an 11 percent decline from 1982 to 1997.

Surveys have also questioned the public on its attitudes toward particular types of hunting. The *Parents* magazine survey of 1989 asked specifically about the hunting and killing of

animals for sport. Thirty-three percent of the respondents thought it should be made illegal, 27 percent disapproved but did not think it should be illegal, and 36 percent felt the practice was acceptable. The Gallup Organization polled the public on behalf of the National Shooting Sports Foundation in 1990 with the following question: "Animal rights groups and their activities have received considerable publicity in recent months. I'd like your opinion of the following actions and goals of animal activities. Certain animal rights groups want a total ban on all types of hunting. Do you strongly support this goal, somewhat support this goal, somewhat oppose this goal, or strongly oppose this goal?" Only 21 percent supported this goal (8 percent strongly) compared with 77 percent who opposed it (50 percent strongly).

Both of the above polls used phrases that might be expected to influence the subject. The question from the first poll adds the phrases "humans assert their dominance over animals" and "hunting and killing animals for sport," while the second question uses the phrase "certain ani-

Table 10
Public Opinion on the Humane Treatment of Specific Farm Animals

Question	Type of Animal	% Believing the Animal Treated Humanely	% Believing the Animal Not Treated Humanely
Turning to your understanding of the way specific kinds of animals are generally treated in this country, is it your feeling that the following animals are treated humanely, or not? (Animal Industry Foundation 1989a)	Egg-laying hens	56	19
	Beef cattle	69	12
	Broiler chickens	51	19
	Turkeys	57	17
	Hogs	63	13
	Dairy cows	79	6
	Veal calves	49	23

mal rights groups want a total ban" (feeding into public concerns about infringement of their own liberties). These phrases influence the subjects to respond more strongly in one way or another and presumably explain the contrasting results from the two polls. Public opposition to sport or trophy hunting is much higher than opposition to subsistence hunting (Rutberg 1997).

Farm Animal Issues

Farm animal welfare and treatment is an issue that has recently begun to appear in public polling results. The Animal Industry Foundation (AIF) conducted the first national public opinion survey on animal agriculture and animal rights in 1989 (AIF 1989a). The findings from the survey show that 79 percent of consumers believed that farmers and producers treat their animals humanely, and that 40 percent believed modern animal husbandry practices are focused primarily on the animal's health and safety. Even so, 25 percent believed that farm animal husbandry practices were cruel. The 1989 survey also questioned the public on its opinions about the treatment of specific farm animals (Table 10). The results suggest that, overall, the public feels farm animals are treated humanely. Table 11 displays opposing views.

In 1992 the *Star Tribune*/WCCO-TV in Minnesota conducted a survey on the same issue, but the sample frame was smaller, 1,009 Minnesotans. The results were similar; the public believed that farm animals are raised without unnecessary cruel treatment. The Minnesota poll found that 69 percent of the public either disagreed strongly or disagreed with the statement, "In general, the way animals are raised for food in this country is unnecessarily cruel." The public did agree that humane treatment is an important ingredient in animal agriculture and felt that it was worth spending more money to make sure humane treatment was provided for the farm animals. Sixty-four percent of the respondents responded positively to the question: "In order to

Table 11
Public Opinion on Farm Animal Treatment

Statement	% Who Strongly/Somewhat Disapprove of the Practice
Confining veal calves for their entire lives in narrow wooden stalls where they are unable to ever turn around.	92
Confining pigs for their entire lives in narrow metal stalls where they are unable ever to turn around.	91
Keeping hens in cages so small that they are never able to stretch their wings.	90

Caravan Opinion Research Corporation 1995

improve the conditions under which animals and poultry are raised, the cost of meat would increase. Would you be willing to pay more for the meat from these specially treated animals?" (Schmickle 1993).

Shortly after the Minnesota survey, an animal rights group commissioned another poll on the same subject (Caravan Opinion Research Corporation 1995). The survey focused on specific farm practices and how the public viewed farm animals (Table 11). The results demonstrate again the importance of how a question is worded, but they do reflect a public concern about closely confined animals. (Close confinement is standard practice in modern intensive systems.)

When the sample was asked which of the following statements reflected their concerns most closely, the sample responded as follows: "Animal pain and suffering should be reduced as much as possible, even though the animals are going to be slaughtered" (93 percent); "Since animals raised for food are going to be slaughtered anyway, it really doesn't matter all that much how they are treated" (5 percent) (Caravan Opinion Research Corporation 1995).

The 1989 AIF survey found that 67 percent of consumers would vote for additional government regulation of farm animal production; of those, 35 percent would vote for additional regulation because of their opposition to inhumane husbandry practices. In 1995 the Caravan survey found that 82 percent of the public believed the "meat and egg industry should be held legally responsible in making sure that the farm animals are protected from cruelty" and 58 percent of the public felt the "companies that buy animal parts and profit by selling them for food, like fast-food restaurants and supermarkets, should be held legally responsible in making sure that farm animals are protected from cruelty" (Caravan Opinion Research Corporation 1995). However, 68 percent of the public felt the "meat and egg industry can be relied on to regulate itself," and 91 percent believed "government agencies, like

Table 12
Public Opinion on Eating Specific Food Items

Type of Food Never Eaten	1994 (%)	1997 (%)
Meat	6	5
Poultry	3	2
Fish/Seafood	4	4
All of the Above	1	1

Stahler 1994

the Department of Agriculture, should be involved in making sure that farm animals are protected from cruelty" (Caravan Opinion Research Corporation 1995). In Europe the public is much more negative about factory farming practices and more supportive of organic farming.

Diet Choice: Animal Agriculture and Consumer Behavior

In 1977–1978 the U.S. Department of Agriculture asked 37,135 people if they refer to themselves as vegetarians (Schmickle 1993). The survey found that only 1.2 percent of the respondents referred to themselves as vegetarians. In 1994 *Vegetarian Times* magazine conducted a survey asking a comparable question; 7 percent of the respondents said they considered themselves vegetarians (Stahler 1994).

In 1994 and 1997, the Vegetarian Resource Group, sponsored by the Roper Center, conducted a more careful survey on this issue. However, as one can see in Table 12, the format of the question was different in important ways. The respondents had to answer that they *never* eat certain foods in order to be included in the results, and the polling was conduct-

ed via a personal interview. This survey illustrates how people may interpret questions differently. Some people who eat meat infrequently and others who eat only seafood call themselves vegetarians.

Despite the apparent growth in the number of self-reported vegetarians, from 1.2 percent to 7 percent between 1975 and 1994, animal welfare does not appear to be a factor in making this diet choice. Forty-six percent of all people who consider themselves vegetarians and 49 percent of *Vegetarian Times* subscribers reportedly made the decision to be vegetarian largely for health-related reasons (Yankelovich et al. 1992). About 20 percent of all vegetarians and 40 percent of *Vegetarian Times* subscribers chose to be vegetarian for animal welfare and/or ethical reasons. The National Opinion Research Center found in the 1994 GSS that 30 percent of the sample sometimes refused to eat meat for moral or environmental reasons.

Several polls have also asked the public about what they look for when eating in restaurants. In 1991 the Gallup Poll Organization found that 20 percent of the public responded that "they look for restaurants that have vegetarian items," and 35 percent suggested that they "would order nonmeat items if listed on the menu" (Richter 1997). The survey found that 20 to 30 percent of the business community voiced an interest in having vegetarian items on their own restaurant menu list (Richter 1997). In 1994 a study commissioned by Land O'Lakes reported that more than half of all American households had two or more meatless suppers each week and that 20 percent of U.S. households ate four or more meatless dinners per week (Richter 1997). Also in 1994 the National Restaurant Association reported that, on any given day, nearly 15 percent of the nation's college students selected a vegetarian option at their dining halls (Richter 1997). However, to place this in perspective, American annual per-capita consumption of meat (beef, pork, poultry) has increased from about 155 to 170 pounds during the last thirty years. Soy "meat" sales have increased five-fold since 1985.

Public Support of Animal Protection Philosophy

Survey questions that ask individuals about using non-human animals for human benefit (i.e., animal research, animal testing, and food) shed light on the attitudes of the public on these particular topics. Yet it is often difficult to ascertain where the public stands on broad philosophical aspects of animal protection. Surveys have produced contradictory data about what the public believes and where the public draws its lines. One way of assessing broad changes in public attitudes is to investigate how many people claim to be members of animal protection groups or to donate money to them.

During the 1980s and 90s, membership in animal protection groups exploded. (The membership of The HSUS expanded by over five-fold, to about four hundred thousand members, from 1980 to 1990.) In 1976 Steven Kellert conducted a survey of more than three thousand American adults to determine their attitudes about wildlife. He asked questions about membership in various organi-

Table 13
Membership of U.S. Adults in Animal and Environmental Organizations; 1976

Organization	Males (%)	Females (%)
Animal Protection	0.6	2.0
Wildlife Preservation	3.4	2.5
Environmental Protection	1.5	0.8

Kellert and Berry 1981

zations (Rowan et al. 1995). Table 13 gives the results, illustrating 1) low levels of membership and 2) a gender gap in the support provided to different types of groups. In 1982 Louis Harris and Associates asked broadly, "Have you or has anyone in your immediate family contributed money to any conservation, wildlife, or environmental organizations in the past twelve months, or not." Twenty-four percent responded that they had. When the question was narrowed down, the expansion of support for animal-related groups became clearer. In 1999 a national poll asked specifically, "Did you donate money to animal rights protection groups in 1998?" (Survey Research Center 1999); 16 percent claimed to have contributed. The 1990 survey mentioned earlier found that 6 percent of the public were members of animal protection groups.

Summary

Despite the complexities and limitations of the survey process, a general picture of how the public views animal protection from 1950 to the present can be drawn. It indicates that public opinion has become more supportive of animal protection issues, although there are still many contradictions. On most issues, the public has a higher degree of concern for the welfare of nonhuman animals than it did in 1950 or even 1975.

Literature Cited

Aldhous, P., A. Coghlan, and J. Copley. 1999. Let the people speak. *New Scientist*. May 22: 26–31.

Amato, P.R., and S.A. Partridge. 1989. *The New Vegetarians*. New York: Plenum Press.

American Medical Association. 1989. Public attitudes about the use of animals in biomedical research: Focus groups and national surveys of adults and children. Unpublished.

Animal Industry Foundation (AIF). 1989a. Survey results on how Americans view modern livestock farming. *Farm Animals* April: A1–A12.

————.1989b. Question 29. Feb. 1989.

Balzar, J. 1993. Creatures great and—equal? *Los Angeles Times*, 23 December: A-1.

Baylor University. 1985. Community Poll of McLennan County and city of Waco. Waco, Tex.: Baylor University, Center for Community Research and Development. April–November. Question 3.

Bowd, A.D. 1984. Development and validation of a scale of attitudes toward the treatment of animals. *Education and Psychological Measurement* 44: 513–15.

Broida, J., L. Tingley, R. Kimball, and J. Miele. 1993. Personality differences between pro- and anti-vivisectionists. *Society and Animals* 1: 129–44.

Caravan Opinion Research Corporation. 1995. *Attitudes toward protecting farm animals from cruelty.* Princeton, N.J.: Opinion Research Corporation.

Doyle, Dane, and Bernbach Inc. 1983. America's binding relationship with the animal kingdom. *Soundings* 12: 9–10.

Eagly, A.H., and S. Chaiken. 1993. *The psychology of attitudes.* Orlando, Fla.: Harcourt Brace Jovanovich College Publishers.

Food Marketing Institute. 1991–1994. Consumer attitudes and the supermarket. Opinion Research Corporation—Food Marketing Institute. Questions USGALLUP.92AMA.R105 (Jan. 1991); R109 (Jan. 1992); R121 (Jan. 1993); R130 (Jan.94).

Galvin, S.L., and H.A. Herzog Jr. 1998. Attitudes and dispositional optimism of animal rights demonstrators. *Society and Animals* 6: 1–11.

Herzog, H.A. Jr. 1993. The movement is my life: The psychology of animal rights activism. *Journal of Social Issues* 46: 103–19.

Herzog, H.A. Jr., N.S. Betchart, and R.B. Pittman. 1991. Gender, sex-role orientation, and attitudes towards animals. *Anthrozoös* 4: 184–91.

Herzog, H.A., and L.B. Dorr (in press). Electronically available surveys of attitudes toward animals. *Society and Animals.*

Jamison, W., and W. Lunch. 1992. The rights of animals, science policy, and political activism. *Science Technology and Human Values* 17: 438–58.

Kellert, S. 1996. *The value of life: Biological diversity and human society.* New York: Island Press.

Kellert, S., and J. Berry. 1981. Knowledge, affection, and basic attitudes toward animals in American society. Document 024-010-00-625-1. Washington, D.C.: U.S. Government Printing Office.

Kruse, C.R. 1999. Gender, views of nature, and support for animal rights. *Society and Animals* 7: 179–98.

National Opinion Research Center. 1949. Public attitudes toward animal experimentation. *Bulletin of the National Society for Medical Research* 3, 5: 1–9.

National Science Board (1985–1998). Science and engineering indicators—1989. Washington, D.C.: U.S. Government Printing Office.

National Society for Medical Research. 1949. Public attitudes toward animal experimentation. *Bulletin of the National Society for Medical Research* 3, 5: 1–9. May–June.

Nickell, D., and H.A. Herzog Jr. 1996. Ethical ideology and moral persuasion: Personal moral philosophy, gender, and judgements of pro- and anti-animal research propaganda. *Society and Animals* 4: 53–64.

O'Connell, V., and P.M. Barrett. 1999. Here's the turnoff: In the market for guns, the customers aren't coming back for more. *Wall Street Journal,* 26 October: A–10.

Peek, C.W., N.J. Bell, and C.C. Dunham. 1996. Gender, gender ideology, and animal rights advocacy. *Gender and Society* 10: 464–78.

Pifer, L., K. Shimuzu, and R. Pifer. 1994. Public attitudes toward animal research: Some international comparisons. *Society and Animals* 2(2): 95–113.

Plous, S. 1991. An attitude survey of animal rights activists. *Psychological Science* 2: 194–96.

————. 1996a. Attitudes toward the use of animals in psychological research and education: Results from a national survey of psychologists. *American Psychologist* 51: 1167–80.

————. 1996b. Attitudes toward the use of animals in psychological research and education: Results from a national survey of psychology majors. *Psychological Science* 7: 352–58.

Princeton Survey Research Associates. 1991. Great American TV Poll #2—USPSRA. 91TV02.R30. Sponsored by Troika Productions and Lifetime Television.

Richards, R.T., and R.S. Krannich. 1991. The ideology of the animal rights movement and activists' attitudes toward wildlife. Pp. 363–71 in *Transactions of the Fifty-Sixth North American Wildlife and Natural Resource Conference,* ed. R.E. McCabe. Washington, D.C.: Wildlife Management Institute.

Richter, T. 1997. How many vegetarians are there? *Vegetarian Journal,* 1–4.

Roper Center for Public Opinion. 1948a. Question USNORC.480246.R21. National Opinion Research Center poll. Animal Experimentation.

————. 1948b. Question USNORC.480246.R13. National Opinion Research Center poll. American Experimentation.

————. 1985a. Question USAPMGEN.8.R16C. Associated Press/ Media General poll. Sept.

————. 1985b. Question: USAPMGEN.8.R16A. Associated Press/ Media General poll. Sept.

————. 1985c. Question USAPMGEN.8.R17. Associated Press/ Media General poll. Sept.

————. 1987. Question USHART.87RS, R29A. *Rolling Stone* Sept. 11.

————. 1989a. Question USKANE.89PM10.RO5. *Parents* magazine. Sept. 22.

————. 1989b. Question USKANE. 89PM10.RO2A. *Parents* magazine. September 22.

————. 1989c. Question USGALLUP.89AMA.R31. American Medical Association. Jan.

————. 1989d. Question USABC.89.R10. ABC News poll

————. 1990. Question USGLLUP.90shot.R1C. Gallup Organization Poll–National Shooting Foundation Public Opinion Study.

————. 1992a. Question USWIRTH.92RDIG.RO6G. *Readers' Digest* poll. Mar. 16.

————. 1992b. Question USGALLUP.29AMA.R35. American Medical Association. Jan. 23.

————. 1993. Question USGALLUP.93AMA.R34. American Medical Association. Jan. 22.

————. 1994a. Question USORC. 94GROG.R19D. Food Marketing Institute. Jan. 14.

—————. 1994b. Question US-NORC. GSS94, Q693D. National Opinion Research Center. Jan 27.

—————. 1994c. Question US-PSRA.092194,R24S. Times Mirror. July 12.

—————. 1995a. Question US-AP.945K, Q2. Associated Press. Nov. 10.

—————. 1995b. Question US-HARRIS.122295. Louis Harris and Associates. Nov. 30.

Rowan, A.N., F.M. Loew, and J. Weer. 1995. The animal research controversy: Protest, process, and public policy; an analysis of strategic issues. North Grafton, Mass.: Tufts Center for Animals and Public Policy.

Rowan, A, and K.J. Shapiro. 1996. Animal rights, a bitten apple. *American Psychologist* 51: 1183–1184.

Rozin, P., M. Markwith, and C. Stoess. 1997. Moralization and becoming a vegetarian: The transformation of preferences into values and the recruitment of disgust. *Psychological Science* 8: 67–73.

Rutberg, A.T. 1997. The science of deer management: An animal welfare perspective. In *The science of overabundance: Deer ecology and population management*. Washington, D.C.: Smithsonian Institution Press.

Schafer Center for Public Policy. 1992. January 16. Questions A3–A5. Baltimore, Md.: University of Baltimore.

Schmickle, S. 1993. One in four thinks farm animals are treated cruelly. *Star Tribune*, 14 February: 1-A and 25–26-A.

Sieber, J. 1986. Students' and scientists' attitudes on animal research. *The American Biology Teacher* 48, 2.

Significance, Inc. 1991. The image of the future. *Self* Magazine, July: 28.

Sperling, S. 1988. Animal liberators: Research and morality. Berkeley: University of California Press.

Stahler, C. 1994. How many vegetarians are there? The Vegetarian Resource Group asks in a 1994 national poll. *Vegetarian Journal*, July/August. 7–9.

Survey Research Center. 1999. National Omnibus 1999 Questionnaire Project #1367. College Park, Md.: University of Maryland.

Takooshian, H. 1988. Opinions on animal research: Scientists versus the public. *PsyETA Bulletin* 7: 5–7.

The University of North Carolina of Chapel Hill, Institute for Research in Social Science. 1989. Kentucky Poll/Survey Research Center. Spring Poll. Animals, Question 60a–h (IRSS Study Number NNSRP-KY-021). Chapel Hill, N.C.

—————. 1991. Kentucky Poll/Survey Research Center. April. Chapel Hill, N.C.

Ward, A. 1990. Consumers at odds with animal testing: Survey finds majority oppose it on beauty aids, but respondents lack information on merits. *Advertising Age*, 26 February: S–2.

Wayman, S. 1966. Concentration camps for dogs. *Life* magazine, 4 February, Vol. 60, No.5: 25–28.

Yankelovich, Clancy, Schulman. 1992. *Vegetarian Times*. October.

From Pets to Companion Animals

4

CHAPTER

Researched by Martha C. Armstrong, Susan Tomasello,
and Christyna Hunter

A Brief History of Shelters and Pounds

Animal shelters in most U.S. communities bear little trace of their historical British roots. Early settlers, most from the British Isles, brought with them the English concepts of towns and town management, including the rules on keeping livestock. Each New England town, for example, had a common, a central grassy area to be used by all townspeople in any manner of benefit, including the grazing of livestock. As long as the livestock remained on the common, the animals could graze at will, but once the animal strayed onto private property or public thoroughfares, a "pound master" took the animal to the pound, a small stone-walled corral that was usually just a few feet away from the common. For a small fine, the owner was able to retrieve his stray livestock.

As the United States began to grow and as towns became more populated, urbanization brought a new type of stray to the city. Stray dogs allowed to roam the streets could present all types of problems: barking at and frightening working horses, creating sanitation problems, and biting passersby. The old stone-walled corrals were not appropriate for dogs. Instead unused warehouses or enclosed barns were employed.

Housed in crude pens or tied to hooks on the side of the wall, pound dogs stood little chance of escaping their destiny: death by starvation, injury, gassing, or drowning. There were no adoption, or rehoming, programs and owners reclaimed few strays. And while early humanitarians, like Henry Bergh, founder of the American Society for the Prevention of Cruelty to Animals (ASPCA), and George Thorndike Angell, founder of the Massachusetts Society for the Prevention of Cruelty to Animals (MSPCA), were concerned about animal abuse, their focus was more on working animals—horses, in particular—than on the fate of stray dogs. It was through the efforts of Caroline Earle White, founder of the Women's SPCA of Pennsylvania, that the fate of stray dogs began to change. White secured the first contract from a city to a humane society to operate a more humane pound or shelter for dogs and cats and implemented an adoption program, as well as more humane ways of housing, caring for, and, if need be, euthanizing the animals in the care of the SPCA.

Shelters at the Turn of the Twentieth Century

Expansion of urban life and contraction of agrarian interests created increased problems for city managers, including protecting the public's health and safety. Stray dogs not only harassed working horses, pedestrians, and shopkeepers, but also spread rabies and other zoonotic diseases.

In outlying areas, unchecked breeding of farm dogs and abandonment of city dwellers' unwanted pets created packs of marauding dogs, which killed wildlife and livestock and posed significant health risks to humans and other animals.

State and local governments were forced to pass laws requiring dog owners to control their animals. Although laws that prohibited deliberate abuse of or cruelty to animals had passed in most states by the turn of the century, few states had laws that provided for the control of dogs beyond their owners' property. Only later in the 1900s were laws requiring leashing and licensing of dogs passed throughout the United States and money allocated to hire dogcatchers and run pounds. Although some laws were passed strictly on the grounds of protecting public safety, most were tied to other laws that required dogs to be vaccinated against rabies and/ or that provided additional penalties for a dog who killed livestock. A proliferation of local ordinances and by-laws were passed in the late 1930s and early 1940s to strengthen state animal control laws and to provide a revenue source to pay for animal control programs.

While most citizens did not want stray dogs roaming the streets, they also did not want the captured strays kept in facilities near their homes. The barking, howling, and fighting among hundreds of strays made pounds unpopular neighbors. As a result, the shelters were usually found near a locality's other dumping ground, the municipal landfill. Early municipal pounds were crudely constructed, lacking heat, cooling, and, in many instances, hot and cold running water. Animals entering a pound were rarely claimed, even more rarely adopted or rehomed, and normally destroyed within hours of arriving. Those who did have some sort of identification—a collar with a license or identification tag—were usually afforded an additional period of holding time before they were destroyed. Irregular cleanings and rarely disinfected cages provided ample opportunity for diseases to run rampant throughout pounds. Coupled with the fact that few strays had received any vaccinations against highly contagious diseases such as distemper, even the "lucky" owner-identified animal who escaped immediate destruction with his fellow strays would usually contract and succumb to disease shortly after entering the pound.

A Half Century of Progress: From Dog Pound to Animal Shelter

After World War II, pounds underwent a massive transformation. Pet owners were no longer willing to let a concrete-block-and-wire building at the town dump represent their community's effort to house and care for homeless and stray animals. They wanted a place that humanely sheltered the animals under its roof, but they also demanded programs that were aimed at decreasing the homeless animal population and shelter staff trained to be more caring and professional in the care and treatment of animals.

While most large U.S. cities already were served by an SPCA, many of which ran shelters, smaller cities and rural communities were either underserved by the local SPCA or relied solely on municipal government to provide animal care and sheltering services for their community's animals. During the early 1950s, humane societies, animal rescue leagues, and other animal welfare groups proliferated. Many were created to fill a void in the locality they served. Others were formed to provide an alternative to a substandard municipal pound.

The new shelters were different not only in their look and location, but also in the programs they offered. They sought more to prevent animal control problems than to provide curative and punitive measures. Humane education, spaying and neutering, and differential licensing were part of the broad menu of services added to the new animal shelters' lists of programs provided to their communities.

As the traditional pound disappeared, the stereotypical dogcatcher followed right behind it. The days when a driver's license and the willingness to be bitten occasionally were the only prerequisites gave way; knowing a bit about animal behavior, animal first aid, conflict resolution, and legal procedures was now required. The new animal control officer was more physically fit than his or her predecessor, as well.

Training opportunities to professionalize the field were also increasing. The MSPCA offered training for executives and law enforcement officers in the early 1950s. The American Humane Association (AHA) launched a series of educational and training venues through universities, state federations, and local shelters. In the late 1970s, The Humane Society of the United States (HSUS) launched its Animal Control Academy in conjunction with the University of Alabama to provide certification to animal control officers. Several state animal control associations offered training through state law enforcement training institutes or academies.

Pound Seizure

The conditions and location of the pound were not the only reasons for the formation of hundreds of new humane societies and animal welfare organizations. The proliferation of stray dogs shortly after World War II, the shortage of sheltering facilities, and the growth of government-funded biomedical research combined to bring about a new policy, pound seizure, which horrified many pet lovers. First passed in Minnesota and then pushed along by the National Society for Medical Research (NSMR) and local research organizations elsewhere, pound seizure laws required municipally run animal shelters or pounds to release unclaimed animals on demand to any accredited research facility or university that requested them.

Local humanitarians found pound seizure to be the antithesis of the true purpose of an animal shelter—to provide a safe haven for stray and lost animals. To avoid the law, local humane societies built their own shelters or contracted with municipalities to run their facilities. By agreeing to run the shelter under contract with the city or county or by establishing a separate facility, these organizations found that they were exempt from being forced to comply with pound seizure laws since they fell outside the definition of covered entities. The MSPCA was one of the first to challenge pound seizure laws by filing suit in court, stating that the Massachusetts law mandating pound seizure violated the mission of animal shelters. Although the case went all the way to the state's Supreme Judicial Court before a decision was finally rendered, the court's ruling still left the subject in limbo. The Court stated that the MSPCA did not have standing to sue, since the pound seizure laws applied only to municipally operated pounds or shelters. Since the MSPCA was a private, nonprofit organization that did not serve as a pound, it was not an aggrieved party.

The controversy surrounding pound seizure was not limited to the local level. AHA found itself embroiled in the battle when legislation was proposed on the federal level that would have regulated the sale, care, and use of dogs and cats in medical research. Seeking to find common ground with the research community, AHA entered into an agreement with NSMR only to find that agreement later discarded. Some members of AHA's board of directors and staff were so angered by the executive director's decision to enter into any discussions that would allow shelter animals to go into research that they forced the issue onto the ballot of the general membership meeting in 1954. Although a membership battle on the issue was ultimately avoided, the dissidents who forced the issue left AHA and formed the National Humane Society, later renamed The Humane Society of the United States.

Thirty years later, The HSUS and AHA joined with nine other animal protection groups to form National ProPets, a coalition organized to overturn pound seizure on the state and local levels. The fight over pound seizure initially concentrated on local referenda in California and Florida. Outspent by and losing to the research community on the local level, ProPets turned its attention to the U.S. Congress when Rep. Bob Mrazek of New York sponsored the Pet Protection Act of 1986. The bill later passed in a very weakened version in 1990.

At the height of the pound seizure era, more than fourteen states and hundreds of localities required local municipally owned and operated shelters to give up unclaimed animals for research purposes. As of 2000 only three states still mandated pound seizure and more than a dozen prohibited it. Even in states that neither required nor prohibited pound seizure, most municipalities had dropped the practice, noting its unpopularity with the public and tiring of the public relations nightmare it created for the local animal shelters.

The New Look of Shelters

As the number of households keeping pets grew, the look and function of the shelter that served the canine and feline population in the community changed drastically. The new shelter was more centrally located and usually had indoor runs to reduce noise and to make it a better neighbor to businesses and residences. It not only had hot *and* cold running water, but also had central heat and air-conditioning, heated floors, and built-in cleaning systems to help keep disease transmission down and odors under control.

On the East and West coasts, larger humane societies also incorporated spay/neuter clinics and education centers into their facilities. Beneficiaries of funding from a large trust established by George Whittel in the 1970s named shelter clinics and humane education centers all along the California coastline after him.

But the look of the shelter was not all that changed in the late 1960s and 1970s. Shelters pushed to win acceptance as an HSUS accredited shelter or to comply with AHA's Standards of Excellence program. The standards for both programs looked at day-to-day operations, as well as adherence to programs to reduce the numbers of homeless animals within the community. Many shelters had as part of their adoption contract a provision that animals adopted from them must be spayed or neutered. Most gave the adopter thirty days from the date of the adoption to comply (or thirty days from the date of the animal's "maturity," since six months was considered the youngest age at which an animal could be surgically sterilized). Some had spay/neuter clinics within the shelter and the adopter could make an appointment for the surgery before leaving with the new family pet. Others worked with area veterinarians and required the adopter to select a veterinarian prior to leaving the shelter. Still others required the adopter to leave a refundable deposit to encourage follow-through. But far too often, shel-

ter efforts proved to be insufficient incentive for the adopter to have the animal sterilized.

Even if the shelter was interested in using the adoption contract to ensure compliance with spay/neuter policies, most were limited to civil action. The shelter would have to sue the adopter to force the sterilization or to recover the animal. Most shelters did not have the resources or the time to pursue this option.

In the late 1970s, the Animal Welfare League of Arlington (Virginia) decided to make sterilization of its adopted animals a requirement by law. After the League convinced the county board that intact animals adopted from the shelter were adding to the potential for animal control problems, the board unanimously approved an ordinance that required any animal adopted from the shelter to be spayed or neutered by the time specified in the adoption contract. Failure to do so would result in a $300 fine and/or a year in jail, with each day beyond the specified time being considered a separate offense. In addition, the local commonwealth attorney stated that he considered each puppy or kitten born to a League-adopted animal to be a separate offense.

Several other humane societies and animal control agencies worked with municipal officials to pass ordinances to help reduce the homeless and stray pet populations within their communities. The Santa Cruz (California) SPCA worked with its city officials to pass an ordinance that required intact animals to be spayed or neutered if they were picked up by animal control for a third time in a twelve-month period.

Differential licensing (charging a higher license fee for intact animals than for sterilized animals) also increased in popularity across the United States in the late 1970s and 1980s. A few brave communities took on the issue of cat licensing and the licensing of breeders. Charlotte/Mecklenburg County (North Carolina) passed cat licensing in 1981, but not without a storm of controversy.

The day after the law went into effect, the headline in the *Charlotte Observer* read, "Charlotte Is Killing Its Cats" (M. Blinn, personal communication, Sept. 13, 2000). The town of Oxford, Massachusetts, passed a cat licensing bylaw in the early 1990s, but had to deflect three separate challenges in town meetings to keep it on the books. Some towns and counties that required cat licensing were issuing almost as many cat licenses as they were dog licenses. While these licensing laws helped to increase the return-to-owner rate of stray cats three- or fourfold, going from 1 percent to 4 percent was still unacceptable.

Opportunities and Challenges in Companion Animal Care

Advances in Medical Care for Companion Animals

Recent advances in companion animal veterinary care have been a leading benchmark for the status of companion animals. The life span of a dog or cat has increased significantly through improved delivery of preventive health care measures, such as vaccines to protect from Parvo virus, feline leukemia, and Lyme disease. New cures and treatments for diseases and injuries that seemed beyond the scope of the veterinary field—as well as the pocketbook of the average pet owner—have become almost commonplace. With more disposable income and delayed commitments to marrying and starting families, pet owners are willing to go to any length to prolong their companion animals' lives. Hip replacement surgeries for dogs, kidney transplants for cats, and chemotherapy or radiation treatment for pets with cancer may now be requested by dog and cat owners. This is par-

ticularly remarkable given that such services are paid for exclusively by the pet owners. Pet owners purchase few third-party or insurance payer systems, and those pet owners who do purchase them rarely find such procedures covered.

The War between the Humane and Veterinary Communities

The growth in the veterinary profession and the growing acceptance of veterinary care by pet owners in the 1970s and 1980s did not produce better relations between the humane and veterinary communities. Shelters, and in some instances, municipal governments, desperate to stop the growing homeless pet population and unable to negotiate agreements with local veterinarians, began opening and running their own low-cost spay/neuter clinics. A few shelters established full-service clinics, setting a sliding fee structure that allowed them to subsidize the costs of caring for indigent or low-income families' pets through fees from those who could afford to pay full price.

Full-scale war broke out between local shelters and veterinarians when veterinarians, seeing some of their clients move over to the shelter-operated clinics, decided to file suit to shut down or halt the growth of these nonprofit clinics. Three major challenges, in Michigan, Virginia, and Louisiana, fueled animosity between the camps.

Veterinarians claimed that humane societies enjoyed an unfair tax advantage over private practitioners. The nonprofit-run clinics sat on land that was exempt from property tax; they enjoyed an exemption from paying sales tax on most items; they were allowed to accept tax-deductible donations of money and property from the public; and they paid no state or federal income tax on the revenue they received. Veterinarians incurred the same costs for equipment, personnel, drugs and medical equip-

ment, but enjoyed none of the tax advantages that nonprofit, humane society-run clinics did.

Each of the lawsuits resulted in different judgments. In Virginia the state legislature passed a law making it illegal for anyone other than a veterinarian to own and operate a veterinary clinic. This effectively forced the Virginia Beach SPCA to sell its clinic and contract with the new owner for services. In Louisiana the state veterinary licensing board refused to license or renew the license of any veterinarian working for the Louisiana SPCA (LA SPCA). LA SPCA filed suit in court to force the state registry board to license or re-license its veterinarians. The resulting ruling found that the passage of an ordinance purporting to make the SPCA an "employee" of the City of New Orleans brought the plaintiffs within the statutory exception found in La.R.S. 37:1514 (l) and rendered this case moot (*The Louisiana Society for the Prevention of Animal Cruelty and the City of New Orleans v. Louisiana Board of Veterinary Medical Association 1990*). In two separate cases in Michigan, the Internal Revenue Service ruled that the running of a spay/neuter clinic by a humane society was a reasonable service of a charitable organization, not a business. As long as the humane society did not advertise its services, it was legally allowed to operate a spay/neuter clinic (HSUS 1985).

In 1986 the American Veterinary Medical Association (AVMA) joined with other organizations to ask Congress to impose taxes on nonprofits that operated any type of business not directly related to their mission. Included business activities were elective surgeries at university or church owned hospitals; sales of toys, games, or other items in nonprofit aquariums, zoos, or other wildlife organizations' shops; and spay/neuter surgeries and vaccinations of animals at humane societyo-perated clinics.

Fortunately, relations between the humane community and the veterinary community improved in the aftermath of a congressional hearing on the matter (no congressional action was taken). Their representatives now jointly advocate for legislation on the state and federal levels to improve anticruelty laws and to increase funding for enforcement; research on myriad issues to help improve animals' lives and welfare is being jointly sponsored by the two communities. This is not to say that there is complete agreement on all issues, but the communities are closer on many issues than they have ever been.

Pet Overpopulation

The humane community has traditionally appeared to be perpetually at odds with all other animal-related interests on the topic of pet overpopulation. In the latter part of the twentieth century, shelters were not primarily a refuge for stray animals, but rather the repository for unwanted animals, most of which were puppies and kittens. Humane societies felt overwhelmed by a tremendous influx of young animals, many just one generation removed from being purebred.

In the 1960s and 1970s, mass commercial dog-breeding establishments known as puppy mills, where dogs were often kept in substandard conditions, quickly outdistanced private hobby breeders in the number of animals being produced each year. For farmers in the Midwest (the location of most of the puppy mills), the returns on producing a crop of purebred puppies—with registration papers—were appealing.

The resulting surge in the number of dogs and puppies registered through the American Kennel Club, the primary registry for purebred dogs in the United States, swelled the coffers of the organization. Large numbers of puppies were pumped into the market by pet stores, which purchased in volume from puppy mills and enjoyed prime retail locations, such as suburban shopping malls.

Sterilization of dogs and cats was considered a costly and undesirable procedure by organized veterinary medicine. As animal control facilities and humane societies struggled to care for thousands of unplanned and homeless puppies, the veterinary community and hobby breeders began to respond to the increased demand for a dialogue on the subject.

In 1974 the first of several meetings among animal-related interests was held in Denver, Colorado. Attendees included the American Dog Owners Association, which traditionally opposed any legislation that would regulate dog breeding or ownership, and the AVMA. A second meeting two years later produced a number of scholarly papers and the beginnings of a consensus on how to reverse the tide of unplanned, and usually homeless, litters. This consensus could be summed up as a strategy promoted by Phyllis Wright of The HSUS known as L.E.S.—legislation, education, and sterilization.

Subsequent meetings of animal-related groups to look at the issue of pet overpopulation were limited to one-time workshops, some of which produced scholarly papers but few other results. Then, in 1993, veterinarians and researchers, humane societies, and breeder organizations met to quantify and qualify "pet overpopulation." This meeting was the beginning of the National Council on Pet Population Study and Policy (NCPPSP), comprised of eleven animal-related organizations. The NCPPSP has the mission to gather and analyze reliable data that further characterize the number, origin, and disposition of pets (cats and dogs) in the United States; to promote responsible stewardship of these companion animals; and, based on data gathered, to recommend programs to reduce the number of surplus/unwanted pets in the United States.

The NCPPSP's efforts to define the scope of pet overpopulation, at least through those animals relinquished or brought to shelters, were no less frustrating than previous efforts. Mailings to more than 4,800 U.S. shelters for four consecutive years produced a 25 percent return rate in any given year. Fewer than four hundred shelters responded all four years.

There were many reasons why no accurate count of the number of animals relinquished to shelters each year was obtained. Among them were a lack of consensus on what constitutes a shelter, a lack of uniformity in record keeping, a lack of any record keeping on the part of some shelters, a distrust on the part of shelters of anyone asking for their data, and a lack of an accurate database of shelters. Some shelters felt that the animals they handled were just the tip of the iceberg and did not want their numbers to be used out of context to quantify the problem of animals "in transition" from one household to another.

Surveys from various sources, including the AVMA and the American Pet Products Manufacturers Association (APPMA), indicated that the majority of Americans acquired their pet from some source other than an animal shelter. Cats, in particular, are more likely to be acquired through a friend, relative, or neighbor or taken in as a stray (76 percent combined) than from all other sources (breeder, shelter, pet shop, etc.).

As difficult as it was to obtain numbers from shelters regarding their intake and disposition of animals, getting data from such other sources as purebred registries, pet stores, and commercial breeding facilities was even more problematic. There was, however, general consensus among most animal-related organizations that the term pet overpopulation was not only difficult to define, but that it was also probably no longer an accurate catchphrase to describe the reasons for animals leaving their original homes, especially for dogs.

Dangerous or Vicious Dogs

In every decade since the 1950s, a breed of dog has emerged as a vicious or dangerous dog. In the 1960s, the German Shepherd was the "bad dog du jour"; in the 1970s, it was the Doberman pinscher. In the 1980s, 1990s, and 2001, it has been the pit bull, also known as the American Pit Bull Terrier.

Originally bred to fight other dogs of their breed, pit bulls have been the breed of choice for illegal dogfighting activities, such as organized fighting in well-hidden barns or warehouses and spur-of-the-moment street fights.

The reputation of a pit bull as a "bad" dog has been enhanced by a number of highly publicized attacks by pit bulls and pit bull-type crosses on children and other human victims. During the 1980s, hundreds of municipalities passed legislation to prohibit the keeping of pit bulls but found breed-specific legislation virtually unenforceable. How dogs were to be identified and by whom proved insurmountable problems. Rarely did laws prohibit the owners of pit bulls—or of other prohibited breeds—from acquiring another dog after the offending animal had been destroyed by the local animal shelter.

Where pit bull owners opposed breed-specific laws, officials found that they were spending more time and money defending a law that would probably not survive court scrutiny than they had budgeted for enforcing the law in the first place. One case that went all the way to the state's Supreme Court placed all breed-specific ban laws at risk. The court ruled that breed-specific ban laws were unconstitutional, violating due process laws, and that such laws were vague in their definitions of what constituted a pit bull. Some laws were over-inclusive, including breeds of dogs not known to be aggressive in any way; others were under-inclusive, leaving out breeds or mixes of breeds that had a record of inflicting serious injury or death on their victims.

Most towns and cities tried to regu-late vicious or dangerous dogs by opting for generic laws that imposed restrictions on dogs and their owners based on the individual dog's past behavior. But, even in these municipalities, rarely was enough funding appropriated for animal control to enforce dangerous-dog laws.

Breed-specific ban legislation has once again surged in various areas of the United States, in part in response to a new "bad breed," the rottweiler. While most of these laws are targeted at pit bulls, some are including new breeds of dogs like the Dogos Argentina, whose reputations as fighting dogs in their country of origin and their physical characteristics make them difficult to distinguish from the American Pit Bull Terrier.

Humane organizations are struggling to create new strategies to combat the proliferation of dogs bred to fight or be aggressive without labeling an entire breed as inherently vicious. The HSUS, which wrote guidelines for regulating dangerous and potentially dangerous dogs in 1985, has recently committed to updating those guidelines and to recommending solutions for targeting breeds for additional regulations when the numbers of attacks and/or incidents of aggressive activities involving the breed are escalating.

Present State of Companion Animals and Animal Shelters

Almost two-thirds of U.S. households have a dog, cat, bird, or reptile as a pet. The number of dogs, and particularly puppies, relinquished to shelters was rapidly diminishing as of mid-2000, to the point that some shelters did not have any puppies for adoption for many months. Those dogs and cats fortunate enough to be in lifelong homes are enjoying a longer life span than those who shared our homes in the first half of the twentieth century.

Additional good news is the way that animal shelters—whether run municipally, privately, or through a combination of municipal and private funding—are different from their predecessors in most communities throughout the United States. Their physical structure and their programs have advanced to include a host of new animals and new challenges that most municipal planners and humane society board members would never have dreamed of fifty—or even twenty—years ago.

Shelters have had to adapt, reconfiguring existing space or adding additional space to handle more cats than dogs; accommodating a growing number of small mammals, reptiles, and exotic pets; and housing livestock and equines confiscated or relinquished due to neglect or abuse. Some shelters have had to deal with an increasing number of large wild cats, such as lions, tigers, cougars and leopards, seized by police or humane officers for ordinance violations.

Shelter programs and services are far more preventive in nature than those of the 1900s. A few municipally owned and operated animal shelters stand out in their progressive tackling of animal control problems within their community and creation of "outside the box" solutions. In 1997 Palm Beach County (Florida) Animal Regulation (PBCAR) launched a Spay Shuttle, a converted camper/recreational vehicle that served the lower-income neighborhoods of Palm Beach County. In addition to low-cost sterilization services, the Spay Shuttle offered low-cost vaccination clinics and pet owner education programs in neighborhoods that represented the highest numbers of animal control complaints. PBCAR also offered low-cost sterilization for qualifying pet owners. All adopted animals were sterilized prior to leaving the facility and new adopters were encouraged to enroll their dogs in training programs offered at the shelter in conjunction with area dog trainers (Palm Beach County Animal Care and Control, personal communication Sept. 14, 2000). Alachua County (Florida) Animal

Services created a two-week internship with the University of Florida College of Veterinary Medicine. This allowed veterinary students the opportunity to see every aspect of the operation of a government animal control agency. Thus exposed, students could educate their clients on how to become more responsible pet owners.

Humane organizations created programs to help pet owners resolve problems with their animals before the problems reached the point at which the pet owner was ready to relinquish the animal. Based on research conducted as part of a master's degree thesis at Tufts University, shelters learned that the decision by the owner to relinquish an animal was neither easy nor impetuous (DiGiacomo, Arluke, and Patronek 1998). Most pet owners spent months agonizing over the decision and tried multiple venues for finding the animal another home before they drove to the shelter. Once there, the decision to relinquish the pet was irreversible.

Studies conducted by the NCPPSP found that behavior problems and lifestyle issues are the top reasons for relinquishment of a pet. More than 90 percent of individuals relinquishing a dog to the twelve shelters that participated in the study had not invested any time in training their dogs (Salman et al. 2000). Focus groups sponsored by The HSUS and conducted by research firm Jacobs Jenner and Kent revealed that pet owners who experienced behavior problems with their companion animals sought help with resolving those issues, but often received incorrect or inappropriate responses from individuals not qualified to deal with the pets' problems. Most of these pet owners were desperate to find solutions that would keep the pets in their homes. Shelters were usually the last choice for most pet owners when relinquishment was necessary. Almost unanimously, the focus groups felt that behavioral assistance should be offered by animal shelters and humane societies to help pet owners resolve their pets' problems (Jacobs 1999).

Many shelters have incorporated assistance with behavior problems into their menus of services offered to the community. One of the most inclusive programs exists at the Dumb Friends League (DFL), serving the greater Denver, Colorado, area. Another in a much smaller community is the Humane Society of Washington County (Maryland) that serves a rural and rather remote area.

The DFL's behavior-assistance program was initiated in conjunction with Suzanne Hetts in 1995. Temperament testing of animals within the shelter coupled with dog training classes and a behavior helpline sought to identify undesirable behaviors earlier and to offer solutions that pet owners could understand and easily incorporate to keep the pets in their new homes. Initially limited to those who had adopted from the DFL and aimed at reducing the recidivism rate of shelter adoptees, the program has now been expanded to include additional prevention programs and to serve the broader petowning community. Pet parenting classes, additional dog-training classes, and a stress reduction program have assisted thousands of additional animals both inside and outside the shelter (Rohde 2000).

The DFL and The HSUS also established the Pets for Life National Training Center at the DFL's facilities to instruct shelter staff from all over the country in creating similar behavior assistance programs for their communities.

Handling less than one-quarter the number of animals of the DFL, the Humane Society of Washington County launched a "Petiquette" program, similar to the DFL's Head Start program, which helped to identify and resolve the problems that brought the animal into the shelter. The Society also offered dog training classes open to all dog owners in the community to keep animals in their homes.

Towards the end of the twentieth century, several shelters run by nonprofit organizations that had contracted with their municipalities for animal control services reevaluated

those relationships. Chronically under-funded for the services they provided the community, these nonprofits informed their localities that without substantial increases in funding, services would be eliminated or their contracts cancelled. In some instances, municipalities responded with the additional resources. In others, the nonprofits revisited their demands when they discovered that municipal funding was covering more than they had initially calculated and that loss of funding would create a crisis for the organization. In other cases, contracts were cancelled.

When the San Francisco SPCA (SF SPCA) gave notice that it would no longer be contracting with the city and county of San Francisco to provide animal care and control services, the municipality was faced with several problems. It had no shelter of its own in which to house stray and homeless animals, and it did not have a general animal control program. The SF SPCA had given the city and county enough notice and cooperation to make the transition work, and some staff of the SF SPCA went to work for the new San Francisco Animal Care and Control agency to smooth the transition.

The situation in New York City was quite different. The five shelters operated by the New York City Center for Animal Care and Control were originally owned and operated by the ASPCA, which gave the shelters to the city. The city created a new nonprofit organization to run them and most of the ASPCA staff who had worked in the shelters became part of the staff of the New York City Center (Fekety 1998).

Sterilization Programs and Breeding Moratoriums

As companion animal populations grew in all parts of the United States, the number of animals entering animal shelters grew as well. Registrations of purebred dogs through the American Kennel Club grew from 442,875 per year in 1960 to 1,111,799,000 in 1980. For every purebred dog born in the late 1950s and early 1960s, it was estimated that there was also one mixed-breed puppy born.

Sterilization of companion animals, and particularly of dogs, was usually not undertaken until the female animal's estrus cycles became a nuisance for the human family members. Sterilization surgery was quite costly, considered unnecessary, and often discouraged by the family's veterinarian until the female dog had given birth to at least one litter or had experienced several estruses. To do otherwise was considered unhealthy for the animal. Neutering of male dogs was almost never undertaken except in cases of severe health problems.

As the costs for caring for the unplanned offspring of both purebreds and mixed breeds grew, national animal protection groups rallied to halt or reverse the burgeoning growth in the number of homeless animals. Phyllis Wright, The HSUS's first vice president for companion animal issues, believed that the impediments to reducing the number of unplanned births of dogs and cats stemmed from pet owners' ignorance of canine and feline estrus cycles; from the high costs—whether real or perceived—of having the sterilization surgery performed on pets; and from the lack of motivation on the part of owners to have pets sterilized until *after* the unplanned puppies or kittens had arrived. In the 1970s Wright's mantra to communities having to deal with homeless animals was "You can do more for animals by doing L.E.S.—Legislation, Education, and Sterilization."

The HSUS, through Wright and her staff, laid out a plan to attack pet overpopulation in communities across the United States. Through the passage of laws and ordinances such as differential licensing, The HSUS believed that those who were not motivated to spay or neuter their pets for population-control reasons would realize that the savings from lower licensing fees for sterilized animals could cover the cost of sterilization over the animal's life. Education programs that explained the health and behavioral benefits of sterilizing a pet were juxtaposed with the consequence of overpopulation in shelter—death. Lower fees for sterilization were urged to encourage those pet owners who were interested in having their pets altered to have the surgery performed. In the 1970s several cities experimented with opening lowcost sterilization (as opposed to full-service) clinics. The City of Los Angeles' clinic, which opened in 1971, resulted in a sea change in the attitudes of private practitioners to surgical sterilization. Boston's municipally owned and operated clinic failed quickly. All such clinics were vehemently opposed by veterinary organizations, many of which believed that government had no place in the veterinary field (Dalmadge 1972).

Despite such setbacks, additional campaigns appeared in the 1980s. The HSUS launched "Be A P.A.L.—Prevent A Litter" month. Friends of Animals expanded its program of issuing sterilization certificates that could be used at local participating veterinary clinics. Several local humane societies opened their own spay/neuter clinics to sterilize pets adopted from the shelter, as well as to serve low-income pet owners. The Doris Day Animal League (DDAL) started Spay Day USA in 1995 and publicized the event heavily through other national, as well as local, groups. It failed, however, to obtain AVMA endorsement of the campaign.

As the veterinary field changed to reflect the focus on animal-keeping, the tensions between the two communities on the issue of sterilization began to diminish. The veterinary student population shifted from being predominantly male to being predominantly female. The "feminization" of the veterinary profession, combined with the increase in pet-keeping (which traditionally involves the women in the home as primary pet caregivers), has brought about increased cooperation between the veterinary and animal protection communities.

Current discussions between the humane community and veterinary organizations to reduce pet populations are focusing on early-age (or prepubescent) sterilization (EAS) and development of nonsurgical means of sterilization, particularly for feral or unsocialized populations of cats and dogs. Some of the concerns with EAS have been the impact of sterilizing an animal at eight weeks of age on longbone growth, behavior, and incontinence. Research to date has revealed no deleterious effects.

Early experiments in nonsurgical alternatives to sterilization failed to provide promising results. But new research being undertaken looks more hopeful. Neutersol, a zinc-arginine drug injected into the testicles of male dogs for sterilization purposes, is being tested at various sites and will probably receive acceptance from the U.S. Food and Drug Administration (FDA) in the near future. Several researchers are experimenting with a porcine zona pellucida (PZP) injection for sterilizing female dogs (see "Fertility Control in Animals" in this volume). Recombinant zona pellucida proteins synthetically produced in laboratories were to be tested in 2000–2001.

Although the homeless dog population in the United States is decreasing, the cat population is increasing. This should not surprise those municipal officials and others responsible for animal control who have resisted attempts to regulate cat populations in the past. Many have turned a deaf ear to repeated warnings from animal-protection advocates and now have to reconfigure housing and revamp laws and policies to accommodate more felines than canines.

Breeding moratoriums, or outright bans, are one such attempt proposed by animal advocates to lower pet populations. In 1990 the Peninsula Humane Society in San Mateo, California, fired the opening round in the local overpopulation debate with a controversial advertisement carried in the Sunday edition of the area newspaper, reaching over 80,000 homes (Maggitti 1992). The four-page insert carried the headline "This is One Hell of a Job..." and opened to show barrels overflowing with the bodies of dead animals, with the tagline "...And We Couldn't Do It Without You." The ad called upon San Mateo County to pass legislation that would prohibit the breeding of dogs and cats until the number of animals entering the shelter and the number of those euthanized were substantially reduced.

Although the resulting legislation was substantially watered-down before being passed, the concept of limiting deliberate breeding of animals jump-started the debate on whether laws could reduce pet overpopulation. In 1992 The HSUS advocated a voluntary breeding moratorium (Handy 1993). Other national humane organizations, as well as dog- and cat-fancy groups, championed other ways of raising awareness about pet overpopulation. Several studies undertaken by or on behalf of the NCPPSP have added to the understanding of the breadth of the problem of homeless pets. But some of the more surprising items discovered by the NCPPSP were the low numbers of shelters keeping accurate data and the absence of a definitive and accurate listing of U.S. shelters (NCPPSP 2000).

Euthanasia: From "How To" to "Should We?"

Early methods of animal destruction were crude and rarely met the criteria of "euthanasia," from the Greek *euthantos*, meaning "good death." Death by gunshot, carbon monoxide exhaust gas, and drowning were not uncommon in the United States in the 1950s and unfortunately still exist in some parts of the country fifty years later.

Moves by national humane organizations to develop and implement more humane methods of destruction began in the early 1970s. AHA worked with U.S. Air Force personnel and engineers to develop a chamber that would euthanize animals through hypoxia. Similar to the chambers used by Air Force pilots when testing the effects of rapid decompression on the human body, the Euthanaire™ chamber was to accelerate the simulated "ascent rate" within the chamber from the 1,000 feet per minute used with humans to 1,000 feet per second. The Euthanaire was designed to hold four to eight medium- to small-sized animals and would cause their death in around fifteen minutes.

The HSUS opposed the decompression chamber method of destruction and was not supportive of any mechanical means of killing animals. It felt the most humane method of destruction was through the injection of an overdose of a barbiturate, preferably sodium pentobarbital. It pushed to change laws that prohibited trained lay personnel from administering barbiturates and also advocated for laws that would allow shelters to be licensed to purchase sodium pentobarbital.

AHA believed that killing animals was an emotionally difficult and sometimes dangerous job and that shelter workers charged with the task should be as physically removed from the actual killing as possible. The use of chambers, according to AHA, provided the worker with physical and emotional distance from the animals. The HSUS felt that the further the technician was away from the animal during euthanasia, the greater the potential for error. The potential for callousness, overcrowding of chambers, and increased distress on the part of the animals was increased when a worker could load a machine, flip a switch, and walk away.

By the end of the 1980s, the Euthanaire Company had gone out of business, thirty states had passed legislation prohibiting the use of decompression chambers, and AHA was supporting the use of sodium pentobarbital as the most humane method of destroying animals. AHA, The HSUS, and AVMA were by 2000 united in their preference for injection of sodium pentobarbital as the means of providing an animal with the most humane death.

In the early 1990s, the debate changed from *how to* to *should we* when the subject was the euthanasia of homeless shelter animals. Although no-kill shelters had been around for decades, the SF SPCA and its leader, Richard Avanzino, brought the issue to national attention. Avanzino, who was known for his controversial and often groundbreaking stances on dog and cat issues, informed the city and county of San Francisco in 1989 that, after one hundred years of contracting for animal control services, the SF SPCA was "getting out of the killing business" and would no longer destroy—by any means—the city's unwanted animals. The city and county were given three years' notice to develop their own program to do so. San Francisco Animal Care and Control was the result.

Taking the life of any animal is difficult to explain to the public, and, given a choice, it is assumed that most animal lovers would rather give their financial support to a shelter that does not euthanize animals than to one that does. Regardless of the level of financial support given a shelter by its municipality, that support rarely covers the costs of implementing progressive animal care and control programs. The loss of charitable dollars from donors who find euthanasia an unacceptable tool in battling pet overpopulation is a threat that a growing number of humane society boards of directors have not been willing to challenge.

In 1995 Avanzino extended the SF SPCA's no-kill philosophy to the entire city and county of San Francisco. He worked with the board of supervisors to pass the Adoption Pact, which called for San Francisco County Animal Care and Control to relinquish all unclaimed "adoptable" animals to the SF SPCA, where they would live until they were adopted. In 1997 Avanzino declared the Pact to be a complete success and declared San Francisco to be the United States' first "no-kill" city.

Since then, other cities have passed resolutions or statements declaring their intention to follow in San Francisco's footsteps. Austin, Texas, the County of San Diego (California), and Pittsburgh, Pennsylvania, among others, have declared their goal of becoming no-kill jurisdictions. Several cities have been served notice by their local humane societies that their contracts to provide animal control services will not be renewed. Some have given a few years' notice of their intentions, but others have withdrawn with little, if any, notice. In New York, Ulster County SPCA abruptly severed its agreement with the county and left animal control officers with no place to take stray animals.

The debate over no-kill (or "limited-admission") shelters versus "open admission" shelters has pitted animal advocates against each other. Charges of manipulating statistics and shifting definitions of "adoptable," "treatable," and "non-rehabilitatable" animals have been flung back and forth by groups attempting to seize the high ground in a debate over a difficult, thankless task.

In 1999 David Duffield, founder of the PeopleSoft company, donated $200 million to create Maddie's Fund, which was to distribute the money throughout the United States to help every community become a no-kill community. *Philanthropy* magazine quoted

Claire Rappaport, a human welfare advocate, as questioning the appropriateness of such a large donation for homeless animals when human suffering and homelessness still exists in San Francisco (Richardson 2000).

Journalist Todd Foster investigated no-kill shelters for *Readers Digest* and concluded that a number did not function humanely and often neglected the care of the animals they were trying to "save," overcrowding them in cages or turning away animals when the shelters were full, only to have other shelters euthanize them due to lack of space (Foster 2000).

The controversy over no-kill facilities has had some positive results. It has caused many shelter boards of directors and executive directors to reexamine their mission, goals, and roles in the community. It has empowered some humane societies in their negotiations with tight-fisted municipalities, which feared that, if they did not provide adequate financial support, they would face the unwelcome prospect of providing all the services residents had come to demand.

The debate has encouraged humane organizations to be more innovative and assertive in solving pet overpopulation and pet relinquishment problems. Sterilization prices have been lowered and spay/neuter clinics put on the road to serve a wider pet-owning community. "Open admission" shelters are doing more to keep animals in their original homes by providing training classes, behavior helplines, and leads on pet-friendly housing to help remove barriers from owners and pets in building lifelong bonds.

From "Property" to "Individual"

Companion animals, like most non-human animals, have had legal rights or status under the law only as property. Basic anticruelty statutes, including the Massachusetts Bay Colony's Bodies of Freedoms, which prohibits the abuse of animals, were promulgated to protect the animal owner's interest rather than to protect the animal. Massachusetts's anticruelty statutes, for example, make killing or beating one's own animal a misdemeanor, but killing or abusing an animal of another—destroying his property—is a felony.

Several attempts have been made in recent years to change the status of companion animals under the law. One of the earliest cases involved a San Francisco pet owner's right to determine the disposition of her animals after her death. Sido's owner had established in her will that upon the owner's death any animals living with her would be euthanized. Expecting to live a long life and thinking that her pets would be similarly advanced in age, the pet owner did not want her pets to languish in a shelter waiting to be adopted, nor did she want them to go through the trauma of trying to adjust to new home at the end of their lives. The pet owner did not provide for an alternative in case she died prematurely while her pets were quite young, which is precisely what occurred.

Richard Avanzino felt that Sido should not be euthanized simply because his owner had suffered a premature death. So Avanzino and others went to court to challenge the terms of the will as it pertained to the pets and to petition to be awarded custody of Sido for the term of his life. The court ruled in favor of saving Sido's life. The dog lived out his years at the SF SPCA, in Avanzino's office with free access to the rest of the shelter.

When pet owners have sued veterinarians in wrongful death or malpractice cases in which the negligence or misdiagnosis and treatment of a pet has resulted in the pet's death, courts traditionally have awarded little or no money to the grieving pet owner. Any damages awarded were based on the value of the animal as determined by the amount the owner had paid to purchase the animal. Therefore, a "free to good home" pet, a stray that had been taken in, or an animal adopted from a shelter, in the court's view, had little or no monetary value. The owner who tried to establish emotional value and therefore recover for pain and suffering at the loss of his pet was laughed out of court.

But that, too, is changing. Several cases concerning the death of pets in the care of veterinarians, groomers, boarding kennel owners, and transporting airlines have awarded pet owners large sums of money for the owner's emotional suffering.

Animal shelters have been put in a difficult position in the debate over the position of companion animals as property. In many instances, the stray dog or cat turned in to a shelter benefits from being considered property. If his original owner does not claim the animal in the prescribed period of time established by law, the animal is deemed "abandoned property" and becomes the property of the shelter. The shelter then has the right to dispose of its property as it sees fit. For responsible, caring shelters, this means the animal will be evaluated and then either placed in a new home or euthanized.

In an effort to change the status quo of animals as property, several humane societies and animal protection organizations have in their adoption contracts, newsletters, and policy statements begun to refer to the keepers of dogs and cats as "guardians" rather than "owners." Other communities have changed the terminology in their local ordinances to better reflect the relationship that companion animals and their caregivers enjoy. San Francisco and Boulder, Colorado, have both considered amending their statutes to remove all references to "owner" as it applies to companion animals and to substitute "guardian" instead. In Boulder owners are now guardians.

As animal rights evolve, and particularly as the role of companion animals in the lives of humans is studied and evaluated, the status of dogs and cats will continue to be elevated. Their days of being thought of as simply property are truly numbered.

The Status of Cats

The APPMA has commissioned surveys of pet owners every two years since the late 1970s. These surveys are used by APPMA's membership to forecast trends in pet ownership to better prepare for the pet owners' needs for pet food, collars, leashes, cat litter, and toys. In 1978, when 31.7 million households owned dogs and 16.2 million households owned cats, APPMA profiled the typical dog owner: a large family with children and with an average annual income of $12,000–$25,000. The APPMA considered cat ownership so insignificant that a profile was not even established (APPMA 1978). Twenty years later, APPMA did profile the typical cat owner: a single woman living in the city with an income lower than that of the dog-owning family.

The fact that in 2000 the United States was a nation of cat owners should surprise no one who has followed other U.S. social trends. In 1958 37 percent of adult women worked outside the home. In 1998 60 percent of adult women did so. More than 50 percent of households in the United States in the 1990s were headed by single mothers. The woman in one- or two-adult household is the primary person responsible for the family pet's veterinary care, feeding, exercising, and grooming and is the primary decision maker when choosing the species of the family pet.

The profile of the typical U.S. family has changed—from having 2.3 kids and living in detached houses with large backyards for the dog to having one child and living in townhouses on postage-stamp lots with a cat and a membership at a health club. Cats, often thought of as low-maintenance pets, are now the pets of choice for busy working women.

Cats now pose the greatest challenge to animal shelters, humane societies, veterinarians, and other animal-related organizations. Most state and local laws do not include cats in their animal control statutes. The sheltering community failed to predict and plan for the increased numbers of both owned and unowned cats. Shelters constructed in the late 1970s and throughout the 1980s still allotted more runs and kennels for dogs than cages for cats. Policies that required sterilization of dogs and puppies adopted from the shelter often failed to mention cats. Holding periods for stray cats, whether mandated by law or through shelter policy, were rarely as lengthy as those for stray dogs.

Some communities tried licensing programs. One of the first was Charlotte/Mecklenberg County, North Carolina, in 1980. While initially criticized by the media and by cat owners, the program slowly began to gain credibility. Twenty years later, Charlotte was licensing more than 39,000 cats and had increased its cat-return-to-owner rate by 2.4 percent. But the battle to increase responsibility among cat owners through licensing laws was far from over.

It is estimated that there may be as many as one feral cat for every owned cat in the United States. To curb the growth of unowned, unsocialized, or feral cats within a community, most municipalities have relied on trap-and-euthanize programs, typically carried out by frustrated homeowners. Attempting to trap and euthanize all of a community's unwanted cats has been a failure. The traps end up being sabotaged by well-meaning people. Most communities are still conducive to ferals (providing a ready supply of food from restaurant trash bins or feral cat caregivers and a modicum of safety from cars, weather, and dogs) so "trapping out" one colony just leaves room for a new one.

In San Mateo County, California, a feral cat pact was established between the humane society, which contracted with the county and several cities for animal control, and feral cat caregivers. In the first three years of the program, more than 200 colonies were registered, representing a total of just under 2,000 feral cats. Over this time period, the number of feral cats was reduced by 29 percent, primarily by the identification, removal, and adoption of socialized animals. The humane society sterilized more than 1,400 of the remaining ferals and reached an agreement to manage a feral cat colony within the a local nature park.

Hawaiian Humane Society (HHS), in conjunction with the City and County of Honolulu, passed a comprehensive Cat Protection Act in 1995 to curb the island of Oahu's burgeoning stray cat population. With a combination of resources from municipal and private funds, HHS worked with local veterinarians to offer low-cost or free sterilization to cat owners and caregivers. As of June 1999, the program had sterilized more than 11,828 cats.

Challenges, Conflicts, and Victories

"Unwanted litter" or "unplanned pregnancy" are rarely the reasons given for surrendering an animal to a shelter. Human lifestyle issues, such as "no time," "allergy," or "moving," or animal behavior problems are the new challenges to shelters trying to keep animals in their original homes.

According to studies conducted in the late 1990s by the NCPPSP and other researchers, behavior issues are a major factor in a pet owner's decision to remove a pet from the home. Although the pet owner may list such other reasons as moving to a new home or allergies of family members, as the primary motivation for relinquishment, further investigation of the animal's life in the home often reveals a different cause for surrendering the animal. Lack of basic training

and increased frustration with house-soiling or other preventable problems cause the pet owner to make the decision to remove the animal from his home. Some shelters, seeing increased numbers of "teenage" animals enter their facilities, as well as more pets who have already been spayed or neutered, have decided that spay/neuter programs alone will no longer provide the answer to ending pet overpopulation. To attack the new reasons for companion animal homelessness, programs beyond low-cost sterilization had to be created.

Veterinary student Alexa Dowdichuk and co-researcher John Wenstrup found that many shelters had not carefully analyzed the true causes for relinquishment of young, healthy animals to their facilities and were investing all of their time and resources into traditional overpopulation solutions of sterilization and education on spaying and neutering. Dowdichuk concluded that if those same resources were redirected toward behavior counseling, dog training, and other programs that assist pet owners with integrating a new pet into the home, fewer animals would be relinquished or returned to shelters (HSUS 2000).

To test the theory that behavior assistance programs readily available to pet owners can change the future for animals whose owners are on the verge of relinquishing them because of "curable" behavior problems, The HSUS contracted with a research firm to conduct focus groups around the country. Pet owners who were experiencing or had experienced behavior problems with a pet were asked about their pets' offending behaviors, steps they had taken to address those behaviors, sources or individuals to whom they had turned for advice, and the outcomes of their efforts. Overwhelmingly, respondents reported frustration at receiving inaccurate or incomplete advice or failure in finding sources for advice on their pets' particular behavioral problems.

Based on this research, as well as other data, The HSUS launched the Pets for Life project, a broad-based

campaign which incorporated several existing campaigns, such as promotion of pet sterilization, with new programs that focused on eliminating bond-breakers or barriers that prevent people from developing and building lifelong bonds with their new pets. The campaign concentrates on five major areas: housing issues (policies which restrict or prohibit pets), human health issues (pets and human allergies, zoonotic diseases and immuno-compromised pet owners, and cats and pregnant women), lifetime commitment (educating pet owners on the costs of pet care and the life span of dogs and cats), animal health (preventive health care, including sterilization) and behavior (house-soiling, scratching/clawing digging, vocalizing, etc).

Additional programs will work on a national basis to eliminate other bond barriers by educating housing managers on responsible pet ownership guidelines and human health care providers on protecting patient health while keeping the pet in the home.

Spaying and Neutering

Although the number of animals entering animal shelters continues to decrease, animal protection organizations can not afford to decrease their emphasis on and commitment to sterilization.

Pediatric, prepubescent, or the previously mentioned early age sterilization (EAS)—the spaying or neutering of animals at eight weeks of age or at two pounds—was introduced by Dr. Leo Lieberman in 1987. Research conducted by Lieberman and others found that young animals could be successfully and safely sterilized under controlled conditions and recover from the surgery in shorter time periods than animals six months of age or older (Lieberman 1998). Subsequent research by The University of Florida College of Veterinary Medicine and Texas A&M University, which examined such issues as long-bone growth, urinary incontinence, and behavioral changes, revealed little or no increase in occurrence in the animal sterilized at eight weeks of age as compared to those who underwent surgery at the traditional age of six months (Howe 1999).

The AVMA initially expressed reluctance in accepting prepubescent sterilization, citing a lack of empirical data indicating few or no adverse long-term effects on animals. It adopted a resolution of support for EAS for shelter animals in 1998. Eventually, at the urging of its animal welfare committee, the AVMA's executive board removed the shelter qualifier from its support of early-age sterilization. With the blessing of the AVMA, humane organizations and animal care and control agencies are hoping that sterilization-at-adoption will become standard practice at shelters across the country.

New York City hoped to take early-age sterilization of newly acquired animals a step further. Under an ordinance passed in 2000 and backed by the New York City Center for Animal Care and Control and other humane organizations, city pet stores and animal shelters were required to spay or neuter all animals purchased or adopted from them. The new law spurred other communities to consider proposing similar laws, although it is being challenged in court by the Pet Industry Joint Advisory Council.

While many breeders had relied on spay/neuter contracts that required proof of surgery before sending the new owner American Kennel Club registration papers for pet-quality puppies, some breeders found that compliance was spotty. Some of these breeders are now having their puppies spayed or neutered at eight weeks of age before the puppies are placed in new homes.

Shelters have found that sterilization at adoption greatly reduces their paperwork and staff time for adoption compliance follow-up. Sterilizing the animal before he leaves the shelter does not satisfy all of the adoption contract provisions, nor does it assure the animal of a life-long home, but it does assure that the adopted animal

won't be contributing to the community's pet overpopulation problem.

The acceptance of sterilization as an important aspect of owning a pet increased dramatically throughout the United States from 1975 to 2000. APPMA and AVMA surveys showed that most pet owners didn't want an intact animal in their home (NCPPSP 2000). Data showing that intact male dogs are more likely to bite than neutered dogs drove many reluctant pet owners to castrate their dog for that reason alone.

Surgical sterilization will most likely continue to be the method of choice for controlling breeding in the United States and wherever veterinary care is readily available. In developing countries, less invasive methods that can be delivered by non-veterinarians hold the key to solving animal control and pet overpopulation problems. Research is progressing on several nonsurgical methods for permanently sterilizing dogs and cats.

Future Challenges

Puppy Mills, Humane Organizations, and the American Kennel Club

Humane organizations have fought for years to improve enforcement of the Animal Welfare Act (AWA) and to force a shake-up within the U.S. Department of Agriculture's Animal and Plant Health Inspection Service (USDA APHIS) to ensure that caring, competent staff will take seriously the agency's congressional mandate to protect animals, including dogs in puppy mill operations. During the Reagan administration (1980–88) the Office of Management and Budget (OMB) requested zero funding for enforcement of the AWA provisions, reflecting the Reagan Administration's philosophy that enforcement would be better carried out by local humane societies. OMB overlooked the fact

that most local humane societies had no law enforcement powers and that no local humane organizations have interstate legal powers. The result would have been zero enforcement to accompany zero funding. (Congress restored the funding but never increased it despite the fact that additional licences were granted annually.)

Criticism of the American Kennel Club's role in puppy mill proliferation has centered around the income it receives from large commercial breeding establishments (Derr 1990). Many breeders feel that it should do more to ensure that only the best quality animals carry an American Kennel Club registration and should do more to force the puppy mills out of business. The American Kennel Club maintains that it is not a quality-assurance organization and can therefore not guarantee the health or quality of animals that carry the Club's registration.

Focus groups conducted by Jacobs Jenner and Kent for The HSUS in 1997 found that people who purchase puppies from pet stores were fully aware of puppy mills' existence, but the majority had convinced themselves that their new dog didn't come from a puppy mill. It is likely that the vast majority of the 500,000 puppies sold in pet stores (Patronek and Rowan 1995) originate in large commercial dog-breeding establishments, or puppy mills.

New appointments and reorganization of USDA APHIS in 2000 improved the situation for some animals in puppy mills. Increased training, more intensive scrutiny of licensed dealers, and a stronger commitment on the part of the USDA hierarchy to cast out the bad apples resulted in many areas of change, including hefty fines and penalties and the closing of some of the worst puppy mills. Thousands of animals, however, still languished in puppy mills.

Lions, Tigers, Bears, (and Iguanas)

At the turn of the millennium, a new wave of exotic pets pushed many shelters to the edge in terms of resources and staffing. Pet stores and want-ads had long offered more than just dogs and cats to anyone with enough cash to buy an animal, but the new exotic pet posed multiple challenges to animal care and control facilities and humane organizations.

U.S. shelters were trying to find ways to care for and offer for adoption, when justified, rabbits, guinea pigs, hamsters, gerbils, sugar gliders (flying squirrels), hedgehogs, and reptiles and amphibians that ranged from tiny lizards and turtles to giant pythons and boa constrictors.

Shelters found themselves playing host to lions, tigers, leopards, bobcats, and jaguars when the animals had become too much for their owners to care for or had been confiscated by police. Some had to add staff and space to accommodate a never-ending stream of large exotic cats. Weak laws regarding the keeping of wild exotic animals put a tremendous burden on shelters, which were never intended to house and care for these species. Questions of jurisdiction over these animals when it came to confiscating, caring for, and disposing of them made it imperative that communities clearly define parameters for keeping wildlife.

In 2000 the USDA issued a statement urging states to pass laws to prohibit the keeping of large exotic cats, citing multiple cases of human injuries and instances of animals being poorly and/or cruelly treated.

In 1999 the Centers for Disease Control and Prevention released data showing a marked increase in salmonellosis in young children (Centers for Disease Control and Prevention 2000). This increase was directly correlated to the increased incidence of keeping iguanas as pets. All reptiles carry the salmonella bacterium, and children under eight are particularly susceptible to salmonella infection.

Although most state laws require pet stores to put warnings on reptile displays to advise parents of the risks of salmonellosis transmission from reptiles to children, most warnings go unheeded. As a result, some shelters refuse to place reptiles, particularly iguanas, in homes with children under twelve years of age.

Into the Future

Among the most pressing challenges in the twenty-first century for advocates of companion animals will be to continue the progress made in reducing the uncontrolled breeding of dogs and to translate that success to the feline population. Creative solutions to cat control that include all stakeholders—animal control, feral cat caregivers, breeders, wildlife advocates, veterinarians, and municipal officials—will have to be developed to ensure that success is long-term and supported by the majority.

More veterinarians are entering the field of animal behavior and are anxious to work with dog trainers and shelters to resolve behavior problems. Shelters will realize that the best way to cut euthanasia rates and increase successful adoptions is to work with animal behaviorists, veterinarians, and dog trainers to ameliorate the effects of animal behavior before the pet owner's frustration becomes insurmountable.

Other barriers to building and maintaining a strong bond with companion animals will fall by the wayside. Landlords and housing managers are already finding out that blanket no-pet policies rarely work and that responsible pet owners are good tenants. Obstetricians, allergists, oncologists, and gerontologists who dispense faulty or outdated information about pets and disease transmission and injury will have to rethink their advice if they want to keep patients who are convinced that life is worth living with a pet.

Literature Cited

American Pet Products Manufacturer Association (APPMA), Inc. 1978. National family opinion survey for the American Pet Products Manufacturers Association. Greenwich, Conn.: APPMA.

Centers for Disease Control and Prevention. 2000. PHLIS surveillance data: Salmonella. Available: *www. cdc.gov/ncidod/dbmd/phlisdata/ salmonella.htm*

Dalmadge, G. 1972. Adoption programs: Quality or quantity. *Shop Talk,* December, 19.

Derr, M. 1990. The politics of dogs. *The Atlantic Monthly*, March, pp. 49–72.

DiGiacomo, N., A. Arluke, and G. Patronek. 1998. Surrendering pets to shelters: The relinquisher's perspective. *Anthrozoös* 2(1), pp. 41–50.

Fekety, S. 1998. Personal communication. Animal Shelters Consultation (ASC) for the Center for Animal Care and Control for the City of New York. Report. May.

Foster, T. 2000. Are these animal shelters truly humane? *Readers Digest*, April, pp. 103–108.

Handy, G. 1993. A moratorium on breeding: The best way to stop the killing is to stop the breeding. *Shelter Sense*, March, pp. 3–7.

Howe, L. M. 1999. Prepubertal gonadectomy in dogs and cats, Part I. *Compendium on Continuing Education for the Practicing Veterinarian*, 21(2): 103–111.

Humane Society of the United States (HSUS). 1985. IRS clears Michigan societies' full service and spay/neuter clinics. *HSUS News*, Winter, p. 36.

————. 2000. Making the numbers count. *Animal Sheltering*, July/August, page 2.

Jacobs, W.H. 1999. HSUS campaign to protect dogs and cats. Research report. Jacobs Jenner and Kent. December.

Lieberman, L. 1998. A case for neutering pups and kittens at two months of age. *Journal of the American Medical Association* 191(5): 518–521.

Louisiana Society for the Prevention of Cruelty to Animals and the City of New Orleans v. Louisiana Board of Veterinary Medicine, 89-C-2689 Consolidated With 89-C-2709 (1990). Jan. 19, 1990.

Maggitti, P. 1992. A banner ordinance for San Mateo. *Cats* Magazine, March, pp. 21–23.

National Council on Pet Population Study and Policy (NCPPSP). 2000. The Shelter Statistics Survey, 1994–1997. Publications Resulting From National Council on Pet Population and Policy. Available: *www. petpopulation.org.*

Patronek, G. and A.N. Rowan. 1995. Determining dog and cat numbers and population dynamics. *Anthrozoös* 8: 199–205.

Richardson, V. 2000. Going to the dogs. *Philanthropy,* April, 18.

Rohde, R. 2000. Denver Dumb Friends League. Available: *www.ddfl.org/ tips.htm.*

Salman, M., J. Hutchison, R. Ruch-Gallie, L. Kogan, J. C. New Jr., P. Kass, and J. Scarlett. 2000. Behavioral reasons for relinquishment of dogs and cats to 12 shelters. *Journal of Applied Animal Welfare Science,* 3(2): 93–106.

Farm Animals and Their Welfare in 2000

5

David Fraser, Joy Mench, and Suzanne Millman

Introduction

Humans use far more animals for agricultural production than for any other purpose. Worldwide 1.9 billion cattle, sheep, and swine, and 39.7 billion chickens and turkeys, were slaughtered in 1998 (UN Food and Agricultural Organization [FAO] 2000). Many other species are farmed for food or fiber in smaller numbers, including agouti and capybara, alligators, alpaca and llamas, bison, deer, emus and ostriches, goats, iguanas, pheasants, pigeons, quail, rabbits, and waterfowl. The most rapidly growing segments of the agricultural industry are probably aquaculture and mariculture (the farming of fish, shellfish, and other aquatic animals), which now produce more than 20,000 metric tons of food annually, according to the FAO. Animal agriculture also generates many important byproducts, including gelatin, hides, horn, inedible fats used for industrial purposes, meat and bone meals, manure, and medicinal products. In developing countries buffalo, camels, and cattle are widely used for draft power as well as for food.

From an animal welfare viewpoint, farm animals present unique challenges. The primary purpose of farming, whether of plants or animals, is to produce abundant, high-quality, and competitively priced products for human consumption. Consumer preferences and economics therefore play a central role in determining how farm animals are treated. As a consequence of real or perceived economic constraints, people have developed many animal-production practices that would not be considered acceptable if used with other types of animals. For example, confining animals for many weeks at a time in such a way that they cannot walk or turn around would not be tolerated for zoo or companion animals but is a common practice with pregnant sows.

Farm animals have been a traditional concern of the modern animal protection movement. In the early 1800s, when the movement emerged as a significant sociopolitical force in the United Kingdom, its first priority was protection of farm animals, with particular emphasis on cattle and horses. Subsequently priorities changed, and throughout most of the 1900s, animal protectionism in Europe and the English-speaking world focused more strongly on the use of animals for scientific research and on the rescue of abandoned or ill-treated companion animals. Today, however, with vigorous public debate over animal agriculture and its effects, farm animals are re-emerging as a major subject of humane concern.

Such attention is timely. Animal agriculture is undergoing significant restructuring worldwide, with major and complex implications for animals, human society, and the environment. At the same time, the public is bombarded with polarized, simplistic depictions of animal agriculture both by its opponents and by its defenders. The result is a public misinformed about the issues despite their great importance. In this chapter we review the major changes that have occurred in animal agriculture since 1950, mainly in the industrialized countries; the resulting implications for animal welfare; and the factors that have contributed to these changes.

The Revolution in Animal Production

Animal Numbers and Distribution

The world's human population has increased by about 2 percent per year for the last forty years, with most of that increase occurring in the developing countries. As the population has increased, so too have the consumption of animal products and the numbers of animals raised for agricultural production (Figure 1a,b). Poultry production has shown the largest increase and, in the United States at least, consumption of poultry has consistently increased as consumption of

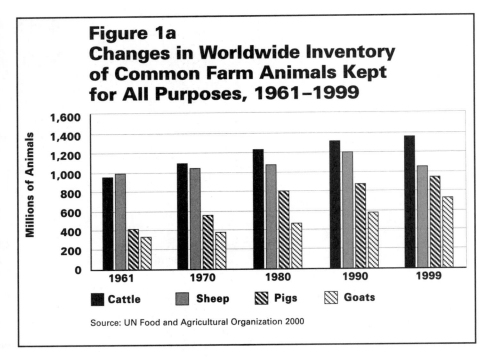

**Figure 1a
Changes in Worldwide Inventory
of Common Farm Animals Kept
for All Purposes, 1961–1999**

Millions of Animals

■ Cattle ▥ Sheep ▨ Pigs ▧ Goats

Source: UN Food and Agricultural Organization 2000

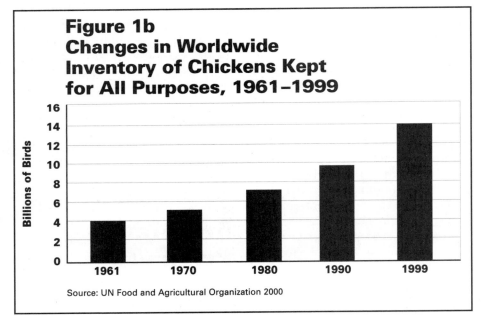

**Figure 1b
Changes in Worldwide
Inventory of Chickens Kept
for All Purposes, 1961–1999**

Billions of Birds

Source: UN Food and Agricultural Organization 2000

red meat has tended to decline (Figure 2). Animal products currently contribute 10 percent of the calories eaten by people in developing countries and nearly 30 percent of the calories eaten in industrialized countries (FAO 1994). By 2020 global demand for meat is projected to increase more than 60 percent over current consumption, with 88 percent of this increase resulting from higher total meat consumption in developing countries (Council for Agricultural

Science and Technology 1999).

Specific types of animal agriculture tend to be concentrated in specific countries or regions of the world. The United States produces about one-fourth of the world's beef and veal; China is by far the world's largest pork producer (Figure 3). The United States produces more than 30 percent of the world's poultry meat, and China and the United States are the world's leading producers of eggs. The United States and India together

produce about 30 percent of the total world production of milk, although the dairy cow populations in the United States are actually low when compared with those of many other countries; high U.S. production is due to high production per cow. Overall, China produces one-third of the world's meat supply, followed by the United States and the European Union, producing approximately 15 to 20 percent each (USDA National Agricultural Statistics Service [NASS] 2000). Animal products play a major role in the economy of many countries. In the United States for example, the value of farm animal products was more than $95 billion in 1999, with about $11.2 billion of that total due to exports (USDA Economic Research Service [ERS] 2000a).

Housing and Handling Methods

Until about 1950 farm animals in industrialized countries were raised using traditional methods that relied on labor to accomplish routine tasks such as feeding and manure removal, and that generally involved keeping animals in outdoor or semi-outdoor environments. (Beef cattle and sheep are still kept in this way, at least during most of their production cycle.) After World War II, however, there emerged a new generation of technology typically called "confinement" or "intensive" animal production. Intensive production systems use hardware and automation instead of human labor for many routine tasks, and the animals are generally kept in specialized indoor environments. In industrialized countries, confinement rearing is now the norm for poultry and swine, while dairy cattle are generally kept in semi-intensive systems where the animals have access to a paddock, cement yard, or pasture for at least part of the year. Worldwide, intensive animal-production systems accounted for 79 percent of the poultry, 39 percent of the pork, and 68 percent of the eggs produced during 1996 (Sere and Steinfeld 1996).

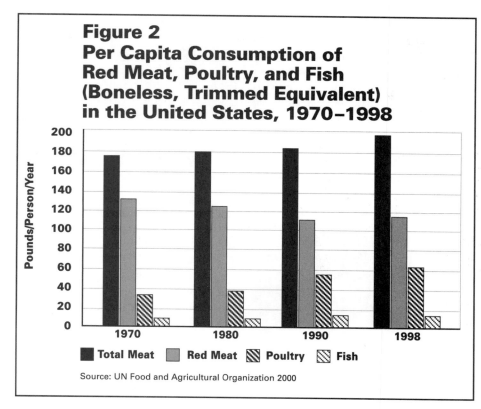

Figure 2
Per Capita Consumption of Red Meat, Poultry, and Fish (Boneless, Trimmed Equivalent) in the United States, 1970–1998

Y-axis: Pounds/Person/Year

Legend: ■ Total Meat ▨ Red Meat ▨ Poultry ▨ Fish

Source: UN Food and Agricultural Organization 2000

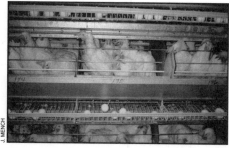

Figure 4.
Laying hens in a battery-cage system

Poultry

Poultry production is the most highly intensified of all the agricultural industries. In the 1950s hens were kept in small flocks outdoors on range. The death rate could be high because of soil-borne diseases, extreme temperatures, and predators. Egg production was largely seasonal, and poultry meat was available mainly when the hens were "retired" from egg-laying and sent to the processing plant. A major, and highly successful, push to use genetic selection (initiat-

ed in the United States by a nationwide "Chicken of Tomorrow" contest) produced strains of chickens suited to either egg-laying (layers) or meat production (broilers). Cage housing systems were developed for layers that allowed better environmental control, including control of the amount of light necessary to stimulate higher levels of egg production.

Most laying hens in North America are now housed in cages (Figure 4), although in response to animal welfare concerns, some countries have moved toward providing more extensive housing, either on range or in housing systems similar to those used for broilers. Wire "battery cages" are arranged in rows and tiers (or batteries), with sloping floors that allow eggs to roll to the front for collection. There are many different designs, but a typical cage houses three to ten hens, and a typical house contains thousands to tens of thousands of cages. Feeding, watering, and egg and manure collection are all automated. Hens are housed in these cages from the start of lay at sixteen to eighteen weeks of age through one or more laying cycles.

Egg production begins to decline as hens age, so if the hens are to be kept after the end of their first laying cycle (at around seventy weeks of age), they are stimulated to resume higher egg production by "forced molting," which induces them to replace their feathers. Forced molting is accomplished by depriving the hens of feed, usually for eight to twelve days or until they lose 30–35 percent of their body weight. Egg production ceases for a period of one to several weeks during

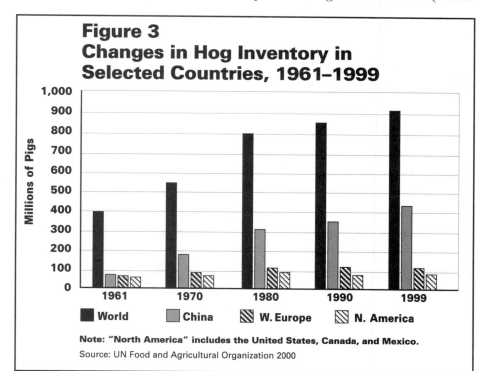

Figure 3
Changes in Hog Inventory in Selected Countries, 1961–1999

Y-axis: Millions of Pigs

Legend: ■ World ▨ China ▨ W. Europe ▨ N. America

Note: "North America" includes the United States, Canada, and Mexico.

Source: UN Food and Agricultural Organization 2000

Figure 5.
Commercial broilers are usually housed in floor systems, sometimes in groups of 10,000 or more birds.

the molt, then the hens resume higher rates of egg production for a second, or even a third, laying cycle.

Hens generally have the distal third or half of their beaks removed (called "beak trimming") to prevent injuries due to pecking, and they may also have part of their toes removed so that they do not scratch one another. Beak and toe trimming are usually performed when chicks are one to two weeks of age, using a hot blade to cauterize the tissues. Male chicks have no commercial value and are considered a by-product of the egg industry. In 1998 219 million chicks were killed in the commercial laying industry in the United States (USDA NASS 1999c), usually in a high-speed macerator or by gas within twenty-four hours after hatching.

Broiler chickens are housed in large groups (usually tens of thousands) in either completely or partially enclosed buildings on a floor covered with bedding (Figure 5). Feeding and watering are automated. Broilers grow rapidly and are marketed at from three to twelve weeks of age. Broiler chickens are usually not beak trimmed, although "broiler breeders" (the parent birds that produce broilers) are both beak- and toe-trimmed.

Broiler breeders are reared to sexual maturity in houses similar to those used in broiler production. However, to prevent fertility problems associated with obesity, broiler breeders are severely feed-restricted. This can lead to excessive drinking; hence, to prevent problems with wet litter, water is often restricted during the rearing

period to four to six hours per day. At twenty-two weeks of age, males and females are housed together, often in flocks of ten thousand birds, and hatching eggs are produced. As with table-egg production, hens may be force-molted for a second or third laying cycle. Turkeys are produced similarly except that artificial insemination is necessary because the males are so large, due to genetic selection for growth, that they cannot mate normally.

Figure 6.
A sow in a farrowing crate with her piglets.

Swine

Swine production in North America has seen a strong trend away from pasture production on small farms toward large-scale confinement systems. Pigs may be kept in one facility from farrowing (birth), through the "growing" phase (to a weight of about ninety lbs.), to "finishing" (market weight), or different facilities may be used for different phases.

During farrowing each sow is usually confined to a "farrowing crate" large enough to permit her to stand, lie, and nurse the piglets, but not large enough for her to turn around (Figure 6); the piglets, attracted to warmth, are induced to rest in a protected, heated area to the side or front of the crate in order to reduce the risk of their being crushed by the sow. Newborn piglets have their "needle teeth" (deciduous canines and corner incisors) clipped short to prevent injuries to other piglets; they may be ear-notched or tattooed for individual identification; and their tails may be clipped short ("docked") to prevent later damage from tail bit-

Figure 7.
Pregnant sows are commonly housed in "gestation crates"; this technology has now been banned in the United Kingdom.

ing by other pigs. Male piglets are surgically castrated, without anesthesia, to prevent "boar taint," an unpleasant odor in the meat. Piglets are usually weaned at three to four weeks of age. Recently, however, there has been a trend toward "segregated early weaning," removing the piglets earlier to an environment some distance from the sow. This isolates piglets from many disease pathogens while they are still protected by maternally derived immunity, thus reducing the risk of disease and the associated slowing of growth later in life.

After the piglets have been weaned, the sows are bred by either natural mating or artificial insemination. During pregnancy, sows are fed a limited amount of food to prevent obesity. Formerly this was often achieved by keeping sows in groups and moving them each day into individual feeding stalls where dominant animals could not monopolize the food. Today individual feeding is usually achieved by housing sows in individual stalls or "gestation crates" for most of their

Figure 8.
Growing and finishing pigs are usually housed in groups until they reach market weight at about six months of age.

pregnancy. To conserve space in the facility, crates provide only enough room for the sow to take about one step forward and back and not enough to walk or turn around (Figure 7). Boars are generally housed in individual pens or stalls to prevent aggression.

Market pigs are housed in groups during the growing and finishing phases (Figure 8), typically in totally or partially enclosed buildings, although they may sometimes be finished on pasture. The buildings typically have flooring constructed of concrete with slats (sections of solid floor alternating with slots that allow manure to fall into a pit below) covering some or all of the floor area. Manure is usually moved as a liquid to outdoor lagoons or sealed tanks and held for several months before being sprayed on the land. Bedding materials, such as straw, are not generally used in these liquid-manure systems.

Dairy cattle

Dairy cattle are usually housed in semi-intensive systems involving some combination of indoor and outdoor environments. According to a USDA survey, 58 percent of dairy operations pastured their lactating cows for at least three months during 1995 (USDA Animal and Plant Health Inspection Service [APHIS] 1996). About a quarter of U.S. dairy operations house cows in free-stall barns (USDA APHIS 1996); these are loose-housing systems with bedded stalls that the cows can enter and leave freely. Roughly 60 percent of U.S. dairy operations use tie-stall

Figure 9.
In some states, such as California, milk is sometimes produced on large "dry lot dairies" housing several thousand cows.

barns in which each cow is confined to an individual stall and held by a neck chain, strap, or stanchion such that she can lie down but cannot turn around. The stalls are usually bedded or covered with a rubber mat. The cows may be released from the stalls for milking, or they may remain in their stalls and be milked by a mobile milker. In some regions of the United States, dairy cattle are managed in "dry lot" systems (Figure 9), where several thousand cows are housed in outdoor padocks with a central parlor for milking.

Dairy cows are usually bred by artificial insemination. Since the cow's milk production is intended for human consumption, most calves are weaned within twenty-four hours of birth (USDA APHIS 1996). Heifers (female calves) are often raised on the dairy farm as replacement animals for the milking herd. However, about one-fifth of large operations (those with more than two hundred cows) contract the rearing of heifers to other farms (USDA APHIS 1996). When young, calves may be kept in group pens, in individual stalls that restrict movement and contact with neighboring calves, or in individual hutches or cubicles that may be associated with a small outdoor area. Male calves are generally considered a byproduct of the dairy industry. Depending on economics and local circumstances, these calves will either be killed shortly after birth or raised for meat. In the latter case, calves may be raised to an age of four months or older on a grain-based diet and marketed as "pink veal" or "baby beef," or they may be fed a low-iron, milk-based or milk-like diet, and marketed as "white" or "special-fed" veal. These calves may be kept in small groups, but white-veal calves are more commonly kept in individual stalls that limit their movement and prevent them from turning around.

To prevent injuries, dairy cattle are dehorned at an early age, usually by the use of a hot iron to cauterize the developing horn buds. Local anesthetic is used for this procedure by some growers (for example, those in

the United Kingdom) but not by others. Tail docking of dairy cattle is increasingly common in Australia, New Zealand, and North America; it is usually performed by placing a tight rubber ring around the tail several inches below the base, whereupon the constricted portion of the tail dies and falls off after several days. The ostensible reason for tail-docking is to improve hygiene and udder health, but there is little evidence that docking has these effects. Docking does, however, make milking easier in milking parlors in which cows are milked from the rear.

Figure 10.
In the United States and Canada, most beef animals are born and raised on pasture or rangeland systems and are "finished" on a grain-based diet in large feedlots.

Beef cattle, sheep, and goats

Beef cattle, sheep, and goats are usually kept on pasture throughout much of their lives. Beef cows are bred either by natural mating or by artificial insemination; embryos from preferred animals may be implanted into others considered of lower quality. Beef calves stay with their mothers until weaning at roughly seven months of age; they may then be shipped to a feedlot (Figure 10) where they are fed grain for four to six months until they reach market weight. Early weaning of beef calves (at three to four months of age), followed by feedlot finishing, is becoming increasingly common. To decrease problems with aggression and to produce more tender meat, male calves not to be used for breeding are castrated. Both surgical and nonsurgical castration methods are used, and all are performed without anesthesia. Beef cattle are also dehorned using several different methods and are usually individually marked by hot-iron or freeze branding. Confinement systems are uncommon for sheep and goats, although lambs are sometimes finished in feedlots or raised in cages. Sheep and goats are castrated and dehorned using methods similar to those used for beef cattle. To prevent fecal contamination of the hindquarters and subsequent infestation with flies, sheep are usually tail-docked through the use of tight rubber rings, a crushing device, or a hot knife.

Other Methods of Enhancing Productivity

While changes were occurring in animal housing and handling methods, other performance-enhancing technologies, including developments in nutrition, veterinary care, and genetic selection, came into widespread use. Vaccines, disease-eradication programs, and disease-prevention measures virtually eliminated some previously common animal diseases. Several hormone products came into use to enhance productivity. In the United States, more than 90 percent of beef cattle now are implanted with hormones or given hormones in their feed to improve their rate of gain and feed efficiency (USDA APHIS 1995a). The United States has also approved the use of recombinant bovine growth hormone (rBST) for injection into dairy cattle as a means of increasing their metabolic efficiency and boosting milk yield. In the United States in 1996, rBST was administered to approximately 10 percent of dairy cows overall and to more than 30 percent of cows on farms with more than two hundred cows (USDA APHIS 1996). An older and more widespread intervention has been the use of low dosages of antibiotics as feed additives to enhance growth; this practice has raised human health concerns about the development of antibiotic-resis-

tant pathogens (National Research Council [NRC] 1999). In the United States during 1994, 55 percent of beef cattle and 59 percent of market hogs were given antibiotics in their feed (USDA APHIS 1995a,b). Low levels of antibiotics are included in most U.S. broiler and turkey feed rations to improve growth and feed conversion (North and Bell 1990).

Farm animals have also undergone significant changes through genetic selection for desirable production traits such as rapid growth, leanness, high milk yield, high egg production, and low feed requirements. In some sectors the use of artificial insemination has allowed males of high genetic merit for production traits to sire huge numbers of offspring on many different farms. The industrial infrastructure of animal breeding has also been evolving. For poultry and egg production, much of the primary breeding is done by a small number of companies. Instead of producing their own breeding sows, many swine producers now buy replacement breeding animals from specialized breeding companies.

These and other changes have resulted in a dramatic increase in the productivity of animal agriculture during the last fifty years. Annual milk yield per cow has doubled or tripled in most developed countries since 1950 (Putnam 1991). Broiler chickens now reach a market weight of 4 lbs. in roughly six weeks—down from twelve weeks in 1950—and they require less than 2 lbs. of feed per pound of live weight—down from 3.25 lbs. in 1950 (Gyles 1989).

By and large, these increases in productivity have not been reflected in the prices paid to farmers for their products. According to the Consumer Price Index, retail costs to consumers for meat and dairy products in the United States have increased approximately 45 percent since 1982–1984, but payments to farmers have not increased at all (USDA NASS 1999a). In some cases they have decreased; for example, farmers in the United States received an average of $74.60 for 100 lbs. of cattle marketed in

1990 but only $58.70 in 1996. Farmers have little control over the margins charged by retailers for their products, and a combination of retail price increases and low farm profit margins no doubt contributes to the pressure on producers to increase production efficiency.

Broader Social Effects

As animal production in industrialized countries has become more mechanized and more concentrated in larger units, farm structure and the sociology of rural communities has changed as well. Fewer and fewer people are directly involved in animal production. In some regions, notably the United States and some of the former Soviet countries, large corporately or collectively owned units have replaced many traditional family-owned units. These changes have been most dramatic in the U.S. poultry industry, where five companies now control 53 percent of the broiler market, and one company, Tyson Foods, alone controls 24 percent of the market (Thornton 2000). Much broiler production has become vertically integrated: birds go from hatch to slaughter under the control of one company, which uses contract labor to raise the birds to market age. For example, Tyson Foods currently produces 98 percent of its broilers under contract, in approximately 20,000 houses on over 6,000 farms, with 45.9 million chicks started per week. The egg-laying industry is less integrated, but similar trends are apparent. In the 1950s the average hen flock contained fewer than a thousand birds; now flocks of tens of thousands to millions of hens are common. Recently the average U.S. flock size for laying hens was reported to be 63,000 birds, and 17 percent of farm sites housed more than 200,000 birds (USDA APHIS 1999). Such units account for a large fraction of the market: by 1998 34 percent of U.S. egg industry was owned by only seven companies (Smith 1998).

Other U.S. industries are following

the model adopted by the poultry industry. In the 1970s approximately one million U.S. farms raised swine (Gillespie 1998), but by 1998 that number had dropped to 114,380 (USDA NASS 1999b). This decline in the number of pig farms is expected to continue, even though the number of pigs being produced in the United States is staying relatively constant (Figure 3). Consequently there has been an increase in unit size; 77.5 percent of the 1998 U.S. hog inventory was raised in units with at least a thousand pigs (Figure 11). Approximately 40 percent of pigs are now grown by contract in the United States, compared with only 3 percent in 1980 (Martinez 1999). In contrast, much beef cow-calf production is still comparatively small-scale. Although beef cattle in the United States tend to be finished to market weight in large feedlots with more than a thousand animals, approximately half of the beef cows are on farms with fewer than a hundred cows (USDA NASS 1999b).

We have concentrated on trends in the United States and other industrialized countries, but developing nations are also seeing rapid changes in animal agriculture. China provides a particularly important example. From the early 1980s to the early 1990s, China's per capita consumption of meat increased by 8.3 percent per year, and animal production in China

began to grow rapidly. Most of China's huge production of pork comes from backyard feeding operations, with 92 percent of farmers raising fewer than five pigs per year (USDA ERS 2000b). However, multinational companies are expanding into developing nations, with animal health companies like the Pharmacia and Upjohn Company building complexes and Tyson Foods investing in giant poultry facilities in China. Developing nations are likely to face difficult adjustments if and as animal agriculture shifts from small-scale labor-based systems to more concentrated, intensive systems that place heavy demands on water and electrical supplies and require reliable transportation and marketing systems. As noted by Hursey (1997), the intensification of animal production in the developing countries will result in "a plethora of interlinked problems and challenges of far-ranging significance" (ii–iii).

Animal Welfare Issues

Some changes in animal agriculture have had positive effects on animal welfare. The use of indoor housing has eliminated some problems related to predation and harsh weather. Confinement sometimes has been used to prevent disease by excluding

common pathogens from flocks or herds. Newer feeding technology, combined with advances in nutritional knowledge, have made it more feasible to meet animals' nutritional needs. Veterinary knowledge and technology allow vaccination, medication, and other disease prevention measures that would not have been possible a half century ago.

However, the various changes in animal agriculture have also created animal welfare problems. Some pertain specifically to the confinement of animals indoors. When large numbers of animals are confined in an enclosed space, inadequate ventilation is common. Harmful levels of respirable dust, heat stress (if the ventilation system cannot generate adequate air flow in hot weather), and irritating or dangerous gases (arising from manure in bedding or stored in pits below the floor) can result. In many confinement units, interruption of the electrical supply can cause complete failure of ventilation systems. Then heat and air-quality problems can rise to deadly levels in a matter of hours.

Agricultural buildings often use concrete as a durable, low-cost flooring material, but concrete surfaces have many possible drawbacks. Slippery concrete can cause accidents; irregular concrete seems to predispose hoofed animals to lameness; and concrete's overall hardness may stress hooves and joints. Under cool conditions unbedded concrete appears to be an uncomfortable lying surface and may disturb normal resting. Metal flooring is sometimes used as an alternative, but many of the same comfort problems remain. Poorly designed flooring in laying hens cages contributes to discomfort and foot and leg problems and can even cause the hens to become trapped.

Space in indoor units tends to be minimal. The recommended space allowance for laying hens in some countries is 60–80 square inches per hen, barely enough for the hen to turn around and not enough for her to perform normal comfort behaviors; how-

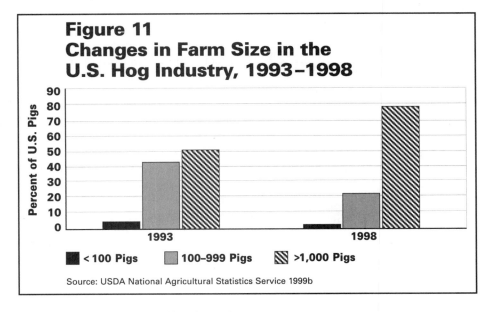

Figure 11
Changes in Farm Size in the U.S. Hog Industry, 1993–1998

■ < 100 Pigs   ▨ 100–999 Pigs   ▨ >1,000 Pigs

Source: USDA National Agricultural Statistics Service 1999b

ever, many hens are allowed less than even that meager amount. Industry codes recommend about 8–10 square feet per market-weight pig—not much more than enough space for all animals in the pen to lie down at the same time. Commercial practice may crowd animals above this level. Amenities such as bedding to improve floor comfort or features of the natural environment such as perches and dust-baths (for hens) or nest-building material (for hens or sows) are usually omitted. Consequently, there is little opportunity for animals to engage in some of their natural behavior, and this may in time affect their health. Restricted space and barren environments may also lead to harmful behavioral abnormalities. Pigs in a restricted, barren space sometimes direct their foraging activities (rooting and chewing) to the bodies of pen-mates to the extent that they damage tails or other body parts, especially if tails have not been docked. Chickens that are not beak-trimmed may peck flockmates to the point of damaging or killing them.

Another set of problems has arisen through genetic selection for production efficiency. Typically, breeders of farm animals have exercised intense genetic selection for a small number of commercially important traits. However, if genetic selection is based on unduly narrow criteria, it can lead to significant animal health and welfare problems. Genetic selection of laying hens for high egg production and low maintenance requirements can create birds that are prone to osteoporosis because bone calcium is mobilized for egg shell formation. Selection for rapid growth in broiler chickens has led to birds that appear to gain weight too quickly relative to their leg strength, resulting in leg abnormalities and lameness. Broiler breeders, which live for much longer than do their offspring killed for meat, show the same very high levels of appetite. These birds have to be kept on restricted diets in order to prevent obesity, and aggression and abnormal behaviors are common

problems, perhaps due to hunger. Among pigs some genetic lines selected strongly for rapid growth and muscle deposition show correlated increases in excitability. Such animals may develop severe, even fatal, physiological stress responses during handling and transportation.

Various other disease conditions can arise from pushing animals' body processes beyond their normal range. Dairy cattle with very high milk yields appear particularly prone to mastitis, lameness, and other health problems. Pigs fed finely ground grains, which help promote efficient feed use, are also predisposed to gastric ulcers. Fast growth in broiler chickens is associated with health problems such as ascites (pulmonary hypertension).

A number of animal management practices also raise animal welfare concerns. Some, such as hot-iron branding, castration without anesthesia, and early removal of dairy calves from their mothers, are traditional but have become controversial because of public concern about causing pain or distress to animals. Others practices, such as the tail docking of pigs and the beak trimming of hens, are controversial because they are seen as stop-gap measures masking basic inadequacies in environment or management. Transportation and management of animals after they leave the farm raise major animal welfare concerns that are covered elsewhere in this volume.

Understanding the Revolution in Animal Agriculture

Why are farm animals kept the way they are? A mix of cultural factors and technology is no doubt involved. Twentieth-century cultural values saw automation and mass production as forms of progress. Perhaps in response to rising standards of living, farmers sought to avoid the arduous

and repetitive manual labor typical of more-traditional animal production systems. Retaining a reliable farm labor force became difficult as more lucrative employment opportunities arose in more mechanized sectors of the economy. The availability of antibiotics and other measures allowed large numbers of animals to be kept close together without major disease outbreaks. Moreover, for several decades agricultural research and development focused on greater productivity, efficiency, and return on investment, while paying little explicit attention to their impact on the environment, worker health, rural communities, or animal welfare.

While all these factors have likely contributed, changes in marketing and economic pressures played—and continue to play—a dominant role in reshaping animal agriculture. In earlier centuries food products made from animals, being highly perishable, tended to be produced and consumed locally. The twentieth century saw the advent of effective refrigeration, fast freezing, and other innovations in product preservation, combined with explosive growth in publicly subsidized road transportation. Meat, milk, and eggs now could be sold into ever larger markets—regional, national, even international. Producers were in effect competing against thousands of other producers, often in various regions of the world.

The resulting price competition and associated need to reduce production costs have had at least three effects. First, price competition has clearly contributed to the increase in farm size. Larger farms often enjoy economies of scale such as greater bargaining power in purchasing feed, and they can generally sell animal products at lower prices. Once larger units began to appear, other producers had to expand their operations in order to compete, even though expansion often involved greater debt and workload. In extreme cases, such as broiler production in the United States, the size of unit typically operated by a farm family ceased to be economically viable at all. Second, production systems that avoided major costs or losses have replaced systems that failed to do so. Many sectors have changed almost universally to confinement systems where labor requirements are reduced and certain common causes of death or illness are avoided. Third, it has become difficult for producers to provide animals with certain traditional amenities. If profit per animal is sufficiently large, producers are free to provide space, veterinary care, bedding, and other amenities beyond what is strictly in the interests of profit; with very low profit margins, the time and resources that can be devoted to each animal are severely constrained.

In fact, many of the animal welfare problems commonly attributed to confinement technology may actually be problems of extreme price competition in a large market. By itself, the practice of penning sows individually during pregnancy may be a defensible way of promoting health and preventing aggression; but restricting the space allowance to a narrow, unbedded stall is a matter of economics. By itself, the use of caging to keep hens in small stable groups, separated from their excreta, may be a defensible means of improving hygiene and preventing social stress; however crowding many hens into a small, barren cage is a decision based on economics. Because confinement methods became the dominant technology during a time of increasing market competition, these methods often minimize the space and amenities provided per animal, but these negative aspects are more a reflection of market-driven economic constraints than of confinement methods themselves. This may help explain why the debate over confinement agriculture tends to run at cross-purposes. Producers defend confinement by citing the health and other benefits it was designed to deliver, while critics attack confinement by citing disadvantages to the animal caused partly by cost cutting.

Measures to Protect Farm Animals

Production Methods and Genetic Selection

One approach producers have used to address public concerns over farm animal welfare has involved returning to more traditional production methods. For example, "free-range" egg systems give laying hens access to outdoor runs as well as to indoor shelters with perches and nest-boxes; pasture systems for dairy cattle allow animals to graze at pasture during the summer months and walk to a parlor for milking twice a day; outdoor farrowing systems house sows in a field with individual huts that provide a protected area for them to give birth and raise their litters. A common public perception is that these older systems of animal production necessarily result in improved standards of animal welfare and food quality. In reality, some of these systems generate significant welfare problems of their own. For example, in the United States, where sheep are typically raised on pasture or range, predation and weather-related losses together account for about 85 percent of lamb deaths (USDA APHIS 1995c). Moreover, some traditional systems languished without research or development during a half century in which they went largely unused. If these systems come back into use, they will need to be developed and evaluated, and appropriate standards will need to be set in order to ensure that the systems meet the needs of the animals and consumers' expectations.

A second approach is to retain the advantages of confinement systems but mitigate the negative effects, partly by restoring a more traditional level of space and amenities. Some indoor farrowing pens allow a degree of freedom and comfort for the sow while providing a warm, draft-free,

and protected environment for the newborn piglets. Enriched cages for laying hens keep the birds in small, stable groups (thus avoiding the social stress of large flocks) while providing amenities such as litter, a perch, and a nest-box. The European Community has announced that it intends to require all new cages for laying hens to be enriched in these ways by the year 2013.

A third alternative, still in its infancy, is to use electronics rather than physical restraint to solve certain animal management problems. For example, gestation crates for pregnant sows arose as a low-cost means of feeding sows individually to prevent bullying and over-eating by dominant animals; now, however, with computerized equipment, group-housed sows can enter an individual feeding station where they are recognized electronically and receive an assigned amount of food which they can eat without harassment. Similarly, new robotic milking systems allow cows to be kept in open pens and enter the milking station at will to be milked.

Virtually all of these approaches require research, testing, and development if they are to meet the health and welfare needs of the animals and the producer's needs for convenient, safe, and reliable production methods. Unfortunately, neither industry nor government invests significantly in such research in North America, and even in Europe the amount of research is inadequate to keep pace with the public's desire to reform animal production methods. Thus, for example, when Sweden announced its intention to ban battery cages for hens, there was substantial concern that available alternative systems were not well enough studied and developed to ensure that the ban would necessarily improve the welfare of the birds.

Partly because narrow genetic selection has contributed to many animal welfare problems, more-appropriate animal breeding can partially improve animal welfare. Broiler chickens can be selected for both skeletal soundness and production traits; this can decrease leg problems with only a small negative effect on growth rate. Appropriate genetic selection can produce pigs that grow efficiently without deleterious reactions to stress and hens that are less predisposed to cannibalistic behavior in confinement. Use of "polled" (genetically hornless) cattle can obviate the need for dehorning. For these changes to occur, animal breeders, large breeding companies in particular, will need to be convinced to include animal welfare considerations in their criteria for genetic selection.

Economic Incentives and Policies

Many alternatives to standard confinement methods involve higher production costs, which must be offset through economic incentives to producers. Additional costs can be substantial if an alternative system involves more labor, less efficient use of feed, or greater losses through disease and death. If these problems are avoided, however, the cost of enhanced housing can be relatively small. Generally, housing is a small fraction of the total cost of animal production—compared with feed, labor, and utilities—so just a small increase in the retail price, if passed on to the producer, could support substantial housing improvements.

One way to compensate producers for using alternative systems is through labeling that identifies products produced according to specified standards or methods. The European Community has established standard definitions for alternative production methods, such as free-range eggs, which normally sell at a premium price. A more comprehensive scheme is the Freedom Foods program in the United Kingdom, originated by the Royal Society for the Prevention of Cruelty to Animals. The program requires certain standards and methods of animal production and inspects subscribing farms for compliance. The products are then eligible to carry the Freedom Foods label, which generally commands a premium price for the producer. Austria has taken a slightly different approach. There a producer-initiated program uses a numerical scoring system to assess standards of hygiene, disease prevention, animal handling skill, and appropriate housing. Producers achieving a certain overall score can use a distinctive label to identify the product. The program is credited with retaining consumer loyalty for small-scale Austrian producers in the face of lower-priced imports from countries where animal production is more intensive. As these programs grow, there may be a need for international standards and definitions in order to avoid confusion.

Some economic policies appear to mitigate farm animal welfare problems. In some countries, subsidization or price controls have kept the profit per animal at a reasonably traditional level, with the result that producers can afford to raise animals in flocks and herds of traditional size and to provide traditional levels of space, amenities, and care. In Norway, for example, price subsidies and the decision to reject free trade with other European countries have allowed small farms with high levels of care and reasonably spacious animal accommodation to remain economically viable.

The supply management system for egg production in Canada provides another example. Under free-market conditions, when egg prices are high, the greatest profit can generally be achieved by crowding extra birds into a cage system to the point of reducing their individual health and rate of lay, yet still increasing the total number of eggs produced. However, the Canadian supply management system limits the number of birds that a producer can house but does not limit the number of eggs that can be sold. The system tends to favor space allowances that maximize the productivity per bird, thus largely eliminating the incentive for extreme crowding, and the price stability created by the system has allowed smaller farms to remain viable (Figure 12).

Economic incentives can also func-tion on a smaller scale. For many years, pig producers in Alberta, Canada, have operated a system for insuring producers against the death of pigs during trucking. The premiums escalate markedly for producers who have a history of substantial claims; this incentive is credited with improving the standards of trucking and greatly reducing losses due to deaths during transportation. Incentives to improve animal welfare can also be given to workers. In several countries catching crews that load and transport chickens are given bonuses if the birds arrive at the processing facility in good condition, with few bruises or injuries, or alternatively are penalized if bruising, injury, and death exceed certain levels.

Legal Measures

At the beginning of the twenty-first century, legal protection of farm animals is in flux. Historically most animal protection laws were intended to prevent animal suffering caused by unusual and socially unacceptable behavior such as deliberate cruelty or gross neglect. Typically these provisions do not apply to suffering caused by common agricultural practices. Many Canadian provinces and U.S. states, for example, forbid the infliction of unnecessary suffering on animals but exempt "generally accepted" or "normal" farm animal management practices from this prohibition. The United Kingdom requires that captive birds in cages have enough space to stretch their wings freely, but commercial poultry are specifically exempted from this requirement.

In the late 1900s, however, a number of European countries introduced legal measures to restrict the use of controversial agricultural practices. In some cases, practices were specifically banned or regulated. Several countries now prohibit the use of battery cages for laying hens; Sweden requires that dairy cows be given access to pasture in the summer; and the United Kingdom does not allow veal calves to be kept in narrow crates. In

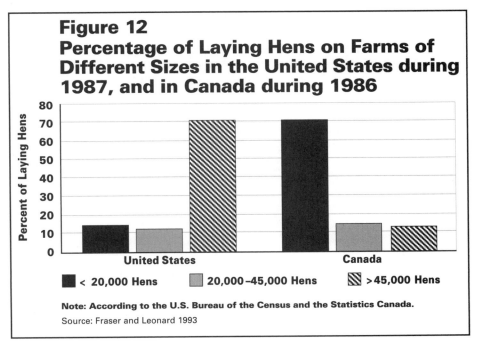

Figure 12
Percentage of Laying Hens on Farms of Different Sizes in the United States during 1987, and in Canada during 1986

Legend:
- ■ < 20,000 Hens
- ▨ (grey) 20,000–45,000 Hens
- ▨ (hatched) >45,000 Hens

Note: According to the U.S. Bureau of the Census and the Statistics Canada.

Source: Fraser and Leonard 1993

other cases, new animal housing systems must be approved for conformity to animal welfare standards before they can be marketed or used; Sweden, Norway, and Switzerland have such provisions. In yet other cases, codes of practice have been created that have some recognition under the law. In the United Kingdom, it is an offense to cause unnecessary pain or distress to farm animals in one's care; failure to follow established codes of practice, while not itself an offense, can be used as evidence against a defendant accused of causing unnecessary pain or distress. In other countries, such as the United States and Canada, industry codes of practice have been written, but compliance is strictly voluntary.

The United States, Canada, and many other countries outside Europe have regulations designed to protect the welfare of animals during transportation and pre-slaughter management, but not while they are being raised on farms. However, surveys in the United States suggest that public support for regulation is growing. For example, 67 percent of consumers polled said they would vote for additional government regulation of production practices (Animal Industry Foundation 1989). Seventy-one percent of U.S. citizens polled said they

would vote "yes" on a measure legally requiring that farm animals be provided with living spaces large enough for animals to turn around and stretch their limbs (Decision Research 1997). In 1998 Coloradons voted 2 to 1 in favor of a statutory amendment to increase regulation of large-scale hog confinement facilities. Thus, the trend toward regulating farming practices may well spread to North America and elsewhere.

Where trade agreements require countries to accept each others' agricultural products, one country's producers can be penalized if they must follow restrictions that do not apply elsewhere. Swiss egg producers are not allowed to use battery cages, but eggs from caged hens are imported into Switzerland from countries where cages are allowed. Similarly since the ban on veal calf crates took effect in the United Kingdom, many calves from British farms have been shipped to continental Europe to be raised in crates. Nothing prevents their meat from then being sold in the United Kingdom. The need for international harmonization is clear, but international trade authorities have so far shown little inclination to provide the necessary leadership.

In fact, great uncertainty surrounds the future effects of international

trade agreements on farm animal welfare. When the European Community created directives on farm animal welfare standards, it was its stated intention to exclude imports from countries that do not require equivalent standards. If this intention can be realized, then international trade might provide an incentive for raising and harmonizing standards. On the other hand, some critics fear that trade panels will disallow trade restrictions based on animal welfare considerations. In that case increased international trade will likely expand further the size of the competitive market, making price competition even more severe and imposing further constraints on the level of animal care that producers can afford to provide.

The Debate about Animal Agriculture

No contemporary account of farm animal production would be complete without mention of the acrimonious clash of views to which it has given rise. On one side are highly negative portrayals of animal agriculture, often originating from vegetarian or animal rights sources, including familiar works such as Peter Singer's *Animal Liberation* and John Robbins's *Diet for a New America*. These materials generally make six interrelated claims about animal agriculture: (1) farm animals live miserable lives, partly because of confinement production methods; (2) greed for profit has replaced traditional animal husbandry ethics in determining how animals are treated; (3) animal agriculture is now controlled by large corporations, not by individuals or farm families; (4) animal agriculture damages the environment through pollution, use of natural resources, and destruction of natural habitats; (5) animal production causes increased world hunger by consuming grain and other resources that could better be used to feed hungry people; and (6) animal products are unhealthy for human consumers.

On the other side of the conflict are highly positive portrayals of animal agriculture, largely originating from animal producers and their organizations. These paint an entirely different picture of modern farming: (1) it is beneficial to animal welfare, partly because of the advantages of indoor environments; (2) it respects traditional animal husbandry values; (3) it is largely owned and operated by traditional farm families; (4) it benefits the environment by recycling nutrients back to the land; (5) it helps to reduce world hunger by creating food from materials not used in human nutrition; and (6) it produces safe, nutritious food.

With an activity as diverse as animal agriculture, proponents of each of these highly simplified views can cite facts and examples to support their claims, yet neither one provides an adequate or accurate description of animal agriculture. Even within a single region, animal production methods can vary from intensive systems such as layer barns to traditional ones such as cow-calf ranching. Corporate control is well established in certain sectors and regions, while families and individuals remain the dominant owners in others. Environmental impacts can be generally positive if animal numbers are commensurate with the land base and if manure is well managed; but environmental impacts can be negative if animal production is highly concentrated and environmental controls are lax.

The debate over animal agriculture, despite the polemical and often misleading way it has been represented to the public, has raised issues of immense importance. The revolution in animal agriculture during the twentieth century had, and continues to have, profound effects on farm animals, on human nutrition, on rural communities, and indeed on the global ecosystem; moreover, the changes have taken place with remarkably little informed public debate or comprehensive policy development. There is an urgent need for careful analysis to understand the effects of the revolution in animal agriculture, to identify better and worse options, and to allow informed consensus building to guide future developments.

Literature Cited

Animal Industry Foundation. 1989. Survey results on how Americans view modern livestock farming. Animal Industry Foundation, CR 2765, April.

Council for Agricultural Science and Technology (CAST). 1999. *Animal agriculture and the global food supply*. Report No. 135. Ames, Iowa: CAST.

Decision Research. 1997. Oregon statewide poll #4971. Washington, D.C.: Decision Research.

Fraser, D., and M.L. Leonard. 1993. Farm animal welfare. In *Animal production in Canada*, eds. J. Martin, R.J. Hudson, and B.A. Young. Edmonton, Canada: University of Alberta Faculty of Extention.

Gillespie, J.R. 1998. *Animal science*. Albany, N.Y.: Delmar Publishers.

Gyles, N.R. 1989. Poultry, people, and progress. *Poultry Science* 68: 1–8.

Hursey, B.S. 1997. Towards the twenty-first century—The challenges facing livestock production. *World Animal Review* 89: ii–iii.

Martinez, S.W. 1999. *Vertical coordination in the pork and broiler industries: Implications for pork and chicken products*. Agricultural Economic Report No. 777. Washington, D.C.: Economic Research Service, U.S. Department of Agriculture.

National Research Council (NRC). 1999. *The use of drugs in food animals. Benefits and risks*. Washington, D.C.: National Academic Press.

North, M.O., and D.D. Bell. 1990. *Commercial chicken production manual*. Fourth edition. New York: Chapman and Hall.

Putnam, P.A. 1991. Demographics of dairy cows and products. In *Handbook of animal science*, ed. P.A. Putnam. New York: Academic Press.

Robbins, J. 1987. *Diet for a new America*. Walpole: Stillpoint Publishing.

Sere, C., and H. Steinfeld. 1996. *World livestock production systems*. Animal Production and Health Paper 127. Rome: Food and Agriculture Organization of the United Nations.

Singer, P. 1990. *Animal liberation*. Revised edition. New York: Avon Books.

Smith, R. 1998. Egg industry warned flock may be getting too large. *Feedstuffs*, November 9.

Thornton, G. 2000. Broiler company rankings. WATT *PoultryUSA* 1(1): 30–40.

UN Food and Agricultural Organization (FAO). 1994. State of food and agriculture, 1994. Electronic product, November 1994.

————————. 2000. Statistical database. *faostat.fao.org/default.htm*. Accessed May and June 2000.

USDA Animal and Plant Health Inspection Service (APHIS). 1995a. *Feedlot management practices*. Washington, D.C.: USDA.

————————. 1995b. *Swine '95: Reference of 1995 swine management practices*. Washington, D.C.: USDA.

————————. 1995c. *Sheep and lamb death loss 1995*. Washington, D.C.: USDA.

————————. 1996. *Dairy '96: Reference of 1996 dairy management practices*. Washington, D.C.: USDA.

————————. 1999. *Layers '99: Reference of 1999 table egg layer management in the United States*. Washington, D.C.: USDA.

USDA Economic Research Service (ERS). 2000a. *U.S. agriculture and food economy at a glance*. *www.econ.ag.gov/Briefing/agfood*. Washington, D.C.: USDA. Accessed June 2000.

————————. 2000b. China: Situation and outlook series. International Agriculture and Trade Reports, WRS-99-4, March 2000. Washington, D.C.: USDA.

USDA National Agricultural Statistics Service (NASS). 1999a. *Agricultural statistics 1999*. Washington, D.C.: USDA.

————————. 1999b. *U.S. livestock summary, statistical highlights 1998/99*. Washington, D.C.: USDA.

———— 1999c. *1998 hatchery production summary*. Washington, D.C.: USDA.

———— 2000. *Agricultural statistics 2000*. Washington, D.C.: USDA.

Further Reading

Appleby, M.C., and B.O. Hughes, eds. *Animal welfare*. Wallingford: CAB International.

Fox, M.W. 1984. *Farm animals: Husbandry, behavior and veterinary practice*. Baltimore: University Park Press.

Fraser, A.F., and D.M. Broom. 1990. *Farm animal behaviour and welfare*. Third edition. London: Baillière Tindall.

Grandin, T., ed. 2000. *Livestock handling and transport*. Second edition. Wallingford: CABI Publishing.

Hodges, J., and I.K. Han, eds. 2000. *Livestock, ethics and quality of life*. Wallingford: CABI Publishing.

Johnson, A. 1991. *Factory farming*. Oxford: Blackwell.

Moss, R., ed. 1994. Animal welfare and veterinary sciences. *Revue scientifique et technique, Office international des épizooties* 13: 1–302 (special issue).

Rollin, B.E. 1995. *Farm animal welfare: Social, bioethical, and research issues*. Ames: Iowa State University Press.

Sainsbury, D. 1986. *Farm animal welfare: Cattle, pigs and poultry*. London: Collins.

Sørensen, J.T., ed. 1997. *Livestock farming systems: More than food production*. Proceedings of the Fourth International Symposium on Livestock Farming Systems. European Association for Animal Production Publication No. 89. Wageningen: Wageningen Pers.

Thompson, P.B. 1998. *Agricultural ethics: Research, teaching, and public policy*. Ames: Iowa State University Press.

Van Zutphen, L.F.M., and P.G.C. Bedford, eds. 1999. Genetics and animal welfare. *Animal Welfare* 8: 307–438 (special issue).

Webster, J. 1994. *Animal welfare: A cool eye towards Eden*. Oxford: Blackwell Science.

Progress in Livestock Handling and Slaughter Techniques in the United States, 1970–2000

6

CHAPTER

Temple Grandin

I have worked as a consultant to the meat industry since the early 1970s. I've been in more than 300 slaughter plants in the United States, Canada, Mexico, Europe, Australia, New Zealand, and South America. During the course of my career, I've seen many changes take place, but I'm going to focus in this paper on my work to improve conditions for the slaughter of cattle and calves and later address transport and other animal-handling issues.

The U.S. Humane Slaughter Act, passed in 1958, required that all meat sold to the federal government had to come from animals that had been humanely slaughtered. Use of the pole axe to render animals unconscious and the bleeding of fully conscious pigs were replaced by use of the captive bolt stunning pistol in cattle and administration of either carbon dioxide (CO_2) or electrical stunning for pigs. This change was a major step forward, since scientific studies show that both electrical stunning and captive bolt stunning will instantly render animals insensible to pain (see reviews by Grandin 1994, 1985/86; Eikelenboom 1983; UFAW 1987; Gregory 1998).

Unfortunately, however, CO_2-induced stunning is not instantaneous, and there has been controversy within the scientific community over whether animals have an adverse reaction to CO_2 gas. Some studies show evidence of aversion; others do not (Forslid 1987; Grandin 1988a; Dodman 1977; Raj et al. 1997). My own observations lead me to believe that some pigs can be anesthetized peacefully with CO_2 while others frantically attempt to escape when they first smell the gas (Grandin 1988a). Genetic factors appear to influence the reaction. Purebred Yorkshire pigs are anesthetized peacefully (Forslid 1987), for example, while other strains become agitated prior to being anesthetized (Grandin 1988a; Dodman 1977). Jongman et al. (2000) found that for Landrace–Large White crossbreeds breathing either 60 percent or 90 percent CO_2 was less aversive than a shock from an electric prod. CO_2, it may be noted, causes highly variable reactions in people. It causes anxiety in some and has little effect on others (Perna et al. 1994; Biber et al. 1999; Perna et al. 1996). It is my opinion that CO_2 is suitable for some genetic types of pigs but causes problems with other genetic types. CO_2 experiments should be conducted with stress-susceptible pigs, in particular. The potential of other gases, such as argon, for use in stunning is also worthy of investigation.

In 1978 the Humane Slaughter Act was amended to cover all federally inspected plants. (Federal inspection allows a plant to engage in interstate commerce, regardless of who the buyer is.) The act was also extended to cover the handling of animals prior to slaughter while they were on the premises of the slaughter plant. Cruel practices such as dragging conscious, crippled, non-ambulatory (downed) animals were prohibited. However, the handling of animals for ritual slaughter was—and is—exempt, as is the slaughter of poultry. In ritual slaughter, both kosher (Jewish) and halal (Muslim), the throat of an unstunned animal is cut.

My First Project

My career started at the Swift Fresh Meats plant in Tolleson, Arizona, in 1973. The plant manager allowed me to visit every week so I could learn the industry. Nobody knew who I was and no attempt was made by the plant employees to be on "good behavior" while I was there.

The equipment available was of poor quality, but at a line speed of 165 cattle per hour, most animals were stunned correctly with one shot from a captive bolt pistol. Swift had a stunning box that consisted of a long, narrow stall in which three cattle at a time were loaded. If the animals became agitated while in the box, they jumped on top of each other. Another problem was that slaughter plants were heavily unionized, and union work rules made it very difficult to discipline any employees who deliberately abused the cattle.

In 1974 I worked on my first equipment project, replacing the stunning box at the Swift plant with a new device, a V conveyor restrainer. This system, a larger version of a system already in use for the slaughter of pigs (Regensberger 1940), had been constructed in the early 1970s by Oscar Schmidt of Cincinnati Butcher's Supply Company and Don Willems of Armour Company. The animals rode along supported by two conveyors. Compared to the old multiple-animal stunning box, it was a great improvement. The V conveyor system was safer for plant employees and much less stressful for the cattle. The one the plant engineer at Swift and I installed was the third V conveyor restrainer system in the United States. By 1980 the V conveyor restrainer had replaced many of the dreadful old stunning boxes that had held several panicked cattle at a time. (Today, stunning boxes are used mainly in small plants; those that hold only one animal work very well in such circumstances, provided they have non-slip floors.)

Kosher Slaughter in the 1970s

Late in the 1970s, I had the opportunity to observe kosher slaughter at Spencer Foods, the world's largest kosher slaughter plant. Cattle weighing 1,200 pounds each were hoisted off the floor by one back leg, and a nose tong attached to a powerful air cylinder was used to stretch their neck so that the schochet, a rabbi who performs kosher slaughtering, could make the throat cut. I was horrified at the sight and sounds of bellowing, thrashing beasts. Workers wore football helmets to protect their heads from the animals' flailing front hooves. I could even hear the cattle bellowing from the plant's office and parking lot. I vowed I would design a system to restrain the cattle in a more comfortable upright position. Many of the smaller kosher slaughter plants that slaughtered large cattle used a holding box called the ASPCA pen (Marshall 1963) (Figure 1). The American Society for the Prevention of Cruelty to Animals (ASPCA) had bought the patents on the box in the 1960s so that any plant could use the box royalty free. Spencer Foods slaughtered 150 cattle per hour, and it would have had to buy two ASPCA pens—and construct a building addition—to accommodate this volume of traffic. Since pre-slaughter handling for kosher slaughter was exempt from the Humane Slaughter Act, shackling and hoisting fully conscious cattle was an economical alternative.

I proposed to plant management the idea of building a head-holding device on the V conveyor restrainer. (It is completely described in Grandin 1980a.) I worked with Spencer to help design the system, which involved no structural alterations to the building already in use. For the large kosher plant, it was a great improvement over shackling and hoisting.

The next big improvement in equipment was the development of upright restraint devices for kosher-

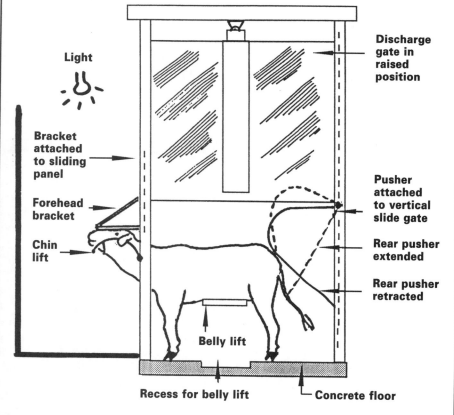

Figure 1
Side View of the ASPCA Pen for Holding Cattle in an Upright Position during Ritual Slaughter

Light

Bracket attached to sliding panel

Forehead bracket

Chin lift

Belly lift

Recess for belly lift

Discharge gate in raised position

Pusher attached to vertical slide gate

Rear pusher extended

Rear pusher retracted

Concrete floor

To reduce stress on the animal, the belly lift should not lift the animal off the floor. All parts of the apparatus that press against the animal should be equipped with pressure-limiting devices and move with a slow, steady, smooth motion.

slaughtered calves and sheep. The Council for Livestock Protection (CLP)—a consortium of The Humane Society of the United States, American Humane Association, The Fund for Animals, Massachusetts Society for the Prevention of Cruelty to Animals, and others—funded research at the University of Connecticut to develop a system for holding calves and sheep in an upright position for kosher slaughter. At that time the only piece of equipment available for holding an animal in an upright position was the ASPCA pen for adult cattle. A restraint device was needed to replace the shackling and hoisting of calves and sheep. A laboratory prototype was completed during the early 1970s (Giger et al. 1977; Westervelt et al. 1976). Stress research conducted at the University of Connecticut demonstrated that having an animal straddle a moving conveyor was a low-stress method of restraint. The laboratory prototype was a major innovation, but many more components had to be developed to make a commercially viable system. Since no slaughter plant was interested in implementing the design, the prototype was put in an old sheep barn.

The 1980s and the Kosher Calf Project

During the early 1980s, plant line speeds increased and the labor unions were no longer so powerful. The old Swift and Armour plants, which had employed union labor, were closed. They could no longer compete with new companies that paid lower wages and had fewer restrictive work rules. The emphasis was now on speed, speed, and more speed. In some large plants, stunning practices actually worsened compared to conditions in the 1970s. Crews were reduced in size, and cattle were being handled at a rate of 250 per hour. It was a bad time for both the animals and the meat industry.

During that decade I completed two

major projects. The first was the design for a curved chute and V conveyor system for Moyer Packing. The second one was the completion of the project that the University of Connecticut had started ten years earlier. Curved chute systems were an important innovation for handling cattle because cattle move more easily around a curve (Figure 2). (These systems are described in Grandin 1980b,c, 1987, 1998c, 2000a.) Curved chutes with solid sides, in particular, facilitate cattle movement because they take advantage of cattle's natural tendency to want to return to where they came from. The chute's solid sides and curves prevent cattle from seeing moving people and equipment ahead of them in the slaughter facility so the animals are less likely to react to the sight by attempting to go backward.

In 1986 the CLP asked me to design and install the University of Connecticut system in a veal calf plant, Utica Veal. We rescued the plywood prototype, which was practically on its way to the landfill, and added several other components to make it work commercially (Grandin 1988b). One was a new entrance design that

positioned the calves' legs on each side of the moving conveyor. For the first time, equipment was available to replace shackling and hoisting of kosher calves and sheep. The new system was later installed in two other veal plants.

The 1990s and Behavioral Principles

By the end of 1999, half of all the cattle in the United States and Canada were being handled in systems I had designed for slaughter plants. I had received a grant to make a large-cattle version of the conveyor system at Utica Veal (Grandin 1991, 2000a) (Figure 3). Cattle entered it more easily and rode more quietly than they had in the V conveyor restrainer. One challenge was that adult cattle are wilder and more difficult to handle than are tame veal calves. The first time the restrainer was run at the Excel plant in Schyler, Nebraska, the cattle refused to enter and they did not ride quietly as had the tame calves at Utica Veal. Two very simple changes solved the problem, and

Figure 2.

Cattle stay calmer because they cannot see the handler on the ramp when they first enter the chute. A curved chute also takes advantage of the natural tendency of cattle to want to head back to where they came from.

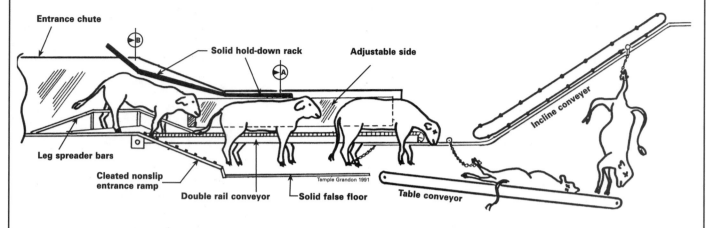

Figure 3
Center Track (Double Rail) Conveyor
Restrainer for Handling Cattle

Entrance chute

B

Solid hold-down rack

Adjustable side

A

Incline conveyer

Leg spreader bars

Cleated nonslip
entrance ramp

Temple Grandon 1991

Double rail conveyor

Solid false floor

Table conveyor

The cattle ride along on the moving conveyor. Design details are very important. Cattle remain calmer if the solid hold-down rack is long enough to block the animals' vision until they are completely off the entrance ramp. The solid false floor prevents cattle from seeing a steep drop-off under the conveyor. In a well-designed system that has proper lighting, 95 percent of the cattle will enter without the use of an electric prod.

their success showed the power of using behavior modification, instead of force, to handle cattle. Both changes calmed the cattle by controlling what they could see.

First, I installed a false floor made of the conveyor belting. Since the restrainer conveyor was seven feet off the floor, the entering cattle had been greeted by a "visual cliff" effect. Ruminants such as cattle and sheep can perceive depth (Lemman and Patterson 1964). The belting under the conveyor provided the animals with the illusion of a solid floor to walk on (Grandin 1991, 2000a).

The second change was even easier. A piece of cardboard positioned six inches above the animals' backs blocked the animals' vision straight ahead. The cardboard was replaced with metal, and the system worked perfectly. Twenty-five of these center-track restrainer systems are now in use around the world.

Although the center-track conveyor restrainer was rapidly adopted by the industry, one of my biggest frustrations has been getting people to fully understand the power of using behavioral principles to handle animals. Equipment companies have often tried to "improve" the restrainer by

removing parts they perceive as unnecessary. They have not been able to understand why a piece of metal that blocked the animal's vision was so important.

At one plant I visited recently, cattle were balking, refusing to enter the restrainer or not riding quietly. The equipment company had left out the false floor and had shortened the piece of metal that blocked the animals' vision. It had also added a hydraulic cylinder to forcibly push rearing cattle down, thinking that this was an improvement! I had the maintenance shop build a false floor and add more metal sheeting to block the cattle's vision. After these parts were installed, the cattle rode calmly. A two-foot difference in a piece of metal was the difference between calm and agitated cattle.

Kosher Slaughter in the 1990s

Between 1993 and 1995, several large shackle-hoist systems were ripped out and replaced with either ASPCA pens or a center-track restrainer system.

I designed a new head-holding device for the center-track restrainer (Figure 4). The new design was a great improvement over the system at Spencer Foods. The new head holder was very similar to the one on an ASPCA pen. It was mounted on two sliding doors, and the two halves of the chin lift slid apart sideways (Grandin 2000a).

Employee safety was a major reason corporations sought to eliminate shackling and hoisting of fully conscious cattle. Another was Henry Spira, a well-known animal activist, who wrote letters pointing out the method's shortcomings to several corporations still using it. Today 90 percent of the kosher-slaughtered cattle in the United States are held in an upright restraint system. (Unfortunately, about half the kosher veal calves and most of the kosher sheep in the United States are still shackled and hoisted prior to the throat cut.) In Europe, Canada, and Australia, upright restraint is now required for all animals. However, countries such as Uruguay and Guatemala still use shackling and hoisting techniques. Both export meat to Israel and the United States.

From an animal welfare perspec-

Figure 4
Head-holding Device Mounted on the End of the Conveyor Restrainer for Kosher Slaughter

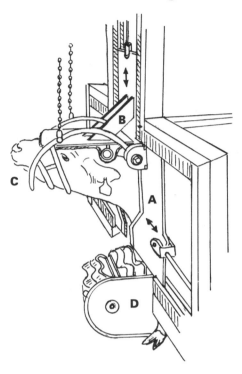

(A) Bi-parting sliding doors with the two halves of the chin lift mounted on them.
(B) Forehead bracket slides up and down. A three-inch-diameter pipe fits behind the animal's poll. (C) A chin-lift yoke raises the head. The chin lift pivots on the sliding doors. (D) The conveyor on which the animal is riding is stopped.

tive, the variables of kosher slaughter—the throat cut and the method of restraint—must be evaluated separately. When conscious animals are shackled and hoisted, it is impossible to observe the reaction to the throat cut itself because the suspended animal is fighting the highly stressful restraint. Once I had built a restraint device that would hold the animal gently, it became possible to observe the reactions to the throat cut, or *shechita*. When the cut is made correctly, the animal appears not to feel it (Grandin 1994, 1992; Grandin and Regenstein 1994). When the head holder was loose enough for the animal to move it, the animal did not move at all when the cut was performed correctly.

From my work with kosher restraint devices, I developed four behavior-based principles of restraint. They are: 1) *the animal's vision should be blocked* so that the animal does not see people and other moving objects; the view of a pathway for escape should also be blocked until the animal is fully restrained; 2) *optimal pressure of holding machinery should not be too tight or too loose*, otherwise the animal will struggle; 3) *equipment should operate with a slow, steady movement*; sudden jerky motion scares the animal; and 4) *the fear-of-falling righting reflex should not be triggered*; the restrainer must either fully support an animal or have non-slip footing (Grandin 2000a, 1994).

How Stressful is Slaughter?

Literature shows equivalent levels of cortisol, a stress hormone, in animals handled at slaughter plants and in animals restrained for vaccinations on the farm. Walking through the chutes at a slaughter plant does cause some stress, but it is similar to that of on-farm restraint and handling (Grandin 1997a reviewed Lay et al. 1992; Crookshank et al. 1979; Ray et al. 1972; Zavy et al. 1992; Mitchell et al. 1988; Ewbank et al. 1992; Dunn 1990; Cockram and Corley 1991; Tume and Shaw 1992.) The cortisol range for both on-farm handling and cattle slaughter was 24 to 63 ng/mL. The one exception was a kosher plant that inverted cattle on their backs for 103 seconds; those animals had 93 ng/mL (Dunn 1990).

Current Cattle Industry Problems

At the beginning of my career, I thought I could fix all plant problems with better engineering. I do not believe this today! By the 1990s the meat industry had cattle handling equipment that was vastly superior to the equipment in the old Swift plant, but good equipment and engineering are only one-third of the equation. Good management and well-trained employees make up the other two-thirds. Good equipment provides the tools that make good handling easier, but it is useless without good management. In a few poorly managed plants, some of the worst acts of cruelty I have witnessed happened with equipment I designed. In these cases, employees were completely unsupervised. For most of my career, I worked with the meat industry primarily as a designer and supervisor of equipment installation, so I was able to witness "normal" employee behavior.

In the mid-1990s, cattle stunning was a definite problem. In 1996 only

30 percent of the plants stunned 95 percent of their cattle correctly—with one shot (Grandin 1997a,b). Cattle were re-stunned prior to bleeding. (Pig stunning was much better, with 90 percent of the plants stunning pigs correctly. Eisnitz [1997] did describe horrific conditions in two terrible plants, where pigs were scalded alive and cattle were skinned alive. I have observed many abuses, such as broken stun guns, the dragging of downed, crippled animals, and deliberately driving animals over the top of a downed animal; but in the vast majority of plants, I have never observed live pigs going into the scalder or live cattle being dismembered. When a live pig is scalded, the USDA will usually condemn the carcass as unfit because water has been aspirated into the lungs. This provides an economic incentive to stun and bleed pigs properly.)

People often mistakenly equate reflexive kicking with animal consciousness. Grandin (1994) and Gregory (1998) explain how to assess insensibility. The beef plant described by Eisnitz (1997) was a small plant where the same employee who bled the animal also skinned the head. Doing something terrible like skinning a live head is more likely to occur in a small plant where the same person performs both bleeding and the initial stages of skinning. In a large plant, stunned and bled cattle carcasses suspended by one rear leg are moved along a power chain. The first part of the animal skinned after bleeding is the free rear leg. Skinning a "live" leg is very dangerous because it will kick the worker in the face. The employees who do "legging," therefore, put a lot of pressure on the stunner operator and bleeder to make sure cattle are dead before they reach the legging stand. (It should be noted, however, that supervisors also put pressure on stunner operators to keep the line moving rapidly, so operators may not always be so careful about making sure that the animals are stunned properly.)

Employee Psychology

I have observed hundreds of people working in slaughter plants. They fall into three basic psychology types: 1) box stapler 2) sacred ritual 3) sadist (Grandin 1988c). The vast majority of the employees who stun cattle become "box staplers." They do their job as if they were stapling boxes on an assembly line. They will seldom engage in deliberate cruelty. Rabbis who perform kosher slaughter view it as a religious ritual and they concentrate on their work within that context. Unfortunately, there are a few people who become sadists, and management should remove them from contact with animals.

The well-managed plant has a manager or quality-control person who acts as a "conscience" to control behavior. In a poorly managed plant, employees may become rough unless someone in authority controls their behavior. It is important not to overwork employees who handle or stun animals. Bad behavior is more likely to occur if the employee is overwhelmed or if equipment is in need of repair. For good conditions, animal-handling and -stunning jobs must not be understaffed.

I have observed that many plants will have good management and good handling in the stockyards, but supervision in the stunning area will be poor. This trend was very evident in my USDA survey (Grandin 1997a,b). People who are too close to killing all the time become callous. The person who supervises employee behavior in the stunning area must be involved enough in the day-to-day operations to care about the process, but not so involved that he/she becomes callous and indifferent to suffering. (In my USDA survey, the two worst-behaved employees were kill foremen.) The supervisor must have the authority to discipline employees who abuse animals.

A Major Change

I saw more improvement in both handling and stunning from 1997 to 1999 than I had seen previously in my entire career. Two fast-food companies started auditing U.S. plants during 1999 to make sure they complied with the American Meat Institute Guidelines (Grandin 1997c). Both federally inspected beef and pork plants were scored objectively. Many plants now have better stunner maintenance, and electric prod usage has been greatly reduced. One company audited forty-one beef plants in 1999; I was present at about half of the audits. By end of 1999, 90 percent of beef plants were stunning 95 percent of the cattle they processed with one shot; 37 percent were stunning 99 percent to 100 percent with one shot (Grandin 2000b). If the first shot missed, the animal was immediately restunned. (This was a big improvement over performance noted in the 1996 USDA survey [Grandin 1997a,b].) Large flags were being used to move pigs, and a piece of plastic on a stick was being used to move cattle. These devices had replaced many electric prods.

In beef production, plants were scored on percentage of cattle stunned with one shot, insensibility on the bleed rail, and vocalization during handling. Vocalization (moos and bellows) is a sensitive indicator of welfare-related problems such as excessive electric prod use, slipping and falling, missed stunner shots, and excessive pressure from a restraint device (Grandin 1998a,b).

Researchers have found that vocalization in both cattle and pigs is correlated with physiological indicators of stress (Dunn 1990; Warriss et al. 1994; White et al. 1995). Vocalization is also correlated with pain (Watts and Stookey 1998; Weary 1998). Vocalization scoring can pinpoint handling problems. Beef plants with good handling practices will have 3 percent or less of their cattle vocalizing during handling in the stunning chute (Grandin 1998b). (To keep scoring simple, vocalization is scored

Table 1
Improvements in Vocalization Percentages in a Cow Slaughter Plant When Practices and Equipment Were Changed

Audits	Vocalization (percentages)	Practices and Equipment
1	17	V conveyor restrainer—cows balked at the restrainer entrance and excessive use of electric prod caused vocalization
2	14	No changes in model
3	7	Employee training on reducing prod usage
4	10	Continued working with employees
5	9	Continued working with employees
6	5	Removed V conveyor restrainer and replaced center-track conveyor
7	2	Improved lighting, installed false floor and sheet metal to block the cattle's vision (these had been left out because the equipment installer did not believe they were important)

on a "yes" and "no" basis—a cow either vocalizes or it does not. Vocalization in the yards where cattle are standing undisturbed is not scored.) In 1999 74 percent of forty-two U.S. beef plants had vocalization scores of 3 percent or less for cattle. In 1996 only 43 percent of the plants had a vocalization score of 3 percent or less. Excessive electric prod use, due to cattle balking, had raised vocalization scores to as high as 17 percent at some plants.

Vocalization scoring can be used to chart handling improvement within a plant. It also works well on feedlots and ranches. Vocalization scores will often be higher than 3 percent when animals are ear-tagged on ranches or feedlots. In contrast, it is easy to have a 0 percent vocalization rate for animals moving through the chutes, being restrained in the squeeze chute, and being vaccinated.

The presence of distractions, which makes cattle balk, makes a 3 percent or less vocalization score almost impossible. The movement of a small chain hanging in a chute, for example, will make an approaching animal stop and impede the flow of the other animals. Lighting a dark restrainer entrance will often improve animal movement. (Information on debugging systems and removing distractions can be found in Grandin 1998c, 1996.)

People manage the things that they measure. Bad practices become "normal" if there is no standard to which they can be compared. Vocalization scoring can be used to chart progress as a plant improves its equipment and practices. Table 1 shows vocalization scored from seven audits of 100 cattle each in a single plant. These audits took place over a period of several months.

Dairy and Pig Industry Problems

The number-one transport problem in the 1970s—and the number-one transport problem today—is loading onto a truck animals who are not fit for transport. The dairy industry has some of the worst such problems. Baby dairy calves, who are too young to walk, are not fit for transport. Emaciated or lame dairy cows are not fit for transport. Downer dairy cows, those who are unable to walk, are more prevalent now than in 1994. Numbers of beef cattle downers have decreased slightly (Smith et al. 1994, 1995; Roeber 2001). The 1999 audit by Smith et al. indicated that 1.5 percent of all culled dairy cows arrived at a slaughter plant down and unable to walk. In the beef industry, 0.77 percent of the cows were downers.

In the past thirty years, although the handling of beef cattle on ranches and feedlots has improved, welfare problems in the transport of old, culled dairy cows have worsened. Genetics is partly to blame. Selection of individuals for milk production has increased the incidence of lameness. John Webster at Bristol University in the United Kingdom states that the typical cow's foot can no longer support its weight. A dairy veterinarian in Florida told me that the incidence and aspects of lameness in dairy cows are horrendous. Leg conformation is heritable, and good conformation will help prevent lameness (Boettcher et al. 1998; Van Dorp et al. 1998). Slaughter plant managers and truck drivers have reported that dairies that use bovine somatrophin (BST), bovine growth hormone, in their dairy herds sometimes have more thin, weak cows. Administration of BST reduced body condition score (Jordan et al. 1991; and West et al. 1990). Unless the cow is fed very well, it may lose body condition. The degree of body condition reduction is related to the dose of BST.

Single-trait selection of pigs for rapid growth and leanness has created pigs who are more fragile and likely to die during transport. I have observed that death losses during transport have tripled in the 1990s compared to the 1980s. Some hybrid pigs are very excitable, which makes handling them more difficult (Grandin 2000a). These pigs act as though they have high sympathetic nervous system arousal. A tap on the rump will make them squeal. Normal pigs are much less likely to startle. Pigs who are selected solely for productivity may have a loss of disease resistance. Genetic factors affect susceptibility to disease.

One of my biggest concerns is the possibility that producers are pushing animals beyond their biological limits. The pig industry, for example, has repeated most of the mistakes that the broiler-chicken industry made. Genetic traits are linked in unexpected ways. Some pigs grow so fast that they have very weak bones. These pigs have large bulging muscles but are so fragile that livestock insurance companies will not sell transport insurance to producers to cover them. Fortunately, some breeders are now selecting for more "moderate" pigs, which will have fewer problems.

Good Stockmanship Pays

Good stockmanship can improve productivity of pigs and dairy cattle by more than 10 percent (Hemsworth 1998; Rushen et al. 1999). Animals who are fearful around their caretakers are less productive. They experience lower weight gain and lower milk production. Pigs have fewer piglets. At the highest-producing dairy in Colorado, the cows are very tame and approach people for petting. Good stockmanship costs very little. Feedlots that handle cattle gently find that the animals go back onto their feed more quickly than those who aren't handled gently. One feed-lot that handled cattle roughly in the squeeze chute recorded a 16 percent drop in feed consumption the following day.

If good stockmanship could be purchased, everybody would buy it immediately. I have observed that people buy twice as many books on corral design as videos on low-stress cattle handling and stockmanship principles. They would rather buy equipment than change their behavior. To be a really good stockman, one has to change one's attitude toward the animals. Animals can no longer be viewed simply as economic units.

I have observed that when people on farms and in feedlots and meat plants start handling animals more gently, their attitudes toward the animals change. In 1999 when one company's audits started, many workers at the company's plants replaced electric prods with other driving aids such as flags. I noticed that the employees' manner towards the animals changed. Instead of aggressively poking at animals with an electric prod, they patted them gently on the rear. Changing the worker's actions helps to change the worker's attitudes.

Conclusions

Promoting better stockmanship is essential to improving animal welfare. Large meat-buying customers such as fast-food restaurants in the United States and supermarket chains in the United Kingdom can motivate great change by insisting that suppliers uphold better animal welfare standards. The greatest advances of the last thirty years have been the result of company audits. To maintain such progress, handling and stunning must be continually audited, measured, and managed. Handlers tend to revert to rough handling unless they are monitored and managed. An objective scoring system provides a standard that can be upheld. An overworked employee cannot do a good job of taking care of animals. Good stockmanship requires adequate staffing levels. More efforts are also needed to address problems of faulty stunning equipment, ever-increasing line speed, and enforcement of the Humane Slaughter Act when violations occur.

Attitudes can be changed, and that change can improve both animal welfare and productivity.

Literature Cited

Biber B., and T. Alkin. 1999. Panic disorder subtypes: differential responses to CO_2 challenge 38% CO_2, 65% O_2. *American Journal of Psychiatry* 156: 739–744.

Boettcher, P.J., J.C. Dekkers, L.O. Warnick, and S.J. Wells. 1998. Genetic analysis of lameness in cattle. *Journal of Dairy Science* 81: 1148–56.

Cockram, M.S., and K.T.T. Corley. 1991. Effect of pre-slaughter handling on the behaviour and blood composition of beef cattle. *British Veterinary Journal* 147: 444–54.

Crookshank, H.R., M.H. Elissalde, R.G. White, D.C. Clanton, and H.E. Smalley. 1979. Effect of transportation and handling of calves on blood serum composition. *Journal of Animal Science* 48: 430–35.

Dodman, N.H. 1977. Observations on the use of the Wernberg dip-lift carbon dioxide apparatus for pre-slaughter anesthesia of pigs. *British Veterinary Journal* 133: 71–80.

Dunn, C.S. 1990. Stress reactions of cattle undergoing ritual slaughter using two methods of restraint. *Veterinary Record* 126: 522–25.

Eikelenboom, G. (ed.). 1983. *Stunning animals for slaughter.* The Hague, Netherlands: Martinus Nijhoff.

Eisnitz, G.A. 1997. *Slaughterhouse.* Amherst, N.Y.: Prometheus Books.

Ewbank, R., M.J. Parker, and C.W. Mason. 1992. Reactions of cattle to head restraint at stunning: A practical dilemma. *Animal Welfare* 1: 55–63.

Forslid, A. 1987. Transient neocortical, hippocampal, and amygdaloid EEG silence induced by one-minute infiltration of high concentration CO_2 in swine. *Acta Physiologica Scandinavica* 130: 1–10.

Giger, W., R.P. Prince, R.G. Westervelt, and D.M. Kinsman. 1977. Equipment for low-stress animal slaughter. *Transactions of the American Society of Agricultural Engineers* 20: 571–78.

Grandin, T. 1980a. Problems with kosher slaughter. *International Journal of the Study of Animal Problems* 1(6): 375–90.

——————. 1980b. Livestock behavior as related to handling-facility design. *International Journal of the Study of Animal Problems* 1: 33–52.

——————. 1980c. Observations of cattle behavior applied to the design of cattle-handling facilities. *Applied Animal Ethology* 6: 10–31.

——————. 1985/86. Cardiac arrest stunning of livestock and poultry. Pp. 1–30 in *Advances in Animal Welfare Science,* ed. M.W. Fox and L.D. Mickley. Boston: Martinus Nijhoff.

——————. 1987. Animal handling. *Veterinary Clinics of North America Food Animal Practice* 3: 323–38.

——————. 1988a. Possible genetic effect on pig's reaction to CO_2 stunning. In *Proceedings, Thirty-fourth International Congress of Meat Science and Technology.* Cannon Hill, Queensland, Australia: CSIRO Meat Research Laboratory.

——————. 1988b. Double-rail restrainer conveyor for livestock handling. *Journal of Agricultural Engineering Research* 41: 327–38.

——————. 1988c. Behavior of slaughter plant and auction employees. *Anthrozoös* 4: 205–13.

——————. 1991. Double-rail restrainer for handling beef cattle. *Paper No. 91-5004.* St. Joseph, Mich.: American Society of Agricultural Engineers.

——————. 1992. Observations of cattle-restraint devices for stunning and slaughtering. *Animal Welfare* 1: 85–91.

——————. 1994. Euthanasia and slaughter of livestock. *Journal of the American Veterinary Medical Association* 204: 1354–60.

——————. 1996. Factors that impede animal movement at slaughter plants. *Journal of the American Veterinary Medical Association* 209: 757–59.

——————. 1997a. Assessment of stress during handling and transport. *Journal of Animal Science* 75: 249–57.

——————. 1997b. Survey of handling and stunning in federally inspected beef, pork, veal, and sheep slaughter plants. *ARS Research Project No. 3602-32000-002-08G.* Washington, D.C.: U.S. Department of Agriculture.

——————. 1997c. *Good management practices for animal handling and stunning.* Washington, D.C.: American Meat Institute.

——————. 1998a. Objective scoring of animal handling and stunning practices in slaughter plants. *Journal of the American Veterinary Medical Association* 212: 36–93.

——————. 1998b. The feasibility of using vocalization scoring as an indicator of poor welfare during slaughter. *Applied Animal Behavior* Science 56: 121–28.

——————. 1998c. Solving livestock handling problems in slaughter plants. In *Animal welfare and meat science,* ed. N.G. Gregory. Wallingford, U.K.: CAB International.

——————. 2000a. *Livestock handling and transport.* Second Edition. Wallingford, U.K.: CAB International.

——————. 2000b. 1999 Audits of stunning and handling in federally inspected beef and pork plants. Paper presented, American Meat Institute 2000 Conference on Handling and Stunning, Kansas City, Mo.

Grandin, T., and J.M. Regenstein. 1994. Religious slaughter and animal welfare: A discussion for meat scientists. Pp. 115–23 in *Meat Focus International.* Wallingford, U.K.: CAB International.

Gregory, N.G., and T. Grandin. 1998. *Animal welfare and meat science.* Wallingford, U.K.: CAB International.

Hemsworth, P.H., and G.J. Coleman. 1998. *Human-livestock interactions.* Wallingford, U.K.: CAB International.

Jongman, E.C., J.C. Barnett, and P.H. Hemsworth. 2000. The aversiveness of carbon dioxide stunning in pigs and a comparison of the CO_2 stunner crate vs. the V restrainer. *Applied Animal Behavior Science* 67: 67–76.

Jordan, D.C., A.A. Aquilar, J.D. Olson, C. Bailey, G.F. Hartnell, and K.S. Madsen. 1991. Effects of recombinant methionyl bovine somatrophic (sometribove) in high-producing cow's milk three times a day. *Journal of Dairy Science* 74: 220–26.

Lay, D.C., T.H. Friend, R.D. Randel, C.I. Bowers, K.K. Grisson, O.C. Jenkins. 1992. Behaviorial and physiological effects of freeze and hot iron branding on crossbred cattle, *Journal of Animal Science* 70: 330–336.

Lemmon, W.B., and G.H. Patterson. 1964. Effects of interrupting the mother-neonate bond. *Science* 145: 835–36.

Marshall, M., E.E. Milburg, and E.W. Schultz. 1963. Apparatus for holding cattle in position for humane slaughtering. U.S. Patent 3,092,871.

Mitchell, G., J. Hattingh, and M. Ganhao. 1988. Stress in cattle assessed after handling, transport, and slaughter. *Veterinary Record* 123: 201–05.

Perna, G., M. Battaglia, A. Garberi, C. Arancio, A. Bertani, L. Bellodi. 1994. Carbon dioxide/oxygen challenge test in panic disorder. *Directory of Psychiatry Residency Training Programs* 52: 159–171.

Perna, G., A. Bertani, D. Caldirola, L. Bellodi. 1996. Family history of panic disorder and hyper-sensitivity to CO_2 in patients with panic disorder. *American Journal of Psychiatry* 153: 1060–1064.

Raj, A.B., S.P. Johnson, S.B. Wotton, and J.L. McInstry. 1997. Welfare implications of gas stunning of pigs: The time to loss of somatosensory-evolved potentials and spontaneous electrocorticogram of pigs during exposure to gasses. *Veteri-*

nary Journal 153: 329–39.

Ray, D.R., W.H. Hansen, B. Theurer, G.H. Stott. 1972. Physical stress and cortisol levels in steers. *Proceedings Western Section: American Society of Animal Science* 23: 255–259.

Regensburger, R.W. 1940. Hog stunning pen. U.S. Patent 2,185,949.

Roeber, D.L., P.D. Mies, C.D. Smith, K.E. Belk, T.G. Field, J.D. Tatum, J.A. Scanga, and G.C. Smith. 2001. National market cow and bull beef quality audit: 1999: A survey of producer-related defects in market cows and bulls. *Journal of Animal Science* 79: 658–65.

Rushen, J., A.A. Taylor, and A.M. de Pasille. 1999. Domestic animals' fear of humans and its effect on their welfare. *Applied Animal Behavior Science* 65: 285–303.

Smith, G.C., J.B. Morgan, J.D. Tatum, C.C. Kukay, M.T. Smith, T.D. Schnell, and G.G. Hilton. 1994. Improving the consistency and competitiveness of non-fed beef; and improving the salvage value of cull cows and bulls. The final report of the National Cattlemen's Beef Association. Fort Collins: Colorado State University.

Smith, G.C., et al. 1995. Improving the quality, consistency, competitiveness, and market share of beef: A blueprint for total quality management in the beef industry. The final report of the National Beef Quality Audit. Fort Collins: Colorado State University.

Tume, R.K., and F.D. Shaw. 1992. Beta-endorphin and cortisol concentrations in plasma of blood samples collected during exsanguination of cattle. *Meat Science* 46: 319–27.

Universities Federation Animal Welfare (UFAW). 1987. *Proceedings, Symposium on Humane Slaughter of Animals.* Potters Bar, U.K.: UFAW.

Warriss, P.D., S.N. Brown, and S.J.M. Adams. 1994. Relationship between subjective and objective assessment of stress at slaughter and meat quality in pigs. *Meat Science* 38: 329–40.

Watts, J.M., and J.M. Stookey. 1998. Effects of restraint and branding on rates and acoustic parameters of vocalization in beef cattle. *Applied Animal Behavior Science* 62: 125–35.

Weary, D.M., L.A. Braithwaite, and D. Fraser. 1998. Vocal response to pain in piglets. *Applied Animal Behavior Science* 56: 161–72.

West, J.W., K. Bondair, and J.C. Johnson. 1990. Effect of bovine somatotropin on milk yield and composition, body weight, and condition score of Holstein and Jersey cows. *Journal of Dairy Science* 73: 1062–68.

Westervelt, R.G., D. Kinsman, R.P. Prince, and W. Giger. 1976. Physiological stress measurement during slaughter of calves and lambs. *Journal of Animal Science* 42: 831–34.

White, R.G., J.A. DeShazer, C.J. Tressler, G.M. Borcher, S. Davey, A. Waninge, A.M. Parkhurst, M.J. Milanuk, and E.T. Clems. 1995. Vocalizations and physiological response of pigs during castration with and without anesthetic. *Journal of Animal Science* 73: 381–86.

Van Dorp, T.E., J.C.M. Dekkers, S.W. Martin, and J.P., Noordhuizen, T.M. 1998. Genetic parameters of health disorders and relationships with 305-day milk yield and information traits in registered dairy cows. *Journal of Dairy Science* 81: 2264–70.

Zavy, M.T., P.E. Juniewicz, W.A. Phillips, and D.L. Von Tungeln. 1992. Effects of initial restraint, weaning, and transport stress on baseline and ACTH-stimulated cortisol responses in beef calves of different genotypes. *American Journal of Veterinary Research* 53: 551–57.

Animal Research: A Review of Developments, 1950–2000

7

CHAPTER

Andrew N. Rowan and Franklin M. Loew

Introduction

One can divide the debate over the use of animals in research and testing into three broad periods. The first started in the 1860s and lasted until World War I. During this period, animal research became established as an important method of laboratory investigation and also as a significant source of public controversy. For a variety of reasons very well researched and analyzed by historians Richard French (1975) and James Turner (1980) (among others), the public found the idea of deliberately inflicting harm on animals in order to learn more about health and medicine particularly disturbing. In the United States, opposition to the use of animals in research appeared to peak around the 1890s and then began to decline. By the end of World War I, following the death in 1916 of two notable advocates for more regulation of animal research (Caroline Earl White of the American Anti-Vivisection Society and Albert Leffingwell, M.D.), the animal research issue became marginalized and of relatively little consequence for politicians and policy makers.

The second phase of the animal research debate lasted from around 1920 to 1950. During this period, animal research continued to develop as a means of discovering new biological data and as a route to potential cures—the discovery of insulin is an oft-quoted example (Bliss 1982). Opposition to the practice was sporadic and of little impact on policy makers, despite the support of such powerful individuals as William Randolph Hearst (owner of a newspaper empire) on the side of the anti-vivisection societies.

The third phase of the animal research debate started around 1950. After World War II the government became a major sponsor of scientific research, including biomedical research. The budget of the National Institutes of Health (NIH) grew dramatically and has continued to grow, with a few minor retrenchment periods, up to the present time (see Figure 1). This growth led to an enormous expansion in publicly funded research. In the private sector, the discovery of penicillin and streptomycin led to a tremendous expansion in pharmaceutical research and in the size of the prescription drug industry. These expansions in government funding for biomedical research and in private-sector investment in drug discovery created an increase in demand for laboratory animals.

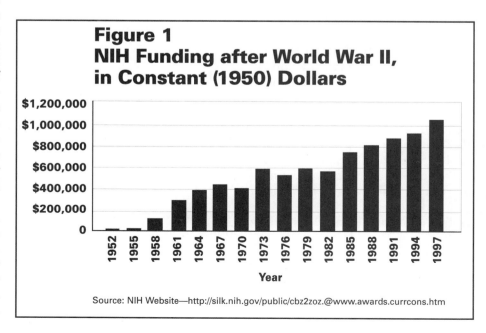

Figure 1
NIH Funding after World War II, in Constant (1950) Dollars

Source: NIH Website—http://silk.nih.gov/public/cbz2zoz.@www.awards.currcons.htm

111

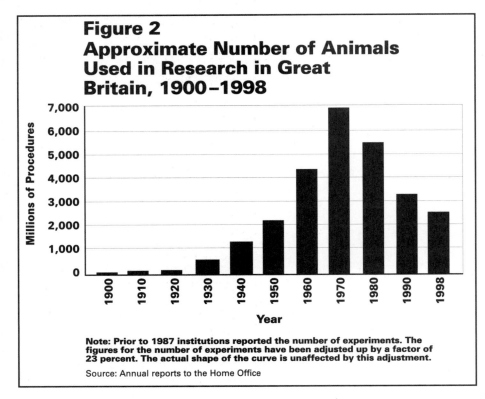

**Figure 2
Approximate Number of Animals
Used in Research in Great
Britain, 1900–1998**

Note: Prior to 1987 institutions reported the number of experiments. The figures for the number of experiments have been adjusted up by a factor of 23 percent. The actual shape of the curve is unaffected by this adjustment.

Source: Annual reports to the Home Office

Trends in Animal Use

Animal User Categories

According to U.S. Department of Agriculture (USDA) statistics, animal use is split almost evenly between commercial and noncommercial users (Newman 1989; Welsh 1991), although these analyses leave out the federal laboratories, which account for somewhere between 15 and 20 percent of national laboratory animal use. It seems as though the ratio between commercial, noncommercial, and government laboratories in the United States may be around 45:40:15. In Great Britain commercial laboratories have always accounted for around two-thirds of the animal use, with educational institutions and government laboratories splitting the remainder.

Much attention has been focused on the use of animals in the testing of personal-care and household products, although such use probably accounts for much less than one per-

cent of the national demand for laboratory animals. In Great Britain the testing of personal-care and household products accounted for fewer than 5,000 animal procedures in 1990, or around 0.15 percent of total animal use. Among commercial organizations the vast majority of animal use is directed toward the discovery, development, and testing of new medicines and therapeutics.

Overall, laboratory animal use can be divided into six basic categories: education; drug discovery and toxicity testing; the development and toxicity testing of other products; the testing of biological agents; medical diagnosis; and other research (immunology, microbiology, oncology, physiology, zoology, ethology, ecology, and a host of other disciplines and subdisciplines). No statistics are sufficiently detailed to provide an accurate estimate of how animal use is distributed among these six categories. However, diagnosis now represents a minor use of research animals (less than 5 percent), while education probably accounts for less than 10 percent. Toxicity and safety testing of all products (including drugs) and the production and testing of vaccines

may account for another 20–25 percent of the total. Drug discovery and the development of new medical devices and treatments may account for about 35 percent of all animal use with other ("basic") research accounting for the remaining 30 percent or so.

Trends: Data from Great Britain and Europe

Unfortunately we do not have good data on laboratory animal use in the United States, but the Home Office in Great Britain has required researchers to report their animal use since the passage of the first act regulating animal research in 1876. Originally, the Home Office counted the number of "animal experiments," where an "experiment" was more or less equivalent to one animal. In 1987 the reporting system was changed and expanded as a result of a new act (1986) regulating animal research. Researchers were now required to report the number of "animal procedures." The reportable use of animals increased approximately 23 percent because some uses of animals (for example, the passaging of tumors) that had not been included under "experiments" were included under the definition of "procedure."

The trends in animal use in Great Britain shown in Figure 2 reflect changes in research during the twentieth century. Briefly, the bulk of animal use prior to World War II came from such laboratory activities as diagnosis of disease and the production and safety testing of various biological agents (for example, insulin; see Bliss 1982, page 172, for comments on the search for rabbits to standardize insulin batches in the early 1920s). After World War II, animal use continued to increase due to many new drug discovery projects and an expansion in university-based research. In the 1970s animal use peaked and has been in decline for the last twenty-five years as the pharmaceutical companies moved from drug development processes that emphasized whole-animal studies to discovery processes that began with studies in cells, cell extracts, and computers. In addition, animal use in vaccine and biological development and testing declined.

The downward trend in animal use seen in Great Britain has also been reported in the Netherlands (a 50-percent reduction since 1978), Switzerland (a 75-percent reduction since 1983), and Germany (a 40-percent decline since 1989).

Trends in the United States to 1990

What little data are available for research animal use in America indicate that the pattern seen in Europe can also be seen in the United States. A survey of animal use in the United States conducted under the auspices of the International Committee for Laboratory Animal Science in the late 1950s found that about 17 million laboratory animals were used in 1957. In the late 1960s, surveys by the Institute for Laboratory Animal Resources (ILAR) of the National Research Council reported that 40–50 million animals were being used annually. Thus, there appears to have been a substantial increase in animal use after World War II. From 1957 to 1969, NIH funding of extramural research increased six-fold in constant dollars, thus a large increase in animal use over this period is hardly surprising.

From 1970 to the early 1990s, we estimate that laboratory animal use declined by about 50 percent from its peak in the early 1970s. This halving of research animal use occurred despite the doubling of NIH extramural funding from 1969 to 1991. It appears that several factors led to the reduction—both in actual numbers and in terms of the number of animals required per unit of funding (see Table 1: dollars spent per animal increased ninefold, indicating a general decline in the research demand for animals).

First, new scientific techniques (for example, radioimmunoassay and cell culture) were developed and improved to the point where animal use could

be greatly reduced or replaced altogether. Second, concern for animal welfare grew dramatically in the second half of the twentieth century and led to changes in practice and regulation. These changes emphasized the need for more attention to animal welfare and the promotion of alternatives to the use of animals. Third, all aspects of research became more expensive, including the purchase and maintenance of the disease-free animals now needed for good research. Finally, the pharmaceutical companies changed their drug discovery programs to rely less on random screening of chemicals in large numbers of animals and more on mechanistic studies in non-animal systems.

For example, during the 1980s Hoffman–La Roche reduced its animal use at its New Jersey research campus from around 1 million to 300,000 per year without reducing its research output (in terms of new drug candidates) at all (Anonymous 1990).

The claim that research animal use has gone down has been challenged (for example, see Orlans 1994) and is not easy to prove conclusively. One has to draw inferences from USDA Annual Reports and from other sources. However, the information is not particularly reliable, and the USDA Annual Reports only account for 10 percent or less of total research animal use (Welsh 1991). This is because research facilities are not

Table 1
NIH Extramural Grants and Research Animal Use in the United States

Year	NIH Extramural Funding ($ Millions, 1950)	U.S. Research Animal Use (Millions)	NIH $/Animal
1957	69	17	4.06
1970	379	ca.50	7.58
1992	937	ca.25	37.48

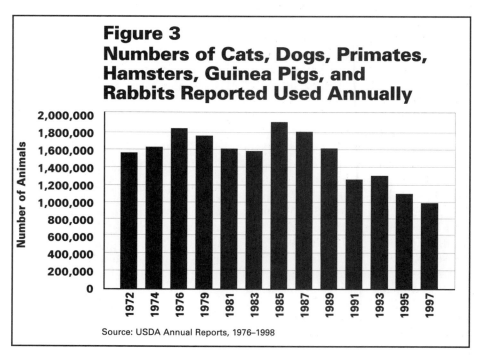

Figure 3
Numbers of Cats, Dogs, Primates, Hamsters, Guinea Pigs, and Rabbits Reported Used Annually

Source: USDA Annual Reports, 1976–1998

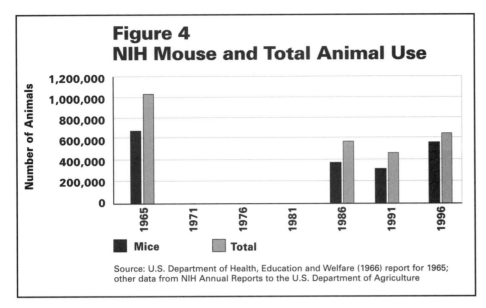

Figure 4
NIH Mouse and Total Animal Use

Number of Animals

1,200,000
1,000,000
800,000
600,000
400,000
200,000
0

1965 1971 1976 1981 1986 1991 1996

■ Mice ▢ Total

Source: U.S. Department of Health, Education and Welfare (1966) report for 1965; other data from NIH Annual Reports to the U.S. Department of Agriculture

required by the USDA to disclose their use of rats, mice, and birds[1]. In addition, individual reports to the USDA vary in their thoroughness and accuracy, and some institutions (including federal laboratories, which do not have to report numbers) may not be included in the annual compilation because their reports were turned in late or not at all. Nonetheless, one can glean some trend information from the USDA reports if one focuses exclusively on the six types of animals (dogs, cats, primates, rabbits, guinea pigs, and hamsters) that have been counted regularly since the 1970s (see Figure 3).

Figure 3 indicates that the number of these animals used annually has fallen from a peak of 1,869,000 in 1985 to 913,000 in 1998. The variation in the use of these animals between 1976 and 1985 is probably due more to reporting and tabulation deficiencies than to real annual fluctuations in animal use. The annual ILAR surveys between 1968 and 1970 reported an average of 3 million dogs, cats, primates, rabbits, guinea pigs, and hamsters used. Therefore, it certainly appears as though, among these six types of animals, there has been a substantial decline in use. It may be that if there has even been a decline in use of rats and mice, it is not so great (see "Trends in the United States since 1990," below). Annu-

al reports submitted to the USDA by NIH indicate that rats and mice accounted for 95.1 percent of all animal use in 1983 but at the end of 2000 account for more than 98 percent of animal use (however, see details of NIH use in "Trends in the United States since 1990," below).

Other studies support the idea that laboratory animal use has declined. The ILAR reported a 40-percent decrease in the number of animals used in the United States in the ten years between 1968 and 1978, based on ILAR's national surveys (NIH 1980). Various large companies (for example, Hoffman–La Roche and Ciba Geigy) have reported substantial declines in animal use since 1980 (Anonymous 1990). A study of U.S. Department of Defense (DOD) laboratory animal use (Weichbrod 1993) indicates that the DOD reduced its use of laboratory animals (including rats and mice) from 412,000 in 1983 (OTA 1986) to 352,000 in 1986, to 267,000 in 1991 (a 35-percent decline in nine years). The National Cancer Institute reported that in looking for anti-cancer drugs it had eliminated the use of several million mice annually by switching from the standard mouse model to a battery of human tumor-cell lines (Rowan 1989).

Trends in the United States since 1990: The Genetic Engineering Impact

While overall laboratory animal use has declined substantially, laboratory mice use has been going up in the last five to ten years. The larger research institutions have begun to house more mice, and annual inventories have increased dramatically (see trends for NIH intramural animal use in Figure 4). Note that mouse use fell from 670,000 in 1965 (DHEW 1966) to a low of 295,000 in 1991. In 1997 mouse use had risen to 647,000. However, this does not mean that "research use" of mice has necessarily increased.

Judging from conversations with animal care professionals, it appears that researchers are creating many new strains of mice using genetic-engineering techniques. These mouse strains are not available from commercial suppliers. Therefore, the institutions have to maintain breeding colonies of these unique strains in their own facilities to provide a continuing supply. Even if a particular strain is not being used at a given moment, the research scientist may still want to maintain it for a possible future project. A researcher who may need no more than 50 of a unique strain of mice a year has to maintain a breeding colony that might total 500 or more. The surplus mice are either kept as breeding stock or euthanized, but they are still counted as part of the annual inventory of animals. Universities also seem to be increasing their colony sizes to maintain more unique strains of mice (see, for example, Southwick 2000 and the note that Baylor University has spent $42 million to triple its rodent holding capacity to 300,000). Laboratory rodent breeding has long been a relatively wasteful process in terms of animal life, and even in economic terms, it is relatively inefficient.

Summary

In general, the animal protection (and research) communities can take heart from the trends in animal use. The use of most laboratory animals (except primates, some farm animals, and mice) is on the decline. Although mouse use is currently on the increase, new developments in cryogenic technologies for storing ova, semen, and fertilized embryos should bring the numbers down again in the next decade. In fact, even with the increase in mouse breeding in research laboratories, overall use may not yet have increased. In Great Britain, where the use of genetically modified animals (mostly mice) has increased from 50,000 a year in 1990 to more than 500,000 a year in 1998, total animal use has fallen from 3.2 million to 2.7 million animal procedures over the same period. Thus, the use of genetically modified animals appears to have replaced—rather than added to—laboratory animal use.

Public Attitudes to Animal Research

In 1949 a poll commissioned by the National Society for Medical Research (NSMR) found that the public was very supportive of animal research—85 percent approved of the use of animals in research and only 8 percent disapproved (NSMR Bulletin 1949). Recent surveys indicate that public attitudes toward animal research have changed substantially since then.

In general, polls indicate that about 75 percent of the public "accepts" the use of animals in research, while about 60 percent "supports" the practice. Support for the use of animals changes according to the type of animal used and the area of research involved. There is much less support for the use of dogs or primates than for the use of mice and rats, and the more useful the research is perceived to be, the more support there is. For example, in a 1985 poll, 88 percent would accept the use of rats but only 55 percent would accept the use of dogs. In the same poll, only 12 percent opposed the use of animals in medical research on cancer or diabetes, but 27 percent opposed the use of animals in allergy testing (FBR 1985).

The public is also concerned about the treatment of research animals, and a majority supports a strengthening of federal regulations and the development and promotion of alternatives. There are indications (but no national poll data) that the public is far less supportive of animal research if the animals are perceived to experience distress or suffering. In a survey of adults in Britain, it was found that public support for animal research dropped by about 20 percent if the animals experienced pain, illness, or surgery (Aldhous et al. 1999). In a survey of psychologists in the United States (only a small percentage of whom actually do animal research), it was reported that for research that involved pain, injury, or death, support dropped dramatically (Plous 1996). While a large majority of the respondents supported the use of dogs or primates in observational research and a majority supported research involving confinement, a large majority opposed the use of dogs or primates in research involving pain or death. The swing was just as large for research on rats, but the respondents tended to be less concerned about the use of rats in general.

Some idea of recent trends in public attitudes can be gleaned from National Science Board (NSB) surveys. In 1985 the NSB added a question on animal research to its regular survey of public attitudes to science. The public was asked if it agreed or disagreed with the statement: "Scientists should be allowed to do research that causes pain and injury to animals like dogs and chimpanzees if it produces new information about health problems." This is a deliberately loaded question in that the costs are high (pain and injury to high-status animals), but the research is posited as providing benefits in the form of new information relevant to human health care. The results of a series of surveys are presented in Table 2. The data in the table endorse the idea that public support for animal research is weakening, especially if compared with the survey data from 1949 (NSMR 1949), when more than 80 percent of respondents supported the use of dogs in research. However, the NSB and 1949 surveys are not strictly comparable.

In conclusion, the public is more

Table 2
Public Attitudes to Animal Research

	1985	1988	1990	1993	1996
Support	63	53	50	53	50
Oppose	30	42	45	42	46
Don't Know	7	5	5	5	4

Source: National Science Board 1987–1997

concerned about the use of animals in research today than at any time in the last fifty years. Research causing pain and distress arouses particular disquiet among both the general public and those with scientific training.

Changes in Animal Research Oversight from 1950 to the Present

In 1950 the only national organizations focusing on the animal research issue were the three major antivivisection organizations (the National, American, and New England Anti-Vivisection Societies). None of the other large animal protection groups was prepared to tackle the issue in any sustained way. However, this was soon to change. New organizations such as the Animal Welfare Institute (AWI) and The Humane Society of the United States (HSUS) (founded in 1951 and 1954, respectively) made the animal research issue a major focus of their work.

For the most part, these groups focused on what they regarded as the inadequate care of laboratory animals, but the AWI also actively promoted the idea of the Three Rs (alternatives) described in a 1959 book by William Russell and Rex Burch (Russell and Burch 1959). By the late 1960s, the idea of alternatives had entered the mainstream of animal protection thought in the United States and was actively advanced in public materials (see "The First Forty Years of the Alternatives Approach" elsewhere in this volume for more information on alternatives).

Animal protection groups focused on the need for some sort of federal regulatory oversight of animal research. Unlike Great Britain, there was no law governing how laboratory animals could be used or treated. The

early efforts at passing legislation promoted the British act as a model for American legislation. There were hearings in 1962, but little progress was made until February 1966, when a *Life* magazine exposé of deplorable conditions in the compound of a dog dealer, "Concentration Camp for Dogs," spurred the U.S. Congress into action. By July 1966 the Laboratory Animal Welfare Act (LAWA) had been passed and signed into law.

However, this legislation regulated only the acquisition and handling of animals by dealers and did not address how animals were cared for or used in laboratories. The LAWA was amended in 1970 (and its name changed to the Animal Welfare Act, or AWA) to include oversight of the care of research animals in research institutions. The USDA was still restricted from "interfering" in how researchers chose and conducted their research projects using animals. Rats and mice, which accounted for about 90 percent of all laboratory animals, were excluded from regulatory oversight by order of the secretary of agriculture. Nonetheless, the AWA began to have an impact and led to improved standards of housing and care in laboratory facilities.

In 1975 the publication of Peter Singer's book *Animal Liberation* was another major landmark in animal protection challenges to animal research. The book empowered animal protectionists, providing them with clear, logical arguments that helped to launch the modern animal rights movement. In the decade after the book appeared, more than a dozen national animal rights groups were founded, and most developed programs against animal research. These groups also were more likely to challenge how animals were used (under the slogan "No cages, not better cages"), and the concept of alternatives became an ever more powerful element in animal protection campaigning.

Pressure continued on federal and state legislators to tighten the laws controlling animal research. Several states either repealed laws permitting

the release of pound animals to research institutions or abolished the practice altogether. At the federal level, two more scandals about animal research in 1981 and 1984 led to a public clamor for more regulation. New legislation was subsequently passed by the U.S. Congress in 1985. One of the bills required the NIH to upgrade its requirements for animal research oversight and the other amended the AWA to require more attention to protocol review and the reduction of animal pain and distress in laboratories. These were major developments, analogous to the 1966/1970 federal legislation.

The critical elements of the 1985 legislation were the focus on animal pain and distress, attention to the use of alternatives, the establishment of a network of Institutional Animal Care and Use Committees (IACUCs), and the requirement that investigators had to justify why and how they wanted to use research animals. The AWA still included a clause that protected academic freedom (in essence), but now researchers were no longer free to pursue a particular scientific puzzle however they wished. They had to obtain permission from an institutional animal care committee. In seeking permission to use animals, they had to take into account the costs to the animals and articulate to some extent how the proposed benefits of the project outweighed those costs. For the most part, the search for new knowledge remains sufficient to justify the confinement of animals in cages and their later euthanasia, but it no longer provides carte blanche for the investigator to do whatever he or she pleases.

Legislative and legal battles continued into the 1990s. Activists campaigned against "pound seizure," product safety testing, and the treatment of nonhuman primates, and they led the debate on whether research should be covered under state anti-cruelty laws, the right of private citizens to sue for enforcement of the AWA, and student rights regarding dissection and animal experimentation. Since 1987 approximately one-

Table 3
Significant Milestones in Animal Research Oversight in the United States

1963	Production of first edition of *The Guide for the Care and Use of Laboratory Animals*
1965	Formation of American Association for the Accreditation of Laboratory Animal Care (AAALAC) as a self-regulating body of scientific organizations
1966	Passage of the Laboratory Animal Welfare Act (LAWA), overseeing treatment and acquisition of dogs and cats destined for research
1970	Amendments to LAWA, changing its name to the Animal Welfare Act (AWA) and extending its reach into research institutions. Specifically, the AWA promoted the idea of "adequate veterinary care" and led to considerable growth in the influence and knowledge of laboratory animal veterinarians

1985	Introduction of revised Public Health Service policy on the use of animals in research requiring the establishment of Institutional Animal Care and Use Committees (IACUCs) for any institution receiving Public Health Service funds for animal research.
	Amendments to the AWA requiring all registered research institutions to establish an IACUC to oversee animal research and approve proposed protocols. Institutions were required to pay particular attention to minimizing pain and distress and to finding alternatives to potentially painful research.
1989	Promulgation of regulations implementing 1985 AWA amendments

fourth of the states have seen the introduction of bills to end the use of animals for educational purposes. On the other side, research scientists have campaigned for protection of research facilities against break-ins and vandalism.

In the last decade, the USDA became more aggressive in pursuing violations of dog and cat acquisition by dealers for sale to research laboratories. As a result, the number of "random source" dogs and cats used in research is down to about 50,000 a year (compared with 500,000 a year in the late 1960s).

There have been a number of legal challenges to the manner in which the USDA is overseeing research animal use. In January 1992 a U.S. District Court decided that the USDA's exclusion of rats, mice, and birds from coverage under the AWA was arbitrary and capricious and in violation of the law. In February 1993 the same federal judge determined that the regulations developed to ensure psychological well-being for primates and exercise for dogs were inadequate because regulated institutions were allowed to develop their own standards. The judge ordered the USDA to redo the regulations. The USDA appealed the judge's ruling, and even-

tually the decision was thrown out by the appeals court because the defendants were deemed not to have standing to sue for legislative relief.

In the last few years, a second lawsuit, filed by the Alternatives Research and Development Foundation to require USDA oversight of mice, rats, and birds used in research, has been wending its way through the courts. Eventually, the courts found that one of the plaintiffs, a student who had used rodents in college laboratory exercises, had standing, and the way was cleared for the case to go forward on its merits. At this point, the USDA sat down with the plaintiffs to negotiate a settlement (the USDA agreed to issue a proposal to regulate rats, mice, and birds under the AWA). Research lobbyists were alarmed by the fact that these negotiations were conducted in secret and were able to persuade the Senate Appropriations Committee to attach language to the U.S. Department of Agriculture's appropriations bill. This language prevented the USDA from taking any action on the rats, mice, and birds issue for one year (until September 30, 2001).

In sum, legislative and regulatory oversight of research animal use has expanded considerably since 1950 (Table 3). What are the animal research issues that will engage the

animal protection movement in the next fifty years?

Issues of the Next Few Decades

Pain and Distress

While overall animal use has declined substantially, there has been less attention paid to the question of reducing pain and distress. Similarly, while there have been developments in laboratory animal anesthesia and analgesia, the larger issue of developing ways to measure animal pain or animal distress so that such states can be identified and addressed when they occur is still in its infancy. Scoring schemes have been developed (see Hendriksen and Morton 1999 for reviews)—and it has been suggested that weight loss could be used as an index of distress (Dallman 2000)—but there are no agreed-upon measures of animal distress that could be applied in the laboratory. Perhaps distress (and pain) are too complex for anyone ever to develop an unequivocal empirical measure, but all should make more of an effort to detect distress and then to alleviate it when it occurs.

The HSUS launched an initiative aimed at generating more attention to detecting and eliminating pain and distress (HSUS 2000). The initiative has already produced some results. During 2000 there were five national meetings involving laboratory-animal-care professionals that focused either exclusively or to a significant degree on the pain and distress issue. The Federation of American Societies of Experimental Biology organized a workshop on the topic that concluded that animal distress was too complex a concept to define or measure unambiguously. The USDA announced its intention to try to develop a workable definition of animal distress and to revise its current pain and distress reporting system.

The HSUS intends to continue to press forward with its initiative and to develop contacts and allies within the research community who will support the development of a more aggressive program to detect and eliminate animal distress in the laboratory.

Primates

Approximately 50,000 primates (1,700 of which are chimpanzees) are in U.S. research facilities. In the past few years, challenges to the use of primates in research have intensified in both the United States and worldwide. The Third World Congress on Alternatives in Bologna, Italy, in 1999, featured a session based on the proposal that the use of primates in laboratories should be "zeroed out." In the United States, various animal activist groups have begun to campaign for such a "zero option" for research primates. On the other hand, primate research enjoys a certain cachet in the United States that makes it very unlikely that a campaign to end it will succeed anytime soon.

The most promising front on primate research in the United States involves laboratory chimpanzees. Widespread support exists among animal protection organizations, scientists, and animal care professionals involved with laboratory chimpanzees for the "retirement" of many of these chimpanzees into appropriate sanctuaries. Estimates of the number that might be retired immediately range from 100 to more than 500. As of late 2000, a bill to provide funding for such sanctuaries had passed the U.S. House of Representatives and awaited action in the Senate. Unfortunately, despite very similar goals, considerable distrust still exists among the various protagonists (both scientific and animal protection) seeking to establish chimpanzee sanctuaries. This distrust has already been one factor (another is the development of problems with moving individuals of an endangered species from one country to another) in a pharmaceutical company's decision not to pursue funding the retirement of some European chimpanzees to a new sanctuary in the United States. It is very likely that the number of chimpanzees in active research programs will continue to fall. What is not so certain is whether appropriate sanctuaries can be built and funded for those chimpanzees who should already be in permanent retirement.

Genetically Modified Animals

Developments in transgenic technology have led to an explosion in the number of mice being kept in the larger research institutions in the United States. Scientists are very excited about some of the possible research projects they might be able to explore using genetically engineered mice (and perhaps rats). For example, scientists have identified about fifty genes linked to heart enlargement, or hypertrophy, in mice, 60 percent of which were previously unknown to be associated with this condition. In the past five to ten years, mouse inventories have doubled at many research institutions. For example, at NIH, the number of mice recorded in the annual report for the USDA jumped from just under 300,000 in 1991 to over 600,000 in 1997. As noted above, Baylor University has increased the size of its facility and can now house 300,000 mice, or three times its previous capacity.

Apart from the natural concern that the animal protection movement would have with this growth in laboratory mouse use, transgenic animals might also experience more distress because they suffer from specific deficits caused by genetic modification. However, we have little specific information on the potential distress experienced by genetically modified mice. Apart from a general exhortation to ICUCs to consider the effects of a particular gene manipulation on animal well-being, there has apparently been no systematic attention to the issue by animal care professionals. The reality is still that mice are small creatures that are easy to overlook and that tend to be given relatively limited clinical care in most research facilities[2]. The whole question of the effects of genetic manipulation is an issue to which the animal protection movement is going to have to pay particular attention. In the immediate future, advances in cryogenic technology could greatly reduce the sum total of animal distress by allowing research institutions to "store" new strains of genetically modified mice as frozen embryos rather than as colonies of living animals.

Reducing Animal Numbers

While the number of genetically modified animals in laboratory facilities continues to rise both in the United States and in Europe, the number of actual animal procedures recorded in Great Britain has declined. In the last few years, however, the decline in procedures has slowed down and may even have stopped. Nonetheless it appears as though research on genetically modified mice is still replacing (rather than adding to) research using standard laboratory mice. Europe is still discussing the idea of setting targets for reducing animal use (by 50 percent, according to one proposal, but no one is sure of what the starting date should be). The United States lacks the necessary reporting structures that would permit the tracking of accurate trends in laboratory animal use. However, both scientific organizations and the animal protection movement have an interest in using as few animals as possible and in eventually eliminating their use altogether (as a representative for the Foundation for Biomedical Research stated to the *Boston Globe*). The challenge (and the policy conflict) resides in deciding what would be an appropriate timetable and how much effort should be put into such a goal. Nonetheless, one can guarantee that there will continue to be pressure from both external and internal sources on research institutions to reduce laboratory animal inventories and use.

Conclusion

There is no question that considerable progress has been made in reducing laboratory animal use and in improving the welfare of laboratory animals in the last fifty years. Improvements in veterinary health management have, for example, eliminated a considerable amount of disease that would have caused animal distress. Higher standards of veterinary care mean fewer animals die before or during the research from unrelated disease and fewer animals are needed for a particular project. In addition, new research technologies and improvements in existing techniques mean that more data can be generated from many fewer animals than was the case in 1950.

There is no question that much more progress is possible. Improvements in monitoring animal distress will benefit both the animals and the scientific projects in which they are used. Primate housing is far from ideal. Keeping a large monkey in a small cage for years at a time cannot be regarded as acceptable. Laboratory animal numbers are still very high and we need aggressively to pursue ways to continue to drive those numbers down while still promoting good

science. In the end, greater attention to animal welfare will not harm biomedical research, it will enhance both its productivity and its reputation in the eyes of the public.

Notes

[1] In 2000 the USDA, in a settlement forced by a legal challenge, agreed to promulgate regulations to include rats, mice, and birds. However, the U.S. Congress then inserted language into the Agriculture Appropriations bill that delayed any implementation of the agreement for at least a year.

[2] Also, in settings more familiar to most citizens, mice and rats are usually considered to be vermin and thus there is the implicit sense that these creatures are not as worthy of attention. Opinion polls usually find that the public is not as concerned about the use of mice and rats as they are about the use of dogs or primates, for example (cf. Herzog, Rowan, and Kossow in this volume).

Literature Cited

Aldhous, P., Coghlan, A., and Copley, J. 1999. Let the people speak. Animal experiments: Where do you draw the line? *New Scientist*, 22 May, 26–31.

Anonymous. 1990. Statistics on the Three Rs. The Alternatives Report 2(2). (Available from the Tufts Center for Animals and Public Policy.)

Bliss, M. 1982. *The discovery of insulin.* Chicago: University of Chicago Press.

Dallman, M.F. 2000. Stress and energy balance: The rationale for and utility of measuring body weight. Presented at FASEB Workshop, August.

Foundation for Biomedical Research (FBR). 1985. Members of the American public comment on the uses of animals in medical research and testing. Washington, D.C.: FBR.

French, R.D. 1975. *Antivivisection and medical science in Victorian England.* Princeton, N.J.: Princeton University Press.

Hendriksen, C.F.M., and D.B. Morton. 1999. Humane endpoints in animal experiments for biomedical research. Proceedings of the International Conference, 22–25 November, 1998, Zeist, The Netherlands. (Inquiries to CFMH, RIVM, P.O. Box 1, 3720 BA Bilthoven, The Netherlands; or DBM, Centre for Biomed-

ical Ethics, University of Birmingham, Birmingham B15 2TT, UK.)

The Humane Society of the United States (HSUS). 2000. Taking animal welfare seriously: Minimizing pain and distress in research animals. Washington, D.C.: HSUS, Animal Research Issues Section.

National Institutes of Health (NIH). 1980. National survey of laboratory animal facilities and resources. In NIH Publication No. 80-2091. Washington, D.C.: U.S. Department of Health and Human Services.

National Science Board (NSB). 1986–1997. *National Science Board: Science and Engineering Indicators.* 1986, 1989, 1991, 1994, 1997. Washington, D.C.: U.S. Government Printing Office.

National Society for Medical Research (NSMR). 1949. *Bulletin.*

Newman, A. 1989. Research versus animal rights: Is there a middle ground? *American Scientist* 77: 135–137.

Office of Technology Assessment. 1986. *Alternatives to animal use in research, testing, and education.* Washington, D.C.: U.S. Government Printing Office.

Orlans, F.B. 1994. Data on animal experimentation in the U.S.: What they do and do not show. *Perspectives in Biology and Medicine* 37: 217–31.

Plous, S. 1996. Attitudes towards the use of animals in psychology research and education: Results from a national survey of psychologists. *American Psychologist* 51: 1167–80. (Also see 1998 paper at *http://altweb.jhsph.edu/science/meetings/pain/plous.htm.*)

Rowan, A.N. 1989. Scientists should institute and publicize programs to reduce the use and abuse of animals in research. *Chronicle of Higher Education*, April 12, B1–3.

Russell, W.M.S., and R.L. Burch. 1959. *The principles of humane experimental technique.* London: Methuen.

Singer, P. 1990/1975. *Animal liberation.* New York: Random House/ New York Review of Books.

Southwick, R. 2000. Animal rights groups gain ground with subtler approaches worrying researchers. *Chronicle of Higher Education*, October 27.

Turner, J. 1980. *Reckoning with the beast*. Baltimore: Thorsons Publishers.

U.S. Department of Health, Education, and Welfare (DHEW). 1966. *The care and management of laboratory animals used in programs of the Department of Health, Education, and Welfare*. Washington, D.C.: DHEW Division of Operations Analysis, Office of the Comptroller.

Weichbrod, R.H. 1993. Animal use in Department of Defense research facilities: An analysis of "Annual Reports of Research Facility," filed with the U.S. Department of Agriculture, 1986–1991. Doctoral dissertation/partial fulfillment, Waldon University Institute for Advanced Studies, Maryland.

Welsh, H. 1991. *Animal testing and consumer products*. Washington, D.C.: Investor Responsibility Research Center.

The First Forty Years of the Alternatives Approach: Refining, Reducing, and Replacing the Use of Laboratory Animals

CHAPTER

An updated version of "Looking Back Thirty-three Years to Russell and Burch: The Development of the Concept of the Three Rs (Alternatives)" (Rowan 1994)

Martin L. Stephens, Alan M. Goldberg, and Andrew N. Rowan

Introduction

The concept of the Three Rs—reduction, refinement, and replacement of animal use in biomedical experimentation—stems from a project launched in 1954 by a British organization, the Universities Federation for Animal Welfare (UFAW). UFAW commissioned William Russell and Rex Burch to analyze the status of humane experimental techniques involving animals. In 1959 these scientists published a book that set out the principles of the Three Rs, which came to be known as alternative methods. Initially, Russell and Burch's book was largely ignored, but their ideas were gradually picked up by the animal protection community in the 1960s and early '70s. In the '80s, spurred by public pressure, the alternatives approach was incorporated into national legislation throughout the developed countries and embraced by industry in Europe and America. Government centers devoted to the validation and regulatory acceptance of alternative methods

were established during the '90s. By 2000 the use of animals in research had fallen by up to fifty percent from its high in the 1970s.

The Alternatives Approach in the Context of the Animal Research Issue

Animals have been used as experimental subjects in biomedical research, testing, and education during the last 150 to 200 years, but the practice began to burgeon in nineteenth century Europe. Alarmed by this increase, early critics of animal research challenged it from several perspectives. They argued variously that animal research was cruel and inhumane; unethical; and medically unproductive, unnecessary, or even misleading. Their criticism largely

proved unpersuasive (French 1975; Turner 1980). Activism in the United States over animal research waned after World War I and remained at a low level until after World War II, when a new dimension in the animal research controversy emerged.

Spurred in part by advances in technological methods, animal protectionists began advocating *for* alternatives to laboratory animal use, not simply advocating *against* animal use or otherwise criticizing the status quo. These alternatives make up the Three Rs: methods that could *replace* or *reduce* laboratory animal use in specific procedures or *refine* such use so that animals experience less suffering. Sympathetic scientists joined in this more constructive approach; indeed, scientists themselves were the ones who first formulated the Three Rs concept. At the dawn of the twenty-first century, this approach is proving to be a powerful force in decreasing the use and distress of animals in experimental biology and medicine.

Table 1
Alternatives Chronology: 1876–1959

1876	Cruelty to Animals Act—the first law to specifically regulate animal experimentation—is enacted in Great Britain.
1927	The LD50 Test is introduced to standardize the potency of digitalis extract.
1938	The Federal Food, Drug, and Cosmetic Act is enacted, marking the first time a U.S. government agency is given the power to regulate consumer products.
1944	Eye irritancy testing is standardized as the Draize Test.
1954	Universities Federation for Animal Welfare (UFAW) establishes a committee to study humane techniques used in laboratory animal experiments.
1957	UFAW holds a symposium, "Humane Techniques in the Laboratory," at which William Russell presents a paper, marking the first time the Three Rs of replacement, reduction, and refinement are discussed in public.
1959	Russell and Burch's study is published as *The Principles of Humane Experimental Technique*, which develops the Three Rs approach at length.

Estimates of the numbers of research animals used annually in the United States and worldwide are highly speculative. The last official estimate for the United States was 17 to 22 million animals (U.S. Office of Technology Assessment 1986), but that study was conducted more than fifteen years ago. There is some evidence that this estimate was made during a period of declining animal use that began in the 1960s and continued into the '90s (Rowan et al. 1995). Consequently, the current figure could be lower. Worldwide animal use was estimated to be between 60 and 85 million animals in the early 1990s (Rowan 1995), but more conservative estimates of rodent use suggest a total of 40 million animals worldwide (D. Kawahara, personal communication with A. Goldberg 1998).

The 1950s: The Three Rs Approach Launched

The British scientists William Russell and Rex Burch formally launched the Three Rs with their book *The Principles of Humane Experimental Technique* (Russell and Burch 1959). However, hints of Russell and Burch's ideas had appeared in earlier discussions about the appropriate use of animals in research. Marshall Hall, a

British experimental physiologist during the first half of the nineteenth century, proposed five principles for animal experimentation that would eliminate unnecessary and repetitive procedures and minimize suffering (Manuel 1987). Hall also recommended the use of phylogenetically "lower," less sentient, animals and praised the findings of a colleague who demonstrated that an animal that had just been killed could be substituted for a living one, thereby eliminating pain.

Fifty years after Hall set out his five principles, a short-lived research foundation—the Leigh Brown Trust—was established to promote and encourage scientific research without inflicting pain on experimental animals (French 1975). Although the Trust commissioned several publications in the 1890s, it never succeeded in developing a research program that convinced a significant proportion of the research community to adopt its principles. From 1900 to 1950, those who opposed the use of animals lost much of their political influence and were relegated to the fringes of political activity. As a result, little attention was paid to the ethical questions posed by the use of animals in research.

After World War II, interest in the animal research issue began to grow again. In the United States, newly formed animal protection groups began to criticize animal research practices. In England the Three Rs concept of alternatives began to

emerge from the work of UFAW. UFAW published a handbook on the care and management of laboratory animals (Worden 1947) that was well received. This gave UFAW the confidence to address the more contentious topic of experimental techniques involving animals (as distinct from animal care). Accordingly, in 1954 Major Charles Hume (the founder of UFAW and its director at the time) established a committee to initiate a systematic examination of the progress of humane technique in the laboratory. Hume served as the committee's secretary, but it is noteworthy that the committee was chaired by Peter Medawar, a well-respected immunologist, and also included among its members William Lane-Petter, secretary of the Research Defence Society, an organization established to defend animal research. The committee employed William Russell (a zoologist) and Rex Burch (a microbiologist) to carry out the project (Hume 1962).

The exact origin of the Three Rs concept is not entirely clear (Russell 1995). In a 1959 talk, Hume indicated that Russell was the originator of the "Three Rs" concept (Hume 1962), while Russell (1995), in a retrospective paper entitled "The Development of the Three Rs Concept," credited Hume as our "inspiration and guide throughout." In that paper Russell recalled that the Three Rs concept evolved sometime between the sum-

Table 2
Alternatives Chronology: 1960–1969

1962	Lawson Tait Trust (UK) is established—the first research fund to support the scientific development of alternatives.	**1967**	United Action for Animals is formed in the United States and later campaigns specifically for replacement alternatives.
1963	The first edition of *The Guide for the Care and Use of Laboratory Animals*, written by the National Academy of Sciences, is published by the National Institutes of Health.	**1969**	The Fund for the Replacement of Animals in Medical Experiments (FRAME) is formed in the United Kingdom to promote to the scientific community the idea of alternatives.
1965	Littlewood Committee Report (UK) concludes that little would be gained by paying special attention to alternatives.	**1969**	Lord Dowding Fund (UK) is established to support alternatives research. Sir Peter Medawar correctly predicts the subsequent worldwide decline in animal use.

mer of 1955 and May 1957. The first recorded mention of the Three Rs was on May 7, 1957, at a meeting, "Humane Technique in the Laboratory," organized by UFAW and chaired by Medawar. Russell (1957) gave a presentation at this meeting in which he described the Three Rs. A brief proceedings (Anonymous 1957) was published later that year by the Laboratory Animals Bureau of the Medical Research Council. Many of the arguments and ideas presented by Russell and the other speakers later appeared in *The Principles of Humane Experimental Technique* (Russell and Burch 1959). See Table 1 for a chronology of these and other early developments.

It is noteworthy from an American perspective that the U.S.-based Animal Welfare Institute (AWI) provided financial support to Russell and Burch's project and that AWI's Christine Stevens made frequent visits to England to encourage their work (Russell 1995).

The 1960s: Dormancy

Although *The Principles of Humane Experimental Technique* has now become the classic text on alternatives, it received little attention when it was published in 1959 despite its promotion by UFAW in England and the AWI in the United States. There are several

examples of the lukewarm reaction to the book within the scientific community. In *Nature*, a leading international science journal based in England, Weatherall (1959) commented:

[It] is useful to have a résumé of ways which have already been adopted to make experimentation as humane as possible…[but the book] is not sufficiently informative to be used as guide either to details of experimental design or to the husbandry of experimental animals. Perhaps its chief purpose is to stimulate thought on both of these topics, and it is to be hoped it will succeed in doing so.

The British journal *Veterinary Record* (Anonymous 1959) commented that the book contained an important message and hoped that it would not be relegated "to the shelves merely for reference," but found the philosophy "somewhat difficult reading." The British medical journal *The Lancet* (Anonymous 1960) also found the book difficult going, noting that "its purpose is admirable, and its matter unexceptionable," but "it is not easy reading." It is not clear whether the tepid reviews reflected a general lack of interest in the topic or were a reaction to the book's arguments (a contemporaneous *Nature* review of a book that defended the use of animals [LaPage 1960] was, by contrast, full of praise).

LaPage's (1960) defense of animal research described the contributions

of animal research to medical advance and mentioned Russell and Burch and the concept of the Three Rs only once, in a final chapter. He noted that distinguished scientists at a UFAW meeting

discussed, among other things, how the numbers of laboratory animals used, and the numbers of experiments done on them, could be reduced, how their welfare could be improved, how the techniques used could be refined and how far, as Russell and Burch (1959) also discuss, animals could be replaced, for certain kinds of experiments at any rate.

After the initial book reviews and aside from the occasional mention of the idea of alternatives in the technical literature, the scientific community largely ignored Russell and Burch's book for nearly two decades. According to an analysis by Phillips and Sechzer (1989), the term "alternatives" did not appear in the scientific literature on the animal research issue in the 1960s, aside from a 1966 paper alluding to the concept.

During the 1960s, the animal protection community occasionally heeded Russell and Burch's 1959 call for alternatives (Table 2). In 1962 three leading antivivisection societies in the United Kingdom (the British Union for the Abolition of Vivisection, the National Antivivisection Society [NAVS], and the Scottish Society for the Prevention of Vivisection) established the Lawson Tait Trust to encourage and support researchers who were not using any animals in their research. In 1967 United Action for Animals was established in the United States to promote alternatives, focusing on the principle of replacement. It's founder, Eleanor Seiling, spent many hours in the New York Public Library poring through scientific journals looking for examples of unnecessary animal research and of alternatives. However, she appears to have been a lone voice in the United States. By and large the animal protection literature of the 1960s did not pay much attention to the idea of alternatives.

Aside from these few examples of individuals taking up Russell and Burch's challenge in the years immediately following publication of their book, their ideas did surface directly or indirectly from time to time. In the early 1960s, the British Home Office set up a Committee of Inquiry into the workings of the 1876 Cruelty to Animals Act, chaired by Sir Sidney Littlewood. The Littlewood Committee report (1965) addressed the question of alternatives only briefly, but the mention at least indicated that the issue was beginning to be raised in public discourse. The Committee reported that it had

> repeatedly questioned scientific witnesses about the existence of alternative methods which would avoid the use of living animals. The replies have been unanimous in assuring us that such methods are actively sought and when found are readily adopted...Discoveries of adequate substitutes for animal tests have, however, so far been uncommon, and we have not been encouraged to believe that they are likely to be more frequent in the future" (paragraph 71).

The Committee accepted these arguments and concluded that the demand for the use of animals in biomedical research was likely to increase in the coming years and that the discovery of substitutes for animal tests was not likely to affect the demand for animal experimentation.

In the United States in the early 1960s, pressure from animal protectionists led to several congressional hearings on bills to regulate animal research. The printed record of the 1962 hearings is 375 pages long but apparently contains only one reference to Russell and Burch and none at all to alternatives (U.S. Congress 1962). The one reference to Russell and Burch came in testimony by Hume, still the director of UFAW, who had been flown to the United States to testify that the Cruelty to Animals Act (1876) was well regarded by British scientists. Also in 1962, The Humane Society of the United States (HSUS) published a booklet, *Animals in Research*, that alluded to the concept of reduction. The booklet reported the results of an analysis commissioned by The HSUS and carried out by Westat Research Analysts of the statistical approach used in published research papers (Anonymous 1962). The analysts concluded that the statistical design of the published studies was usually inadequate and that at least 25 percent fewer animals could have been used without altering the validity of the results.

Arguably the most significant development on the alternatives front during the 1960s was the establishment in 1969 of the U.K.-based charitable organization FRAME (Fund for the Replacement of Animals in Medical Experiments) to promote the concept of alternatives among scientists. Although small in size and influence in its early years, FRAME has become a powerful force for advancing alternative methods. Also in 1969 the U.K.-based NAVS set up the Lord Dowding Fund to support alternatives research. Both FRAME and the Dowding Fund were relatively well received by some popular science magazines (both the *New Scientist* and *World Medicine* praised the new, more scientific approach represented by the two organizations). Attitudes in the United States were more negative. A 1971 editorial in the *Journal of the American Medical Association* (Anonymous 1971) criticized FRAME in scathing terms, commenting that FRAME might be better named FRAUDS (Fund for the Replacement of Animals Used in the Discovery of Science).

By the close of the 1960s, Peter Medawar, the British scientist who had encouraged UFAW to undertake the Russell and Burch project, had won a Nobel Prize for his work in immunology and had been knighted by the British Crown. In a 1969 essay published a few years later, Medawar commented presciently on the prospects for alternatives and a decrease in animal use:

> The use of animals in laboratories to enlarge our understanding of nature is part of a far wider exploratory process, and one cannot assay its value in isolation—as if it were an activity which, if prohibited, would deprive us only of the material benefits that grow directly out of its own use. Any such prohibition of learning or confinement of the understanding would have widespread and damaging consequences; but *this does not imply that we are forevermore, and in increasing numbers, to enlist animals in the scientific service of man. I think that the use of experimental animals on the present scale is a temporary episode in biological and medical history, and that its peak will be reached in ten years time, or perhaps even sooner. In the meantime, we must grapple with the paradox that nothing but research on animals will provide us with the knowledge that will make it possible for us, one day, to dispense with the use of them altogether"* (Medawar 1972, emphasis added).

Table 3
Alternatives Chronology: 1970–1979

1970	FRAME publishes *Is the Laboratory Obsolete?*, which outlines replacement methodologies such as computer modeling, tissue culture studies, and the use of lower organisms.
1971	Council of Europe Resolution 621 suggests that an alternatives database be established, the first significant government recommendation on alternatives.
	Bruce Ames of the University of California at Berkeley introduces a nonanimal test for detecting mutation-causing substances, later known as the Ames Test, using a bacterium.
1972	The Felix Wankel Prize (now 50,000 deutsche marks) for advancing the field of alternatives is offered for the first time.
1973	FRAME begins to publish *ATLA* (Alternatives to Laboratory Animals).
1975	The U.S. National Academy of Sciences holds the United States' first major scientific meeting on alternatives.
1977	The Netherlands Animal Protection Law includes a specific section on alternatives that has grown into a program in which the government provides the equivalent of hundreds of thousands of dollars to support alternatives research.

1978	FRAME hosts "Alternatives in Drug Development and Testing" at the Royal Society—Europe's first big scientific meeting on alternatives.
	David Smyth, president of the United Kingdom Research Defense Society—established to support animal research—publishes the first book examining alternatives since the publication of Russell and Burch's 1959 work.
1979	At the urging of United Action for Animals, the Research Modernization Act (H.R. 4805), which would redirect 30–50 percent of animal research funding to alternatives, is introduced in Congress.
	The Swedish government allocates $90,000 in funding for alternatives—the first government funding for alternatives.
	The Dutch Minister of Health states that the government supports the use of alternatives.

The 1970s: Animal Protectionists Heed the Call

During the 1970s, the alternatives approach became a key theme for the animal protection movement, which was growing in both size and political clout (Rowan 1989). The HSUS established a committee of experts on alternatives in the early '70s and later in the decade published a twenty-five page booklet on the subject (Rowan 1979). The political and scientific establishments also began to be drawn into the debate, as indicated by some selected events (Table 3). The first major political initiative on alternatives came in 1971 when the Council of Europe passed Resolution 621. This proposed, among other things, the establishment of a documenta-tion and information center on alternatives and tissue banks for research. Deliberations on Resolution 621 did not begin until the late '70s, and the ensuing final Council of Europe Convention dropped some of the specific recommendations on alternatives. Instead, the Convention reflected the broad concern over animal research and made some rather general recommendations on alternatives.

In Europe a number of countries (for example, Denmark, the Federal Republic of Germany, the Netherlands, Sweden, and Switzerland) enacted animal research legislation that included specific support for alternatives. In Sweden the government established an advisory Central Committee on Experimental Animals to develop and promote alternatives and allocated the equivalent of $90,000 annually for the support of research on alternatives. This represented the first government funding for alternatives.

In 1977 the Netherlands Animal Protection Law included a specific section on alternatives that has grown into a program in which the government provides the equivalent of hundreds of thousands of dollars to support alternatives research.

In the United Kingdom, FRAME began publishing *ATLA Abstracts* to identify articles in the scientific literature that focused on alternatives. While the journal had little impact when it was simply publishing abstracts, it started to include review articles in 1976 and then, early in the '80s, dropped the abstracts altogether and adopted its current format, which is centered on original articles. *ATLA* (Alternatives to Laboratory Animals) is now well enough established to be covered by the Science Citation Index.

In the United States, interest in alternatives grew slowly. By the mid-'70s, the term had entered the

Table 4
Alternatives Chronology: 1980–1989

1980 American activist Henry Spira launches the Draize campaign against the rabbit-based eye irritancy test.

As a result of the Draize campaign, Revlon gives a $750,000 grant to Rockefeller University to establish an alternatives research program.

The New England Antivivisection Society gives $100,000 for alternatives research on tissue culture, and a second animal-welfare consortium provides $176,000 for Chorio-Allantoic Membrane (CAM) test development.

1981 As a result of the Draize campaign, the cosmetics industry gives $1 million to Johns Hopkins University to establish the Center for Alternatives to Animal Testing (CAAT) (Avon and Bristol-Myers Squibb were the leading donors).

Swiss animal legislation specifically requires consideration of alternatives.

Zbinden and Flury-Roversi publish a critique of the LD50 Test.

1982 Colgate Palmolive provides $300,000 to investigate the CAM system.

CAAT holds its first symposium.

1983 Switzerland provides two million Swiss francs over two years for alternatives research.

The Food and Drug Administration (FDA) formally announces that it no longer requires data from the classical LD50 Test.

Utrecht University in the Netherlands establishes research and education programs directed towards further implementation of the Three Rs.

1984 FRAME receives £160,000 from the Home Office—the first UK government funding for alternatives research.

1985 The Health Research Extension Act is passed, requiring the NIH to develop a plan for alternatives.

Animal Welfare Act amendments are passed, requiring greater attention to alternatives to research techniques that cause pain and distress.

Index Medicus, an index of published biomedical studies, adds the subject heading "Alternatives to Animal Testing."

The European Research Group into Alternatives to Toxicity Testing (ERGATT) is formed.

The Soap and Detergent Association (USA) initiates the In Vitro Alternatives Program.

1986 CAAT and Bausch and Lomb sponsor a workshop on alternatives and acute ocular irritation testing.

The UK's Animals (Scientific Procedures) Act replaces the 1876 act.

The U.S. Congress's Office of Technology Assessment issues a landmark report, "Alternatives to Animal Use in Research, Testing and Education."

The Council of Environmental Ministers of the European Community enacts EC Directive 86/609, requiring that member countries develop legislation promoting the Three Rs.

An FDA survey reports a 96 percent decrease in the use of the classic LD50 tests in 1985 compared with the period 1975–1979.

Two new cell toxicology journals, *Toxicology In Vitro* and *Molecular Toxicology*, are established.

The Organization for Economic Cooperation and Development (OECD) announces changes in its guidelines for acute oral and dermal toxicity and starts to discuss alternatives.

British Industrial Biological Research Association (BIBRA) increases funding of alternatives research to £700,000 per annum.

The Industrial In Vitro Toxicology Society (IVTS) is established in the United Kingdom.

Federal Republic of Germany enacts new laws on animal protection requiring consideration of alternatives in animal research.

1987 The HSUS publishes an analysis of the historical importance of alternative methods in biomedical research awarded Nobel Prizes.

The Dutch Alternatives to Animal Experiments Platform is established with participation from government, industry, and animal welfare organizations.

In Vitro Toxicology: A Journal of Molecular and Cellular Toxicology is established.

The Swiss Foundation "Finanzpool 3 R" is established to support alternatives research with one million Swiss francs.

(continued on next page)

continued from previous page

Table 4
Alternatives Chronology: 1980–1989

1988	A government/industry workshop is held on alternatives in ocular irritancy testing, to review the Soap and Detergent Association's Alternatives Program.	1989	The Center for the Documentation and Evaluation of Alternative Methods to Animal Experiments, known by its German acronym ZEBET, is established in Germany.
	The Industrial In Vitro Toxicology Group holds its first meeting.		Procter and Gamble announces that it is contributing $450,000 per year for three years to its University Animal Alternative Research Program.
	The U.S. Republican presidential platform encourages the implementation of alternatives to animal testing.		Avon Products announces that it will no longer use the Draize Test.
	The J.F. Morgan Foundation for Alternatives Research is established in Canada.		The Scandinavian Society for Cell Biology establishes the Multicenter Evaluation of In Vitro Cytotoxicity (MEIC) to assess alternatives to LD50 testing for acute toxicity.
	The Swiss government's Office for Animal Experiments and Alternatives is established.		The Second International Conference on Practical In Vitro Toxicology is held in the United Kingdom.
			The Swedish Fund for Scientific Research without Animal Experiments invests 700,000 Swedish crowns in alternatives projects.
			The Clonetics Corporation begins to market cells and cell testing methods.
			The American Anti-Vivisection Society establishes the Demeter Fund (later known as the Alternatives Research and Development Foundation) in order to support nonanimal research, funding up to $50,000 annually for one or more projects.

vocabulary of the animal movement on a large scale and had begun to find its way into the scientific literature (Phillips and Sechzer 1989). The National Academy of Sciences (NAS) organized a meeting on alternatives in 1975 (NAS 1977), but the broader scientific community was not happy about the idea of alternatives, and there was much criticism of the Academy for providing a platform for "antivivisectionists" by organizing the meeting. In the late '70s, Seiling of United Action for Animals managed to persuade a New York congressman to introduce the Research Modernization Act, which called on the National Institutes of Health (NIH) to reallocate 30 to 50 percent of all money spent on animal research to "alternatives" (in the narrow sense of replacement, not the full Three Rs). The Act caught the imagination of the animal protection movement in spite of its vague language and lack of contact

with political realities. This public pressure then forced Congress to start to pay attention to alternatives.

The 1980s: Government and Industry Begin to Heed the Call

The growing pressure from the animal protection community for alternatives paid dividends in the '80s, as industry in Europe and America began to embrace the alternatives concept and governments played an increasingly important role (Table 4).

In 1983 Switzerland enacted a legislative requirement for consideration of alternatives and the government earmarked two million Swiss francs over two years for alternatives

research. Five years later the Swiss government established an office for animal experiments and alternatives.

In 1986 the Council of Environmental Ministers of the European Communities passed EEC Directive 86/609, which required member countries to develop enabling legislation promoting the Three Rs. The Animals (Scientific Procedures) Act of 1986, replacing the 1876 Cruelty to Animals Act, was passed in the United Kingdom. It required greater attention to the issue of animal suffering (refinement). Also in 1986 the Federal Republic of Germany enacted new laws on animal protection requiring consideration of alternatives in animal research. Three years later Germany established the Center for the Documentation and Evaluation of Alternative Methods to Animal Experiments, known by its German acronym ZEBET, which spearheaded several government initiatives to validate alternative tests. In the Netherlands government officials began collecting data on the extent of the suffering experienced by laboratory animals, and the Organization for Economic Cooperation and Development (OECD), driven by representatives from Europe, began to address the Three Rs in their guidelines for toxicity testing.

Worldwide, probably the most significant event in the '80s was the launching of campaigns in many of the developed countries against animal testing of cosmetics, toiletries, and household products. These campaigns built on the efforts and publications during the late '70s by scientists and organizations such as FRAME, which laid out the scientific challenges to the routine use of animals in toxicity testing (Balls et al. 1983; Zbinden and Flury-Roversi 1981). The main actor in the U.S. animal protection campaign was labor and civil rights activist Henry Spira, who turned his attention to animals after reading an article by Australian philosopher Peter Singer (1973). Spira contacted with activists in England (such as Jean Pink of Animal Aid, who had been targeting cosmetics testing since 1977), Europe, and Australia and helped to focus and coordinate protests against the eye irritancy testing (the Draize Test) of cosmetics worldwide.

In the United States, Spira's campaign built a coalition of four hundred animal protection organizations that targeted the use of the Draize Test by cosmetic companies in general and Revlon in particular. Within twelve months, the coalition's activities resulted in more than $1.75 million of funding for alternatives research. The Rockefeller University received $750,000 from Revlon to establish a laboratory for *in vitro* toxicological assay development, and the Johns Hopkins University Center for Alternatives to Animal Testing (CAAT) was established with $1 million from the Cosmetic, Toiletry, and Fragrance Association. Avon Products, Bristol-Myers Squibb, and other companies provided the bulk of the funds for CAAT and also provided funds for FRAME programs in the United Kingdom.

The effectiveness of Spira's campaign was based on several factors. First, he engaged in extensive preliminary planning and preparation. For example, Spira acquired numerous copies of the government Draize Test training film and slides (showing inflamed and damaged rabbit eyes) *before* the campaign started. (By late 1980 these materials were no longer being handed out for free by the government to anyone who asked.) Second, he did not shy away from the hard-nosed street politics he had learned in the labor and civil rights campaigns; he made skillful use of demonstrations and the media. Third, he was always willing to negotiate with the opposition and he avoided *ad hominem* attacks and insults. This earned him the respect of his opponents. Fourth, he engaged in a constant search for solutions in which everyone could feel he or she had won something. (Importantly, he did not boast to the media about victories over corporate targets.) When Revlon finally negotiated a settlement with Spira that set up the Rockefeller alternatives research program, Spira not only stopped his campaign, but he also praised Revlon for its innovative program and invited other cosmetic companies to take similarly progressive steps.

The Draize campaign initiated enormous changes in the field of alternatives in toxicity testing. From 1981 to 1991, there was a tremendous shift in attitude toward alternatives in toxicity testing within industry. Corporate toxicologists who had gone along with the initial grants for alternatives research in 1980 and 1981 because they felt such actions were necessary for public relations reasons, became excited by the technical and scientific challenge of alternatives by the end of the decade. Colgate-Palmolive began to fund research into the Chorio-Allantoic Membrane (CAM) test in 1982 (to the tune of $300,000) and within three years had set up an alternatives program in its in-house laboratories. Procter and Gamble and Bristol-Myers Squibb made the search for alternatives part of their corporate culture; they currently provide millions of dollars annually for intramural and extramural alternatives programs. Industrial *in vitro* toxicology associations have been started in both Europe and the United States, and several toxicology journals specializing in *in vitro* approaches were established in the late 1980s. For-profit companies that develop and market *in vitro* tests, such as the Clonetics Corporation and the National Testing Corporation, later known as In Vitro International, were established.

Despite all the interest, however, scientists were still cautious about relying too heavily on the new *in vitro* techniques. Toxicological risk evaluation is a difficult art, and the transformation of alternative methods from screening tools for preliminary decision-making to their use as replacements for whole animals did not begin to come to fruition until the 1990s. However, a widespread consensus emerged during the '80s that toxicology testing needed to move in a different direction. Thus, at CAAT's first symposium (in 1982), the participants mostly wondered *if* an alternative to the Draize Test could be found (Goldberg 1983), but within five years, participants at CAAT symposia were discussing *when* such an alternative would be available.

While similar developments were evident in Europe, there were large segments of scientists outside industry that resisted the concept of alternatives in the United States. In fact, important research institutions such as the NIH avoided use of the term "alternatives" whenever possible. For example, the Health Research Extension Act of 1985 required the NIH to establish an alternatives program, to which the NIH gave the awkward title "Biomedical Models and Materials Resources." A few years later, a Public Health Service draft document on animal welfare commented that "efforts have led to the discovery of research methods that are useful as 'adjuncts' to animal research, in that they complement animal models but rarely replace them. Thus, these adjuncts are not true 'alternatives'—even the use of this latter term can be misleading" (Public Health Service 1989).

A more balanced approach to the issue was evident in the U.S. Office of Technology Assessment's landmark report, "Alternatives to Animal Use in Research, Testing and Education," which was produced by a government office outside the orbit of the NIH and Public Heath Service. In fact, in drafting the Animal Welfare Act, Congress stipulated that the U.S. Department of Agriculture, and not the Public Health Service or its parent agency (the Department of Health, Education, and Welfare, as it was then known), oversee animal use in biomedical research.

The 1990s: Alternatives Begin to Be Validated and Accepted for Regulatory Use

If the 1970s were marked by an increase in interest in alternatives and the '80s by an increase in activity on this front, the 1990s was a period of maturation for the alternatives approach. The field already had a few academic centers, high-technology companies, and journals dedicated to the cause, as well as backing from national laws. What it needed was a better sense of when a new alternative test was qualified to replace an animal test; in other words, What constituted adequate "validation" (Goldberg 1987)? The field also needed more government-based centers not only to partner with industry and others in validating alternative tests, but perhaps more importantly, to give their stamp of approval to adequately validated tests, which would then

allow for regulatory acceptance.

In Europe both needs were addressed by the establishment in 1992 of the European Centre for the Validation of Alternative Methods (ECVAM), headed by Michael Balls of FRAME (Table 5). ECVAM took an active role in establishing validation criteria and in funding and managing validation programs for promising alternative methods, and it was the European Union's (EU) primary authority for approving alternative tests.

ECVAM's counterpart in the United States is the Interagency Coordinating Committee on the Validation of Alternative Methods (ICCVAM), established in 1994. ICCVAM was the successor to the informal Interagency Regulatory Alternatives Group and was an outgrowth of the NIH Revitalization Act of 1993. This legislation directed the National Institute of Environmental Health Sciences (NIEHS, one of the NIH institutes) to establish criteria for the validation and regulatory acceptance of alternative testing and to outline a process for regulatory review of potential alternative methods. To accomplish these tasks, the NIEHS asked the various federal regulatory and research-oriented agencies to appoint representatives to an ad hoc interagency committee to draft a report. The ICCVAM report, "Validation and Regulatory Acceptance of Toxicological Test Methods," was issued in 1997 (ICCVAM 1997). With ICCVAM's original mission accomplished, the participating federal agencies decided to change ICCVAM's status from an ad hoc entity to a standing committee to facilitate the ongoing regulatory review and acceptance of alternative methods. ICCVAM is staffed by employees who have other responsibilities to their parent agencies, so to facilitate ICCVAM's new role, the NIEHS established a support center, the National Toxicology Program Interagency Center for the Evaluation of Alternative Toxicological Methods (NICEATM) in 1998.

Several large-scale validation efforts were launched during the 1990s, and ECVAM played a role in many of these

through coordination, participation, or funding. The establishment of ECVAM and ICCVAM gave industry the confidence to invest in new tests and their validation, knowing that regulatory authorities were available to give advice on validation and acceptance criteria and foster the administrative process of regulatory acceptance. The efforts of ECVAM, ICCVAM, industry, and others began to bear fruit in the late 1990s. In 1998 ECVAM endorsed the 3T3 Neutral Red Uptake Phototoxicity Test for assessing phototoxicity and the Transepithelial Electrical Resistance Test and Episkin (and similar bioengineered skin constructs) for assessing skin corrosivity. The same year ECVAM also endorsed *in vitro* methods as alternatives to the ascites (mouse-based) method for producing monoclonal antibodies. The following year, ICCVAM recommended Corrositex® for assessing skin corrosivity and the Local Lymph Node Assay (a reduction and refinement alternative) for assessing allergic contact dermatitis. ICCVAM's recommendations are not binding on the individual regulatory agencies (for example, the Food and Drug Administration), but may be accepted (or not) according to agency needs; so far the agencies have acted favorably on ICCVAM's recommendations.

In addition to ICCVAM and ECVAM, the OECD has emerged as a significant authority in the acceptance of alternative methods. The OECD, an international organization that facilitates trade, formally accepted the Fixed Dose Procedure (in 1991), the Acute Toxic Class Method (1993), and the Up and Down Method (1997) as reduction alternatives to the LD50 Test for acute toxicity (the Fixed Dose Procedure is also a refinement alternative). In 1996 the OECD hosted a workshop to develop internationally harmonized criteria for the validation and regulatory acceptance of alternative methods (OECD 1996).

The "internationalization" of the alternatives field has also been aided by the establishment of the triennial World Congress on Alternatives and

Table 5
Alternatives Chronology: 1990–1999

1990 CAAT and ERGATT hold a workshop on validation of alternative methods.

The University of California Alternatives Center is established at UC–Davis.

The Platform for Alternatives to Animal Experiments in the Netherlands allocates the equivalent of $700,000 annually for the promotion and validation of research into the Three Rs and the improvement of housing and care systems.

The HSUS establishes the Russell and Burch Award for scientists who have made outstanding contributions to alternative methods.

The Japanese Society for Alternatives to Animal Experimentation begins publishing the journal AATEX (Alternatives to Animal Testing and Experimentation).

1991 The Interagency Regulatory Alternatives Group holds a workshop, "Eye Irritation Testing Alternatives: Proposals for Regulatory Consensus," in Washington, D.C.

The HSUS presents Alan Goldberg, director of CAAT, with the first Russell and Burch Award.

The OECD accepts the Fixed Dose Procedure as an alternative to the LD50 Test.

Representatives of regulatory agencies in Japan, Europe, and the United States agree to drop the classic LD50 Test as a required measure of acute toxicity.

The UK Home Office announces a grant program for the funding of alternatives research.

The Second Report of the FRAME Toxicity Committee is published in *ATLA*.

The Swiss Institute for Alternatives to Animal Testing (SIAT) is established in Zurich.

1992 The European Centre for the Validation of Alternative Methods (ECVAM) is established.

The European Parliament amends the Cosmetic Directive 76/768 to ban the marketing of cosmetics tested on animals after January 1, 1998 (a decision on the ban is later postponed until June 30, 2000).

CAAT hosts a tenth anniversary conference in Baltimore, Md., giving Founders' Awards to Dr. D.A. Henderson, the CTFA, and Henry Spira.

1993 The NIH Revitalization Act of 1993 directs the NIEHS to establish criteria for the validation and regulatory acceptance of alternative testing and to outline a process for regulatory review of potential alternative methods; it also directs the NIH director to establish an alternatives program and to report on its progress annually.

The first World Congress on Alternatives and Animal Use in the Life Sciences: Education, Research, and Testing, takes place in Baltimore.

Member states of the European Union agree on the goal that everything possible should be done to achieve a reduction of 50 percent in the use of vertebrate animals for experimentation and other scientific purposes by the year 2000.

The Interagency Regulatory Alternatives Group holds its second meeting on alternatives, in Washington, D.C.

Dr. Michael Balls of FRAME is appointed director of ECVAM.

1994 The U.S. federal government establishes the Interagency Coordinating Committee on the Validation of Alternative Methods (ICCVAM), co-chaired by William Stokes of NIEHS and Richard Hill of EPA, in response to the 1993 NIH Revitalization Act.

The Netherlands Centre for Alternatives to Animal Use (NCA) is established as a national information center on alternatives.

1995 The Gillette Company and The HSUS launch a program to fund research and development of alternative methods; two grants of $50,000 each are awarded annually.

1996 The second World Congress on Alternatives and Animal Use in the Life Sciences is held in Utrecht, the Netherlands.

The OECD holds a workshop to develop internationally harmonized criteria on validation and regulatory acceptance.

CAAT, The HSUS, Procter and Gamble, and other organizations establish Altweb, a website devoted to information on alternative methods.

1997 ICCVAM issues guidelines on criteria for validation and regulatory acceptance of alternative methods.

The Institute for In Vitro Sciences is established in Gaithersburg, Md.

(continued on next page)

continued from previous page

Table 5
Alternatives Chronology: 1990–1999

1998	The HSUS presents the FDA's Neil Wilcox and ICCVAM's William Stokes with the Russell and Burch award for their contribution to the development of alternatives. ECVAM accepts the following alternative methods: 3T3 NRU PT test as an alternative for assessing phototoxicity, Episkin and similar methods for assessing skin corrosivity, and TER (transepithelial electrical resistance) test for assessing skin corrosivity. ECVAM endorses *in vitro* methods as alternatives to the ascites method for the production of monoclonal antibodies. The National Toxicology Program Interagency Center for the Evaluation of Alternative Toxicological Methods (NICEATM) is established to provide support to ICCVAM.
1999	The third World Congress on Alternatives and Animal Use in the Life Sciences is held in Bologna, Italy. The HSUS presents Procter and Gamble scientist Dr. Katherine Stitzel with the Russell and Burch award for her contribution to the development of alternatives. CAAT holds TestSmart (a humane and efficient approach to regulatory toxicity data) workshops in order to discuss alternatives to animal testing in the Environmental Protection Agency's High Production Volume (HPV) chemical testing program. The EPA announces major changes in its HPV program, including funding for alternative methods, following the TestSmart workshops and negotiations with animal protection organizations. ICCVAM endorses Corrositex® for the assessment of skin corrosivity and the Murine Local Lymph Node Assay for the assessment of allergic contact dermatitis.

Animal Use in the Life Sciences, the first of which was held in Baltimore in 1993 (Goldberg and van Zutphen 1995); the second in Utrecht, the Netherlands, in 1996 (van Zutphen and Balls 1997); and the third in Bologna, Italy, in 1999. The international exchange of information on alternatives was also given a boost in 1996 with the establishment of Altweb, an Internet web site spearheaded by CAAT, Procter and Gamble, The HSUS, and others.

Political pressure played a significant role in moving the alternatives issue during the 1990s, more directly in Europe than in the United States. The issue had some momentum of its own, but outside pressure spurred progress. In Europe, for example, the European Parliament amended the Cosmetic Directive 76/768 to ban the marketing of cosmetics tested on animals after January 1, 1998, regardless of whether such testing was conducted in Europe. Although a decision on the marketing ban was later postponed until June 30, 2000, the Cosmetic Directive amendment led to the formation of ECVAM and encouraged research and development of alternatives by the European cosmetics trade association (COLIPA) and others. The marketing ban would have affected companies in the United States as well as in Europe, so the amendment also kept some political pressure focused on the issue in the United States.

Since the most recent postponement of the marketing ban, a new amendment (the seventh) has been proposed. It calls for: (1) a ban on animal testing of finished products in the European Union as soon as the directive comes into force, (2) a ban on animal testing of cosmetic ingredients where alternatives are available, and (3) a complete ban on animal testing of cosmetic ingredients within three years of implementation of the directive, regardless of the availability of alternatives. The European Commission has stated that only one two-year postponement of the ingredients-testing ban would be considered. Consequently, an absolute ban on ingredients testing could become effective within five years of implementation of the directive. Finally, the directive states that a marketing ban, which would have affected countries outside of the European Union, will not occur due to potential problems with World Trade Organization rules; this effectively "kills" the proposed sixth amendment.

Alternatives legislation in the United States in the 1990s was largely a cooperative venture between industry and animal protection. The alternatives language in the NIH Revitalization Act of 1993, which led to the creation of ICCVAM, was the product of efforts of several industry and animal protection representatives working with Rep. Henry Waxman. A similar coalition led to the introduction of the ICCVAM Authorization Act in the Senate (1999) and House (2000) in an effort to strengthen ICCVAM and make it a permanent entity. As of October 2000, this legislation was pending.

Discussion

Many animal protectionists are frustrated with the pace at which the use of animals in research and testing is being replaced, reduced, and refined. However, the growth of the alterna-

Abbreviations

ATLA	Alternatives to Laboratory Animals
CAAT	Center for Alternatives to Animal Testing
CAM	Chorio-Allantoic Membrane
ERGATT	European Research Group into Alternatives in Toxicity Testing
FRAME	Fund for the Replacement of Animals in Medical Experiments
HPLC	High Pressure Liquid Chromatography
IACUC	Institutional Animal Care and Use Committee
NAS	National Academy of Sciences (USA)
NAVS	National Anti-Vivisection Society (UK)
NIH	National Institutes of Health (USA)
OECD	Organization for Economic Cooperation and Development
UFAW	Universities Federation for Animal Welfare
ZEBET	Zentralstelle zur Erfassung und Bewertung von Ergänzungs und Ersatzmethoden zum Tierversuch

tives field since the publication of Russell and Burch's seminal book in 1959 has been remarkable, especially considering that the animal protection community itself did not embrace the alternatives issue in a significant way until the late 1970s. During the 1980s cosmetics and consumer products companies began investing millions of dollars into research and development of alternatives, national governments incorporated the alternatives approach into their animal protection legislation and, in some cases, began funding research and development of alterna-

tives, some companies began developing and marketing alternative test kits, academic centers devoted to the issue began to be established, and the field of *in vitro* toxicology blossomed. During the 1990s government centers devoted to the validation and regulatory acceptance of alternative methods were established in Europe and the United States, the triennial World Congresses on Alternatives began, and alternative tests began to be formally approved and accepted by regulatory agencies.

Have these developments translated into a decrease in the use of laboratory animals and in their levels of pain and distress? Most countries that keep records on the use of research animals report a fall in laboratory animal numbers during the 1980s and 1990s, in some cases a dramatic fall (Rowan et al. 1995). The statistics from the United Kingdom show a decline in annual animal use from around 5.5 million in 1976 to 2.7 million in 1998. Sir Peter Medawar, who predicted in 1969 that such a decline would begin in 1979 or even earlier (Medawar 1972), was obviously more far-sighted than the Littlewood Committee, which reported in 1965 that animal use would not be influenced by the development of new (alternative) technology.

However, a key question is this: How much of the decline in research animal use in the United Kingdom and in other countries has resulted from pressure to develop and use alternative methods? The available data is not adequate to provide an unequivocal answer. While other factors such as the cost of research animals and the increased sensitivity and specificity of new techniques have no doubt been important, it is also likely that pressure from animal groups (and progressive scientists) calling for the development and use of "alternative" techniques has played a role in reducing animal use. Animal protectionists certainly increased awareness of the Three Rs and humane issues within the scientific community.

Technical developments over the past thirty years have, for example,

reduced the demand for animals in the production and testing of polio vaccine and insulin (Hendriksen 1988; Trethewey 1989). Hendriksen describes how the number of monkeys used in the production and testing of polio vaccine in the Netherlands was reduced from 4,570 in 1965 to 30 in 1984 by a series of technical improvements, even though the actual amount of polio vaccine produced was about the same in the two years. The technical improvements were the result of advances in molecular techniques and cell culture biology.

Trethewey describes a similar process in insulin testing that reduced the demand for mice by 95 percent between 1970 and 1986. The major technical advance was the introduction of a mouse blood glucose test in place of the mouse convulsion test. This relatively nonstressful assay permitted the re-use of the same mouse for more than one assay leading to a further reduction in the number of animals required. High Pressure Liquid Chromatography (HPLC) techniques have been developed and introduced, and it is now possible to standardize insulin preparations using only a handful of mice to ensure that each batch is biologically active. A life-time supply of insulin for one diabetic now requires testing on the equivalent of only a single mouse and it is possible that mice will be eliminated altogether as further technical advances are made.

Innovations in toxicity testing and the standardization of therapeutics such as insulin have reduced the demand for animals in some procedures. However, the most significant reductions have come in the search for new drugs. As pharmaceutical companies have switched from animal to *in vitro* screens for agents with potential therapeutic activity, they have recorded dramatic decreases in animal use. Hoffman–La Roche, for example, reduced its annual animal use from one million to about 300,000 without changing the number of new drug entities under investigation (Anonymous 1990). A switch by the National Cancer Institute from a mouse screen for potential anti-cancer agents to human cancer cell culture screens has resulted in a saving of several million mice per year (Rowan and Andrutis 1990).

Russell (1995) attributes the development of replacement technology, and the consequent decreases in laboratory animal use, to the waning influence of what he and Burch (1959) called the "high fidelity" fallacy—that models had to look like the organism being modeled, no matter what the power of the model to "discriminate" or elucidate the process under study. Thus mammals such as mice, dogs, and primates have historically been preferred as models of humans because they have high fidelity to humans, not necessarily because they have high discrimination. The high fidelity fallacy has lost its currency as the power of low fidelity–high discrimination techniques, such as tissue culture and use of invertebrate species (for example, *C. elegans*) has been demonstrated.

The impact of refinements on animal pain and distress is even harder to gauge than the impact of replacements and reductions on animal numbers. While animal numbers declined during the 1980s and 1990s, increasing attention was being paid to the neglected "R"—refinement—thanks in part to new legislation in Europe and the United States. In the United Kingdom, the passage of the 1986 Scientific Procedures (Animals) Act focused more attention on animal distress and led to a virtual doubling (from 21 percent to 36 percent of all procedures) in the rate of anesthetic use in animal research in six years (Anonymous 1990). In the United States, protocol review by Institutional Animal Care and Use Committees is increasingly focusing on reducing animal pain and distress.

Two technical advances that will significantly decrease pain and distress in laboratory animals are non-invasive imaging and telemetric approaches to animal data (Stokstad 1999). These approaches not only reduce or eliminate pain and distress, they also allow for a 75 to 80 percent

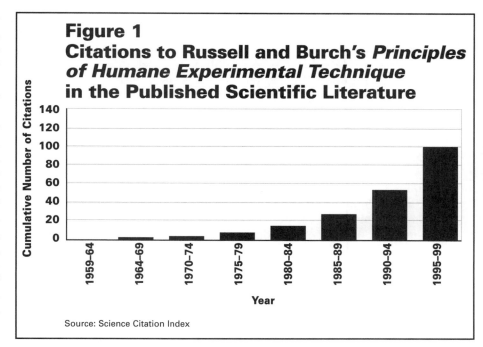

Figure 1
Citations to Russell and Burch's *Principles of Humane Experimental Technique* in the Published Scientific Literature

Source: Science Citation Index

reduction in animal numbers by increasing the reliability of the data and improving experimental design.

One of the major challenges in making further progress in alternative methods is the indifference, if not the antagonism, to the alternatives approach on the part of many academic researchers worldwide. While the NIH no longer automatically characterizes alternatives as mere "adjuncts" of animal research, and the NIEHS actively promotes alternative methods, some biomedical research advocates have argued that use of the term "alternatives" implies that one needs to apologize for using animals in research and that this gives the public the wrong impression (Goodwin 1992). While such hostility to the alternatives approach is abating, the field of alternatives would progress much faster if academic researchers were more sympathetic to the approach.

Another challenge in implementing alternatives and in decreasing animal use is the growth of genetic engineering, particularly in mice. The NIH's in-house use of mice reached a low of about 300,000 in 1991 but has more than doubled since then, according to NIH Annual Reports and NIH Reports to the USDA. Genetic engineering can sometimes be harnessed to

reduce (and refine) animal use (Gordon 1991). It can also be argued that the increasing numbers of genetically engineered mice are at least somewhat offset by a corresponding decrease in the use of other mice or species, thereby nullifying any increase in overall numbers. This seems to be what is happening in the United Kingdom, where the use of genetically modified mice has gone up tenfold, to around 500,000, but total mouse use has fallen slightly. At the very least, the impact of genetic engineering on animal use should be carefully monitored, given its potential to reverse the decreases in animal use seen during the 1980s and 1990s.

Conclusion

The program that UFAW set in motion in 1954 has born significant fruit. Although Major Hume would no doubt be surprised at the scope and potential of biomedical science today, he would be pleased at the growing recognition accorded to Russell and Burch (1959). The number of citations to Russell and Burch's book in the scientific literature increased dramatically during the 1980s and, especially, the 1990s (Figure 1).

In 1959 Hume spoke to an Animal Care Panel meeting in Washington, D.C.:

A more recent event has been the publication of a remarkable book by Russell and Burch entitled *The Principles of Humane Experimental Technique*. This deserves to become a classic for all time, and we have great hopes that it will inaugurate a new field of systematic study. We hope that others will follow up the lead it has given, and that a generalized study of humane technique, as a systematic component of the methodology of research, will come to be considered essential to the training of a biologist (Hume 1962).

This has indeed come to pass in the Netherlands and other parts of Europe (van Zutphen, Baumans, and Beynen 1993), and we are hopeful that the Three Rs will become fully incorporated into the training of biologists in the United States.

Literature Cited

Anonymous. 1957. *Laboratory animals bureau collected papers,* Vol. 6. Hampstead, London: Laboratory Animals Bureau.

Anonymous. 1959. Review of the principles of humane experimental technique. *Veterinary Record* 71: 650.

Anonymous. 1960. Review of the principles of humane experimental technique. *The Lancet* i: 34.

Anonymous. 1962. *Animals in research.* Washington, D.C.: The Humane Society of the United States.

Anonymous. 1971. Antivivisection rides again. *Journal of the American Medical Association* 217: 70.

Anonymous. 1990. Statistics on the Three R's. *The Alternatives Report* 2(2): 1–5.

Balls, M., R.J. Riddell, and A.N. Worden, eds. 1983. *Animals and alternatives in toxicity testing.* London: Academic Press.

French, R.D. 1975. *Antivivisection and medical science in Victorian society.* Princeton, N.J.: Princeton University Press.

Goldberg, A.M., ed. 1983. *Product safety evaluation: Alternative methods in toxicology,* Vol. 1. New York: Mary Ann Liebert.

—————. 1987. *In vitro approaches to validation: Alternative methods in toxicology,* Vol. 5. New York: Mary Ann Liebert.

Goldberg, A.M., and L.F.M. van Zutphen, eds. 1995. *The World Congress on alternatives and animal use in the life sciences: Education, research, testing.* New York: Mary Ann Liebert.

Goodwin, F.K. 1992. Animal research, animal rights and public health. *Conquest, the Journal of the Research Defence Society* 181: 1–10.

Gordon, J. 1991. Viewpoint: Transgenic animals as "alternatives" to animal use. *CAAT [Center for Alternatives to Animal Testing]* Newsletter 9 (#2): 8. See *http://caat.jhsph.edu.*

Hendriksen, C.F.M. 1988. *Laboratory animals in vaccine production and control.* Dordrecht, the Netherlands: Kluwer Academic Publishers.

Hume, C.W. 1962. The vivisection controversy in Britain. In *Man and beast,* ed. C.W. Hume. Potters Bar, U.K.: Universities Federation for Animal Welfare.

Interagency Coordinating Committee on the Validation of Alternative Methods. 1997. *Validation and regulatory acceptance of toxicological test methods.* Research Triangle Park, N.C.: National Institute of Environmental Health Science.

LaPage, G. 1960. *Achievement: Some contributions of animal experiments to the conquest of disease.* Cambridge, U.K.: W. Heffer & Sons.

Littlewood Committee. 1965. *Report of the departmental committee on experiments in animals.* London: Her Majesty's Stationery Office.

Manuel, D. 1987. Marshall Hall (1770–1857): Vivisection and the development of experimental physiology. In *Vivisection in historical perspective,* ed. N.A. Rupke. London: Croom Helm.

Medawar, P.B. 1972. *The hope of progress.* London: Methuen.

National Academy of Sciences (NAS). 1977. *The future of animals, cells, models and systems in research, development, education and testing.* Washington, D.C.: NAS.

Office of Technology Assessment. 1986. *Alternatives to animal use in research, testing, and education.* Washington, D.C.: U.S. Government Printing Office.

Organization for Economic Cooperation and Development (OECD). 1996. *Final report of the OECD workshop on harmonization of validation and acceptance criteria for alternative toxicological test methods.* Paris: OECD.

Phillips, M.T., and J.A. Sechzer. 1989. *Animal research and ethical conflict: An analysis of the scientific literature, 1966–1986.* Berlin: Springer Verlag.

Public Health Service. 1989. *Final report of the Public Health Service Animal Welfare Working Group, Phase I.* Washington, D.C.: Department of Health and Human Services.

Rowan, A.N. 1979. *Alternatives to laboratory animals: Definition and discussion.* Washington, D.C.: The Humane Society of the United States.

—————. 1989. The development of the animal protection movement. *Journal of NIH Research* 1(Nov/ Dec): 97–100.

—————. 1994. Looking back thirty-three years to Russell and Burch: The development of the concept of the Three Rs (alternatives). In *Alternatives to animal testing: New ways in the biomedical sciences, trends and progress,* ed. C.A. Reinhardt. New York: VCH.

—————. 1995. Replacement alternatives and the concept of alternatives. In *The World Congress on alternatives and animal use in the life sciences: Education, research, testing,* eds. A.M. Goldberg and L.F.M. van Zutphen. New York: Mary Ann Liebert.

Rowan, A.N., and K.A. Andrutis. 1990. NCI's developmental therapeutics program. *The Alternatives Report* 2(3): 1, 3.

Rowan, A.N., F.M. Loew, and J.C. Weer. 1995. *The animal research controversy: Protest, process, and public policy—An analysis of strategic issues*. Grafton, Mass.: Tufts University School of Veterinary Medicine.

Russell, W.M.S. 1957. The increase of humanity in experimentation: Replacement, reduction and refinement. Laboratory Animals Bureau, *Collected Papers* 6: 23–26.

——————. 1995. The development of the Three Rs concept. *ATLA* 23: 298–304.

Russell, W.M.S., and R.L. Burch. 1959. *The principles of humane experimental technique*. London: Methuen.

Singer, P. 1973. Review of *Animals, men and morals*, eds. S. Godlovitch, R. Godlovitch, and J. Harris. *The New York Review of Books*, April 5, 1973.

Stokstad, E. 1999. Humane science finds sharper and kinder tools. *Science* 286 (Nov. 5): 1068–71.

Trethewey, J. 1989. The development of insulin assays without the use of animals. In *In vitro toxicology—new directions: Alternative methods in toxicology*, Vol. 7. New York: Mary Ann Liebert.

Turner, J. 1980. *Reckoning with the beast: Animals, pain and humanity in the Victorian mind*. Baltimore, Md.: Johns Hopkins University Press.

U.S. Congress. 1962. *Hearings before a subcommittee of the Committee on Interstate and Foreign Commerce; House of Representatives, 87th Congress on H.R. 1937 and H.R. 3556, September 28 and 29*. Washington, D.C.: U.S. Government Printing Office.

van Zutphen, L.F.M., and M. Balls, eds. 1997. Animal alternatives, welfare and ethics: Proceedings of the Second World Congress on Alternatives and Animal Use in the Life Sciences, Utrecht, the Netherlands, 20–24 October 1996. New York: Elsevier.

van Zutphen, L.F.M., V. Baumans, and A.C. Beynen, eds. 1993. *Principles of laboratory animal science*. Amsterdam: Elsevier.

Weatherall, M. 1959. Review of the principles of humane experimental technique. *Nature* 184: 1675–76.

Worden, A.N., ed. 1947. *The UFAW handbook on the care and management of laboratory animals*. London: Bailliere, Tindall, and Cox.

Zbinden, G., and M. Flury-Roversi. 1981. Significance of the LD50 test for the toxicological evaluation of chemical substances. *Archives of Toxicology* 47: 77–99.

Is There a Place in the World for Zoos?

9

CHAPTER

David Hancocks

We human animals make rapid technological and cultural advancements because we have the ability to pass definitive information to succeeding generations. But we also accept too much from the past without challenge. The good, the bad, and the indifferent are muddled together, accumulating in layers that smother each succeeding age. Cultural mores ranging from the silly to the profane, from charming to dangerous, clutter our world. They exist only because, as the British are wont to say, "We have always done things this way." One very troubling example is the public zoological parks found in almost every city: they are fundamentally unchanged from the first public zoo that opened in The Regent's Park in London in 1828. Although significant modifications have taken place since then, particularly recently, for the most part, zoos continue to do things the way they have done them for almost two centuries. An objective reevaluation is long overdue.

One improvement that has taken place is that an accredited, professionally operated modern zoo is no longer likely to present animals to the public in rows of tiny, barred cages. Such zoos now display animals in simulated natural habitats. Modern veterinary medicine, too, has brought enormous benefits to zoo animals.

Preventive medicine and overall health care are now usually at very competent and professional levels of expertise. The zoo animals of today receive fresh and wholesome food in contrast to their predecessors, and their diets are carefully researched and evaluated. Zoo education programs reach millions of students each year. Keeper staffs are highly trained, knowledgeable, and dedicated.

When examined from the point of view of the visitor or the staff, in fact, conditions in today's accredited zoos are far better than those of yesteryear. But an examination from the animals' point of view reveals that many of the problems of nineteenth-century menageries remain, inexcusably, in common practice.

If you examine the daily routine of a chimpanzee, lion, tiger, bear, or any other typical zoo animal, you will not find it unusual for animals in even the best zoos to spend the far greater part of each twenty-four-hour day locked in holding cages, "off display." Far too commonly, these cages are almost exact replicas of the old menagerie cages that were viewed by zoo visitors, the only difference is that the cages are out of public sight. Night cages for zoo animals are invariably noisy, harsh, barred cubicles, lit by cold fluorescent tubes, with no attention given to acoustic comfort, soft lighting, or any behavioral or psycho-

logical needs of the inhabitants. Their only function, like the old menagerie cages, is secure containment. Everything in them is fixed and hard, immovable, never changing, and largely unusable by the animals.

The public display areas may be luxuriantly green in the best of the new zoos, but behind the scenes the nineteenth century still exists. Even worse, all too often the supposedly naturalistic display areas of the modern zoo are, as far as the animals are concerned, of even less functional value than were iron-barred menagerie cages. At least they had bars to climb on and swing from! Today electric wires and hidden moats all too often keep the animals away from the lush vegetation of the new habitat exhibits. Appearances to the contrary, the animals on display may have nothing but a small area to sit in all day and nothing natural with which to interact. Trees and shrubs that appear to be an integral part of the animals' habitat are likely to be untouchable.

To add insult to injury, it is not unusual for the "natural habitat" to be composed of nothing but concrete and plastic. Some zoos and their designers boast of their skill in creating scenes that closely mimic the appearance of natural habitats by using entirely artificial components and materials. This public face of the new zoo may convince the visitors and their video-camera view of the authenticity of the scene, but a "tree" made of epoxy resin or a "mud wallow" made of concrete is of no more use to a wild animal than is a plastic beach ball.

These shortcomings are especially evident in many of the "rainforest" exhibits that have mushroomed in American zoos in recent years. Unlike real rainforests, which are hushed, dark, daunting, and contemplative environments, zoo rainforest exhibits are invariably bright, colorful, and full of noise—more like a suburban garden center than the somber splendor of the Amazon. They are usually filled to overcrowding with the most colorful and noisy species, since quantity has always counted when it comes to zoo species, and zoos have never been able to resist the flashy and the cute. The mistaken impression left in zoo visitors' minds is that rainforests are crammed with chattering monkeys and boldly colored birds. Botanical gardens fall prey to the same trap, preferring to present the grotesque and unusual rather than a true picture of nature.

The sense of awe inspired by the all-embracing quietude of the tropical forest is replaced by a gaudy, oversimplified spectacle. Overhead there is no closed green canopy, only the steel and concrete slabs of a glass roof. It is a kindergarten view of the natural world: to your right is the café, on your left is the public restroom, and ahead of you is the gift shop.

Animals as Jewels

Zoos have always had one overriding concern—that their animals must always be on view and easily seen. The general curator at the Bronx Zoo describes a recent instance in which he was consulted on the design of a new jaguar exhibit at an unspecified but "well known zoological park" (Seidensticker and Doherty 1996). The designers wanted to create the effect of a jaguar lying on a log in the sun at the edge of a tropical river

backwater. They had allocated less than 300 square feet for this tableau and were insistent that not only was more space not available, but it was also unnecessary.

This type of problem is found in zoos worldwide. It stems from a lack of awareness that zoo animals are living creatures and an apparent inability to place the animal's needs—psychological and behavioral, as well as physiological—at the top of the list of design criteria. This myopia is typically exacerbated in zoo rainforest exhibits: their extremely high construction costs result in minimal space to the animals. Thus, zoo rainforest exhibits can virtually guarantee that both the quantity and the quality of space allocated to the animals are inadequate. Kept in tiny spaces with no access to any natural vegetation, animals have to learn to live with plastic. In the worst examples, such as Omaha Zoo's Lied Jungle building, many animals spend their entire lives in cramped, completely artificial environments and never have contact with anything natural. The general design approach is closer to that used in store window displays, with the animals perched like jewels in the spotlight, dimensions calculated to the inch, than to habitats for living animals. No space is wasted, unless you take the philosophical position that the entire space is wasted, since these multi-million-dollar extravaganzas typically claim little authenticity and provide minimal educational value.

The attitude that a zoo animal is merely an object for display is disquietingly prevalent in many zoos, but fortunately there are some exceptions. When Zoo Atlanta built a large exhibition habitat for gorillas in the late 1980s, it included several big trees in the animal areas. The designers were aghast when the gorillas began to inflict heavy damage on these trees and asked the zoo director, Terry Maple, to install electric wires to protect them. His response was, "Plant cheaper trees!" (Croke 1997). There are other refreshing signs, particularly of a new trend in zoo employees. Zoo keepers, in particular, are

these days likely to be well educated, well trained, and dedicated to the well being of the animals in their care. Many of the younger zoo directors, too, bring compassion and powerful intellects to their profession. What is generally lacking within the profession, however, is an eagerness to look for fundamental changes to the whole zoo concept. Few recognize that a complete reexamination of zoos is necessary: there are too few zoo heretics.

The most urgent and fundamental change needed for the new millennium is for zoos to recognize that they do not need to focus exclusively on animals, particularly on those species traditionally kept in zoos. If we compare the zoo collections of today with those of one hundred years ago, we find the same distorted emphasis on big, colorful, and charismatic species. The richness and the complexity of nature is completely overshadowed by this obsession to an astonishing degree. About 1,640 of the 30 million species of animals on the planet are mammals. The average American zoo contains 53 of these known mammalian species, a ratio of 1:31. For birds, the ratio is 1:98; for reptiles, 1:104. Amphibians are represented in the average American zoo at a ratio of only 1:2,000. For invertebrates it drops to one in several millions (Boyd 1997). Zoos present an upside down view of the animal world. More than 95 percent of all species are small enough to fit in the cup of your hand and are completely unknown in zoos.

This is particularly galling, since invertebrates, especially, typically have more biological mass than any other species in a natural habitat, and thus greater biological importance and influence. As Harvard biologist E. O. Wilson has suggested, we need to better demonstrate that in many critical ways it is often the little critters that run this world. Zoos are missing a golden opportunity to do so.

The persistent dedication of zoos to a very small segment of the animal world raises the question of why zoos should limit themselves to the field of zoology. That restriction is after all completely anti-natural. The Victorian zoo visitors were most suitably impressed to see the new scientific tool of taxonomy made clear to them through the invention of the public zoo that put all the primates together in one building, all the parrots in another, all the hoofed beasts over there, the bears over there. That they could go to the zoo to see wild animals, and try to make comparisons between the different orders, was sufficiently edifying for the day. But nature does not function in tidy packages of separated scientific disciplines, and although it is of value to study the natural world in distinct related components, there is no virtue in presenting it to the general public in such a manner. We need natural history institutions that can reveal the connectedness, not the separateness, of the natural world. Zoos must metamorphose (Hancocks 1996). Instead of restricting themselves to displaying wild animals, they must become places that celebrate nature in its entirety. For this, zoos must first appreciate that it is impossible to tell the critically important stories of nature with exhibits that represent only a very small fragment of the cast of characters. Complex interdependencies between plants and animals that have evolved over millions of years, for example, are becoming increasingly vulnerable, because of pesticide use, habitat loss, and decreasing diversity. Zoology exhibits alone cannot reveal the reasons for and the ramifications of this story, nor can solely botanical displays. We need "zoos" that focus on biology, on ecology, and on nature.

Our general level of understanding of nature is declining precipitously as people become ever more separated from the natural world and more reliant upon a technological and domesticated environment. Children speed along the information superhighway instead of walking along country lanes. They browse the World Wide Web rather than observe a spider spin. They are exposed more to rap than to bird song and spend more time in shopping malls than in mead-

ows. This is why we need partnerships among zoos, botanical gardens, arboretums, natural history and geology museums, aquariums, science centers, even libraries and art galleries. With shared programs or connected thematic exhibits, our cultural, scientific, and natural history institutions could collectively engage a public debate about new ways to look at nature and about sound ecological practices, and they could devise many different ways to promote conservation. People are hungry for this information.

Most of all, we need to rekindle a love for all wildlife, and a respect that goes beyond the aesthetics of the television documentary or the IMAX spectacular. To this end we also need zoos to desist from perpetuating the image that only the cute and the cuddly animals are worthy of our concern. Furry mammals elicit far more support for our affections than "slimy" snakes or "warty" toads, and we seem to be instinctively fascinated with what we perceive as the bizarre and the peculiar, such as albino tigers or oversized specimens. Zoos have the ability and the opportunity to dispel myths and to help people realise that "ugliness" in the animal world is nothing more than a product of our cultural bias.

We have an innate affinity for and a deeply embedded fascination with animals. E. O. Wilson has coined the term "biophilia" to describe this phenomenon (Kellert and Wilson 1993). This attachment reveals itself in both beneficial and harmful ways. Animals that reflect human infantile features, such as large heads and big eyes, are especially popular for zoo displays. (The giant panda is the classic example.) Appeals to the public to help save the tiger, or the koala, or some other charismatic creature fall easily upon sympathetic ears. Zoos can quite easily find people to champion their pretty, or cute, or spectacular animals. Conversely, they can always draw a crowd with spiders and snakes because the public finds these species repulsive. The fascination does not seem to extend to concerns about their welfare or survival, however. It would be a most useful challenge for

zoos to try to change the public's thinking on both fronts.

If people are to accept responsibility for the enormous damage that humankind has inflicted on wildlife, they must learn to act and think like good custodians of the earth. Objective, carefully considered, and extraordinarily difficult decisions will have to be made about the conservation of wild animals and their wild habitats. How much? Where? When? At what cost? For the specific benefit of which species or ecosystems? Such judgments will tax new generations for decades, even centuries, to come. Zoos can, if they will accept the challenge, be an effective medium for helping people to consider such questions.

The western mind learned to make sense of the apparent chaos of nature by dissecting it and sorting its component parts into degrees of relatedness. In doing so we lost the holistic view, in which, in the words of John Muir, "everything is hitched to everything else."

Hediger's Philosophies

Our urgent need for institutions that reveal the complexities and the connections within nature in no way diminishes zoos' responsibilities to the animals in their care. The standards of a zoo's animal care should be above reproach. It's as simple as that. Ironically, if the typical zoo would shift away from big mammals and focus instead on smaller species, it could find that its abilities to meet its inmates' requirements would be greatly enhanced. It is easier to satisfy the needs of a group of meerkats than a herd of elephants or of a beetle than an orangutan.

Large, social, strong, intelligent animals with a high level of awareness place very great demands upon their caregivers. This is not to suggest that the husbandry for small animals or for creatures such as reptiles and amphibians is in any way facile, nor does it imply that such animals do not have their own very specific and sometimes elaborate psychological and social requirements. But there is a more acute sense of failure in not meeting the needs of a more highly perceptive animal. One is not making value judgments when one acknowledges that a dog or an elephant or a baboon demands more work than does a beetle or a starfish.

These complex needs have too rarely been considered in zoos. There are far too many instances of misery and deprivation in these public institutions. Seldom are these the product of any deliberate callousness or sadism. Much more likely is a situation like that of the gorillas at Zoo Atlanta, who were going to be deprived of contact with live trees because they were inflicting damage upon them. When Maple called for "cheaper trees" he may simply have been espousing a natural affinity for the needs of these apes, but it is probably not coincidental that he is also a disciple of Heini Hediger.

In 1950 Hediger, director of the Basel Zoo in Switzerland, published *Wild Animals in Captivity*. If more zoo professionals had embraced Hediger's teachings and philosophies, much of the suffering and inadequacies of care endured by thousands of zoo animals over the past fifty years could have been avoided. Hediger believed that zoo environments should be managed in such a way that critical aspects of the animals' lives mirror as closely as possible those of their wild conspecifics. He advocated an ethological approach to zoo management. Hediger was not particularly concerned with how a zoo exhibit looked to the public, at least in terms of whether or not it looked "natural," but he was adamant that it should duplicate the animal's spatial, social, and environmental needs and challenges. He argued the need for recognizing animal territories, and flight distances, in the zoo, and he strongly advocated occupational therapy, based upon natural behaviors, to relieve the omnipresent boredom of zoo animals. He spoke eloquently of the need for considering the animal as a whole being, a *living* being, drawing a parallel between the standard zoo enclosures of the time and the cabinet displays of a natural history museum: "The death chambers of the menagerie were, in a way, the ante-rooms of the museums… the animal in its narrow cage was provided with food, the stuffed one with preservative."

Zoo managers were offered much practical advice in Hediger's writings, all based upon the principle of using nature as the norm. He described everything from types of flooring substrates and the quality of the ambient environment to the different foods—and methods of food presentation—for captive animals. Much of what Hediger advocated was labor intensive and sometimes a bit difficult. It did not appeal to managers looking only at the bottom line. His attention to the needs of the animals was easily shoved aside by promoters who wanted only baby animals for the Spring Break and bean counters who wanted a minimal labor force. Ever since the first huckster put a lion in a cage and charged a penny to see it and the first public menageries opened their doors, the click of the turnstile and the chink of a coin in the cash box have drowned out the cries of those that need wallows to roll in, trees to climb, and thick grass to sleep in.

Hediger argued that zoo enclosures should be planted with shrubs and bushes left untrimmed and landscaped with boulders and fallen trees, because the animals need such things. They provide cover for individuals that may wish to get out of view and hours of entertainment for those that prefer to peel the bark off a fallen tree. Rubbing his way past shrubs or scraping against tree branches combs and freshens an animal's coat. Such natural components of the environment provide opportunities to interact. He has places to scent mark, for example. Natural components change and decompose with time. An object as simple as a big root ball, with clods of mud and dirt sticking to it, offers ever-changing opportunities for investigation as it slowly rots and falls apart. Concrete and plastic objects, by contrast, never change from one day to another.

Big cats, Hediger implored, should be given whole carcasses to tear up and thus exercise their muscles and clean their teeth. When Seattle's Woodland Park Zoo began offering uncut sheep carcasses to lions in the early 1970s, there were vitriolic letters of complaint from visitors repelled by such a sight. "In the good old days," complained one letter to the local newspaper, "the lions were fed nice chunks of meat." It seems that visitors have always been ready to participate in the old zoo game of delusion, preferring not to see the zoo animals as real, "wild" animals with real needs. It shouldn't be all that surprising. If zoo environments place wild animals in completely artificial environments then it is inevitable that visitors will see zoo animals as somehow *different*. They may look like wild bears and tigers but, see, they pose for our cameras! The monkeys bring their babies to the front of the cage to show them off to us! They listen to what we say!! The distortions in the zoo mirror can be disturbingly profound.

Of Cages and Habitats

Zoos have traditionally served as places for human recreation. Whereas some people have traditionally attended zoos to gaze in wonder at big wild animals or to marvel at the colors and patterns of exotic creatures, others have wanted only to laugh at the animals and see in their dumb captivity a reassurance that here, at least, were beings that fell below a man. Zoos historically have reinforced this amusement-park attitude, offering camels and elephants to ride in circles. Animals could be made to beg for nothing but peanuts, and until recently, feeding the animals was an integral part of going to the zoo. No wonder that after any summer weekend zoo inmates suffered abundant diarrhea, vomiting, and nausea.

If the principle reason for going to the zoo was entertainment, then it was essential for zoo managers to ensure that the cages were full and the animals clearly visible, typically in barren concrete cages elevated to human eye level. Traders became wealthy obtaining animals from the wild to restock zoos each season. If changes were to be made they were to be only technical. Zoo managers wanted progress, not philosophies. They looked for technological solutions and called it science. Thus, the antithesis of Hediger's thinking prevailed throughout the zoo world, especially during the 1950s and 1960s. It was the age of B. F. Skinner, the psychologist who invented the Aircrib, a soundproof, air-conditioned box for raising babies in during the first critical years of their life. Vitamin pills were going to meet all our dietary needs. Formica was modern and wood was unhygienic. From Frankfurt to Philadelphia, zoos promoted the concept of reducing animal diets to a selection of formulated biscuits, full of proteins and vitamins but devoid of any sensual or therapeutic value. Iron bars were replaced with even more restrictive glass panels. Modernity was manifest in tiled cages. For zoos, it was the Disinfectant Age. Designers concentrated on meeting the needs of the hose and the mop and ignored the needs of the animal inhabitants.

Zoo managers not only ignored the behavioral and biological needs of the animals in their care, but they also provided equally sterile and miserable environments for their visitors. Zoo food service was awful. (Indeed, it often still is. Fresh fruit, healthy produce, or vegetarian alternatives is rarely available, but hot dogs remain ubiquitous.) Clean restrooms were a novelty (though they are a little less so now), but useful gift shops and worthy bookstores have always been in the minority. Contemplative spaces and edifying experiences are as elusive as ever.

Visits to public zoos in the 1950s and 1960s left strange memories: over-heated, stuffy, and vaguely grubby buildings; forlorn animals isolated on concrete slabs, the smell of hay and feces the only evidence of life; pop-

corn-strewn sidewalks; clipped hedges and chain-link fences. Do Not Walk On The Grass. A shackled elephant swaying trance-like to some internal rhythm. Glass-fronted boxes in the Reptile House containing snakes that never uncoiled. Completely immobile crocodiles. Slimy pools edged by tidily laid stones. A chimpanzee that screamed incessantly. Birds perched on bare branches greasy from overuse. Spilled seed from food dishes scattered across the sour earth.

The media at this time occasionally railed against the unsightly iron bars that were still a common feature in zoos, but only because they reminded them of prisons. Sentimentality and aesthetics were of greatest concern, with virtually no public debate about the physical spaces in which the animals were maintained and the repetitive regimes that controlled their days. It seemed to be accepted that zoo animals had to live empty lives in bare spaces that provided nothing of value. They were there only to satisfy our curiosity.

In the late 1960s, Desmond Morris, ex-curator at the London Zoo, wrote a scathing public attack on the "naked cage" (Morris 1968). Just as Hediger before him, Morris argued the need for more elaborate and intricate environments for zoo animals to match their behavioral and psychological requirements. Hediger's writings had been confined to specialist and relatively obscure scientific publishers, but Morris had become a household name with his book *The Naked Ape*, and suddenly he was able to use the powerful pulpit of *Life* magazine to promote these ideas. The public began to take notice of the inherent inadequacies of zoos. A steadily growing dissatisfaction began to swell in the 1970s. Attendance, especially in Britain and northern Europe, started to slide.

Over the next thirty years, zoos completely turned the game around. More visits are made now to professionally run zoos in North America than to all professional sports events combined. Newspapers and television stations pay lavish attention to their

local zoos. Booster clubs raise vast sums of money to build new zoo exhibits. Much has also improved for the zoo inhabitants, since zookeepers are now selected for qualities beyond their dexterity with a hose and a shovel. Many of them now dedicate much of their time to finding ways to keep the animals in their care more active and alert.

Children visiting an accredited zoo today are much more likely to find themselves exploring trails through densely planted jungles, seeing animals in more natural-sized groupings, absorbing images of replicated habitats that sometimes look surprisingly realistic. The old shabby wardrobe still pokes through in places, but for the most part modern zoos have dressed themselves in new finery, wearing green coats with a veneer of wildness.

The changes began in the late 1970s, with the adoption of a new zoo design ethic, called "landscape immersion." The term was coined by landscape architect Grant Jones, whose design firm developed the first such exhibits at Seattle's Woodland Park Zoo (Jones et al. 1976). It has since become the catchphrase for all modern zoo design, even as at the same time the purpose behind the nomenclature has been forgotten. Landscape immersion was a philosophy by which animals were to be given living spaces that as closely as possible replicated their natural habitat. It was Hediger's philosophy of practical biology expanded into naturalistic aesthetics. The landscape was intended not only to meet the animals' psychological, behavioral, and physiological needs but also to convincingly relate to zoo visitors the visual power and drama of wild places. The "immersion experience" came from the notion that the animals' replicated habitat was to be extended beyond the barriers and engulf the human visitors in the very same landscape. The hope and intent was that by engaging all their senses within a naturalistic habitat, zoo visitors would—at least subconsciously—come to a greater awareness of the connections between the animals they were seeing and the habitat they were experiencing. Landscape immersion was to bond the images of wild animals and wild places in the visitors' experiential memory.

Initially rejected, and quite savagely, by other zoos, which saw so much space and money dedicated to landscaping as wasteful and unnecessary, and which chafed at the idea that animals could not now be so easily exposed to public view, this new design technique also took time to be accepted by traditional zoo visitors. Used to concrete sidewalks and neat flowerbeds, several complained vociferously about the new style. Few zoos of the time even kept animals on grass, and those that did, such as San Diego's, regularly mowed the grass in their animal enclosures, keeping it short and tidy.

The wild appearance of landscape immersion exhibits has now gained wide favor. A new specialty, zoo horticulture, has emerged from the concept, and skilled practitioners devote their budgets and energies to creating scenes that mimic the wilderness. The public likes it.

It might seem that with the greening of our zoos, especially in North America, all is now well. But zoos still have enormous progress to make if the animals in their care are to find themselves the beneficiaries of this trend. A typical zoo animal's day remains as devoid of contact with anything from nature as it did in the old menageries. The deception is simply more subtle than the painted scenes of desert and forest on the old zoo exhibit walls.

Species Survival

At about the same time that Seattle's zoo was pioneering new concepts in exhibit design, the zoo world was beginning to pay more attention to its breeding programs. For their entire history, zoos had succeeded in breeding animals only accidentally and with no projected outcomes. The main objective had always been to have baby animals available for the first flush of visitors in the spring. If animals died and cages became emp-

ty, a call could be made to an animal trader to find out what new specimens were available for trade or for sale. These animals came from other zoos' surplus stock or from the wild. In either case the source was fairly arbitrary and with little thought to provenance. If standard museum procedures were not considered, neither was much sleep lost over ethics. Killing several adult wild gorillas to obtain an infant, for example, and the subsequent high mortality rates involved in shipping such young animals, meant that each new ape introduced into a zoo carried a hidden toll—the deaths of many other apes. Breeding failures among captive stock compounded the problem.

In 1979 Katherine Ralls, a researcher at the National Zoo, in Washington, D.C., examined juvenile mortality rates correlated with inbreeding for sixteen species of animals at the zoo. The death rate for inbred animals was markedly higher than for those born from unrelated parents. Ralls made a follow-up study on forty-four species. This study reinforced her initial findings. It became apparent that a management program was needed. Intensive Population Management became the new catchphrase, and the American Association of Zoological Parks and Aquariums (now known as the AZA) began to strenuously promote the breeding of animals in genetically regulated programs.

The Species Survival Plan (SSP) of the AZA was founded in 1981. Its purpose was to ensure cooperative breeding programs for selected rare species in North America's zoos. The intent was to maintain healthy and self-sustaining populations of rare and endangered species.

Although landscape immersion, with its emphasis on strange expenditures like plantings for the sake of public perceptions, had first received a hostile reaction from zoo curators, the idea of controlled and managed breeding programs was enthusiastically adopted. This, after all, was an activity dear to the hearts of zoo specialists and one that they understood. Maintaining studbooks and tracking

births, deaths, transfers, and family lineage so as to develop breeding programs based on genetics and demographics was instantly understandable to them.

The ardor with which these managed breeding programs was adopted made itself evident in one unpleasant manner. Some zoo directors, wedded to their new role as the savior of endangered species, began euthanizing animals that were not considered pure or that occupied space that could be devoted to rare sub-species. The howls of protest in the animal welfare community were dismissed as mere sentimentality. The spurious defense was that only the purest-bred individuals, those with the most perfect bloodlines, could have space in the Ark. Even today, many zoo professionals will brook no criticism of their actions, cloaking themselves in the holy mantle of Conservation, protected from censure by the purity of their mission to save wild animals from extinction.

The pursuit of this role as guardian of the world's rare and endangered species sometimes brings to mind the horrible fervor of the American eugenics movement of the 1920s and its misconceptions about preserving the "purity of races." Although the prevalence of this element of zoo fanaticism has declined, some zoos continue to euthanize animals almost routinely, because they do not have room or to avoid financial inconvenience. Responsible zookeepers today try hard to prevent unwanted births, but even they typically fall back on euthanasia as a management tool. The gift of life should not be treated casually. For the individual animal, its life is precious. To take that away because it imposes upon the zoo's resources is not a justifiable action. We will have made significant progress when zoos come to realize that there should be no such thing as a "surplus" animal.

Zoos are not farms, where animals are produced specifically for consumption. They should be places that inspire and encourage sympathy for and awareness of wildlife. On one level, zoos accept this premise: zoo marketers and promoters have no trouble slipping into sentimentality when they talk about individual zoo animals. At the same time, curators are expected pragmatically to discuss how to manage "collections" of animals.

That said, the SSP program *has* proven to be a success in many practical ways. Animals in accredited zoos are now bred sensibly and wisely, with a great reduction in capricious or erratic breeding of unwanted babies. Genetically viable collections of species have been established in zoos around the world. This is a significant mark of progress in zoos, and it reflects particularly well on the two individuals who championed it—William Conway, at New York's Bronx Zoo, and George Rabb, at Chicago's Brookfield Zoo.

SSP is essentially a sound business strategy: zoos must breed and maintain their captive populations if they are to have animals to display. SSP could more accurately stand for Self Sustaining Program than for Species Survival Plan. But in the 1980s the notion grew (probably with the help of someone in the marketing division of some zoo) that the SSP was to be the sanctuary for rare and endangered animals, and zoos launched themselves as the new Noah's Ark. The media loved this simple imagery. Zoo publicists pushed the idea strongly, and the public quite eagerly devoured it. The plight of wild animals was becoming more evident, and the volume of news about the destruction of wilderness was increasing. Any indication that zoos could solve or ameliorate this horrific dilemma was welcomed. Up until that time, the only contact most people had had with exotic wild animals was through zoo visits. Zoos had for generations perpetuated the myth that they were displaying the abundance and diversity of animal life, so it is not surprising that the public could be bamboozled into believing that zoos could save the world's wildlife. Each time a member of a rare species gave birth, zoo publicists proudly proclaimed it another example of America's zoos saving the endangered animals of the planet.

Today, thankfully, more zoos are acknowledging the depth and the breadth of the problem of species extinction and no longer claim to be providing a (self-serving) quick fix to the loss of wild species. Claims that zoos are breeding animals for future reintroduction to the wild are also being muted: the success rates in such endeavours are minuscule. When they do happen, such as in the unique example of the golden tamarin (in a long-term program led by the National Zoo's Devra Kleiman), we all have reason to rejoice, but expectations that zoo-bred animals will repopulate the earth have sadly come to roost on a rather barren tree.

Present-day hopes that we can clone endangered animals will surely arrive at a similar destination. Some zoos have been promoting themselves as frozen Arks, with cryogenic repositories of flash-frozen sperm or the eggs of rare animal species. Once the cloning of animals became a viable tool and debate over replicating dinosaurs from preserved tissue hit the headlines, the public, as in the past, heaved yet another sigh of relief. It seemed that we had been saved from ecological disaster by the skin of our teeth, or at least some bit of it with a DNA component.

People are much more willing to accept the Pandora's box of cloning than the possibility that they may have to change lifestyle and values in order to slow the massive levels of predation we are currently inflicting on the natural world. We seem unable to conceive that the problem is not loss of species but loss of entire habitats and the eradication of complete, functioning, balanced ecosystems. In this regard, zoos—and indeed all of our natural-history institutions—have failed utterly. The western world has several hundred years' worth of public zoological parks, botanical gardens and arboretums, public aquariums, and natural history museums. Yet all of their accumulated scholarship, massive plundering of the planet for their displays, and bil-

lions of hours of study have failed to generate in the general public even the most rudimentary understanding of the realities of nature. We maintain attitudes of dominance, believing that everything on the planet is here for our unbridled use. In a survey (Louis Harris Associates 1994) on biodiversity and the reasons for its collapse, only 8 percent of Americans were aware that destruction of wild habitats caused reduction in biological diversity.

The New Institutions

Zoos are not likely to go away. It would take an enormous effort and too much time to get rid of them, even if it were possible. Better, instead, that we should encourage zoos to recognize that it is time for them to accept a new role. They may continue to call themselves "zoos" but they will have a new purpose, a new look, a new goal.

More than any other kind of natural-history institution, zoos have the capacity to modify themselves to a remarkable degree and to become places that champion and celebrate the natural world. The move of humans into urban areas, and the even more insidious suburban sprawl, is accelerating around the world. Our demands on the natural resources of this planet are increasing. And the decimation of wild animals and plants is reaching proportions that beggar belief. Twenty-five percent of all birds have been driven to extinction in the past two hundred years. Almost all the big mammal species are in serious trouble. Ninety percent of the black rhinos have been eradicated in the past eighteen years. One-third of the world's 226 turtle species are threatened with imminent extinction. It is not just the animals that are disappearing—their habitats are evaporating. Terborgh (1999) calculates that if the clearing of tropical forests were to continue at the 1979–1989 rate, the last tree in those forests would fall in 2045. The rate of deforestation is increasing, however, not holding steady.

Bill Conway, retired president of the Wildlife Conservation Society and director of New York's Bronx Zoo, has said, "Wildlife conservation is destined to be among the main adventures, as well as challenges, of the twenty-first century" (Conway 1999). Many of the new adventurers are already aboard ship, on vessels bearing names like the Audubon Society, Friends of the Earth, Greenpeace, Earthwatch, and Nature Conservancy. It is imperative, however, that the public join this great expedition. For this purpose zoos are admirably suited. They reach vast numbers of people who come to them each year eager for contact with the world of nature. With imagination, creativity, and most of all commitment, zoos can fashion a strong and public voice for conservation. Instead of directing their educational programs to schoolchildren, they can educate the voters and decision-makers in our society. They can bring the beauty and fragility of wild places directly into our city centers, reaching and energizing an urban audience that needs to become more aware of the real need for wildlife conservation.

Ironically, zoos can achieve this with less dependence upon animal displays. New technologies, new techniques, and an acknowledgement of their true mission can transform zoos into champions of conservation. The wonder that is inherent in very small life forms can be magical, when presented in the right way. It is certainly more edifying and uplifting than watching the aimless shuffling of a captive elephant. Interactive zoo exhibits that reveal the connections in nature can benefit and inspire us intellectually, spiritually, and aesthetically. New types of zoo displays can help us to understand the interdependencies of flowers and bats, elephants and savannas, mushrooms and trees, ants and butterflies, minerals and bones. An example of this new approach, called Wildscreen, has recently opened in Bristol, England. It uses multi-media to reveal behaviors and explain natural processes as well as the majestic splendor of wildlife spectacles, and it incorporates live-animal exhibits that focus on small life forms. It also has a very sound conservation philosophy. It dramatically illustrates how the benefits of such an approach are immeasurably greater than those derived from any bored zoo ape, listless lion, or pacing bear.

Zoos need to boldly broaden their focus, sharpen their mission, and form new partnerships with other cultural, scientific, and arts and humanities institutions. Then all of them can tell the story that wild places and wild animals are essential as well as wonderful and that we must learn to share the world with them.

Literature Cited

American Zoo and Aquarium Association (AZA). 1994. *Species survival plan*. Bethesda, Md.: AZA.

Boyd, L. 1997. *Zoological parks and aquariums in the Americas*. Bethesda, Md.: American Zoo and Aquarium Association.

Conway, W. 1999. The changing role of zoos in the twenty-first century. Keynote address, Annual Conference of the World Zoo Organisation, Pretoria, South Africa.

Croke, V. 1997. *The modern ark*. New York: Scribner.

Hancocks, D. 1996. Gardens of ecology. In *Keepers of the kingdom: The new American zoo,* ed. N. Richardson. Charlottesville, Va.: Thomasson-Grant Lickle.

Harris, L. and Associates. 1994. *Science and nature survey*. N.Y: American Museum of Natural History.

Hediger, H. 1950. *Wild animals in captivity: An outline of the biology of zoological gardens*. London: Butterworth.

Jones, G., J.C. Coe, and D.R. Paulson. 1976. *Woodland Park Zoo: Long range plan, development guidelines and exhibit scenarios*. Seattle, Wash.: Department of Parks and Recreation.

Kellert, S.R., and E.O. Wilson, eds. 1993. *The biophilia hypothesis*. Washington, D.C.: Island Press.

Morris, D. 1968. Must we have zoos? yes, but....In *Life magazine*, December 9, 78–86.

Seidensticker, J., and J.G. Doherty. 1996. Integrating animal behavior and exhibit design. In *Wild mammals in captivity: Principles and techniques*, eds. D. Kleiman et al. Chicago: University of Chicago Press.

Terborgh, J. 1999. *Requiem for nature*. Washington, D.C.: Island Press.

Another View of Zoos

Richard Farinato

Zoos have engendered strong feelings in people ever since emperors and kings began assembling private menageries for themselves.

Although zoos have some ardent supporters, zoo critics have often succeeded in disseminating their view of zoos as little more than animal jails, concrete warehouses in which blameless inmates live out lives of desperate misery. In an effort to combat that negative image, during the past decade a small minority of zoos has gone out of its way to create the myth of the "good zoo." This visible, vocal minority declares that gone are the days when zoo animals existed only to provide a family's afternoon entertainment. Conservation and education are now the avowed purposes of zoos, they say. Endangered species are micromanaged down to the gene level for the enhancement of their survival. The zoo is an ark with a precious cargo to save. As animals disappear in the wild, zoos offer a last hope for such species' survival and a last chance for visitors to learn about them. So they say.

Such cheerful pronouncements, however, haven't changed what the average American zoo is or what the average American zoo does. The truth isn't easily reconcilable with the new image. It is difficult to argue the merits of concepts like "precious cargo" and "education" when bears still endlessly pace the cement floors of zoo cages all over the country and chained elephants rock the decades away in dusty, barren enclosures better suited to the pony ride concession than to habitat for natives of the African savanna. It remains hard to understand how the sale or loan of endangered tigers and orangutans to birthday-party entertainers "enhances the survival" of their species. No one seems eager to explain that when the spring crop of baby animals featured in the local newspaper's "What's New at the Zoo" article displaces last year's crop, last year's babies sit unnoticed in bleak "off exhibit" holding areas. Yet it should be impossible for everyone but the perky, positive, vocal pro-zoo few to ignore reality—that the vast majority of public-display facilities are not cutting-edge conservation societies underwriting conservation research in remote rainforests.

Zoos exist primarily to entertain people. They are businesses. The first concern of any business is the satisfaction of the customer, and a zoo, whether public or private, depends on repeat business from satisfied customers. Whatever the zoo has identified as necessary to visitor satisfaction will determine the zoo's priorities. It shares with all other animal-based industries the same building blocks of business: produce or acquire animals; display and otherwise market those animals; and dispose of surplus, excess, or otherwise unwanted animals. In the course of conducting their business, zoos say, the public is educated, conservation is fostered, and visitors are entertained through the use or mere presence of captive wild animals.

For the most part, the public seems to believe them, judging from the popularity of zoos in general. Some ten thousand zoos are estimated to exist worldwide. Annual attendance is estimated at 700 million (IUDZG 1993). No one knows exactly how many zoos exist in the United States. In order to exhibit wild animals to the public, however, U.S. law does requires that an exhibitor be licensed by the U.S. Department of Agriculture (USDA). Currently, approximately 2,300 USDA-licensed exhibitors are in operation. Since 1996 USDA figures show that exhibitor numbers have increased by an average of a hundred licensees each fiscal year. The USDA doesn't categorize its exhibitors by size, number of animals displayed, or any other criterion. It simply requires that they display or exhibit animals to the public. USDA-licensed exhibitors therefore can range from a gas station owner displaying a single moth-eaten tiger in a cage to the world-renowned San Diego Zoo.

For the purposes of discussion, let us arbitrarily cut the number of licensed exhibitors in half to eliminate the gas station tigers, mobile petting zoos, and birthday party monkeys for hire. Even so, the remaining thousand would still be enough to allocate twenty wild-animal display attractions to every state in the Union. Such operations may call themselves preserves, reserves, sanctuaries, rescue centers, wildlife parks, or nature centers, but since they all exhibit wild animals to the public on a predictable basis, they function for all intents and purposes as traditional zoos. Of this arbitrarily assigned thousand, less than 20 percent—185—are accredited by the American Zoo and Aquarium Association (AZA) (formerly AAZPA, the American Association of Zoological Parks and Aquariums), the professional membership association for zoos in this country. Within even this small subset, the quality of the facilities, staff, and animal care varies widely. In general, however, it is only a relative handful of these AZA-accredited institutions that has led the zoo field in innovative animal care and display, *in situ* conservation programs, and animal welfare. The remaining uber-majority are by-and-large silent and far, far behind.

Whenever the public reads that zoos are dedicated to the conservation of endangered species or are working to teach the public about the natural world, the story is likely to have originated with the comment of an AZA spokesperson or facility. It typically does not include the numbers of zoos actually involved in these laudable endeavors. Instead, the impression is left that all zoos are doing all these things all the time, and that the specific facility mentioned is simply a shining example of a pervasive state of affairs. Indeed, the zoo community is a unified and consistent entity, vastly changed for the better from what it used to be.

This is very different from the reality The HSUS and other animal protection organizations deal with annually: the shabby reality of outdated facilities, miserable animals, unenlightened and misguided management, and suspect sales practices of zoos receiving public and/or private support. From 1996–1998, the USDA received more than eighty thousand inquiries from citizens, groups, and legislators concerned about animal welfare in regulated facilities in general (out of a total of 7,800 facilities regulated by USDA) (USDA APHIS 1998). Over that same time period and to the present, The HSUS routinely has received letters, e-mails, and phone calls of concern about zoo facilities on an average of three to five times a week. Green (1999) followed "de-accessioned" zoo animals via a paper trail from roadside menageries to exotic animal auctions to exotic-animal dealers back to zoos in a persuasive account that makes zoos' affirmations of ethical treatment of animals disingenuous at best.

The AZA zoos that dominate the media present themselves as dedicated to educating the public and to conserving wildlife. Some zoos have made great strides in both areas, but relatively few AZA zoos, and virtually none of the non-AZA member facilities, are involved or effective in either conservation or education. Those that have anything tangible to show for such efforts rely on intuition, anecdotes, projections, and hypotheses built on hypotheses to imply that the whole zoo community shares in any successes. Studies (Kellert and Dunlap 1989; World Society for the Protection of Animals and the Born Free Foundation 1994) found little evidence of any substantive education taking place among zoogoers; although the potential for it was and may be present, education has not replaced entertainment during a zoo visit.

It is accurate to say that people

respond on a basic, emotional level to seeing a live animal on display and that such observation can create a bond with an individual animal. But the bond between zoo animal and visitor is more likely to have been manufactured by the facility through sophisticated signage, favorable publicity (such as baby-animal "naming" contests and charity outings), and gift-shop novelties than through any spontaneous or genuine interaction. For that reason the quality of the interactions varies wildly, from negative to positive, depending on staff sophistication, physical resources, and institutional goals.

According to traditional zoo philosophy, people must see live animals in order to learn about a species (and consequently to care about the species and its habitat). To prove their educational effectiveness, zoos frequently cite their annual attendance figures, as though visitors learn about animals simply by walking through a turnstile. But does mere exposure to captive animals translate directly into practical action—or even heightened ecological awareness—as zoos claim? One could argue that it does exactly the opposite. Instead of sensitizing the visitor to animals and their (unportrayed) natural habitats, such exposure may plant the notion that wild animals belong in confinement and that artificial, visitor-friendly surroundings are natural or at the least representative of the animal's native habitat. Viewing an orangutan sitting in a grassy, moated outdoor yard or a concrete enclosure teaches nothing about the nature of the animal or its role in the non-zoo environment. It encourages people to consider wild animals as isolated objects rather than as integral elements of an ecosystem with their own intrinsic value.

If the basic educational tool in the zoo's classroom is the living animal and its surroundings, we must look closely at what a zoo exhibit tells a visitor. Some zoos teach that gorillas, orangutans, and chimpanzees are found in nature on grassy lawns at the bases of sheer cliffs. Visitors of other zoos may learn that these apes prefer

living with stainless steel, rope hammocks, and cardboard boxes. Still others will experience highly detailed re-creations of tropical rainforests. With little consensus and/or regulation within either the AZA or non-AZA zoo communities on the design and execution of exhibits, there is little consistency in the educational messages being delivered by zoos. What is being taught? What message does the visitor get? What has he or she learned about the animal? Should it vary according to each zoo's display budget, geographical location, and educational mission?

The issue of education aside, vocal, visible zoos have increasingly promoted themselves as conservation centers, in some cases even changing their names to reinforce this image. Through skillful marketing and public relations, they miss no opportunity to emphasize their role as modern arks, hedges against the extinction of endangered species in the wild. The majority of zoos, however, do no more than produce multiple generations of common—as well as endangered—species. They label this breeding "conservation," when the most that can be claimed for it is that it replenishes available zoo stock to minimize capture from the wild. Facilities with the financial resources, staff expertise, and commitment to engage in or support real conservation programs have always been few in number. Perhaps 10 percent of AZA zoos are involved in such substantial conservation programs, either *in* or *ex situ*, so to call conservation a purpose of zoos in general is misleading.

Yet there is no doubt that claims of conservation by a few zoos insulate all zoos from criticism and wrap them in a mantle of noble endeavor. Certainly, as the capture and import of wild animals have become more controversial, zoos have made captive breeding a central project, if only to provide themselves with a steady supply of replacement animals, but the captive birth of an animal does not necessarily enhance its species' prospects for survival. Most captive-breeding programs ensure a supply of animals for display or trade, and often create a growing number of surplus animals of questionable genetic backgrounds. Neither these animals nor their progeny can be considered as hedges against a species' extinction. All face uncertain futures at best.

Zoos claim that they foster not only education and conservation, but also research and scientific study of animals that benefits conservation. However, much of what can be learned from captive animals has limited application to the conservation of free-living populations. The majority of zoo-based research addresses husbandry techniques or other issues specifically aimed at the management of animals in captivity, and has little if anything to do with issues involving wild animals or populations. Conservation funding from various sources administered by AZA has been awarded to 130 projects from 1991 through 1999; 70 percent of these projects were dedicated to captive animal management or in-house education activities as opposed to conservation of species in the wild (www.AZA.org).

Zoos have a better reputation than they deserve. The same four to eight prominent zoos are trotted out over and over again so the media can pay homage to a handful of people or exhibits. The institutions that engage in meaningful programs for conservation and education and place a high priority on animal welfare are not typical zoos. They do not represent what commonly exists in so many municipalities, in city parks, on scenic routes in rural tourist areas, or in the multitude of other locations that have animals in cages on display. They ignore or deny or forget the squalid facilities that make up the large majority of zoos in this country. It is a disservice to the public and to the animals for the zoo community to act otherwise.

Zoo professionals need to accept that the welfare of any animal in any captive situation is ultimately their responsibility. They must engage in honest acknowledgement of conditions that are prevalent—rather than those that are desirable—in the zoo world. Then they must do something to ensure that the ideals of the small percentage of "good" zoos becomes the standard by which all zoos are judged.

Literature Cited

Green, A. 1999. *Animal underworld: Inside America's black market for rare and exotic species.* New York: Public Affairs.

IUDZG—The World Zoo Organization and the Captive Breeding Specialist Group of IUCN/SSC. 1993. *The world zoo conservation strategy: The role of the zoos and aquaria of the world in global conservation.* Brookfield, Ill.: Chicago Zoological Society.

Kellert, S.R., and J. Dunlap. 1989. *Learning at the zoo: A study of attitude and knowledge impact.* Philadelphia: Philadelphia Zoological Society.

U.S. Department of Agriculture Animal and Plant Health Inspection Service (USDA APHIS). 1998. Animal welfare report: Fiscal year 1998. APHIS 41-35-059. Washington, D.C.

World Society for the Protection of Animals (WSPA) and The Born Free Foundation. 1994. *The zoo inquiry.* London and Surrey, U.K.: WSPA and The Born Free Foundation.

Animal Protection in a World Dominated by the World Trade Organization

10

CHAPTER

Leesteffy Jenkins and Robert Stumberg

During the last decade, animal protection suffered a profound setback as a result of global trade rules. Until recently, the harm has remained almost invisible to the general public because international trade has seemed only tangentially related to animal protection. Much like Magellan, whose great ships appeared on the horizon of Terra del Fuego yet remained unseen by the natives,[1] an elite few have been making global trade rules out of sight of the rest of the world—acting as an invisible hand affecting economic and social policy.

However, that is beginning to change, and animal issues are playing a crucial role in making the World Trade Organization (WTO), the international body responsible for initiating and enforcing global trade rules, publicly visible. Current WTO rules prohibit the types of enforcement mechanisms relied upon by sovereign nations to make animal protection initiatives effective; as a result, many animal protection measures in this country and abroad have been reversed or stymied in the face of WTO challenges or threatened challenges. The WTO's adverse impact on animal protection is one of the reasons why the WTO's new-found public image is increasingly a negative one.

Where We Are Now

The Third WTO Ministerial in Seattle, Washington, in December 1999, dramatically revealed for the first time many segments of the public's growing discontent with WTO rules.[2] An attempt to launch a new round of trade negotiations[3] ignited street clashes between protesters, including some in sea turtle costumes (to symbolize the WTO's anti-environment policies), and law enforcement officials. The protesters, flashed across television sets around the globe.[4] The ministerial meeting collapsed as a result of the upheaval, and sea turtles quickly became a symbol in Seattle of what is wrong with the WTO.[5]

Laws protecting sea turtles,[6] dolphins,[7] and dogs[8]; laws banning cosmetic testing on animals[9] or the use of steel-jaw leghold traps[10]; laws promoting the production of hormone-free beef[11]—all have been challenged or threatened with challenge as a barrier to trade under WTO rules or its precursor, the General Agreement on Tariffs and Trade (GATT). In each case, when global trade rules were applied, the laws were modified or revoked. These laws represent decades of effort to establish strong animal protection legislation in the United States, Canada, and Europe.

At stake is the democratic stewardship of animals and their environment. Global trade rules govern not only trade, but also the values a country reflects within its marketplace. WTO supporters say that the WTO Agreements permit countries to set high environmental and social standards. But WTO and GATT case law demonstrate the Orwellian nature of this statement. Under WTO rules, animals cannot be protected if protection results in any adverse market impact.[12] In effect, free-market theory preempts all other social values.

The WTO does not specifically prohibit governments from establishing strong animal protection or environmental policy, as WTO supporters point out. The effect is more subtle. WTO rules narrow the range of mechanisms available to governments to create or modify social policy. Specifically, WTO rules prohibit government-initiated, market-based remedies such as sanctions, standards, and even ecolabeling, if they are used to implement and enforce animal protection and environmental policies.[13] Yet today, much of the harm done to animals and the environment is the result of market-based problems—including fishing for tuna by killing dolphins, factory farming, and scientific research on animals to reduce product liability. In each case the ultimate consumer contributes to the market's impact on animals.

149

Conflict or Compromise?

Government policy is meaningless if no viable ways exist of implementing and enforcing its substantive provisions. In the context of global economic integration, this realization in part, led to the strengthening of the institutional and enforcement provisions of the WTO.[14] Similarly, without viable options for implementing and enforcing animal protection policy, including market-based remedies, the sovereign authority to set high anima protection standards is an anachronism.

The 1990s were characterized by conflict and competition initiated as GATT/WTO proponents sought to impose a dominant global economic order. A strategy of "winner take all" was pursued,[15] and it extended to challenges to animal welfare.[16] Principles of free trade, not pragmatism, governed decisions to challenge legitimate animal welfare laws.[17] The public seemed asleep. Free market theorists had free rein. But by 1999 the climate was changing, as demonstrated by the broad public interest piqued by the protests against the Seattle Ministerial. The question for the new millennium is whether compromise can be found.

Each new WTO challenge to an existing national or international policy—environmental; animal protection; or consumer-related—creates an atmosphere of insecurity that can be exploited by those who wish to undermine protection. In the short term, social policy seems to be the loser. In the long term, however, the viability of the international trade regime will be at issue. Any WTO solution that does not take into account social policy will inevitably create further conflict rather than reduce or eliminate tension.

WTO rules are constitution in nature: while they are vague and broad in scope, they can also be reinterpreted to reflect changing public perceptions and opinion. It is possible to change the impact of WTO rules.

The question is whether WTO supporters perceive the need to change the rules to accommodate social values—values other than free-market theory, comparative advantage, and competition based only on the lowest price.

Comparative Advantage Theory Does Not Apply to Social Policy

At the core of GATT theory is the concept of "comparative advantage." Comparative advantage is the rationale underlying GATT Articles I (Most Favored Nation) and III (Nation Treatment).[18] It is also the rationale used to discredit the enforcement of environmental and animal protection policy with standards that regulate the production or process of goods.[19] The objective of comparative advantage was first incorporated in an early GATT decision known as the *Belgian Family Allowances*.[20]

In the *Belgian Family Allowances* case,[21] Norway and Denmark brought a complaint against Belgium because Belgium placed a levy on products purchased by public bodies from states that did not have a system of family allowances meeting specific requirements. The panel decided that Belgium's levy violated Article I:1 and possibly Article III and that the levy was inconsistent with the spirit of GATT.[22]

The rationale behind the decision was comparative advantage. By requiring that all countries have similar social/economic requirements, Belgium was undermining the comparative advantage that some countries gained by not having such economic legislation. The objective of comparative advantage was again articulated in a later panel decision, *United States—Section 337 of the Tariff Act of 1930*.[23] In that case the panel found that the purpose of Article III was to

"ensure effective equality of competitive opportunity and to protect the expectations on the competitive relationship between imported and domestic products."[24]

As compelling as the theory of comparative advantage may be in the economic realm, it is not applicable to social or moral policy typically embodied in environmental or animal protection regulation. At issue in environmental or animal protection policy-making is the legitimacy of the goods produced, or more typically, the legitimacy of the process by which the goods are produced. To use a real example, the European Union (EU) has implemented a regulation banning the sale within the European Union of pelts caught by using steel-jaw leghold traps. At issue for the EU electorate were ethical concerns regarding the appropriateness of producing a product in such a way as to cause extreme animal suffering. Comparative advantage has no meaning in this context. The issue is not whether pelts can be produced at a lower economic cost by using steel-jaw leghold traps. Rather, the electorate determined that the moral cost of producing pelts in this manner outweighs any economic advantage. The electorate did not want such pelts, no matter what the economic price.

Applying WTO rules to this type of regulation results in decisions which technically may be consistent within the context of GATT, but which nonetheless may be viewed as illegitimate or irrational by national policymakers and their electorate.[25] When GATT rules are applied to social/moral regulations, the goal of preserving comparative advantage is input into social policy. This insures that economic considerations will override or outweigh the underlying social purpose of the regulation. The net effect is to stymie the ability of policymakers to use the democratic process to balance competing policy interests of the societies which they govern.

In a democratic political process, the concerns of various stakeholders, including affected industries, are balanced so as to preclude an absolute

150

win or absolute loss for any particular segment of society. In this way, policymakers attempt to devise solutions that harm the fewest number of stakeholders. Establishing a presumption that global economic concerns must be given priority in the context of noneconomic regulation promotes autocratic, rather than democratic, policy regimes. This is because a presumption of trade supremacy precludes policymakers from balancing the diverse needs of their political community.

A Balance Originally Envisioned

Trade agreement history reveals that the original framework of GATT trade principles and exceptions envisioned a dynamic system that could balance trade and domestic policy needs, as well as global economic integration, with national sovereignty.

Adopted in 1947, GATT-the-document reflects a theoretical balance of interests that has not characterized interpretations by GATT-the-institution (now the WTO). That balance between trade and environment or other domestic policy interests is achieved not only in the GATT, but in numerous places throughout the WTO Agreements adopted or modified in 1994. For example, the Preamble to the Agreement on Technical Barriers to Trade ("TBT Agreement") provides:

no country should be prevented from taking measures necessary... for the protection of human, animal or plant life or health, or the environment...subject to the requirement that they are not applied in a manner which would constitute a means of arbitrary or unjustifiable discrimination between countries where the same conditions prevail or a disguised restriction on international trade.[26]

Similarly, the Preamble to the Agreement on the Application of Sanitary and Phytosanitary Measures (the "SPS Agreement") states that "no Member should be prevented from adopting or enforcing measures necessary to protect human, animal, or plant life or health, subject to" the same requirements set forth in the TBT Agreement.[27] The Preamble to the Agreement Establishing the WTO specifically recognizes the need to

[allow] for the optimal use of the world's resources in accordance with the objective of sustainable development, seeking both to protect and preserve the environment and to enhance the means for doing so in a manner consistent with [countries'] respective needs and concerns at different levels of economic development.

While this language admittedly is not proscriptive, it nonetheless conveys an implicit intent to balance economic growth with social values.

Proscriptive language to this affect, however, is contained in at least two places in the WTO Agreements. Article XIV (the exceptions clause) of the General Agreement on Trade in Services (the "GATS") states

Subject to the requirement that such measures are not applied in a manner which would constitute a means of arbitrary or unjustifiable discrimination between countries where like condition prevail, or a disguised restriction on trade in services, nothing in this Agreement shall be construed to prevent the adoption or enforcement by any Member of measures:

(a) necessary to protect public morals or to maintain public order;

(b) necessary to protect human, animal or plant life or health.

Similarly, Article XX of the GATT provides that subject to the safeguards in its preamble, "*nothing* in this Agreement shall be construed to prevent the adoption or enforcement by any contracting party of measures" (emphasis added) that are included in the list of "general" exceptions.[28] Article XX has three general exceptions that have great relevance to the relationship between the WTO and animal protection. They include measures:

(a) necessary to protect public morals;

(b) necessary to protect human, animal or plant life or health ...[and]

(g) relating to the conservation of exhaustible natural resources if such measures are made effective in conjunction with restrictions on domestic production or consumption.

Article XX dramatically protects the measures listed against conflict with *every* trade rule save the two safeguard tests written into the Article's preamble. By supplanting the sum of all other trade considerations, the safeguards play a crucial role in preserving the balance between trade and environment (and the other protected domestic policies). The preamble requires that protected measures:

are not applied in a manner which would constitute a means of [1] arbitrary or unjustifiable discrimination between countries where the same conditions prevail, or [2] a disguised restriction on international trade.

This framework for balancing trade and noneconomic interests was debated and designed well in advance of GATT 1947.[29] Two global trade documents developed the approach of balancing trade rules on one hand with general exceptions and a preamble with safeguards on the other, however neither ever took effect. The first was the 1927 International Convention for the Abolition of Import and Export Prohibitions and Restrictions (or the 1927 Convention), which was drafted by committees and conferences of the League of Nations. The second was the charter for creation of the International Trade Organization (or the ITO Charter), which was sponsored by committees of the United Nations. While the ITO Charter was still being drafted after 1947, the seminal proposals from the United States and other countries did predate the GATT, and they help to illustrate contemporaneous thinking.

As the first serious effort to promote global economic integration, the deliberations over Article 4 of the 1927 Convention yield the most extensive historical record regarding the structure and purpose of the GATT general exceptions and their preamble. From the start, the goal of the 1927 Convention was to develop a formula for abolishing import and export restrictions while preserving deference for legitimate noneconomic policies.[30]

The League of Nations Economic Committee (LoN Economic Committee) went so far as to describe the Article 4 prohibitions of restrictions on trade as "outside the scope" of the Convention.[31] It is clear from the discussion at several committee meetings that the delegates distinguished between "economic," or "financial," regulations and "noneconomic" regulations. The 1927 Convention was designed to govern the former, not the latter.

As an example, the delegation of India expressed the view that only sovereign nations could determine the need for trade restrictions.[32] The Japanese delegate emphasized that "[e]ach country must be allowed sufficient liberty to take those measures of prohibition or restriction which it considered necessary for non-financial or noneconomic reasons...."[33] In this context, the balance between sovereignty and economic integration was a central issue for the 1927 Convention.

The delegates frequently asked whether particular laws of interest would be covered by the proposed general exceptions. These were most often questions about quasi-economic regulations,[34] but noneconomic laws were discussed as well.[35] In response to the discussion of whether various quasi-economic trade restrictions would be protected by Article 4, the Austrian delegate raised the possibility of more detailed disclosure in order to "get rid of the skeletons."[36] However, most delegations opposed developing a detailed list or a policy of strict construction. The committee eventually arrived at a consensus that

generic exceptions would strike the best balance. The British delegate articulated the rationale upon which the committee reached consensus:

If these noneconomic prohibitions were not covered by the scheme of the Convention [that is, protected by general exceptions], there was ground for hope that the danger of abuse would... not be serious. In pursuing this course the Conference would be taking the only step possible at this stage. It should not set up machinery relating to these noneconomic prohibitions....The time has not yet come to include noneconomic prohibitions and restrictions, for Governments had their special and peculiar obligations to their peoples in matters to which they related.[37]

While generic exceptions would strike the balance with sovereignty concerns, the LoN Economic Committee also wanted to assure that such broad exceptions would not lead to abuses of the trade rules.[38] At the same time, the committee wanted to avoid drafting the agreement "so strictly and with so little regard to local conditions as to make it impossible to obtain general adhesion."[39] In this context the committee drafted the two safeguards for the preamble to Article 4. Thus did the 1927 Convention explain its framework of using general exceptions and preamble safeguards to preserve the balance between trade and noneconomic policy interests.

The ITO Charter debates followed much the same pattern. India, among others, continued to express general concern about losing its sovereignty over noneconomic matters, particularly resource conservation.[40] The alternating concern was still the potential for abusing the exceptions, as was expressed by the delegates from France and the United Kingdom, among others.[41]

Based on a proposal from the United States, the ITO committee that worked on general exceptions began with a list of exceptions, but without a preamble citing safeguards against

abuse. The committee inserted the same structure of preamble safeguards that the 1927 Convention used.[42] The ITO preamble stated that trade measures could not be "applied in such a manner as to constitute a means of arbitrary discrimination between countries where the same conditions prevail, or a disguised restriction on international trade."[43]

While the exact language of GATT general exceptions continued to develop, the framework of exceptions with a preamble to safeguard against abuses carried through from the 1927 Convention to the ITO Charter to GATT 1947. That original framework for maintaining a balance between trade and noneconomic concerns remains as a prominent feature of GATT architecture.[44]

WTO Decisions Undercut Measures for Animals

Recent GATT/WTO dispute panel decisions have increasingly curtailed the capacity of policymakers to use trade measures for environmental or animal protection purposes. For example, Article III (the "National Treatment" clause) of the GATT permits the application of domestic regulations to foreign products so long as they are not applied in excess of those applied to "like" domestic products. The term "like product" has been interpreted by dispute panels to exclude regulation based on differences in production or processing methods,[45] which is often a key concern for environmental or animal protection.

Dispute panels also have narrowed the exceptions contained in Article XX of the GATT for measures "necessary to protect human, animal, or plant life or health" (Article XX(b)) or "relating to the conservation of exhaustible natural resources" (Article XX(g)). They have interpreted the term "necessary" in Article XX(b) as a least-trade-restrictive test for health measures.[46] According to dispute panels, trade measures are only "necessary" if there is no other conceivable means of achieving the policy goal. As a result of this interpretation, dispute panel members who are not experts in the policy at stake have substituted their judgment of what is "necessary" for that of the legislature. They have often rejected pragmatic solutions in favor of hypotheticals that are not politically feasible or have been tried and have not worked.[47]

Dispute panels have also narrowed the general exception in Article XX(g), "relating to the conservation of exhaustible resources." Panels have interpreted the term "relating to conservation" to mean "primarily aimed at conservation," which in turn has been narrowly interpreted to permit only those regulations that directly accomplish the stated policy goal. Regulations that accomplish the goal indirectly or over a period of time do not qualify for Article XX(g) protection.[48] Although this rigorous standard has been modified somewhat by the Appellate Body's rulings in *Shrimp-Turtle AB* and *Reformulated Gasoline*, these cases have simply constructed a new hurdle or test in terms of the preamble (known as the "*chapeau*") to Article XX.

The Article XX chapeau provides: Subject to the requirement that such measures are not applied in a manner which would constitute a means of arbitrary or unjustifiable discrimination between countries where the same conditions prevail, or a disguised restriction on international trade, nothing in this Agreement shall be construed to prevent the adoption or enforcement by and contracting party of a measure.

When the Appellate Body addressed the issue of the *chapeau* requirements in *Reformulated Gasoline,* it applied what was essentially a "least-trade-restrictive" test, although the Appellate Body did not use this specific language.[49] The Appellate Body determined that an alternative means could have been used to achieve the conservation goal and therefore, the measure was both *arbitrary* and *unjustifiable* and *a disguised restriction on trade*. In so deciding, the Appellate Body substituted its policy judgment for that of U.S. environmental regulators and found that an alternative non-trade restrictive method of achieving U.S. policy could have been equally effective from a conservation point of view."[50] In *Shrimp-Turtle AB*, the Appellate Body again substituted its own judgment for that of domestic environmental regulators, and again found that alternatives measures were available to achieve the particular conservation goal.[51] These decisions affect not only Article XX, but also other WTO Agreements including, the TBT Agreement, the SPS Agreement, and GATS, where identical language is found.

The dynamic relationship between local innovation and global solutions is important. If the WTO uses its power to block the use of trade measures for environmental or animal protection at the local (domestic) level, the direct result will be to limit the options at the global level. Limited options at the multilateral level means that multilateral environmental agreements (MEAs) lose their efficacy. This in turn decreases the incentive for multilateral environmental cooperation, increases the pressure for unilateral (domestic) action, and consequently, may temper the enthusiasm of some governments for further global economic integration, thereby stunting the evolution of both environmental and economic law.

MEAs Require Strong Protective Legislation

Previous GATT and WTO dispute resolution panels have suggested in *dicta* that multilateral solutions are more appropriate than unilateral action by a single nation.[52] While international cooperation is ideal, it is not always possible or even desirable for environmental or animal protection problems.[53] In most cases, international cooperation is a slow process, with necessary consensus resulting only at the point of crisis.

MEAs are the high-water mark of pragmatic, bottom-up problem-solving. They do not emanate top-down from an international center of power. Most MEAs come into existence only after their substantive policies are first implemented at a "local" level, either nationally or subnationally within a state or province.

Consensus usually builds from the bottom up. The first communities to act are usually the ones that experience a problem more acutely than others. For example, a maritime province may feel the economic brunt of depleted fishing stocks, or a nation with particular religious or moral values may recoil at the commercial treatment of animals it reveres.

A community may not be specially or acutely affected by a problem, but it may still see itself as *part* of the problem and therefore demand domestic regulation. For example, the State of Vermont was one of the first governments at any level to limit the sale or use of chemicals that deplete the ozone layer of the atmosphere.

Local initiative is essential to solving global-scale problems in three different ways. First, local initiatives help build critical mass to make a real ecological or economic difference on a global scale. Second, the movement toward a solution has to start somewhere: local initiatives are often the first step toward political risk-taking without which a global solution cannot be achieved. Third, local initiatives are necessary as experiments. Nation-states, whether they act alone or in unison, depend on ideas that work to solve environmental and animal protection problems. Global environmental solutions cannot be developed in a test tube; the only laboratory that works is policy implementation on a national or subnational scale.

Many environmental and animal protection problems do not respect national borders. Although a single domestic policy is a necessary beginning, it is not sufficient in scope to conserve a resource (like fish) or protect a sentient species (like dolphins) that live in the global commons.

The point at which nation-states move beyond their own domestic consensus is the point at which an MEA is born. An MEA is to environmental protection what the WTO is to global economic integration. If the WTO's trade rules interfere with MEAs, the risks to the global trade regime will increase, not diminish: if local and national leaders are prevented from devising environmental solutions that work, they and their electorate will associate the WTO with their own political and environmental impotence. If the WTO does not achieve an effective balance for trade and environment, the movement for global economic integration will lose credibility.

Multilateral Agreements Are Hard to Enforce

International environmental cooperation has led to the adoption of more than 180 treaties or agreements to protect the global environment and conserve natural resources. The need for continued international cooperation is undisputed by trade and environmental experts alike. International cooperation increases the resources available for enforcement, monitoring, and scientific innovation. It can also be a mechanism for providing technological, educational, and monitoring resources to countries that do not have the resources to address a particular problem. If MEAs are to be a viable option for addressing global and regional animal-related problems, they will need enforcement tools that work.

Developing the enforcement powers of MEA organizations is conceptually and practically difficult.[54] Historically, enforcement powers have been inextricably tied to the concept of sovereignty, and only nation-states have the sovereign right to enforce laws within their own jurisdiction. With some exceptions, the concept of enforcement jurisdiction is territorially based.[55] Theoretically, no international juridical body may interfere with that right, and granting an MEA organization enforcement powers may result in infringing upon the sovereignty of its member countries. Because of the limited options for international enforcement, the use of trade measures by MEA members will increasingly become necessary for enforcement. While member states have the means to implement and enforce MEA objectives within their territory through their police powers, they have few means of implementing and enforcing objectives *outside* their territorial boundaries, even when their interests are directly threatened. This would suggest an increase in attempts to use trade measures to implement and enforce both national and international environmental and animal protection policy.

The WTO's Committee on Trade and Environment (CTE) has addressed the issue of the relationship between the WTO and MEAs but has come to no conclusions. The question of whether MEA-derived trade measures are WTO-consistent is unresolved. There have been no GATT or WTO challenges to such trade measures. This is primarily because there are so few of them.[56] A third treaty, the Convention on International Trade in Endangered and Threatened Species of Wild Fauna and Flora (CITES), regulates commercial trade in endangered and threatened animal and plant species through the use of a trade permitting system, but doesn't specifically authorize the use of trade measures or sanctions. The permitting system is basically an honor system. Members agree to abide by their obligations in good faith. The only recourse to trade measures *per se* has been in the form of a recommendation from the CITES Standing Committee, the juridical body which has authority over such matters. In September 1993 the Standing Committee issued a decision which provided *interalia*, "Parties should consider implementing stricter domestic measures up to and including prohibition in trade in wildlife species now" (see Press Release of CITES Secretariat, September 9, 1993, announcing Decision of the Standing Committee, para. 6). This came in response to the most visible use of MEA-authorized trade measures yet—the U.S. imposition of trade measures against China and Taiwan for the continued trade in rhinoceros horn in violation of CITES. In that case, the CITES Standing Committee, the judicial body with authority over such matters, issued a decision strongly recommending that Parties "consider implementing stricter domestic measures up to and including prohibition in trade in wildlife species now."[57] The purpose of the decision was to encourage China and Taiwan to comply with CITES. The United States took action by imposing a ban on the importation of animal-related products. Because neither China nor Taiwan was a member of GATT, no GATT challenge was possible.

Some governments, most notably those of the United States and the European Union, assert that trade measures taken to enforce MEAs are consistent with WTO rules and that MEAs and the WTO are theoretically international equals.[58] The U.S. Trade Representative's office has said this repeatedly in public briefings in order to quell the qualms of environmental and animal protection advocates regarding the WTO.

Such statements, however, are at odds with U.S. policy positions. While claiming that nothing in the WTO preempts the use of trade measures by MEAs, the U.S. government has actively pursued a policy of ensuring that WTO rules trump MEA policy by including "savings clauses" in new MEAs in which the use of trade measures are most likely to occur. For example, in the Biosafety Protocol negotiations, the United States pushed vigorously for language that would ensure that members did not take action which would interfere with implementation and enforcement of Trade-Related Intellectual Property Rights (TRIPS) Agreement, a WTO Agreement.[59] (A savings clause is the legal mechanism by which countries agree and ensure that a new agreement does not supercede obligations under an existing international agreement, such as the WTO.[60] It is the means by which the United States and others are ensuring that MEAs do not supercede WTO rules.)

Where Do We Go From Here?

The conflict between the WTO and national and international animal protection legislation is ultimately a question of social policy and sovereignty. These concepts stand between the WTO and its vision of a global economy. The thrust of this chapter has been to emphasize how the original framework of GATT trade principles and exceptions envisioned the task of striking a balance not only between trade and environment/animal protection, but between economic integration and sovereignty as well. That balance has been lost as trade negotiators push to further integrate the global economy, imposing free-market theories and ignoring social policy.

At issue is the type of global society being created by the current push for global economic integration. From an animal protection perspective, current WTO rules create a global society devoid of humane considerations, where the bottom line is profit and competition, rather than cooperation, compassion, and conservation. The former promotes over-consumption—characterized by a need to create increased market access—while the latter helps encourage responsible consumerism. Economists would argue that WTO rules form a value-neutral system. But the impact of the system belies such statements. WTO/GATT case law and practical application of WTO rules reveal a global economic order that shuns ethical concerns and brands them as "technical trade barriers." The imposition of comparative advantage to social norms ensures that ethical considerations do not affect the marketplace in any meaningful way. Instead, low-cost consumerism has become the global economic mantra. It is a system that lacks grace and long-term durability. The system is subject to attack precisely because it has no moral rectitude. The original balance envisioned must be regained if the WTO hopes to retain public legitimacy.

Revising the Rules

From an animal welfare perspective, revision or reinterpretation of WTO rules is essential to making the global economy animal friendly. Of greatest concern are the issues of national treatment, burden of proof, the scope of the GATT Article XX Exceptions, including the *chapeau* (which has implications for several other agreements including, the SPS Agreement, the TBT Agreement and GATS) and the issue of risk assessment with respect to the SPS Agreement.

National Treatment

Article III of GATT provides for national treatment on internal taxation and regulations, that is, all similar products must be treated in a like manner. For example, Article III(2) specifically provides:

> The products of the territory of any contracting party imported into the territory of any other contracting party shall not be subject, directly or indirectly, to internal taxes or other internal charges of any kind in excess of those applied, directly or indirectly, to *like domestic products* (emphasis added).

Dispute panels have interpreted Article III to preclude internal regulations governing the production or processing of a product.[61] From an environmental and animal protection perspective, however, the way a product is produced is often more important than the product itself. In the life-cycle of a product, the production process may be where environmental degradation or animal suffering occurs.[62]

The precautionary principle, accepted at the UN Conference on Environment and Development and elsewhere,[63] embodies the belief that environmental degradation should be prevented rather than controlled, that conclusive proof of harm should not be a prerequisite to environmental or animal welfare regulation, and that even limited evidence of a causal nexus between production and harm should be sufficient to justify regulation. Production and process method (PPM) measures are often the most effective means of preventing environmental degradation and promoting animal welfare. One of the main goals of the animal protection community is to make trade rules acknowledge the value of process-related standards and thereby embody the precautionary principle.

PPMs can be divided into two categories: "product-related PPM requirements" and "non-product-related PPM requirements." A product-related PPM must be embodied in and somehow alter the final characteristics of a product. An example of a product-related PPM is the EU regulation requiring heat treatment of wood to prevent the importation and proliferation of nematodes. The heat treatment alters the chemical properties of the wood, which makes results of the process physically measurable and detectable.

A non-product-related PPM affects the production or processing of the product, but it is not actually incorporated or reflected in the final product. Examples of non-product-related PPMs are the EU regulation banning the importation of certain fur products caught in steel-jaw leghold traps and the U.S. law banning the importation of fish caught in driftnets that exceed the UN standard of 2.5 kilometers.

Only product-related PPMs are specifically permitted under GATT[64]; non-product-related PPMs are not. However, in two GATT cases, *Tuna-Dolphin I* and *Tuna-Dolphin II,* dispute panels found that non-product-related environmental PPMs violate GATT. In both, the panel held that a U.S. law restricting imports of canned yellowfin tuna caught using purse-seine nets (a "process" or "production" regulation) were quantitative restrictions prohibited under Article IX of GATT. Moreover, the U.S. regulation was not an internal measure as contemplated under Article III[65] of GATT because the U.S. law did not regulate tuna as a product. Rather, it regulated the method by which tuna was harvested. Both panels ignored the distinction between tuna caught by encircling dolphins with purse-seine nets and tuna caught by other methods, because this was a distinction based on production, not the physical characteristics of the tuna. The panels concluded that the U.S. law was discriminatory because the United States banned the import of tuna from any country that did not adopt a dolphin conservation regime comparable to that of the United States.

Many animal welfare laws—such as the EU Leghold Regulation and Cosmetics Testing Directive and the U.S. Marine Mammal Protection Act, Wild Bird Conservation Act, Humane Slaughter Act, sea turtle protection law, African Elephant Conservation Act, and High Seas Driftnet Enforcement Act—incorporate non-product-related PPMs. Under the reasoning of both the *Tuna Dolphin I* and *II* decisions, these and many other noneconomic laws are vulnerable to a WTO challenge.

To remedy this, the WTO Council of Ministers should establish an interpretive rule (giving as little discretion as possible to dispute panels or the Appellate Body) that the term "like product" as used in Article III, and as applied to environmental and animal protection policy, permits differentiation based on process or production methods so long as the environmental and animal protection measures are not intended as disguised restrictions on trade. Such types of products and production method standards should be permissible at both the domestic level (i.e., unilaterally) and in terms of MEA enforcement. Such an interpretation by the Council of Ministers would reflect the principle that environmentally sound "production or process" methods are an essential component of the precautionary approach. The WTO should provide the

following interpretative guidance:
(a) Discrimination: Domestic producers should be prevented from utilizing production or process methods which foreign producers are either *de facto* or *de jure* prohibited from using if they want market access.
(b) Assistance to developing countries: If developing country producers are affected, sufficient financial and technological assistance (including transfer of technology) should be forthcoming from the regulating country in order that the developing country producer can bring its production into compliance with the PPM standard.
(c) Dispute panel composition: To ensure an accurate and comprehensive review of disputes involving animal protection or environmental concerns, dispute panels considering newly interpreted Article III defenses should include at least one panelist who is a recognized environmental or animal welfare expert.

Burden of Proof

As noted above, the plain language of GATT Article XX is that *"nothing in this Agreement* shall be construed to prevent the adoption or enforcement by any contracting party of measures"* (emphasis added) that are included in the list of "general" exceptions.[66] Thus, Article XX preserved the historical deference to sovereignty in the sphere of noneconomic policy.

Unfortunately, GATT dispute panels have required countries defending their laws under Article XX to carry the burden of proof to justify use of a trade measure to enforce a environmental objective.[67] This interpretation was codified within the GATT 1994 Dispute Settlement Understanding (DSU), which provides that:

> the action is considered *prima facie* to constitute a case of nullification or impairment. This means that there is normally a presumption that a breach of the rules has an adverse impact on other Members...[and] it shall be up to the Member against whom the complaint has been brought to rebut the charge.[68]

Although it is now codified in the DSU, this interpretation on burden of proof is inconsistent with the framework of the GATT regarding Article XX exceptions. First, the very purpose of Article XX was to countenance the kind of "adverse impacts" to which the DSU refers. Second, Article XX explicitly provides that except for the two safeguards built into its preamble,[69] *"nothing* in this Agreement" prevents a member nation from adopting or enforcing exempted measures. The dictionary definition of "nothing" as it is used (as a noun) in Article XX means "no thing at all" or "no share, element or part."[70] In other words, for purposes of Article XX general exceptions, a dispute panel may consider only the safeguards in the preamble—otherwise, no dispute settlement presumptions, no externally imposed limitations on policy alternatives, nothing. As one commentator puts it, "if the 'nothing in this Agreement' clause in Article XX means what it says, why are any conditions outside the Preamble relevant?"[71]

The WTO should adopt the position that the DSU presumption that a defending nation must bear the burden of proof does not apply to defenses under Article XX. To the contrary, the policy of deference implied by Article XX shifts the burden of proof on the complaining nation, once a defending nation raises an Article XX defense.

Scope of GATT Exceptions

Over the years, GATT dispute panels have narrowed the Article XX exceptions. This narrowing also affects several other WTO Agreements, including the TBT Agreement, SPS Agreement, and GATS.[72] As with the burden of proof, the restrictive interpretations go beyond the plain language and historical deference, which the structure of GATT provided in order that sovereign nations could define their own interests regarding noneconomic matters, so long as the Article XX safeguards are applied.

Protecting Life or Health

Article XX(b) exempts measures that are "necessary to protect human, animal or plant life or health." The general scope of this exemption is constrained on two fronts. The first involves interpretation of whether a given measure is "necessary," and the second involves the meaning of "life or health."

The Meaning of "Necessity"[73]

WTO Dispute panels have interpreted the term "necessary" from the "trade impact" point of view. The initial point of inquiry has been: What is the impact on trade and is this impact strictly "necessary?" The development of the least-trade-restrictive "test" was an attempt to judicially codify an easily applicable test to determine the impact of various health and safety measures on trade. This test, however, ignores the deference that the structure of the WTO provided to sovereign nations to define their own noneconomic interests.

Democratic legislatures are designed to draft measures that balance competing interests; the result is a politically feasible compromise. Rarely do consumers or affected industries get all they want. But WTO panels have ruled that in order for a human or animal health measure to be "necessary," a defending nation must prove that it chose the least-WTO-inconsistent measure available based upon the panel's own speculation about what the alternatives might be.[74] An interpretation of "necessary" that requires sovereign states to choose the least-WTO-inconsistent measure to qualify under Article XX exceptions denies any deference to national problem-solving as envisioned by the drafters of GATT and the earlier trade agreements. This runs counter to the deference to national problem-solving envisioned by the drafters of GATT and the earlier trade agreements. There is virtually always a less-trade-restrictive alternative. No WTO panel can presume to know what action is "necessary" based on the diverse factors that a

legislature must take into account.[75]

If the balance between trade concerns and deference to sovereign nations in the noneconomic realm is to be preserved, any "test" regarding what is "necessary" should be defined from the perspective of *the relevant legislative body*. A WTO panel does not have the capacity to evaluate whether an environmental or animal-related threat is real or significant. Factors relevant to determining the *scope* of the environmental threat include public interest in the perceived problem by constituents other than an "affected industry," the degree of public discussion about available options, and limitations on effective enforcement due to the scope of the problem.

The Meaning of "Life and Health"[76]

A dispute panel could interpret the meaning of "life or health" as parallel to the definition used in the SPS Agreement, which is limited to "risks arising from the entry, establishment or spread of pests, diseases, disease-carrying organisms, or disease-causing organisms."[77] This definition, however, excludes environmental threats to animal life or health—such as loss of habitat, excessive hunting, and pollution and other ecological imbalance caused by human commerce—as well as humane considerations.

When GATT 1947 was being drafted, there was little discussion of the scope of Article XX(b), perhaps because it was so similar to language in the ITO Charter, the 1927 Convention, and bilateral treaties; it had become "boilerplate," in the words of a U.S. delegate.[78] Prior to the 1927 Convention, the LoN Economic Committee recommended a health exception that included protection from disease and "degeneration or extinction."[79] This additional phrase was dropped from the text adopted by the Convention, but it was retained in an explanatory protocol to the Convention.[80]

The model for this GATT exception was established when the U.S. and British delegations proposed simplifying the 1927 exception even further into its present form.[81] Sanitary and

phytosanitary measures were clearly the foremost concern. However, there is no hint on the record that the simplification of Article XX(b) language was anything more than a decision to use the most general phrase possible to include the various health risks that were mentioned in predecessor documents. The movement away from detailed list-type definitions to generic definitions is consistent with a policy of GATT deference to sovereign articulation of policy purposes.

A much broader interpretation of Article XX(b) can be supported by both the plain language of the terms "life" and "health" as well as by the drafting history of this provision. Defining "life" and "health" as pertaining only to sanitary and phytosanitary measures focuses the inquiry on "impact" or harm to others (that is, the spread of disease). The terms "life" and "health," however, also have meaning in the context of the impact on the individual: How is the individual affected? For example, in the human realm, human rights violations could significantly affect an individual. Similarly, the conditions in a dog breeding facility could significantly affect the life or health of an individual dog.

Possible Solutions

As a solution, either the WTO Council of Ministers or the Appellate Body established under the DSU[82] should establish a new "interpretive rule" with respect to the term "necessary" as used in Article XX. The rule should focus on the scope of the moral, health, or conservation problem *as it is perceived by the sovereign legislator or regulator*. Factors such as public interest in the issue, enforcement limitations, and public debate about various policy options could be considered by a dispute panel to determine the scope of the problem as perceived by the legislature. The necessity to protect life or health should not limit WTO members to only a theoretical measure that is least inconsistent with the WTO Agreement.

This precludes solutions that are politically or practically feasible and ignores the original spirit of providing a general exception.

Furthermore, the meaning of "life or health" should not be limited to "sanitary or phytosanitary" concerns. Particularly in the case of animals, life or health is often dependent on protecting animals from undue stress, pain, loss of habitat, or other environmental threats. A new WTO interpretative rule should be established to clarify this point.

Conserving Exhaustible Resources

Article XX(g) exempts measures "relating to the conservation of exhaustible natural resources if such measures are made effective in conjunction with restrictions on domestic production or consumption." GATT panels have interpreted broad terms like "relating to" conservation and "in conjunction with" domestic restrictions very narrowly. The plain meaning of "relating to" would suggest that either a direct or indirect causal link between the perceived harm and the chosen mode of regulation would suffice. Past GATT panels, however, have interpreted the term, "relating to," to mean "primarily aimed at," which in turn has been interpreted to require a direct causal link between the asserted policy goal and the means chosen to attain the goal.[83] This narrow interpretation has permitted panels to substitute their subjective judgment regarding what constitutes "effective policy" for that of sovereign legislators, which contravenes the purpose of the Article XX exceptions.

Another way of limiting the application of this exemption is to narrow the substantive scope of what is "exhaustible." Some analysts have suggested that "exhaustible resources" include only minerals that are available in finite quantities.[84] However, within the constraints of such a standard, the WTO precludes the use of an environmental exception to safeguard creative responses

by MEAs and sovereign states to address some of the most serious environmental problems of our time (such as ozone depletion).

If the term "exhaustible resources" is narrowed, the only alternative available to a country whose environmental measure is challenged is to argue that the trade-related measure fall within another exception (public morals or life/health) that has a "necessity" test. As previously noted, the term "necessary" has been construed by previous GATT panels to require that only the least-trade-restrictive policy option be implemented. In either case, the balance envisioned in Article XX between GATT authority in the economic and financial realm and sovereign authority in the noneconomic realm will be eviscerated.

The question of whether a resource is exhaustible is a factual one that is not limited by whether a resource *can* renew itself. Obviously, species can die to the point of extinction. While the ecosystem of trees and oceans renews the atmosphere, a significant change through global warming or ozone depletion can exhaust the specific balance that makes the atmosphere a life-supporting resource. While rivers renew their own purity, pollution can overwhelm their restorative powers.

In this case, dispute panels have recognized that not just minerals but also animals, plants, and ecosystems can be exhausted.[85] The risk is that without interpretive guidance from the Council of Ministers, future panels will not continue to give deference to member-nations' assessment of whether a resource is exhaustible.

The WTO should require that dispute panels respect the plain meaning of the term "relating to conservation," which could include trade-related environmental measures that either directly or indirectly achieve the stated environmental objective. Alternate tests (such as "primarily aimed at") that rely on the subjective judgment of a dispute panel regarding the underlying economic impact of a trade-related environmental mea-

sure are not appropriate.

Dispute panels should also continue to apply an open analysis of whether a resource is exhaustible, not a more limited definition based on presumed categories of what is exhaustible and what is not.

Public Morals

GATT Article XX(a) and GATS Article XIV(a) exempt measures that are "necessary to protect public morals."[86] While this is one of the most relevant GATT exceptions regarding animal protection, it is mentioned last because it has not been used before, at least in the context of a GATT challenge before a dispute panel.

Like Article XX(b), XX(a) requires a measure to be "necessary" to accomplish its purpose. The previous comments regarding the term "necessary" in the context of Article XX(b) are equally applicable here. The difference between the two exceptions is that articulation of public morals by policymakers is an inherently subjective task, much more so that determining whether there is a threat to life or health. Therefore, the legislative determination of whether a measure is "necessary" to serve a subjective purpose can be likewise more of a subjective judgment.

The history of debate from the 1927 Convention through the adoption of GATT 1947 confirms a common sense understanding that the scope of the public morals exception is broader than the other exceptions and that nation-states were allowed to determine public morals within the context of their own culture.

The history of trade agreements since the League of Nations shows that protecting public morals has been a constant concern and that language has gradually evolved from specific to more generic terms. As noted above, Article XX(a) of GATT 1947 had two predecessor documents, which never took effect. The first was article 4(2) of the 1927 Convention. The second was article 45(1)(a)(I) of the initial proposals for the ITO Charter, which was sponsored by committees of the United Nations.

The 1927 Convention exempted "prohibitions or restrictions imposed on moral or humanitarian grounds."[87] Like the other exceptions in Article 4, the Economic Committee reported that moral prohibitions or restrictions on trade were "outside the scope" of the Convention.[88] The delegates frequently asked whether particular laws of interest would be covered by the proposed general language. Examples of morally based trade restrictions included prohibitions on obscene materials (Ireland)[89] and prohibitions on lotteries (Egypt).[90] The 1927 Conference ended with a morals exception close to what the Economic Committee originally recommended, except that the language on morals became even more general.

As drafted by the Economic Committee of the 1927 Convention, the morals exception covered trade restrictions for "moral or humanitarian reasons *or for the suppression of improper traffic, provided that the manufacture of and trade in the goods to which the prohibitions relate are also prohibited or restricted in the interior of the country*" (emphasis added).[91] The Conference shortened the entire section to read, "moral or humanitarian grounds."[92] While there was no comment on why the Conference moved to shorten the section, its action was consistent with the policies of (1) using the most generic language, and (2) using the safeguards in the preamble to protect against discrimination or disguised trade barriers.

Apart from the generic exception debate, there was no further discussion of whether animal or environmental protection would be considered a moral exception to trade rules. However, it is worth noting that during the same period, another branch of the League of Nations was negotiating a convention that included a clause to prevent unnecessary suffering of animals during transport.[93] This suggests that in 1927 international institutions recognized animal protection as both a moral issue and

a sanitary or phytosanitary issue, as they do today.

The morals exception within the ITO Charter was initially proposed by the United States as part of its comprehensive charter proposal. The proposed exception covered measures "necessary to protect public morals,"[94] which is the same language as Article XX(a) of GATT 1947. When compared to its predecessor language from article 4(2) of the 1927 Convention, "moral or humanitarian grounds," the ITO proposal carried on the trend toward ever more general language.

There was literally no comment on the general exceptions recommended by the United States within the first ITO report (the London conference).[95] Nor was there further comment on the "public morals" exception in later reports. It is clear that the drafters of GATT 1947 began their work with the pre-1947 ITO Charter drafts, which were based on the original U.S. proposal.[96]

Without any further insight into the internal U.S. rationale for adopting "public morals" rather than its older 1927 cousin, "moral and humanitarian grounds," the most likely explanation remains the preference for using general terms rather than specific examples.[97] For example, "humanitarian" concerns would be a type of "public morals," and therefore the broader term, "public morals," is all that is necessary.

The issue of whether trade-related environmental or animal protection measures are protected by Article XX(a) is more than simply a theoretical question. Many of the highly politicized trade challenges that have occurred, or are likely to occur in the near future, are animal related. It was the infamous tuna-dolphin dispute that first alerted broad sectors of the international public to the limits on law-making authority posed by trade agreements. Policies affecting sea turtles (as symbolized in 1999 by the widely photographed costumed demonstrators) became synonymous with the WTO Seattle Ministerial.

Trade conflicts involving animals

will likely increase public ire about trade agreements. It would seem prudent, therefore, for the WTO to address the issue of how Article XX(a) applies to trade-related animal protection measures and provide interpretive guidance to ensure that dispute resolution panels afford the appropriate deference to sovereignty that the drafters of GATT envisioned under the Article XX exceptions.

As in the case of life or health, the phrase "necessary to protect public morality" should be interpreted to include solutions that are practical and politically feasible, which would preserve the original spirit of providing a general exception.

Public morals are defined by each respective nation based on its unique cultural, ethical, or religious norms. A generic deference to national determination of public morals clearly includes protection of animals, among other values of respect for life.

Arbitrary or Unjustifiable Discrimination or a Disguised Restriction[98]

The Appellate Body in both *Reformulated Gasoline AB* and *Shrimp-Turtle AB* employed a type of least-trade-restrictive test in analyzing the meaning of the *chapeau* to Article XX. In so doing, it substituted its judgment for that of domestic environmental policymakers by determining that, from a conservation perspective, nontrade-related alternatives were available to achieve the conservation goals in question. It also made the language of the *chapeau* nearly equivalent to the WTO interpretative meaning of the word "necessary," thus obfuscating the meaning of particular words. The result is an overall presumption that trade will always preempt social concerns.

In order to remedy this problem, the WTO Council of Ministers should instruct the Appellate Body to take heed of Article 31 of the Vienna Convention of the Law of Treaties, which provides: "A treaty shall be interpreted in good faith in accordance with the ordinary meaning to be given to the terms of the treaty in their context and in the light of its object and purpose." The ordinary meaning of the word "arbitrary," as defined in *The American Heritage Dictionary of English Language*, is: "determined by chance, whim or impulse, and not by necessity, reason, or principle," while the meaning of "unjustifiable" is: "impossible to excuse, pardon, or justify." Application of the *chapeau* (or in the case of other WTO Agreements, where similar language is used) should be limited to an inquiry of whether the relevant policymakers had a rationale, unrelated to trade, for choosing the policy mechanism in dispute. If there is a non-trade rationale, regardless of whether a universe of other possible alternatives exist, the law or regulation in question should, as a matter of law, meet the requirements of the *chapeau*. Application of any other rule results in an infringement by trade experts on nontrade policy objectives and domestic legislative authority.

Risk Assessment Under the SPS Agreement

By its terms the SPS Agreement specifically applies to risks to animals resulting from disease, contaminants, toxins, additives, and a host of other harms.[99] It applies both to risks to humans arising from contaminants from animal food sources and to direct harm to animals. Thus, the SPS Agreement is very important from an animal welfare perspective. Despite this, there have been no animal cases arising under the SPS Agreement. Although the *Beef Hormone*[100] case involved questions of human health rather than animal harm, the case is instructive of how a panel would treat the issue of risk assessment should a case arise in the context of animal life or health.

In *Beef Hormone* the dispute panel found that Article 2.2 of the SPS Agreement required that risk assessments specifically be based on scientific principles and that SPS measures could not be maintained without sufficient scientific evidence.[101] Although the panel determined that

the European Union had conducted a risk assessment,[102] it said that the European Union nonetheless provided no evidence that it had taken such assessments into account in enacting the measure in question.[103] The panel also determined that application of the precautionary principle did not override the explicit wording of Articles 5.1 and 5.2 and that the precautionary principle had been incorporated in *inter alia* Article 5.7.[104] Furthermore, according to the panel, none of the scientific evidence presented by the European Union specifically addressed the identifiable risk arising to human health from the hormones in question if so-called "good practice" was followed. Because of these and other reasons, the panel found that the EU hormone ban was not based on a risk assessment as required by Article 5.1 of the SPS and, in addition, the ban resulted in discrimination or a disguised restriction on international trade and therefore was inconsistent with Article 5.5.

The Appellate Body agreed with the panel that the precautionary principle does not override the provisions of the SPS Agreement. It reversed the panel's decision, however, with respect to Article 5.2 and whether the SPS required a measure to be "based on" a risk assessment. The Appellate Body found that as long as the measure is reasonably supported by the conclusions of a risk assessment, no proof that the measure was based on that assessment is necessary,[105] nor does a particular risk assessment need to reflect a "majority" scientific viewpoint.[106] The Appellate Body nonetheless held that the EU measure was not consistent with the SPS because, among other reasons, the evidence presented concluded that there was little risk so long as "good practice" was followed and the EU presented no evidence regarding the risk resulting from nonconformity.[107]

There are many potential harms to animals for which no risk assessment could be conducted before severe harm occurred. Risk assessments are based on scientific evidence which itself is typically based on years (or at

least some quantifiable amount) of empirical evidence. The die-off of the Monarch butterflies is an example of harm that can only be quantified after severe harm has occurred.[108] The introduction of a foreign invasive species is another example where empirical evidence is often gathered after harm has occurred. For an SPS Agreement to effectively protect animals from harm (rather than simply to ensure that no barriers to trade occur) the WTO Council of Ministers or the Appellate Body must apply the precautionary principle are part of customary international law.[109] This will safeguard actions taken when no effective risk assessment can be conducted before harm occurs.

Conclusion

The WTO, with its eighteen global trade agreements including the GATT, represents a vision of global economic reform. It also represents fifty years of work by multinational corporations, which now represent a powerful constituency for the WTO as a top-down instrument to promote the supremacy of trade rules over nontrade objectives such as animal welfare.

The animal welfare movement and the broader environmental movement are no less a vision of global reform. The evolution of well over one hundred MEAs represents a bottom-up process of multilateral cooperation. This progress is now at risk because the WTO agreements threaten to stunt the further evolution of viable enforcement mechanisms for MEAs. The trade agreements pose an even greater threat to domestic trade measures that protect animals and the environment.

The failure of the WTO, and before it the GATT, to defer to nontrade policies is a threat to the bottom-up process of developing a global economy that is humane and environmentally sustainable, not merely efficient and profitable. We have stressed that this democratic deficit on the part of trade institutions is not only a threat to animal welfare and other non-trade objectives; ultimately, it also risks the sustainability of the trade institutions themselves. This argument is based on political reality.

A nationwide study of public attitudes toward trade reveals that 62 percent of the American people are comfortable with the pace of trade liberalization.[110] But in even stronger numbers, Americans believe that environmental problems are global in nature (78 percent) and that there should be more international agreements on environmental standards (77 percent).[111] Three-quarters of the American people support the proposition: "Countries should be able to restrict the imports of products if they are produced in a way that damages the environment, because protecting the environment is at least as important as trade."[112] But even more specifically, 72 percent of Americans favor restricting the importation of tuna from Mexico because the fishing methods kill dolphins, and 63 percent favor restricting the importation of shrimp from both India and Pakistan because the fishing methods kill sea turtles.[113] In short, the diverse interests at the Seattle Ministerial expressing resistance to trade rules were not a fringe movement, as trade promoters have argued, but a reflection of public opinion on a massive scale.

The American people know that they can enjoy the benefits of free trade without sacrificing their humane and environmental values. If trade institutions, including the trade representatives of the United States, persist in promoting trade supremacy over the nontrade values that define our democratic society, then those institutions are the ones at risk of becoming endangered species.

Notes

[1]Mattingly, J. W. 1987. In *The cancer cure that worked: Fifty years of suppression*, ed. B. Lynes. Mexico: Marcus Books.

[2]Anonymous. 1999. Thousands protest meeting of WTO. *The Washington Times*, Dec. 1, 1999; BBC News. 1999. Anti-WTO protesters claim victory, December 1, 1999, at A1, column 2. ("Protesters from all walks of life—among them environmentalist, anarchists, union members, and lobbyists from non-governmental organisations—took to the streets over the past week to make their concerns heard.")

[3]BBC News. World trade talks collapse, December 4, 1999 (online news service at *http://news.bbc.co.uk/hi/english/business/newsid_549000/549439.stm*); Environmental News Service. WTO talks fail to launch new trade round, December 4, 1999 (online news service at *http://ens.lycos.com/ens/dec99/1999l-12-04-01.html*). ("After a week of meetings marked by protest marches and demonstrations against the WTO environmental and labor policies...the trade officials were not able to agree on an agenda for future talks."); Pigott, R. 1999. *WTO tarnished by Seattle failure*, BBC News, December 4, 1999, (online news service at *http:// news.bbc.co.uk/hi/english/special_report/1999/11/99battle_for_free_trad.../549794.st*).("After such a public relations disaster on the streets, failure in the talks as well, seemed unthinkable.")

[4]On December 1, 1999, several new stations covered the environmental/labor march and protest, including Fox News, ABC, NBC, Northwest News, and CNN.

[5]See, *The Washington Times*, editorial cartoon, December 1, 1999, page A16. (Protest signs read save the cockroach; save the snail darter; free trade=dead sea turtles.)

[6]See, WTO, *United States—Import Prohibition of Certain Shrimp and Shrimp Products* (WT/DS58/R), Final Report, May 15, 1998, *("Shrimp I")* at para 9.1. ("WTO Members are bound to implement [environmental] objectives in such a way that is consistent with their WTO obligations, not depriving the WTO Agreement of its object and purpose.") The United States appealed this ruling. The WTO Appellate Body reversed the reasoning of the lower panel but reaffirmed the decision. WTO, United States—Import Prohibition of Certain Shrimp and Shrimp Products (WT/DS58/AB/R), Report of the Appellate Body, October 12, 1998, *("Shrimp- Turtle AB")* at para 187.

[7]In 1988 the United States, pursuant to the MMPA, embargoed tuna caught in purse-seine nets from countries whose fishers killed dolphins in a number in excess of 125 percent of the dolphins killed by U.S. fishers. For reasons unknown, yellowfin tuna congregate under schools of dolphin and follow the schools. Fishers chase and capture the dolphins in order to harvest the tuna swimming below. It is estimated that hundreds of thousands of dolphins have been killed in this fishery. Nafziger, J.A.R., and J T. Armstrong. 1977. The porpoise-tuna controversy: Management of marine resources after Committee for Humane Legislation, Inc. v. Richardson, 7 *Environmental Law* 223, 227–29. The Department of Commerce estimates that 529,000 dolphins were killed as a direct result of international fishers using purse-seine netting techniques. On August 16, 1991, the U.S. embargo placed on the importation of yellowfin tuna from Mexico was found to be in violation of the GATT. *See, United States—Restrictions on Imports of Tuna* (unpublished decision), GATT Doc. DS21/R (September 3, 1991) *("Tuna-Dolphin I")*. Two years later, a second case was brought by the European Union, among others, and again a GATT dispute panel ruled against the United States. *See, United States—Restrictions on Imports of Tuna* (unpublished decision), GATT Doc DS29/R (June 23, 1994) *("Tuna-Dolphin II")*.

[8]In 1992 Canada proposed regulations that would ban the importation and sale of dogs bred in substandard facilities (commonly known as "puppy mills"). Studies showed that puppy mill dogs had higher incidences of contagious and congenital diseases, many of which were not detectable until sometime during the first year of the dogs' lives. In response to these proposed regulations, the United States threatened to take action against Canada under the Canadian/U.S. Free Trade Agreement (FTA), even though the trade value of the dogs in question was a mere few million dollars. *See*, 1993 National Trade Estimate Report on Foreign Trade Barriers, Office of the United States Trade Representative at 34. As a result, Canada revoked its proposed law.

[9]In response to public demand, EU legislation was adopted in 1993 to prevent the use of animals in cosmetics testing beginning in 1998. (Anonymous. Council Directive 93/35 EEC—amending for the sixth time Directive 76/768EEC on the approximation of the laws of the Member States relating to cosmetic products, *Official Journal of the European Communities* L151/32–36 1993.) However, because the Directive was based on a trade-related measure (a non-product-related PPM), the measure was thought to be incompatible with WTO rules and therefore, it was never implemented. Anonymous. *Report on the development, validation and legal acceptance of alternative methods to animal experiments in the field of cosmetics*, COM(97) 182 finals, European Commission, Brussels 1997.

[10]In 1991 the European Union enacted a law prohibiting the sale and importation of fur pelts caught with steel-jaw leghold traps, as of 1995. Because of the difficulty in determining the difference between fur pelts caught with this method and one that is more humane, the Directive provided that furs from countries that do not ban the use of steel-jaw leghold traps or meet other humane trapping standards are banned from the European Union. The United States, Russia, and Canada threatened to challenge the European Union at the WTO if it implemented this law. The WTO threat succeeded in halting the EU humane policy. The outcome allows fur caught with steel-jaw leghold traps to continue to be sold in Europe, providing no incentive for the U.S. fur industry to switch to less cruel techniques.

[11]In 1988, the European Union banned the sale of beef from cattle treated with artificial hormones. The ban applies equally to domestic and foreign-source beef. *See*, European Economic Council Directive 88/146/EEC. Exposure to artificial hormones has been linked to cancer and premature pubescence in girls (Bulger and Kupfer. 1985. Estrogenic activity of pesticides and other xenobiotics on the uterus and male reproductive tract. In *Endocrine technology*, eds. J.A. Thomas, et al., at 1–33.), although the risk to humans of artificial hormone residues in meat is uncertain. On the basis of the unknown risk and consumer demand, the European Union adopted a "zero risk" standard. The European Union made this policy choice after prolonged and effective policy campaigns in numerous EU member countries.

In 1996 the United States challenged the ban at the WTO. In 1998 a WTO panel ruled that the beef hormone ban was an illegal measure under the SPS in part because it was not based on a WTO-approved risk assessment. See, WTO, European Communities—Measures Affecting Meat and Meat Products (Hormones) (WT/ DS26R), Report of the Panel, Aug. 8, 1977, at para. 8.159. The WTO Appellate Body affirmed the panel decision, and the European Union was ordered to begin imports of U.S. artificial- hormone-treated beef by May 13, 1999. See, WTO, EU communities—Measures Affecting Meat and Meat Products (Hormones) (WT/DS26AB), Report of the Appellate Body, April 16, 1998.

[12]See, *Shrimp I supra* at 6. The dispute panel held: "[T]he chapeau Article XX, interpreted within its context and in the light of the object and purpose of GATT and the WTO Agreement, only allow Members to derogate from GATT provisions as long as, in doing so, they do not undermine the WTO multilateral trading system." Id at para.7.45. Although, the Appellate Panel specifically reversed this finding and the interpretive analysis embodied therein, *see, Shrimp-Turtle AB, supra* at 6, para 122, it nonetheless held that the U.S. law did not meet the requirements of the chapeau as the measure in question was both *unjustifiable* and *arbitrary discrimination* between countries where the same conditions prevail. Id. at para 184. In other words, while using different reasoning, the Appellate Body came to the same result.

[13]While some GATT/WTO panels, including the Appellate Body in *Shrimp-Turtle AB,* have held that countries may pursue a high level of environmental protection consistent with the WTO, in actuality this has not been the case. Although few would deny that a country has the sovereign right to establish its own environmental policies, to date, GATT/WTO jurisprudence has limited the range of enforcement mechanisms a country may use to ensure that the policy is implemented. For instance, in *Tuna-Dolphin I* and *Tuna-Dolphin II supra.,* the U.S. policy (as established in the MMPA) was to reduce to zero mortality the number of marine mammals killed as a result of the commercial tuna fishery. In *Tuna-Dolphin II* it was the means by which the United States pursed this goal (that is, trade measures) rather than the goal itself, that the panel found objectionable. *See, Tuna-Dolphin II supra.* note 7, at para 5.27. Similarly, in *Shrimp-Turtle AB* it was means of protection rather than the goal itself (protecting sea turtles) which the Appellate Body found ran afoul of WTO rules. No GATT or WTO panel has ever found that application of trade measures to protect animals or the environment are consistent with GATT/WTO obligations. But a policy can only be successful as long as it can be enforced. When cooperation and persuasion fail, short of establishing international police powers or the naked use of violence by countries (such as sinking vessels), there is no effective international means of enforcing environmental policy other than through the use of trade measures. *See,* Jenkins, L., Using trade measures to protect biodiversity. In *Biodiversity and the law,* ed. W. Snape. Washington, D.C.: Island Press.

[14]Dispute Panel rulings under GATT could be vetoed by a single GATT Member, including by the Member against whom the ruling was made. The Uruguay Round Agreement on dispute settlement, adopted in 1994, provides for automatic acceptance of a dispute panel ruling by the WTO Council within sixty days unless there is a consensus within the Council to reject it. *See,* Article 16.4 of the DSU.

[15]Numerous social initiatives were challenged during the 1990s, including an EU policy to give preferential treatment to banana farmers in former colonies in Africa and the Caribbean *(See, e.g., European Communities—Regime for the Importation, Sale and Distribution of Bananas—Recourse to Arbitration by the European Communities Under Article 22.6 of the DSU,* WT/DS27/ARB, April 9); and a Massachusetts state law (Mass. Gen.L.A. ch. 7. Sections 226–22M (West 1998 Supp.) prohibiting companies that do business with Burma from doing business with the Massachusetts government *(See Crosby v. National Foreign Trade Council,* 530 U.S. ___, 120 S.Ct. 2288; 147 L.Ed.2d 352; 68 USLW 4545 (2000)).

[16]See, Canadian puppy example, note 8 *supra.*

[17]In connection with the *shrimp-turtle* case, the Thai WTO ambassador admitted that the cost of conversion to TEDs (turtle-excluded devices) was minimal and that all Thai boats had been converted in a few months, but that it was the principle of using trade measures to protect animals and the environment that the Thai government opposed. EURONEWS. 1997. Trade and environment: Preserving biodiversity and health. Broadcast by EURONEWS in *Correspondent,* May/June, 1997.

[18]Snape, W.J., III, and N.B. Lefkowitz. 1994. Searching for GATT's environmental Miranda: Are "process standards" getting "due process." 27 *Cornell International Law Journal* 77 at 781.

[19]This is otherwise known as a "production or process method" (PPM). According to previous GATT panels, PPMs are not covered by Article III, nor have past GATT panels determined that environmental PPM measures are protected by the exceptions set forth in Article XX. *See, Tuna-Dolphin I* and *Tuna-Dolphin II.*

[20]*Belgian Family Allowances,* GATT BISD 1S/59 (Nov. 1952).

[21]GATT BISD 1S/59, 1st Supp. (1953).

[22]Id.

[23]GATT BISD 36S/345 (November 1989).

[24]Id. at para. 5.13.

[25]Dunne, N. 1992. Fears over "Gattzilla the trade monster." *Financial Times* Jan. 30, 1992, 3.

[26]Furthermore, Article 2.2 of the TBT provides that "technical regulations shall not be more trade-restrictive than necessary to fulfill a legitimate objective, taking into account the risks non-fulfillment would create. Such legitimate objectives are, *inter alia...*protection of human health or safety, animal or plant life or health, or the environment."

[27]Article 2.1. provides further that "Members have the right to take sanitary and phytosantiary measures necessary for the protection of human, animal or plant life or health, provided that such measures are not inconsistent with the provisions of this Agreement."

[28]GATT art. XX. See, Charnovitz, S. 1992. The environmental exceptions in GATT Article XX, *Journal of World Trade,* 49.

[29]Because the language in the *chapeau* and various sections of Article XX is virtually identical to that found in the newer WTO Agreements, the GATT 1947 legislative history and case law is illustrative of the meaning and purpose of the social provisions in those Agreements as well.

[30]Economic Committee, *Report Submitted to the Seventh Session of the Assembly,* A.55, 1926.II[B] (September 13, 1926) 21. [Economic Committee—7th Session Report]

[31]*Preliminary Draft Agreement Established by the Economic Committee,* 228. [Economic Committee, *Preliminary Draft.*]

[32]The Indian delegate said that "...the Government of a country was the only possible arbiter of the necessity for restrictions and that it could not afford to surrender the responsibilities placed upon it and submit the case to any foreign or extraneous body...[T]he Indian Government....would prefer to see all measures connected with prohibitions relating to national security, revenue, finance, health or morals removed altogether from the Convention." *International Conference for the Abolition of Import and Export Prohibitions and Restrictions, Proceedings of the Conference [1927 Convention], Minutes of Preliminary Meetings [Minutes],* A.559. M.201.1927.II[B] (October 17—November 8, 1927), 228.

[33]Comment by Mr. Ito (Japan). 1927 *Convention—Minutes,* 84.

[34]*1927 Convention—Minutes.* Examples of quasi-economic concerns included grading standards (United States, 82 and 86), import/export restrictions (India, 87), stabilization of currency (Greece, 83), and marks of origin (Britain, 80).

[35]Examples of noneconomic concerns included prohibitions on obscene materials (Ireland, 108) and lottery tickets (Egypt, 110). *Minutes of Plenary Meetings,* 1927 Convention, at respective page cites above.

[36]The Austrian delegate said that "...the sooner the skeletons were got rid of the better...The danger was that, by discussing general formulas, the Conference might adopt exceptions more general than was desired, and therefore it must ascertain which were the points on which restrictions were necessary and leave for later discussion the way in which those restrictions could be expressed. The formulas finally adopted should be made as light as possible on account of the unavoidable exceptions which it was impossible to remove at present." *1927 Convention—Minutes,* 87.

[37]Comment by Sir Sidney Chapman. *1927 of Plenary Meetings,* 1927 Convention, 84.

[38]Economic Committee, *7th Session Report,* 27.

[39]Economic Committee, *Report of the Economic Committee to the Council, 15th Session,* C.309(I)M.114.1925.II[B] (May 25–June 3, 1927), 309. *[15th Session Report]*

[40]Comments by Mr. Gangudi (India), *Minutes of the Preparatory Committee of the International Conference on Trade and Employment [Preparatory Committee II Minutes]* (November 13, 1946), 5.

[41]Comments by Mr. Roux (France) and Mr. Rhydderch (United Kingdom), *Preparatory Committee II Minutes,* 3 and 7.

[42]Proposal by Mr. Rhydderch (United Kingdom), *Preparatory Committee II Minutes,* 7.

[43]UN Docs. E/PC/T/C.II/32, ll and E/PC/T/C.II/50, 3–7.

[44]See, the Preambles Contained in the Agreement Establishing the WTO, The SPS Agreement, the TBT Agreement, Article XX of the GATT, and Article XIV of the GATS.

[45]See, *Tuna-Dolphin I* and *Tuna-Dolphin II* at note 7 *supra.*

[46]See, *United States—Standards for Reformulated and Conventional Gasoline* (WT/DS2/R), Report of the Panel, January 26, 1996 ("*Reformulated Gas*"); *Thailand—Restrictions on Importation of and Internal Taxes on Cigarettes,* GATT Doc. DS10/R, BISD 37S/200 (Nov. 7, 1990) *(Thai Cigarettes).*

[47]See, e.g., *In the Matter of Lobsters from Canada,* Panel No USA 89-1897-01, U.S.— Canada Free Trade Agreement (FTA), Binational Panel Review. At issue in this case was the application of GATT Article XX(g), not (b), yet the panel's reasoning is instructive. The United States had adopted a conservation measure prohibiting the sale of undersized lobsters. Size in lobsters is related to maturation, and both U.S. and Canadian scientists believed that harvesting undersized lobsters had contributed to the fishery's rapid decline. Despite this, the FTA panel ruled that the measure in question was not *primarily aimed at conservation* (and thus not safeguarded by GATT

Article XX(g)). The panel's reasoning was based on the fact that it could not determine that conservation was the only objective of the measure and further, that the United States engaged in only a limited discussion of possible alternative solutions. According to the panel, the United States did not address the reasons for which its conservation objectives could not be met by special marking of Canadian small lobsters (which apparently reached maturation before U.S. lobsters). Of course, the reason the United States eventually banned all undersized lobsters (originally it had allowed the sale of Canadian undersized lobsters with proof of Canadian origin) was because it was very difficult to enforce anything other than a total ban on the sale of small-sized lobsters, and there was evidence that rampant cheating had been occurring under the original measure. *See, id.* at para. 9.5.1–9.8.

[48]In *Tuna-Dolphin II*, the GATT panel reasoned that only if other governments changed their policies would U.S. conservation objectives be met.

[49]The Appellate Body in both *Reformulated Gasoline AB* and *Shrimp-Turtle AB* determined that there were alternative means available to achieve the conservation goal in question and that therefore the chosen measure was either an *arbitrary and unjustifiable* or *a disguised restriction on* trade. The effect of these rulings is no different than if a *least-trade-restrictive test* had been employed. *See, note 46 supra* and discussion of "necessity" *infra*.

[50]The United States argued that there was no viable alternative (from an enforcement point of view) to the measure in question. Though clearly not experts in air quality control, the Appellate Body nonetheless felt it appropriate to determine that alternative measures were viable. *See, Reformulated Gasoline* at paras. 4.10–4.17.

[51]In this case, the Appellate Body found that the United States 1) had failed to try to negotiate an international agreement to protect sea turtles from the complaining countries; 2) had discriminated in its efforts to transfer technology; and 3) had established no procedure for review of, or appeal from , a denial of an application, as well as other basic elements of due process. Therefore, the measure in question did not pass the requirements set forth in the *chapeau*. *Shrimp-Turtle AB* at paras. 171, 175, and 180–184.

[52]*See, e.g., Shrimp I,* note 6 *supra.* at para. 7.50. ("We are of the view that these treaties show that environmental protection through international agreement—as opposed to unilateral measures—have for a long time been a recognized course of action for environmental protection....We are not dealing with measures taken by the United States in application of an agreement to which it is a party, as the United States does not claim that it is allowed or required by any international agreement [sic] to impose an import ban on shrimp in order to protect sea turtles.") *See also, Tuna-Dolphin I,* note 7 *supra.* at *para 5.24* ("[T]he import prohibition imposed by the United States was not necessary because alternative means consistent with the General Agreement were available to it to protect dolphin lives or health, namely international co-operation between the countries concerned.")

[53]A requirement of consensus can lead to downward harmonization to the least common denominator. Invariably, there are environmental and animal problems that affect countries differently. For example, to some, the elimination of fishing subsidies may be a hardship, while to others it is the inevitable solution to over-fishing. Those to whom it is a hardship may balk at strong international regulation, even though such regulation is in the long-term interest of all countries. (In this regard, in preparation for the 1999 Ministerial Conference, seven countries, including the United States, submitted a paper to the WTO regarding the elimination of fishing subsidies. WT/GC/W/XXX, July 30, 1999 [99-2779] Despite clear evidence regarding the harm of over-fishing, discussions regarding the elimination of fishing subsidies has been met with hostility by many countries, including Japan and the European Union.) Consensus in such circumstance may result in weak international solutions that do not adequately resolve the harm at hand.

[54]Examples of MEA organizations include the International Whaling Commission, the Inter-American Tropical Tuna Commission, and CITES.

[55]*See,* Jenkins, L. 1993. Trade sanctions: An effective enforcement tool. *2 Review of European Community & Environmental Law [Trade Sanctions]* 362.

[56]There are three animal/environmental-related treaties that use or have recommended the use of trade measures. The International Commission for the Conservation of Atlantic Tunas (ICCAT) adopted a provision that allows for trade sanctions to be taken against non-ICCAT members who refuse to cooperate with the commission's conservation program for bluefin tuna and swordfish. See, Resolution adopted by the Commission at its Ninth Special Meeting (Madrid, November-December 1994). Report for Biennial Period, 194–95, Part 1.

Similarly, the Montreal Protocol on Substances that Deplete the Ozone Layer (the "Protocol") regulates trade in chlorofluorocarbons, carbon tetrachloride, and trichloromethane but provides for the use of trade measures only against non-complying non-parties. *See,* Art 4. para. 4 of the Protocol which provides that "the parties shall determine the feasibility of banning or restricting, from States not a party to this Protocol, the import of products produced with, but not containing, controlled substances."

[57]*See, note 56 supra.*

[58]*See, e.g.,* statement of Sir Leon Brittan, vice president of the European Commission, contained in Policing the Global Economy, Proceedings of the International Conference organized by the Bellerive Foundation and GLOBE International, Geneva, March 1998, at 37. ("My view is clear: where there is an MEA which commands wide support among WTO members, we need to be more confident than at present that WTO trade rules do accommodate the aims of the parties to the MEA, and therefore allow trade measures to be taken under such an MEA. WTO rules should not be capable of being used to frustrate the objective on an MEA.")

[59]The Biosafety Agreement Preamble provides in relevant part:

Recognizing that trade and environment agreements should be mutually supportive with a view to achieving sustainable development,

Emphasizing that this Protocol shall not be interpreted as implying a change in the rights and obligations of a Party under any existing international agreements,

Understanding that the above recital is not intended to subordinate this Protocol to other international agreements.

[60]Article 30 of the Vienna Convention on the Law of Treaties provides a procedure for resolving conflicts between treaties. The general rule is that the agreement negotiated later in time prevails. Because these new MEAs are being negotiated subsequent to the WTO Agreements, governments like the United States are taking precautions to ensure that the new MEA provisions do not trump WTO rules. Specifically, Article 30 provides:

...2. When a treaty specifies that it is subject to, or that it is not considered as incompatible with, an earlier or later treaty, the provisions of that other treaty prevail.

3. When all the parties to the earlier treaty are parties also to the later treaty...the earlier treaty applies only to the extent that its provisions are compatible with those of the later treaty.

4. When the parties to the later treaty do not include all the parties to the earlier one:...b) as between a State party to both treaties and a State party to only one of the treaties, the treaty to which both States are parties governs their mutual rights and obligations.

[61]*See, Tuna-Dolphin I and Tuna-Dolphin II.*

[62]For instance, in the case of tuna caught by killing dolphins, the issue is not that the tuna cans contain dolphin meat; rather, in harvesting tuna, dolphins are killed. The encircling and netting of dolphins and tuna is part of the production process rather than the end-product of canned tuna.

[63]The most recent endorsements of the principle include the 1987 Second International Conference on the Protection of the North Sea, the 1990 Bergen Ministerial Declaration, the 1990 Ministerial Declaration on Environmentally Sound and Sustainable Development in Asia and the Pacific, and the 1991 meeting of the United Nations Environmental Program (UNEP) Governing Council. *See* Naomi Roth-Arriaza, Precaution and the 'greening' of international trade law, 7 *Journal of Environmental Law and Litigation,* 60–63 (1992).

[64]The TBT was amended in the Uruguay Round Negotiations and now provides that the terms "standard" and "technical regulations" include product-related processes and production methods.

[65]Article III, para. 1 recognizes the validity of "internal taxes and other internal charges and laws, regulations and requirements affecting the internal sale, offering for sale, purchase, transportation, distribution, or use of products" so long as the measure in question is not applied to imported or domestic products "so as to afford protection to domestic production."

[66]GATT art. XX.

[67]*See Tuna-Dolphin I; Tuna-Dolphin II;* and *Eurocars.*

[68]DSU art. 3.8.

[69]These include the requirements that "measures are not applied in a manner which would constitute (1) a means of arbitrary or unjustifiable discrimination between countries where the same conditions prevail, or (2) a disguised restriction on international trade..." GATT 1947 art. XX (preamble).

[70]*Webster's Third New International Dictionary,* unabridged. 1971. 1544.

[71]Charnovitz, S. 1992. The environmental exceptions in GATT Article XX, *Journal of World Trade,* 49.

[72]To date, there has been no direct challenge under either GATS or the TBT Agreement. The Article XX case law, therefore, is illustrative of how a Dispute panel would interpret similar language contained in GATS and the TBT Agreement.

73The term "necessary" is used in GATT Article XX, GATS Article XIV, and the preambles of both the SPS and TBT Agreements.

74See, e.g., *United States—Restrictions on Imports of Tuna* (unpublished decision), GATT Doc. DS29/R (May 23, 1994); *Thailand— Restrictions on Importation of and Internal Taxes on Cigarettes,* GATT Doc. DS10/R, BISD 37S/200 (Nov. 7, 1990).

75Charnovitz, Environmental exceptions, *note 71 supra.* Charnovitz points out the dilemma of an exempt-purpose measure that conflicts with multiple parts of the GATT. For example, a tax preference for local industry to use less dirty fuel might be less restrictive than a ban on dirty fuel under GATT 1947 article XIII (quantitative restrictions), but it could be attacked as a subsidy under the Agreement on Subsidies and Countervailing Measures.

76The term "life and health" is used in GATT Article XX, GATS Article XIV, the Preamble and throughout the SPS Agreement, and the Preamble and Article II of the TBT Agreement.

77SPS Annex A.1(a).

78Charnovitz, Environmental exceptions, *note 71 supra. (citing International Trade Organization,* Hearings Before the Committee on Finance, Part 1, U.S. Senate, 84th Congress, 1st Session, at 442), 44.

79*1927 Convention,* 224.

80*1927 Convention,* 18.

81UN Doc. E/PC/T/A/PV/30 at 7–13.

82Understanding on Rules and Procedures Governing the Settlement of Disputes ("DSU"). Article 17 of the DSU establishes that a standing Appellate Body shall be established by the Dispute Settlement Body (which is comprised of the Members of the WTO Agreements).

83*See, Tuna-Dolphin II.*

84Those who espouse this view rely on the fact that original GATT drafting committees described a resource as "raw material" or "mineral." UN Doc. E/PC/T/C.H/50, 4; *see,* Charnovitz, Environmental exceptions, *note 71 supra.*

85*See, e.g., Tuna-Dolphin II* at para 5.13 and *Shrimp-Turtle AB* at para. 132.

86GATS Article XIV(a) states: "necessary to protect public morals or to maintain public order." Footnote 5 to this section further provides that the public order exception may be invoked only where a genuine and sufficiently serious threat is posed to one of the fundamental interests of society."

87*1927 Convention,* art. 4(2), 8.

88*Preliminary Draft Agreement Established by the Economic Committee, 1927 Convention,* 228.

89*Minutes, 1927 Convention,* 108.

90*Minutes, 1927 Convention,* 110.

91*Preliminary Draft, 1927 Convention,* 224.

92*1927 Convention, Official Instruments,* 8. At one point, the "moral and humanitarian" exception had been deleted during the drafting process. When the Egyptian and British delegates moved to put it back in, the committee's rapporteur explained that the intent had not been to delete the moral exception but to consider that it was included within the terms of a broader section that protected restrictions that applied to like national products. While the committe chose to reinsert the moral exception, this episode illustrates the effort that the committee was making to develop the broadest possible generic categories. *Minutes, 1927 Convention,* 107–108.

93*International Convention Concerning the Transit of Animals, Meat and Other Products of Animal Origin,* art. 5, C.78.M.34.1935.II[B] (March 1935), 3.

94*Report of the First Session of the Preparatory Committee of the United Nations Conference on Trade and Employment [ITO London Report],* United States Draft Charter, Annexure 11, art. 32(a), 60.

95*ITO London Report,* 32.

96 "The [New York] draft Agreement reproduces many provisions of the Charter. Reservations entered by delegates to those provisions of the Charter...apply equally to the corresponding provisions of the draft Agreement." *Report of the Drafting Committee of the Preparatory Committee of the United Nations Conference on Trade and Employment [ITO New York Report],* Part III, Draft General Agreement on Tariffs and Trade, Introduction, para. 1, 65. *See also, Report of the Second Session of the Preparatory Committee of the United Nations Conference on Trade and Employment* (Geneva, August 1947), 70.

97Apart from the ITO reports and appendices, neither the State Department Library nor the National Archives was able to locate any documents that would explain the U.S. rationale.

98This language appears in GATT Article XX, GATS Article XIV, and the SPS and TBT Agreements.

99*See,* SPS, Annex A (Definitions).

100*European Communities—Measures Concerning Meat and Meat Products (Hormones),* United States (WT/DS26/R), Report of the Panel, June 30, 1997 *("Beef Hormones I"); European Communities—Measures Concerning Meat and Meat Products (Hormones), United States* (WT/DS26/AB/R and WT/DS48/AB/R), Report of the Appellate Body, adopted, February 13, 1998 *("Beef Hormones AB".)*

101*Beef Hormone* at para. 8.96.

102*Id.* at para. 8.114.

103*Id.* at para. 8.117.

104*Id.* at para. 8.157. The European Union argued that the precautionary principle was part of customary international law and should be used to interpret Articles 5.1 and 5.2. The United States said it did not consider the precautionary principle international law and suggested it was more an "approach" than a "principle." *See, Beef Hormone AB* at para. 122.

105*Id* at para. 193.

106*Id.* at para. 194.

107*Id* at para. 207 and 208. ("The [European Union] did not actually proceed to an assessment...of the risks arising from the failure of observance of good veterinary practice combined with problems of control of the use of hormones for growth promotion purposes.")

108The effects of Bt corn on the monarch butterfly is a case in point. The widespread global distribution of this genetically modified seed occurred long before laboratory tests confirmed Bt corn kills monarch butterfly larvae. Consequently, the effects of this seed on adult monarchs in the field is totally uncertain. Literally, the earth had become the petri dish to prove or disprove biological harm. Such potentially devastating implications should be well understood in containment—prior to release.

109In *Shrimp-Turtle AB* the Appellate Body relied on an international principle called "Abuse of Rights" to find that the U.S. law in question was a violation of U.S. obligations under the WTO. *See, note 7 supra* at para 158.

110Program on International Policy Attitudes, Center on Policy Attitudes of the University of Maryland. 2000. Americans on globalization: A study of U.S. public attitudes, 5 (Mar. 28, 2000), available at *<http://www.pipa.org/>.*

111*Id.* at 23.

112*Id.* at 24.

113*Id.* at 25.

Urban Wildlife

11
CHAPTER

John Hadidian and Sydney Smith

Introduction

Humans have been experimenting with "urban living" for at least the last six millennia. The scope of this experiment has been described as "massive" and "unplanned" (McDonnell and Pickett 1990), an apt characterization of a phenomenon that is also known by such terms as "sprawl" and "blight." Urbanization is both a biophysical and a social phenomenon. Among its many measurable physical characteristics are greater concentrations of airborne dust, carbon dioxide, and sulfur compounds and slightly higher precipitation, annual mean temperature, and ultraviolet radiation at ground level than is typical in surrounding hinterlands (Trefil 1994). Among its social consequences are the inhabitants' alienation and disassociation from natural environments, juxtaposed with attitude and value scales that indicate greater concern for the protection and preservation of such environments and the wildlife that inhabit them than is the case among nonurbanites (Kellert 1996).

While cities cover no more than 1 or 2 percent of a typical habitable land mass, they have an impact that far exceeds their physical presence. In much of the world (and soon in all of it), the urban populace outnumbers the rural. Today, eight of every ten Americans live in towns of fifty thousand or more, with more than half of

the population living in cities of a million residents or more. If projected trends hold true, the majority of all humans on Earth will be urbanites sometime early in the twenty-first century (United Nations 1987). Urban ecosystems demand natural resources and raw materials far in excess of what they can produce and thus have the potential to influence the global ecology. Rees (1996) defines the "ecological footprint" of the city as the area required to supply raw materials, resources, and other opportunities, such as recreation, for urbanites. Direct and indirect ecosystem impacts of cities, varying from air pollution to nitrogen loading, have reached the point at which human influences now extend to the most remote and previously pristine global reaches (Vitousek et al. 1997).

Despite the dominance of humans in the urban environment, other animals flourish there as well. It is almost certain that when humans first began to aggregate in urban communities, specific conditions were established that favored certain plants and animals, which joined humanity in colonizing what were, for them, preferred habitats. These synanthropes have been far less studied than their counterparts elsewhere, and it is tempting to suggest that this is because those who pursue such knowledge have been biased to regard

urban ecosystems and habitats as "artificial" when compared with "natural" ones found outside the human-built environment. Of course, the same ecological processes that affect the "natural" world "out there" affect the "artificial" world of cities "in here." Undoubtedly, their form, rate, and effects vary with the influence of the built environment, but this may only make their study more relevant and interesting.

Indeed, urbanization may be better understood from an ecological perspective than it is from a socioeconomic one, as is much more common. That said, the consequences of urbanization on natural communities of plants and animals remain largely unknown and may be difficult to understand at all, given the rapidity with which cities and the areas they influence are changing.

Despite the potential for difficulty, there are several reasons why urban wildlife should be valued and better understood. First is its scientific and heuristic value. Urban wildlife populations are essentially parts of ongoing natural experiments in adaptation to anthropogenic stress. How urban animals are affected by human activities—and how they cope with them—can represent, on a highly accelerated scale, a model of what is happening to species in other biomes. No other wild animals live in such intimate contact and under such constant constraint from human activities as do synanthropes. Second, urban animals are exposed to many environmental hazards and should be considered sentinels on our behalf. Additionally, wildlife in urban environments is apparently quite important to people (Adams 1994; Kellert 1996; Reiter et al. 1999). It may be critical that these coinhabitants maintain a connection between people within the most densely settled human developments and the natural environment. Finally, we argue that there is an inherent value and right for wildlife species to exist, in whatever type of environment they are found. Human beings have a moral obligation to recognize and appreciate the diversity of life and celebrate it by acknowledging the rights of others.

Historical Background

The formal study of urban wildlife is of quite recent origin, although human involvement with wild animals in cities and towns is deeply rooted in history. The Roman historian Josephus, for example, in the first century A.D., mentioned the use of metal spires on the rooftops of Jerusalem to deter birds (possibly storks) from nesting there. Wild animals were undoubtedly tolerated, controlled, or ignored in cities and towns for many centuries without a Josephus to take note. Occasional records surface to detail events as well as afford us a glimpse into changing social mores. In at least two cases, documented from medieval times, efforts were made to use the device of excommunication to control unruly sparrows around places of worship, in the one case for defecating on pews and in the other for "scandalous unchastity" that occurred during the delivery of a sermon (Evans 1906; Ryder 1989). The development of an interest in life's diversity during the Age of Discovery fueled an understanding of animal lives as phenomena worthy of study, an understanding that previous-

ly had not occurred (Thomas 1983). The subsequent heyday of natural history (Barber 1980) coincided with the onset of the Darwinian revolution and led to increasingly objective, scientific study of animals as well as to a heightened interest in and sympathy for human impact on animals and their habitats. Representative of many general works arising from the increased interest in natural history is Ernest Ingersoll's *Wild Neighbors* (1899), a combination of natural history, anecdote, and scientific speculation about common urban, as well as decidedly nonurban, species.

In one of the first scientific publications on any aspect of urban wildlife, Shenstone (1912) described the flora of building sites in London, including the role of both wild and domestic animals in transporting seeds to various locations within the city. Probably the first comprehensive description of an urban fauna is Richard S. R. Fitter's *The Natural History of London* (1945). John Kieran's *A Natural History of New York City* (1959), is the American counterpart to Fitter's work. The French geographer Jean Gottman (1961) devoted a chapter in his seminal description of the urban future, *Megalopolis*, to wildlife and forests, but restricted his discussion largely to the role of game species and the conflicts that were caused by the overabundance of animals such as white-tailed deer.

More concerted and focused interest in urban wildlife arose in the late 1960s. The first technical session among wildlife professionals that focused specifically on urban wildlife was organized in 1967 at the Thirty-second North American Fish and Wildlife Conference (Scheffey 1967). That session, "Farm and Urban Resources," included papers by Stuart Davey (1967) on the role of wildlife in an urban environment, Forest Stearns (1967) on wildlife habitat, and Robert Twiss (1967) on wildlife in the metropolitan environment. The first truly national conference on the subject was convened under the auspices of the U.S. Fish and Wildlife Service (then the Bureau of Wildlife and

Sport Fisheries). "Man and Nature in the City," held in Washington, D.C., in 1968, marked the emergence of the field of urban wildlife from its previous anonymity. It was followed in 1974 by a symposium organized in Great Britain around the theme of the place of nature in cities and towns, and Laurie (1979) summarized the two events in a collection of papers on the idea of urban green space. Over the next decades, a number of conferences were held (Noyes and Progulske 1974; Euler et al. 1975; Stenberg and Shaw 1986; Adams and Leedy 1987, 1991), each broadening the basis for the discipline. Texts or collected works on urban wildlife were not so forthcoming, although Gill and Bonnett (1973) co-authored an early general work on urban ecosystems that emphasized urban wildlife. Gilbert (1989) published a general work on the ecology of urban habitats that included much information on wildlife, and Adams (1994) issued a general text on urban wildlife habitats that went into almost immediate use in college courses in wildlife management. Platt et al. (1994) contributed a broad overview of the "ecological" city to introduce and emphasize the preservation and conservation of urban biodiversity, thus continuing a tradition of looking at wildlife as a component of the larger urban ecosystem. This tradition has been even better observed in Europe, where studies of urban ecosystems (e.g., Marcuzzi 1979; Sukopp et al. 1995) have probably been more comprehensive, longstanding, and widespread than have those in the United States, if less available.

Works on urban wildlife intended for the general public have long constituted their own literary genre. In the United States, these have ranged from popular works and general natural histories (Beebe 1953; Kieran 1959; Garber 1987) to backyard field guides (Villard 1975; Mitchell 1985) and works that focus on specific urban species (Rublowsky 1967; Kinkead 1974, 1978). Goode (1986) published in England a general description of the wildlife of London and its environs and Shirley (1996) a general natural history of urban wildlife, both of which, while written for lay audiences, were more science based than many earlier works. Baines (1986) combined a more popular account of English urban wildlife with advice for improving the habitat in backyards to encourage and support wildlife. An interesting variation on the general theme of urban natural history is provided in both English and American examples of the ecological history of a single human dwelling over the passage of several centuries for each (Ordish 1959, 1981).

Although academic interest and focus on urban wildlife is gradually increasing, the field clearly remains under-emphasized in comparison with traditional (resource management, consumptive use) orientations in university curricula. Adams et al. (1985) surveyed ninety-five colleges and universities that offered a wildlife sciences curriculum to determine their involvement in urban wildlife issues. Of the eighty responding, most (92 percent) did not have a recognized urban wildlife program. Of those that did, only 5 percent of all wildlife projects ongoing in the questionnaire year focused on urban wildlife; they devoted only 2 percent of their research budgets to urban wildlife studies. Follow-up surveys have not been conducted, but change, if any, over the intervening fifteen years appears to have been slight. A quick review of articles in the *Journal of Wildlife Management*, the foremost American journal dealing with wildlife study, shows only one of more than three hundred articles published in 1999 containing the words "urban" or "suburban" in its title (it is a study of a nesting raptor population).

The efforts of state and federal agencies to recognize and deal systematically with urban wildlife issues have not seemed equal to the need of urban residents (San Julien 1987). The federal government had launched the field of urban wildlife as a formal pursuit in 1968 and followed with a series of publications on urban eco-

systems (Sudia 1971 et seq.), including one focusing specifically on urban wildlife (Sudia 1978). A National Park Service research facility (the Center for Urban Ecology) was dedicated in 1985, praised six years after that opening (Hester 1991) and closed four years later. The only private-sector nonprofit urban wildlife organization, the National Institute for Urban Wildlife, also closed its doors in the mid-1990s. A few years later, Babbitt (1999) suggested that urban ecology was being "rediscovered" at high levels in American government. State involvement with urban wildlife programs appears to have been minimal as well, although it certainly was increasing faster than were university programs. Lyons and Leedy (1984) asked state wildlife agencies in 1983 if they had urban wildlife programs. Only six responded positively, noting programs whose principal functions were identified as extension, public education, and management. Only three states reported research as part of their activities, and only 8 percent of staff time and 5 percent of budget were devoted to this activity.

Federal and state involvement in urban wildlife issues and programs has been complicated by at least three factors. First, tradition has dictated that wildlife agencies and wildlife professionals looked to rural areas and their constituencies as the places where wildlife work should be done (San Julien 1987). Funding mechanisms, such as federal Pittman-Roberston Act monies, which stem from a federal excise tax on firearms and ammunition, have focused on projects more of service to rural than to urban constituencies and for consumptive more than for nonconsumptive wildlife users. Finally, the unspoken but apparently real bias against urban areas as suitable for research has tended to focus academic interest and resources away from our demographic centers. With increasing environmental awareness and activism, ecological understanding, and the demands of the urban populace for help in resolving wildlife conflicts, this situation is slowly changing. Unfortu-

nately, many unique opportunities to conduct definitive research on wild animals in urban and suburban environments during periods where colonization, population growth, and diversification were under way have been lost, to the detriment of future understanding.

Cities as Wildlife Habitat

Cities, as well as suburbs, encompass diverse and complex habitats to which many wild animals show affinity. What to the observer may seem to be a "biological desert" (the inner city) may in fact be suitable habitat for even such highly specialized predators as peregrine falcons (*Falco peregrinus*). Less noticed, but of equal or greater biological significance, would be the microfauna of these places, such as the detritus feeders that might live upon organic material blown into and stopped by the building faces. Generally, the biota of urban places have not been documented as well as they have been for other systems, but inventories and descriptions clearly tell us that even such "waste" places as vacant lots can have complex biological communities adapted, and adapting still, to the special biophysical characteristics of the sites they occupy (Vessel and Wong 1987). The complex, varied, and changing landscapes of cities and towns must certainly constrain attempts by many animals to successfully colonize them and maintain viable populations. Urban wildlife habitats are characterized by dynamic and changing environmental conditions in which both natural changes (e.g., the maturation of vegetation) and anthropogenic changes (e.g., the clearing of vegetation) constantly impose demands for accommodation. Thus, if urban landscapes have any defining characteristic as wildlife habitat, it must be their heterogeneity and variability.

Numerous schemes have been proposed to identify the various components of the urban landscape and describe its ecological properties.

Brady et al. (1979) proposed a hierarchical landscape scheme based on biogeographical units to help visualize both the richness of urban habitats and the landscape scales that could be imposed on urban areas, from regional to highly local and site-specific perspectives. Dickman (1987) proposed a structural classification of the urban lands of Oxford, England, in a scheme that included woodland, scrub (regenerating woodland), orchard, long grass, short grass (lawns, parks, playing fields), allotments, churchyards, and gardens of detached and semi-detached houses. Other possible habitats in the urban environment include cemeteries, utility corridors, university and corporate campuses, storm sewers, waterfronts, and garbage disposal sites (Stearns 1967). To these areas Davis and Glick (1978) add roadsides and median strips, city-center highrises, apartment blocks and condominiums, parking lots, golf courses, railroad tracks, and old residential neighborhoods. A basic dichotomy of urban habitats distinguishes between "open space," such as parklands and woodlots, and "built areas," such as residential housing, commercial buildings, and industrial areas (Foreman 1995).

Some generalizations about urban habitats are possible, although they may not hold true everywhere. Urban areas tend to sustain low species diversity (Dickman 1987; Gilbert 1989). This may be attributable to anthropogenic impacts, low habitat diversity, missing habitat types, species sensitivity, fragmentation, absence of successional stages, or simply the altered "geometry" (Goldstein et al. 1981) of vegetation in urban and suburban areas. The species that do adapt to and survive in urban areas tend to be present at greater concentrations than is typical for them in other types of habitats (Gilbert 1989; Riley at al. 1998). This could be attributed to relatively greater food abundance, absence of competitors, absence of predators, or a combination of these factors. The extreme fragmentation of the landscape in cities tends also to create habitat "islands" (Davis and Glick 1978) that may promote some species while suppressing others.

Ecology of Urban Wildlife

Wildlife inventories for urban areas are generally lacking, although specialty groups, such as birds, have been fairly well documented for some cities (Montier 1977; Guth 1979; Cousin 1983; Hadidian et al. 1997b). Large animals undoubtedly tend to disappear with increasing urbanization, as do habitat specialists or species sensitive to habitat fragmentation, such as many reptiles and amphibians (Campbell 1974). The survival and extinction rates of local and regional populations under various forms of anthropogenic stress need to be better studied, as do virtually all aspects of genetic change and variation within populations of "urban" organisms.

Even less studied than the biophysical effects of urbanization on animal distribution and abundance are the life histories and general ecological relations of urbanized species. Perhaps the best-studied urban mammal is the red fox, *Vulpes vulpes* (Harris 1977, 1981, 1994; MacDonald and Newdick 1982; Lloyd 1981; Page 1981; Kolb 1984). The studies conducted by Stephen Harris on the urban fox population of Bristol, England, span more than twenty years of observation and research and are unquestionably the most comprehensive study of any urban species. Harris found that this urban fox population was heavily provisioned by human residents, many of whom deliberately engaged in feeding programs. Bristol fox population densities were found to be extremely high, while territory sizes were small, and fox groups with multiple adult members were observed in a species that elsewhere was classically identified as solitary. Profound changes in the population density and, concurrently, the social organization of Bristol foxes occurred as a result of an outbreak in 1994 of sarcoptic mange, a disease that in foxes can lead to high mortality. The outbreak led to more than 80 percent annual mortality in the Bristol fox population until by 1996 nearly all the foxes in the study population were dead. Four years later the population recovery was still proceeding slowly, with social behavior, territory size, movement and activity patterns, and virtually all other aspects of fox life reverting toward the norm described in other studies (Harris 2000). Beyond demonstrating the extreme adaptability and social flexibility of fox populations, the long-term studies by Harris and colleagues challenge preexisting assumptions concerning the "normal" behavior of wildlife populations and call into question the meaning of "normal" itself.

Wildlife and Land Development

The urban population of Earth increased tenfold in the last century (Platt 1994). One consequence has been the rapid transformation of land from agricultural and undeveloped natural zones to expanding suburbs and the consumption of open space within existing urban zones. The term "sprawl" has been coined to describe the haphazard and chaotic pattern of suburban expansion, although long before that name appeared the issue had been identified and described (Dassmann 1972). The impacts of development on wildlife range from the direct physical destruction of animals and their habitats as land is cleared to the loss of habitat "values" such as size and connectivity, which can lead to local extirpations or failure of some fauna to be able to recolonize an area that has been isolated. Although there may be ways to indirectly measure the effects of development activities on wildlife, such as through estimates of change in the amount of available wetlands habitat, there is little that can be done to more than guess at the overall magnitude of impacts. Enough concern exists for the deleterious short- and long-term impacts of development, however, to have created professional responses in the form of alternative development schemes, mitigation strategies, and an emerging body of scientific information that addresses the value of landscape features such as patch size, habitat mosaics, and corridors to link natural areas and open space (Foreman and Godron 1986). The concept of linking design and environment is personified historically by the seminal work of Ian McHarg (1969), whose *Design with Nature* ushered in an era of attention to the greater schemes of nature and human interaction with landscapes.

Loss of habitat and habitat fragmentation are critical issues in urbanizing environments and are cited as the most common reasons for population reduction or loss of species in such places (Davis and Glick 1978; Adams 1994). Because private land ownership decentralizes the planning process, habitat destruction and alteration can occur on a parcel-by-parcel basis, with little attention paid to such needs as preserving habitat connectivity. The results are truncated corridors, habitat islands, and mosaics of different types of land at different stages of development. By the theory of island biogeography (MacArthur and Wilson 1967), the larger islands of habitat should contain greater species diversity and experience lower rates of "extinction" as populations within them dip below thresholds of sustainability. Under such configurations habitat areas can also function as population sinks, demanding a constant influx of animals from outside to sustain themselves (Pulliam 1988). The same effect can be caused by human activities such as trapping and removal of "nuisance" animals or culling of local populations. Isolated urban habitat areas also should adversely affect the genetic interchange between populations, although the consequences of this are as yet little understood (Davis and Glick 1978).

Another consequence of fragmentation is that it leads to an increase in landscape edge. Edges, or ecotones, provide critical habitat for some wildlife species, such as deer, allowing access to cover within one habitat type (e.g., forest) and food in another (e.g., fields). Such edge habitat may favor nonnative species, particularly plant species, with corresponding changes in animal community structure. Roads can create significant edge across a landscape and can be a major factor in causing habitat fragmentation. They also can burden animal populations as a direct cause of mortality. For some groups, such as amphibians, arthropods, and small mammals, roads may essentially be complete barriers (Mader 1990; Richardson et al. 1997). Wildlife mortalities from roadways are documented for only a few of the larger and economically more important species, but those that are known are considerable. Conover et al. (1995) estimated more than a million deer-vehicle collisions annually for the United States, with approximately two hundred people killed and a billion dollars in property damage as the consequences.

The process of land development includes such activities as clearing, grading, soil compression, lake draining, and infill, all of which profoundly affect everything that lives on sites in the pre-development stage. Surprisingly, there seem to be no studies on such sites in which total species composition and pre-and post-development distribution and abundance of species have been documented over time. On-site impacts on nonvolant species—for example, small- and medium-sized mammals, invertebrates, amphibians, and reptiles—will be immediate and direct and typically end in almost complete destruction. Larger mammals and volant species will be displaced, with potential for increased mortality as well as conflict and competition with conspecifics, as those displaced attempt to become reestablished elsewhere. The effects of displacement will be difficult to measure and depend on so many external factors and conditions that it may be

some time before a body of information sufficient to identifying trends could be collected. This complexity is similar to that faced by investigators seeking to understand the effects and consequences of wildlife translocation (Craven et al. 1998), and it is possible that studies of such phenomena could be approached under the same conceptual framework.

Certainly, the timing of land clearing would be critical to determining whether animals with dependent young were affected. However, decisions to schedule an event to avoid birth or weaning periods in any wildlife species would be entirely voluntary under most development schemes, excepting those in which state or federally protected threatened or endangered species are involved. Few laws exist to curb or shape the development process in ways that mitigate or minimize impact on wildlife. Those that do exist, such as the Migratory Bird Treaty Act (MBTA), could theoretically be used to afford protection to some species, but are probably so little known to developers that they might as well not be there. The MBTA makes it unlawful for anyone to "pursue," "take," or otherwise harm any migratory bird or to destroy nests or eggs unless under a federal permit, but it is clearly abrogated on a large scale when development incidentally "takes" birds, their nests and eggs, or their flightless young as land is cleared. To bring a claim on such activities under the MBTA it would be necessary to prove a willful violation of the act, beyond simple knowledge of the presence or potential presence of nesting birds.

Land clearing can be timed to minimize impact on specific species' nesting, birthing, and weaning schedules, and pre-development surveys and efforts to conduct "salvage" operations to remove specific species can be conducted. It may simply be that a greater awareness and more information about these practices could lead to some voluntary compliance or that local ordinances could be crafted that would allow such factors to be taken into account during the development permitting process. Few wildlife professionals or organizations, however, have focused on wildlife in these contexts or attempted to communicate with developers about these needs. Little is known about the attitudes of the public on these issues or whether such consequences as increased expense would be supported if developers were engaging in salvage or rescue efforts.

Much of today's land-use policy is determined within a utilitarian framework in which economic considerations predominate (Beatley 1994). The potential economic benefits of development schemes that include wildlife habitat (more frequently termed open space or conservation areas) as part of the overall planning concept have been gaining attention and where examined indicate some positive influences on property value (King et al. 1991). Beyond that, with the public moving toward a greater environmental consciousness, the preservation of ecosystems, conservation of biological diversity, and protection of small and unique habitats and their wildlife are receiving more advocacy (Nash 1989). Arguments are being made for planners to anticipate and counteract threats to vulnerable wildlife populations (Hough 1994). Still, despite twenty of the forty national policies of the American Society of Landscape Architects focused on environmental issues, there is no policy regarding wildlife (Wacker 1987).

In an ideal world for urban wildlife, development sites would be assessed by qualified personnel to determine what species occur on year-round and seasonal bases, how development is likely to affect resident wildlife or transients (e.g., neotropical migratory songbirds), and what can be done, at all stages of development, to minimize the impacts that might occur (SCWF 1997). To some extent, experiments in this approach have begun, as in the King County, Washington, effort to identify significant wildlife habitat and review development plans to ensure that critical amenities and values are maintained under zoning

prescriptions. Another approach to determining wildlife presence and potential, rather than focusing on biological inventories of fauna, involves an inventory and assessment of habitat (Burns et al. 1986; Geis 1986; Matthews 1986; Houck 1987). Once identified, such areas can be manipulated within a landscape ecological scheme to determine how physical factors such as patch size and connectivity interact with specific faunal groups, such as songbirds, to create predictive models that help prioritize land units from which maximum conservation value will be realized (Darr et al. 1998).

The concept of urban open-space management from an ecological perspective is widely recognized by urban wildlife specialists as both critical to conserving wildlife in urbanizing environments and beneficial to enjoyment by human residents (Adams and Dove 1989; Gilbert 1989; Hough 1994). Ecological landscape planning and design intends to integrate known concepts of landscape design and ecological process to understand and manage land-human relationships on a broad scale. It is characterized by viewing nature as a partner from a bioregional vantage point, integrating design with soils, vegetation, topography, and human culture. It embraces an inclusive process of discussion and debate, challenging the notion that architecture and design are pure processes that "should not be 'contaminated' by any real-world constraints or needs: social, environmental, or economic" (Van der Ryn and Cowan 1996).

The historical development of the field has been traced by Richard Foreman (1995) through three broad phases. The first, which extended to about 1950, encompassed a period of emphasis on natural history and the environment in which identification of many of the underlying principles and factors of landscapes and animal populations was a necessary prerequisite to a synthesis of information into a conceptual framework. A second, so-called "weaving" phase, between 1950 and 1980, involved the drawing

together of previously established threads to set the stage for the current "land mosaic" or "coalescence" phase. The current period is marked by the attempt to create an overall conceptual framework that explains landscapes from a regional perspective, incorporating the ecological processes and ecosystem functions subsumed at that scale. It is made possible by advances in our understanding of ecological process and functioning and by tools, such as the Geographic Information Systems (GIS), that allow regional perspectives to be drawn on what are complex and interconnected landscape elements.

In a broad sense, ecological design is a process whereby each community member can be considered a "participant-designer," and the balance of knowledge is shifted from the experts to all. Ecological design advocates the identification and protection of core reserves of habitat that are off-limits to human disturbance, surrounded by expanding buffer zones that allow a range of uses, from nature trails to low-density housing to more-intense land use. These core reserves ought to be connected by wildlife corridors (Adams and Dove 1989; Van der Ryn and Cowan 1996). Employing techniques such as following the natural contour of the land, clearing and grading less, retaining and replacing topsoil, reducing impervious surface coverage, and retaining as much natural vegetation as possible will go far in reducing the immediate destruction of animals from construction practices and subsequent loss of populations and communities as a result of habitat loss.

By recognizing the need to better understand and plan development, not only to maximize benefits to wildlife but also to provide amenities for humans, both theoretical and practical models can be developed to predict the outcome of various approaches. From a landscape perspective, an overriding principle to seek maximum environmental benefits during development can be subsumed under the concept of "aggregate-with-outliers" (Foreman 1995). This principle states that "one should aggregate land uses, yet maintain corridors and small patches of nature throughout developed areas, as well as outliers of human activity spatially arranged along major boundaries" (437).

In general, the understanding of the landscape-ecological factors involved in this principle, ranging from patch size to landscape mosaic grain, is better established than the responses of wildlife to the various landscape categories that have been identified.

Several types of development have been planned to enhance natural area and corridor presence. They include (1) planned unit development (PUD), usually applied to a large site, often allowing for more-flexible design, housing variety, and compatible commercial uses; (2) cluster zoning, which permits groups of homes on one portion of the property, with the remainder left as open space; and (3) conservation subdivisions, which in their purest form, can be defined as residential developments in which half or more of the buildable land area is designated as undivided, permanent open space (Arendt 1996). All three are zoning alternatives that involve density transfers. Normally, if a developer were to set aside a portion of the developable land, it would reduce his yield (the number of lots that he could build under current zoning), which translates into less profit. Density transfer addresses this financial disincentive by allowing the developer to site the same or greater number of homes onto smaller lots in a more compressed area, with the remaining open space left undeveloped and serving as a community and natural resource. The natural area can be put into a conservation easement (a legal agreement between the property owner and a nonprofit organization or government agency that permanently restricts the uses of the property) with the developer or the homeowners' association retaining ownership of the land and the right to use it consistent with the easement.

Human-Wildlife Interactions in Urbanizing Environments

Human-wildlife interactions in urbanizing environments can be positive or negative. Conflicts between humans and wildlife in suburban and urban areas are inevitable. Human-altered landscapes create highly suitable habitats for some species of wild animals. Absent hunting and trapping, many urban areas may harbor species that elsewhere occur below ecological carrying capacity (Robinson and Bolen 1984). Other human activities—such as poor trash management, landscaping that provides food resources, and structures that increase available harborage—can affect local wildlife populations. Many urbanites seeking interaction with wild animals deliberately feed and provision them, which can cause problems such as localized concentrations of animals.

The conflicts that arise between people and wild animals in urbanizing environments can involve individual animals, local groups of animals, or increasingly, regional populations of some species. A homeowner may have a problem with an individual animal that has taken up residence in a chimney, leading to action to resolve an immediate and highly site-specific issue. A municipal park may have a population of animals, such as gray squirrels, that is causing damage to plantings (Manski et al. 1981). A neighborhood or community may have widely distributed conflicts (with animals such as white-tailed deer or Canada geese) that affect multiple households and involve public lands and buildings, corporate parks, or specific sites such as golf courses. The conflicts experienced by urbanites range from "nuisance" situations (that aren't really problems at all) to situations in which measurable damage to homes or yards is occurring, to circumstances where complex types of impacts (e.g., deer browsing on

sensitive plant species on public lands) or human health and safety concerns are claimed (e.g., Ankney 1996). Problems with individuals or local groups may be self-correcting or resolvable with a small commitment of time and effort. Problems with larger populations may not be resolvable without a considerable commitment of time and effort through a coordinated regional planning approach.

The type and variety of human-wildlife conflicts in urban and suburban environments, as well as their economic consequences, are little documented, but what studies have been conducted are suggestive of trends. Overall, less than a third of the general population has reported experiencing problems with urban wildlife. In one survey of the six metropolitan areas in New York City, 20 percent of all respondents said they had wildlife problems (Brown et al. 1979), while in the upstate population of metropolitan Syracuse about 30 percent had experienced problems (O'Donnell and VanDruff 1983). Another study focused on three metropolitan areas in Missouri, where about 13 percent of the respondents indicated they had experienced wildlife problems (Witter et al. 1981). More recently, Mankin et al. (1999) reported that 18 percent of both urban and rural respondents to a questionnaire about wildlife conflicts in Illinois reported damage within the past year. Problems in metropolitan Syracuse varied from one neighborhood area to another (O'Donnell and VanDruff 1983), suggesting site- and area-specific factors contributing to the type and intensity of wildlife problems at the local level. Where it has been surveyed, measurable damage by wildlife, usually as structural damage to buildings or landscape plantings, ranges from about 20 to 50 percent of the complaints reported (Brown et al. 1979; O'Donnell and VanDruff 1983; Mankin et al. 1999).

The most frequently reported complaint regarding wildlife in urban and suburban areas is that an animal has become a general "nuisance" around a primary residence (Brown et al.

1979; Witter et al. 1981; O'Donnell and VanDruff 1983). The use of the term "nuisance" in characterizing human-wildlife encounters is problematic, however, since it predefines an emotional condition that can range from the imagined to the very real. Often, what constitutes an animal's being termed a "nuisance" may simply be misunderstanding or ignorance. Almost 40 percent of the complaints about wildlife received by two suburban Maryland wildlife offices resulted from a misunderstanding of wildlife activity and an unnecessary fear of wildlife itself (Hotten and McKegg 1984). Such findings almost certainly forebode that many wild animals are "controlled" in urban habitats for no offense other than simply being considered "nuisances."

As dramatic as wildlife conflicts may be, by far the most frequent and substantive interactions between people and wild animals are positive ones. People value, and often cherish, contact with other living things (Kellert 1996), and it may be especially compelling and urgent that such opportunities occur for urbanites, who are most likely to be divorced from contact with the natural world. Mankin et al. (1999) report that nearly all respondents to their questionnaire of urban and rural residents of Illinois indicated that wildlife was important to them, with nearly 60 percent indicating that it was very important. Nearly half of the urban respondents indicated they valued wildlife as much as pets, with a quarter assigning equal value to humans. Goode (1993) notes that urban wildlife programs and natural-area conservation in Great Britain give considerable weight to the "value and benefits of ordinary wildlife to local people," an extremely important concept that is often overlooked in this time when wildlife's scarcity, rarity, and disappearance command such attention.

Attributing value to wildlife or to wildlife habitat can be difficult. Concepts regarding wildlife valuation range from the idea of inherent or intrinsic value (Norton 1987), through those addressing the legal rights and status of animals (e.g., Singer 1975), to the notion that human well-being is enhanced by contact with animals. Benefits provided by wildlife may be simple pleasure and enjoyment, enhanced health and well-being, educational opportunities for adults and children, and increased economic returns through recreational, nonconsumptive pursuits, such as birdwatching, and functions that enhance ecosystem-level stability (Shaw and Magnum 1984; Rolston 1986; Beatley 1994; Kellert 1997; Warren 1997). Improved psychological and even physical health is often associated with contact with natural environments and with wild animals themselves (VanDruff et al. 1995). Better environmental health has long been associated with juxtaposition of natural areas with human-built environments (e.g., Foreman 1995); and because of the position of most species at higher trophic (or distance from plant food source) levels, wildlife has been suggested as a good indicator of environmental quality (Evenden 1974). In fact, wild animals are often used as sentinels to detect and monitor environmental contaminants (National Academy of Sciences 1991).

The benefits of working with wildlife species to maintain or complement environmental factors important to humans has only recently begun to be explored. Beavers, for example, can improve watersheds negatively affected by human activity, but because of their early and near-complete extirpation from most of North America (Novak 1987), few people recognize their potential contributions. Among these are reduction in the extent and severity of floods due to the buffering effect of beaver impoundments; settling of turbid, sediment-laden urban runoff to include the precipitation of harmful industrial products such as heavy metal residues; a net increase in the area of urban wetlands; the creation of new wetlands; and the addition of habitat for sensitive and threatened plant and animal species (Hammerson 1994). Public attitudes concerning conflicts with such animals could change dramatically were their contribution to urban ecosystems better known. Better public education and understanding lies at the heart of much of the effort to deal with human-wildlife conflicts in urban areas.

Attitudes toward Urban Wildlife

American attitudes toward, and knowledge and perception of, animals have been measured in a series of pioneering studies by Stephen Kellert and his colleagues (cf. Kellert 1996). Historically, the predominant attitude toward animals in the United States has been a utilitarian one, focusing on the practical and material value people derive from animals or their products (Kellert and Westervelt 1982). Roughly contemporaneous with the population shift to urbanized areas has been the growth of humanistic feelings, defined as a strong interest in and affection for individual animals (Kellert 1980) and, in cities with a million or more residents, high moralistic sentiments characterized by a primary concern for the right or wrong treatment of animals (Kellert and Berry 1980). These changing values have influenced how Americans view such activities as hunting and trapping (Gentile 1987); nonconsumptive uses of wild animals (Shaw and Mangun 1984); wildlife education (Adams and Leedy 1987); wildlife conservation (Hunter 1989); and wildlife damage control (Flyger et al. 1983). Urbanites can be selective, however. Some animal groups, such as songbirds, are held in high esteem (Dagg 1974; Szot 1975; Brown et al. 1979), while others, such as coyotes and snakes, are much less appreciated and sometimes even completely untolerated (Flyger et al. 1983; Kellert 1996).

However urbanites feel about specific wildlife species, their attitudes toward control practices tend to strongly favor nonlethal approaches. Marion (1988) found in a survey of state extension service offices that 55 percent of the public contacted regarding urban wildlife conflicts did not want animals to be harmed by control procedures. An even higher percentage (78 percent) were willing to implement prevention and control measures. Braband and Clark (1992) found that 89 percent of the customers they contacted in conjunction with a private wildlife control business felt that humane treatment (i.e., people's feelings about the reduction of pain felt by an animal in a nuisance control situation) was either "very" or "moderately" important. Almost half (44 percent) of those responding indicated they would pay more for services that ensured this sort of treatment. However, attitudes about lethal control as an appropriate means of resolving conflicts was high for many species, including rats and mice (95 percent), bats (71 percent), pigeons (60 percent), and skunks (57 percent), indicating that negative feelings about some species overrode any broader concept of animal welfare. Marion et al. (1999), while not specifically querying for lethal versus nonlethal control, found more than 80 percent of respondents indicating that they tolerated the "nuisance" presented by wildlife during conflict situations, with fewer than 10 percent of the urbanites questioned having tried lethal control for an offending animal.

The relationship between positive feelings about an individual animal species and its status as a "problem" or "nuisance" animal should be intuitively an inverse one, but this is apparently not always the case. The gray squirrel (Sciurus carolinensis), for example, ranks very high as a nuisance species while maintaining a position as an animal for which affection remains high (Dagg 1973; Brown et al. 1979; Witter et al. 1981; O'Donnell and VanDruff 1983; Gilbert 1989). This suggests that public opinion is strongly situational, at least for some species. Rapid change in public sentiment may be indicated by shifting attitudes toward species such as deer and geese. While they were not

mentioned as problems in most urban wildlife damage surveys conducted throughout the 1970s, white-tailed deer increasingly have been mentioned as an emerging problem in urban areas (Witham and Jones 1990; Decker and Gavin 1987), and public attitudes seem to be shifting to more negative sentiments as a consequence. Canada geese, as well, seem to be attracting more widespread disapproval as they enter into greater contact with urban and suburban residents (Addison and Amernic 1983; Conover and Chasko 1985; Ankney 1996; Hope 2000). The rapidity with which animals such as geese and deer have not only accommodated to urban and suburban living but also become problematic suggests that other species may rapidly follow suit. Every effort should be made at an early stage in urban wildlife planning to anticipate and head off such situations. Given the physical and socioeconomic heterogeneity of cities, as well as the social and cultural variation within urban populations, the existing attitude surveys on urban wildlife probably reflect only a small part of the range of potential values and sentiments about urban wildlife and human-wildlife conflict-resolution strategies. More contemporary and comprehensive surveys must be conducted to explain both this variability and the potential for rapid change in the nature of, and attitudes toward, future conflicts.

Urban Wildlife Management

Interest in wildlife conservation—as well as recognition that good scientific information was needed to achieve conservation goals—arose around the turn of the twentieth century as a response to the near-complete destruction of many animal species and their habitats on a continent-wide basis (Matthiessen 1987). Nonetheless, traditional wildlife management perspectives grew out of a view of wild animals as a renewable resource and emphasized management from utili-

tarian and materialistic perspectives (e.g., Robinson and Bolen 1984). The consumptive use of animals superceded other concerns. "Surplus," "excess," or "expendable" segments of wildlife populations were to be "taken" under regulated hunting and trapping protocols that did not influence the overall health of the population but maintained numbers at desired levels. Those levels were typically set at a point where harvesters and recreational users had a maximum number of animals available to them, while commercial interests, typically agriculture, suffered a minimum of economic damage from those animals.

This traditionalist orientation in the United States led to wildlife management being considered synonymous with "game management," the title of the first text on the subject (Leopold 1933). "Nongame management," a term that came into use during the 1970s (Clawson 1986), refers to managers' activities that involve species not typically pursued for commercial or utilitarian purposes.

Temple (1986) recognizes four categories of animals within a nongame classification scheme: pest species, endangered species, rare species, and species that do not require management. Pest species largely included animals found in urban and suburban environments. Unlike funding for game programs, which is largely supported through the federal Pittman-Roberston initiative, funding for nongame species comes from voluntary contributions, income-tax check-offs, and a variety of special taxes (Robinson and Bolen 1984). Federal legislation to fund comprehensive conservation planning was enacted as the Fish and Wildlife Conservation Act of 1980. Unlike Pittman-Robertson monies, which are funded through excise taxes, this initiative was to be funded through appropriations from the federal budget—appropriations that were never approved (Manville 1989). Both endangered and rare species are the focus of special funding efforts and regulatory and statutory attention, but little if any attention is focused on the "pest" and "other" species categories, into which a majority of urban wildlife would fall.

Once urban species become more noticeable, they may be branded "overabundant" and subjected to calls for management from a traditionalist perspective (e.g., Ankney 1996; McCombie 1999). However, by far the majority of calls for management of urban wildlife comes from concern over "nuisance" or "pest" species near individual houses. Ironically, this may be one of the reasons that traditional wildlife managers have eschewed involvement in urban wildlife issues (Lyons and Leedy 1984). Another may be that traditional approaches in wildlife management may not be applicable to urban settings (San Julian 1987; Hadidian et al. 1997a). A shift to "problem-oriented" management of urban wildlife means that other factors have to be taken into consideration, including human health and safety issues, environmental damage, biological diversity, and protection of private property. The "control" of "problem" urban wildlife is likely to be needed at times that don't coincide with hunting and trapping seasons.

Conflicts with urban species may, in fact, be greatest at such biologically sensitive times as when young are being reared, raising moral and ethical questions concerning how management programs are implemented. In the past, private citizens (animal rescuers and rehabilitators), law enforcement personnel, university extension specialists, and nature centers were often the only resources available to guide urbanites in resolving conflicts with wildlife or responding to wildlife emergencies. Forces are now emerging to address human-wildlife conflict resolution in urban areas: animal shelter and control agencies, wildlife rehabilitators, the private wildlife control industry, and others.

Municipal animal shelters and animal control agencies, as well as law enforcement agencies, typically do not have a mandate to deal with wildlife issues but become involved in handling significant numbers of wild animals (Kirkwood 1998). Shelter personnel are often the first to respond to wildlife emergencies or to be called to a scene by law enforcement. Shelters may routinely handle sick and injured wild animals, respond to road fatalities, and extricate animals roaming at large in buildings. Shelter personnel often are untrained for these tasks, but may be highly skilled and motivated to learn; have law enforcement authority, and can work from within established infrastructures. Although funding and resource limitations might be seen as obstacles to such individuals' involvement, they are concerns for which solutions can readily be found. For example, a local animal shelter might run a wildlife control advice and response service as a for-fee option under its larger nonprofit operation. Costs for both advice and service could be covered by service charges competitive with private-sector rates.

The private-sector nuisance-wildlife control industry will also increasingly play a role in urban wildlife conflict resolution. This industry has developed partly from within and partly from outside the context of traditional wildlife management (Braband and Clark 1992; Barnes 1993; Curtis et al. 1995). The growth of the industry has been rapid. In New York private wildlife control operations grew by 309 percent over a six-year period in the mid-1980s, with more than eleven thousand wildlife complaints handled in 1989–90 alone (Curtis et al. 1995). Little is known of the nature, scope, and extent of the activities of nuisance-wildlife control operators, and virtually nothing can be said yet of the biological and ecological consequences of this industry's activities. Thousands, perhaps tens of thousands, of "nuisance" animals are taken by trapping businesses in hundreds of municipal areas annually, but virtually nothing is done to document and publish summary statistics regarding this activity.

The "nuisance" wildlife control industry is in a formative period in which its "professionals" range from recreational wildlife trappers, with little understanding of the behavior and ecology of urban wild animals beyond what is needed to capture them, to highly skilled wildlife professionals, who often hold advanced academic degrees. Organization of these businesses through franchising operations places many practitioners on a solid footing in a business sense, while "fly-by-night" operators engage in irresponsible business practices such as price-gouging. The fly-by-nighters are of particular concern to animal protection interests, since the wildlife control industry is particularly susceptible to profiting from the provision of incomplete or inadequate services. A practitioner may not recommend that a chimney be capped to permanently seal out future occupancy by a raccoon or squirrel, for example, virtually guaranteeing that another visit (and payment for service) will be necessary. Eventually, state and municipal oversight, public vigilance, better public education, and peer influence, should force standardization and policing of the industry. Animal protection interests and the private wildlife control industry will always argue over whether a majority of "nuisance" complaints can be resolved without handling, much less killing, the animal. Private operators will always be torn between earning a service fee and providing free advice that allows homeowners to resolve conflicts themselves.

Another emerging resource is the wildlife rehabilitation community. Wildlife rehabilitators range from individuals with little or no background and training with wild animals to highly skilled professionals with advanced degrees in wildlife science or veterinary medicine. Once a "kitchen operation" in which injured and orphaned animals were taken into private homes and given compassionate, if sometimes misguided, care, wildlife rehabilitation is now emerging as an organized discipline. An established body of knowledge is applied to diverse species and situations, sometimes through "kitchen operations" but increasingly through professional-

174

The State of the Animals: 2001

ly staffed wildlife centers. Rehabilitators are increasingly at the center of "nuisance" wildlife control, even though the only reason may be their inherent interest in limiting the number of "orphaned" animals that come to them for care. Many such orphaned young are by-products of wildlife control activities during which adult animals are either forcibly separated from dependent offspring or euthanized under state law. As a result, rehabilitation facilities are often swamped with incoming floods of orphans. Larger centers, especially, may decide to solve problems for homeowners in self-defense. Wildlife hotlines that provide advice or referrals to "humane" wildlife control operators are providing such proactive outreach.

Regulatory authority and programmatic responsibility for urban wildlife remain with federal, state, and municipal agencies and wildlife organizations. Absent a funding breakthrough, it is unlikely that state wildlife agencies will greatly augment their urban wildlife programs and activities in the near future. Instead, their role in regulatory oversight and program planning appears to be where they will have the most impact. Current regulations in most states are insufficient to ensure either the protection of public interest or the humane treatment of animals themselves. Several surveys of state regulatory and statutory oversight of the wildlife-control industry suggest that regulations or statutes advising operators to humanely handle, transport, or euthanize "problem" wild animals generally don't exist, and that even licensing and reporting requirements are absent in many of the states (Brammer et al. 1994; LaVine et al. 1996; Barnes 1997; Hadidian et al. in press). In a recent poll of the fifty states by The Humane Society of the United States (HSUS) (Hadidian et al. in press), a rating of 1 or 0 was given in each of ten categories (license and permit requirements; training, examination, and related requirements; re-certification; reporting; translocation[1]; humane treatment;

euthanasia[2]; consumer education and protection; threshold of damage; and use of integrated pest management [IPM][3] strategies) to yield an ideal score of 10 for any state that provided regulatory oversight for each category. The mean score for states was 2.16 (range 0–7), with a mode of 0 (fourteen states received this score) and a median of 1.75.

Changes in the social acceptance of animal damage management and vertebrate pest control require reexamination of the structure of federal and state programs and more input from these programs into private-industry initiatives. Traditional wildlife damage control programs must ask fundamental questions with greater scientific rigor (Hone 1996); address growing public demand for accountability in the use of chemicals, particularly toxicants; and satisfy growing public demand for solutions that include nonlethal options before lethal alternatives are considered. Borrowing from IPM, many specialists are acquiescing to this demand. They advocate approaches to wildlife damage management that, depending on the species and nature of the problem involved, move from nonlethal to lethal control only when circumstances dictate no other recourse (Dent 1995; Hone 1996). Federal agencies are directed to use IPM approaches (U.S. Government 1979), and the principal federal agency responsible for wildlife damage control, the U.S. Department of Agriculture's Wildlife Services (WS) has created an Integrated Wildlife Damage Management concept to direct its activities (USDA 1994). Slate et al. (1992) describe a decision-making model to determine the need for action and appropriate responses that emphasize nonlethal methods.

Relatively few case histories demonstrating the IPM approach in urban areas can be found outside of commensal rodent management, but there is information on the use of such an approach to relieve a gray squirrel (Sciurus carolinensis) problem. Substantial damage had been claimed to bulbs, flowers, and histori-

cally valuable trees in a downtown Washington, D.C., park, and efforts to trap and relocate squirrels had been under way for some time before local and national humane organizations challenged the National Park Service to document and authenticate its claims (Manski et al. 1981). This was done, and a management plan was created under which a one-time removal of squirrels was to be coupled with the removal of older den trees and some artificial nest boxes that provided harborage (Hadidian et al. 1987). These actions, together with voluntary reduction in feeding activities by a small but active group of individuals, led to a long-term stabilization of the population that left damage at an acceptable level. Unknown, however, are the consequences of "humane" control of populations through limiting access to food, water, and shelter. Did the stabilization of the squirrel population in this small park cause increased mortality in subsequent litters? Were "surplus" squirrels forced to leave the area, at greater risk for mortality? To date, relatively little attention has focused on such questions.

As such issues remain, The HSUS has begun to identify a multi-step process of problem evaluation and response (Hadidian et al. 1997) for homeowners and the general public. The approach is based on using solutions to conflicts that are "environmentally sound, lasting, and humane." It is fundamentally hierarchical, moving from least to most invasive in its applied procedures.

Understanding is an important component in any wildlife conflict, since the magnitude of the problem must be weighed against the consequences of human intervention. Tolerance of a wild animal's presence—and the ability to accept some "damage"—should always be the first option considered. If tolerance clearly is not enough of a response, then other nonlethal approaches should be considered. These range from changing human activity (such as trash management), modifying habitat, and using scaring and mild harassment strategies to employing repellents and exclusionary strategies. Trapping and relocating or killing offending animals is far more problematic and always unacceptable when it is the sole response to a wildlife conflict. Lethal approaches should never be employed unless all other practicable options have been considered and/or tried or unless conditions can be changed to modify or eliminate the circumstances that led to the problem. Even then, killing as a means of "solving" a wildlife conflict is offensive to large segments of the public (Reiter et al. 1999) and will be opposed by animal protection interests.

With more than eight of every ten Americans living in urban and suburban areas, public and private resources and attention must be focused on their issues with wildlife. Currently, no clear responsibilities or roles exist for any private or public entities to address urban wildlife issues. The conflict that often accompanies issues should therefore be of no surprise. Clearly, better understanding of the issues and the positions of stakeholders is needed, and compromise and synthesis will be important in determining the outcome of future programs.

The core elements of one such approach have been outlined by Robert Dorney (1989) as the framework for a new field, environmental management. It is envisioned as a consulting practice that combines elements of the "social, natural, engineering, design, and geographic services" working under a shared conceptual framework based on "a systems approach, a human ecology view, an environmental ethic, and a willingness to work for private, government, or community groups in a political and legal context" (p. 5). Given the need in many emerging human-wildlife conflicts for coordination among planners, public health specialists, wildlife specialists, technical personnel, and the public, it is difficult to envision how the urban wildlife specialist of the future could successfully operate with as narrow a focus as the field now has. The more than a dozen specializations, ranging

from hydrologist to social scientist, proposed by Dorney as necessary to environmental management, combined with the need for political support, suggest a new approach may be in order.

Animal Welfare and Protection Concerns

In the nineteenth century, Henry Bergh founded the American Society for the Prevention of Cruelty to Animals, the first animal welfare organization in the United States, in response to the treatment of the horses used as draft animals in New York City (Zawistowski 1998). Once he was given the power under law to prosecute cases of animal abuse, however, one of the first cases he brought to court was against a sea captain and his crew for the mistreatment of sea turtles kept alive as food aboard ship. The judge threw the case out of court, ruling that turtles were not animals and thus not covered in the newly promulgated cruelty statutes. Not a great deal has changed in the treatment of many wildlife species since then. Although the welfare of domestic and companion animals is an ongoing concern, any such consideration for wildlife has barely begun.

Potential topics range from the highly specific, such as the humaneness of capture and handling techniques for "nuisance" animals, to the very broad, such as conservation of biological diversity in urbanizing areas. Several animal protection organizations—The HSUS, the Fund for Animals, People for the Ethical Treatment of Animals, Animal Alliance of Canada, the Massachusetts Society for the Prevention of Cruelty to Animals, and the Progressive Animal Welfare Society, in Washington State—staff programs on wildlife issues. Clifton (1992) expressed what were some of the first published concerns from this perspective. Numerous activist and local groups have formed around particular issues, often incor-

porating themselves as nonprofit organizations.

It is often said that urbanites are so ignorant of wildlife ecology that their concerns for the protection of urban wildlife and the humane treatment of wild animals are misplaced (Howard 1990). Where measured, this ecological ignorance does seem to exist; however, it can be found among people living in rural areas as well (Kellert 1996). This ignorance can lead to unrealistic and misguided attempts to impose "humane" solutions, such as wildlife translocation, on wildlife problems (Craven et al. 1998). But attention should first be placed on obvious human mistreatment of wild animals. Wild animals may be mistreated by people (including animal damage professionals or animal control professionals) out of ignorance or through deliberate acts of cruelty or indifference. They may be mistreated on an institutional level by instruments of policy or regulation that allow mass poisoning or lethal control on a recurring and cyclical basis.

It is hardly surprising that we have little information on how wild animals and people interact in urban environments. What happens even in the average backyard may always be a mystery, but increased attention to the links between childhood and adult violence toward animals and violence toward humans (Lockwood and Ascione 1998) may result in better efforts to collect information on extremely negative human-wildlife interactions, at the least.

Few in the professional communities have called for better understanding of animal welfare in the context of wildlife damage or management concerns (but see Schmidt 1989a,b). Even among regulatory agencies, such as state wildlife departments, oversight may be lacking. Of the states polled by The HSUS for a recent survey of state oversight of the wildlife control industry (Hadidian et al. in press), only thirty-two (slightly more than 60 percent) required individual homeowners or their agents to apply for permits to "control" wildlife on their property. Fewer (seventeen) required private nuisance-wildlife control businesses to be licensed, and only three states required licensed nuisance-wildlife control operators to comply with established handling, transportation, and care standards.

Beyond animal protection advocates' concern for the fate of individual animals in urban and suburban environments lies the broader need to consider the fate of entire animal populations and communities of organisms. The example of government oversight of Canada geese is illuminating. Early in the last century, giant Canada goose (*Branta canadensis maxima*) populations were so victimized by overhunting and exploitation for market that there was concern that they had been driven to extinction (Hansen 1965). When a few small breeding populations were discovered in the mid-1960s, extensive efforts were undertaken to repatriate this race of Canada goose to its former—and to new—ranges. These restocking programs proved successful, and goose populations grew to the point where, by the mid-1980s, many were considered problematic (Conover and Chasko 1985). As year-round residents, geese quickly adapted to the prime urban and suburban sites that provided shelter and food, including golf courses, playing fields, and public open space where humans and geese were bound to come into conflict. The debate over the extent of goose "damage" to landscapes, the potential for human health and safety issues associated with growing populations of these birds, and the extent to which nonlethal strategies (including habitat management) have been attempted prior to adoption of lethal-control programs has led to confrontations between wildlife management agencies and animal protection groups. A complex interplay between federal authority (largely derived from the MBTA) and federal and state responsibilities (largely derived from statutory trust or tradition) appears to be unfolding. Federal managers are struggling with adhering to the MBTA while at the same time allowing "nuisance" geese to be taken under permit. Some states have assumed responsibility for overseeing "nuisance" goose programs, some of which involve capturing geese that are molting and killing them in commercial poultry houses. Others are allowing private nuisance wildlife control businesses and federal animal damage control agents to engage in lethal control programs without state involvement. With the increasing interest in urban wildlife management, the reluctance of many regulatory and oversight agencies to engage more immediately in emerging programs will set precedents that will affect them for years to come.

Concern for land and ecosystem protection has traditionally been an interest of conservationists and environmentalists. Clearly, however, the animal protection community's wildlife concerns cannot be addressed without considering ecosystem and environmental concepts. Aldo Leopold's 1949 articulation of the concept of a land ethic marks the emergence in contemporary environmental thinking of a holistic concept that embraces people, animals, and land. Largely neglected for two decades, the concept of a land ethic was joined in the mid-1970s by the concern for environmental injury that had been articulated in Rachel Carson's *Silent Spring* (1962).

Leopold (1949) called for a land ethic as a revolutionary shift in the way humans viewed their relationship to the land and the animals and plants supported by it. He lamented that the relationship between people and the land was primarily economic and entailed "privileges, but not obligations." Leopold was a hunter, and his concern for the land and its biotic community has been called antithetical to that of the movement for individual animals and extending rights to nonhumans. In fact, Regan (1983) went so far as to suggest that Leopold's biotic community viewpoint could be dubbed "environmental fascism" (p. 362). This characterization springs from the premise that, even when nonhuman members of the biotic community are accorded rights, those rights become prioritized based on the contribution of each to that community. Thus a rare wildflower could be accorded higher priority within the community than would a human, since humans are plentiful. But the concept of biotic right as a cornerstone of the land ethic advocated by Leopold, and the environmental ethic that derives from it, is not so estranged from the animal rights concepts advocated by Regan and others that common ground cannot be reached. A Leopold essay written in 1923 but published only recently argued that the earth is an "organism possessing a certain kind and degree of life" (1979), suggesting common ground between Leopold and much of the thinking that comes from the Deep Ecology and animal rights movements (Nash 1989).

It is the concept of biocentrism (Nash 1989) that provides proponents of the environment and advocates of those parts of the environment that exhibit unusually high levels of sentience and sensitivity (i.e., animals) with common ground. Biocentrism seeks the extension of the rights, privileges, and protection given as our moral responsibility to fellow humans to other living things and, potentially, to the nonliving as well. Biocentric thinking incorporates the idea of recognizing the rights of every form of life to function normally in an ecosystem (Nash 1989). It understandably conflicts with traditional conceptions of humans as preeminent over other living things (e.g., Bidinotto 1992). From this derives the fundamental, underlying tenet of an animal welfare perspective on urban wildlife: to seek and advocate life-affirming solutions to conflicts with wild animals.

Prognosis: Cities and Wildlife

The demands and requirements of the urban human population control the global ecosystem (Vitousek et al. 1997). Wildlife is a preferred component of natural systems, one in which humans typically vest more interest and attention than they do to physical environments or even other living communities. How the quality of the human environment is improved and enhanced by wildlife is an issue that will engage much attention as human populations become increasingly urban. It would be truly unfortunate if we could not resolve the paradox raised by Raymond Dassmann: "…Cities, man's greatest creation and the place where most people must live, are in many ways becoming least suited for human occupancy" (1972, 339).

It may be that as we begin to understand ourselves better and explore our deepest roots in affiliation with nature—our "biophilia" (Kellert 1997)—we are becoming isolated from and inured to the natural world in perhaps irreversible ways. It is no coincidence that the converging streams of contemporary thought in environmentalism, animal welfare and protection, ecological understanding and human affinity for nature are all focused within the prism of urban wildlife. It is not surprising that the visionary efforts to resolve human–wild-animal and human–natural-world conflicts would be addressed within new fields such as Dorney's discipline of environmental management, which was to be founded on an "ethical triad" of "reverence for land, life, and diversity" (Dorney 1989, 37).

If one promise of urbanization is to facilitate greater concern for the welfare and treatment of animals, then its peril may lie in the possibility of large segments of the urban population losing their connection to wild things and becoming indifferent and uncaring. Urban wildlife problems must be approached as ecosystem problems where, along with the goal of controlling animal damage, successful strategies will stress the development of harmonious relationships within which the needs of all species are properly balanced. We stand at that crossroads.

Notes

[1] Translocation is defined as the transport and release of wild animals from one location to another (Craven et al. 1998).

[2] Euthanasia literally means "good death" and is a term frequently used to describe veterinary-approved methods of killing companion animals.

[3] IPM is defined as a decision-making process that emphasizes monitoring and action when needed using a blend of cultural, physical, and chemical methods to keep pest problems at an acceptable level of management (Dent 1995).

Literature Cited

Adams, L. 1994. *Urban wildlife habitats.* Minneapolis: University of Minnesota Press.

Adams, L., and D.L. Leedy, eds. 1987. *Integrating man and nature in the metropolitan environment.* Columbia, Md.: National Institute for Urban Wildlife.

———. 1991. *Wildlife conservation in metropolitan environments.* Columbia, Md.: National Institute for Urban Wildlife.

Adams, L.W., D.L. Leedy, and W.C. McComb. 1985. Urban wildlife research and education in North American colleges and universities. *Wildlife Society Bulletin* 15: 591–95.

Adams, L.W., and L.E. Dove. 1989. *Wildlife reserves and corridors in the urban environment.* Columbia, Md.: National Institute for Urban Wildlife.

Addison, L.R., and J. Amernic. 1983. An uneasy truce with the Canada goose. *International Wildlife* 13: 12–14.

Ankney, C.D. 1996. An embarrassment of riches: too many geese. *Journal of Wildlife Management* 60: 217–23.

Arendt, R. 1996. *Conservation design for subdivisions.* Washington, D.C.: Island Press.

Babbitt, B. 1999. Noah's mandate and the birth of urban bioplanning. *Conservation Biology* 13: 677–78.

Baines, C. 1986. *The wild side of town.* London: BBC Publications and Elm Tree Books.

Barber, L. 1980. *The heyday of natural history.* Garden City, N.Y.: Doubleday and Company, Inc.

Barnes, T.G. 1993. A survey comparison of pest control and nuisance wildlife control operators in Kentucky. In Proceedings of the Sixth Eastern Wildlife Damage Control Conference.

———. 1997. State agency oversight of the nuisance wildlife control industry. *Wildlife Society Bulletin* 25(1): 185–88.

Beatley, T. 1994. *Ethical land use.* Baltimore: The Johns Hopkins University Press.

Beebe, W. 1953. *Unseen life of New York: As a naturalist sees it.* Boston: Little, Brown and Company.

Bidinotto, R.J. 1992. The most dangerous pest: "Homo environmentalus." In Proceedings of the Fifteenth Vertebrate Pest Conference. Newport Beach, California, March 3–5.

Braband, L.A., and K.D. Clark. 1992. Perspectives on wildlife nuisance control: Results of a wildlife damage control firm's customer survey. In Proceedings of the Fifth Eastern Wildlife Damage Control Conference.

Brady, R.F., T. Tobias, P.F.J. Eagles, R. Ohrner, J. Micak, B. Veale, and R.S. Dorney. 1979. A typology for the urban ecosystem and its relationship to larger biogeographical landscape units. *Urban Ecology* 4: 11–28.

Brammer, T.J., P.T. Bromley, and R. Wilson. 1994. The status of nuisance wildlife policy in the United States. In Proceedings of the Annual Conference of the Southeastern Association of Fish and Wildlife Agencies, 48: 331–35.

Brown, T.L., C.P. Dawson, and R.L. Miller. 1979. Interests and attitudes of metropolitan New York residents about wildlife. In Transactions of the Forty-fourth North

American Wildlife and Natural Resources Conference.

Burns, J., K. Stenberg, and W.W. Shaw. 1986. Critical and sensitive wildlife habitats in Tucson, Arizona. In *Wildlife conservation and new residential developments*, eds. K. Stenberg and W.W. Shaw. Tucson: University of Arizona.

Campbell, C.A. 1974. Survival of reptiles and amphibians in urban environments. In *Wildlife in an urbanizing environment*, eds. J.H. Noyes and D.R. Progulske. Planning and Resource Development Series, No. 28. Amherst: University of Massachusetts.

Carson, R. 1962. *Silent spring*. Cambridge, Mass.: The Riverside Press.

Clawson, R.L. 1986. Introduction. In *Management of nongame wildlife in the Midwest: A developing art,* eds. J.B. Hales, L.B. Best, and R.L. Clawson. Chelsea, Mich.: BookCrafters.

Clifton, M. 1992. Urban wildlife: reclaiming their birthright. *The Animals' Agenda,* January/February: 12–24.

Conover, M.R., and G.G. Chasko. 1985. Nuisance Canada goose problems in the eastern United States. *Wildlife Society Bulletin* 13: 228–33.

Conover, M.R., W.C. Pitt, K.K. Kessler, T.J. DuBow, and W.A. Sanborn. 1995. Review of human injuries, illness, and economic losses caused by wildlife in the United States. *Wildlife Society Bulletin* 23: 407–14.

Cousin, S.H. 1983. Species size distributions of birds and snails in an urban area. In *Urban ecology*, eds. R. Borkham, J.A. Lee, and M.R.D. Steward. London: Blackwell Scientific Publications.

Craven, S., T.G. Barnes, and G. Kania. 1998. Toward a professional position on the translocation of problem wildlife. *Wildlife Society Bulletin* 26: 171–77.

Curtis, P.D., M.E. Richmond, P.A. Wellner, and B. Tullar. 1995. Characteristics of the private nuisance wildlife control industry in New York. In Proceedings of the Sixth Eastern Wildlife Damage Control Conference.

Dagg, A.I. 1974. Reactions of people to urban wildlife. In *Wildlife in an urbanizing environment*, eds. J.H. Noyes and D.R. Progulski. Planning and Resource Development Series, No. 28. Amherst: University of Massachusetts.

Darr, L.J., D.K. Dawson, and C.S. Robbins. 1998. Land-use planning to conserve habitat for area-sensitive forest birds. *Urban Ecosystems* 2: 75–84.

Dassmann, R.F. 1972. *Environmental conservation*. New York: John Wiley and Sons, Inc.

Davey, S.P. 1967. The role of wildlife in an urban environment. In Transactions of the Thirty-second North American Fish and Wildlife Conference.

Davis, A.M., and T.F. Glick. 1978. Urban ecosystems and island biogeography. *Environmental Conservation* 5: 299–304.

Decker, D.J., and T.A. Gavin. 1987. Public attitudes toward a suburban deer herd. *Wildlife Society Bulletin* 15: 173–80.

Dent, D. 1995. *Integrated pest management.* London: Chapman and Hall.

Dickman, C.R. 1987. Habitat utilization and diet of the harvest mouse, *Micromys minutus*, in an urban environment. *Acta Theriologica* 31: 249–56.

Dorney, R.S. 1989. *The professional practice of environmental management,* ed. L. Dorney. New York: Springer-Verlag.

Euler, D., F. Gilbert, and G. McKeating. 1975. *Wildlife in urban Canada,* eds. David Euler, Frederick Gilbert, and Gerald McKeating. Guelph, Ontario: University of Guelph.

Evans, E. Payson. 1906. *The criminal prosecution and capital punishment of animals.* London: William Heinemann Ltd.

Evenden, F.G. 1974. Wildlife as an indicator of a quality environment. In *Wildlife in an urbanizing environment,* eds. J.H. Noyes and D.R. Progulske. Planning and Resource Development Series, No. 28. Amherst: University of Massachusetts.

Fitter, R.S.R. 1945. *London's natural history.* London: Bloomsbury Books.

Flyger, V., D.L. Leedy, and T.M. Fanklain. 1983. Wildlife damage control in eastern cities and suburbs. In Proceedings of the First Eastern Wildlife Damage Control Conference. Ithaca, N.Y.: Cornell University. September 27–30.

Forbush, E.H. 1916. The domestic cat. *Massachusetts State Board of Agricultural Economics Bulletin 2.*

Forman, R.T.T. 1995. *Land mosaics: The ecology of landscapes and regions.* Cambridge, England: Cambridge University Press.

Foreman, R.T.T., and M. Godron. 1986. *Landscape ecology.* New York: John Wiley and Sons.

Garber, S.D. 1987. *The urban naturalist.* New York: John Wiley and Sons.

Geis, A.D. 1986. Planning and design for wildlife conservation in new residential developments—Columbia, Maryland. In *Wildlife conservation and new residential developments,* eds. K. Stenberg and W.W. Shaw. Tucson: University of Arizona.

Gentile, J.R. 1987. The evolution of antitrapping sentiment in the United States: A review and commentary. *Wildlife Society Bulletin* 10: 245–53.

Gilbert, O.L. 1989. *The ecology of urban habitats.* New York: Chapman and Hall.

Gill, D., and P. Bonnett. 1973. *Nature in the urban landscape: A study of city ecosystems.* Baltimore: York Press.

Goldstein, E.L., M. Gross, and R.M. DeGraaf. 1981. Explorations in bird–land geometry. *Urban Ecology* 5: 113–24.

Goode, D. 1986. *Wild in London.* London: Michael Joseph Ltd.

———. 1993. Local authorities and urban conservation. In *Conservation in progress,* eds. F.B. Goldsmith and A. Warren. London: John Wiley and Sons, Ltd.

Gottmann, J. 1961. *Megalopolis.* New York: The Twentieth Century Fund.

Guth, R.W. 1979. Breeding bird survey of the Chicago metropolitan area, Illinois. In *Natural history miscellania.* Chicago: Chicago Academy of Sciences.

Hadidian, J. 1992. Interaction between people and wildlife in urbanizing landscapes. In Proceedings of the Fifth Eastern Wildlife Damage Control Conference. Ithaca, N.Y.: Cornell University Press.

Hadidian, J., D. Manski, V. Flyger, C. Cox, and G. Hodge. 1987. Urban gray squirrel damage and population management: A case history. In Proceedings of the Third Eastern Wildlife Damage Control Conference. Gulf Shores, Ala.: Auburn University. October 18–21.

Hadidian, J., J. Grandy, and G. Hodge, eds. 1997a. *Wild neighbors: The humane approach to living with wildlife.* Golden, Colo.: Fulcrum Publishing.

Hadidian, J., J. Sauer, C. Swarth, P. Handly, S. Droege, C. Williams, J. Duff, and G. Didden. 1997b. A citywide breeding bird survey for Washington, D.C. *Urban Ecosystems* 1: 87–102.

Hadidian, J., M.R. Childs, R.H. Schmidt, L.J. Simon, and A. Church. In press. Nuisance wildlife control practices, policies and procedures in the United States. In Proceedings of the Second International Wildlife Management Conference. Godollo, Hungary.

Hammerson, G.A. 1994. Beaver (*Castor canadensis*): Ecosystem alterations, management, and monitoring. *Natural Areas Journal* 14(1): 44–57.

Hanson, H.C. 1965. *The giant Canada goose.* Carbondale, Ill.: Southern Illinois University Press.

Harris, S. 1977. Distribution, habitat utilization and age structure of a suburban fox (*Vulpes vulpes*) population. *Mammalian Review* 7: 25–39.

—————. 1981. The food of suburban foxes (*Vulpes vulpes*), with special reference to London. *Mammalian Review* 11: 151–68.

—————. 1994. *Urban foxes.* London: Whittet Books.

—————. 2000. Rise of the reds. *BBC Wildlife* 18: 48–55.

Hester, F.E. 1991. The National Park Service experience with urban wildlife. In *Wildlife conservation in metropolitan environments,* eds.

L.W. Adams and D.R. Leedy. Columbia, Md.: National Institute for Urban Wildlife.

Hone, J. 1996. Analysis of vertebrate pest research. In Proceedings of the Seventeenth Vertebrate Pest Conference. Davis, Calif.: University of California. March 5–7.

Hope, J. 2000. The geese that came in from the wild. *Audubon* 102: 122–27.

Hotten, L.D., and J.S. McKegg. 1984. Wildlife complaints and their resolution in Maryland. In Proceedings of the Annual Conference of Southeastern Fish and Wildlife Agencies.

Houck, M.C. 1987. Urban wildlife habitat inventory: The Willamette River Greenway, Portland Oregon. In *Integrating man and nature in the metropolitan environment,* eds. L.W. Adams and D.L. Leedy. Columbia, Md.: The National Institute for Urban Wildlife.

Hough, M. 1994. Design with city nature: An overview of some issues. In *The ecological city,* eds. R.H. Platt, R.A. Rowntree, and P.C. Muick. Amherst: The University of Massachusetts.

Howard, W.E. 1990. *Animal rights vs. nature.* United States: W.E. Howard.

Hunter, M.L. 1989. Conservation biology, wildlife management, and spaceship earth. *Wildlife Society Bulletin* 17: 351–54.

Ingersoll, E. 1899. *Wild neighbors: Outdoor studies in the United States.* New York: The Macmillan Company.

Kellert, S.R. 1980. American's attitudes and knowledge of animals. In Transactions of the Forty-fifth North American Wildlife and Natural Resources Conference.

—————. 1996. *The value of life.* Washington, D.C.: Island Press.

—————. 1997. Kinship to mastery. Washington, D.C.: Island Press.

Kellert, S.R., and J. Berry. 1980. Phase III: Knowledge, affection and basic attitudes toward animals in American Society. U.S. Fish and Wildlife Service Report.

Kellert, S.R., and M.O. Westervelt. 1982. Historical trends in American animal use and perception.

Transactions of the Forty-seventh North American Wildlife and Natural Resources Conference. Washington, D.C.: Wildlife Management Institute.

Kieran, J. 1959. *A natural history of New York.* Boston: Houghton Mifflin Company.

King, D.A., J.L. White, and W.W. Shaw. 1991. Influence of urban wildlife habitats on the value of residential properties. In *Wildlife conservation in metropolitan environments,* eds. L.W. Adams and D.L. Leedy. Columbia, Md.: National Institute for Urban Wildlife.

Kinkead, E. 1974. *A concrete look at nature.* New York: Quadrangle/The New York Times Book Co.

—————. 1978. *Wildness is all around us.* New York: E.P. Dutton.

Kirkwood, S. 1998. Answering the call of the wild. *Animal Sheltering* 21: 4–11.

Kolb, H.H. 1984. Factors affecting the movements of dog foxes in Edinburgh. *Journal of Applied Ecology* 21: 161–73.

La Vine, K., M.J. Reeff, J.A. DiCamillo, and G.S. Kania. 1996. The status of nuisance wildlife damage control in the states. In Proceedings of the Seventeenth Vertebrate Pest Conference, eds., R.M. Timm and A.C. Crabb. Davis, Calif.: University of California.

Laurie, I.C., ed. 1979. *Nature in cities.* Chichester: John Wiley and Sons.

Leopold, A. 1933. *Game management.* New York: Charles Scribner's Sons.

—————. 1949. *A sand county almanac.* New York: Oxford University Press.

—————. 1979. Some fundamentals of conservation in the Southwest. *Environmental Ethics* 1: 131–41.

Lloyd, H.G. 1981. *The red fox.* London: B.T. Batsford, Ltd.

Lockwood, R., and F.R. Ascione, eds. 1998. *Cruelty to animals and interpersonal violence.* West Lafayette, Ind.: Purdue University Press.

Lyons, J.R., and D.L. Leedy. 1984. The status of urban wildlife programs. In Transactions of the Forty-ninth North American Wildlife and Natural Resources Conference.

MacArthur, R.H., and E.O. Wilson. 1967. *The theory of island biogeography.* Princeton, N.J.: Princeton University Press.

MacDonald, D.W., and M.T. Newdick. 1982. The distribution and ecology of foxes, *Vulpes vulpes* (L.) in urban areas. In *Urban ecology,* eds. R. Bornkamm, J.A. Lee, and M.R.D. Seaward. Oxford: Blackwell Scientific Publications.

Mader, H.J., C. Schell, and P. Kornacker. 1990. Linear barriers to arthropod movements in the landscape. *Biological Conservation* 54: 209–222.

Mankin, P.C., R.E. Warner, and W.L. Anderson. 1999. Wildlife and the Illinois public: A benchmark study of attitudes and perceptions. Wildlife Society Bulletin 27, no. 2: 465–72.

Manski, D.A., L.W. VanDruff, and V. Flyger. 1981. Activities of gray squirrels and people in a downtown Washington, D.C., park: Management implications. In Transactions of the Forty-sixth North American Wildlife and Natural Resources Conference.

Manville, A.M. III. 1989. A funding dilemma: The Fish and Wildlife Conservation Act. In *Preserving communities and corridors,* ed. G. Mackintosh. Washington, D.C.: Defenders of Wildlife.

Marcuzzi, G. 1979. *European ecosystems.* The Hague–Boston–London: Dr. W. Junk B.V.

Marion, W.R. 1988. Urban wildlife: Can we live with them? In Proceedings of the Thirteenth Vertebrate Pest Conference, eds. A.C. Crabb and R.E. Marsh. Davis, Calif.: University of California.

Matthews, M.J. 1986. An inventory of wildlife habitat in an urban setting. In *Wildlife conservation and new residential developments,* eds. K. Stenberg and W.W. Shaw. Tucson: University of Arizona.

Matthiessen, P. 1987. *Wildlife in America.* New York: Elisabeth Sifton Books.

McCombie, B. 1999. Those dirty raccoons. *Field and Stream* 104: 8.

McDonnell, M.J., and S.T.A. Pickett. 1990. Ecosystem structure and function along urban-rural gradients: An unexploited opportunity for ecology. *Ecology* 7: 1232–37.

McHarg, I. 1969. *Design with nature.* New York: Garden City Press.

Mitchell, J.H. 1985. *A field guide to your own back yard.* New York: W.W. Norton and Co.

Montier, D.J. 1977. *Atlas of breeding birds of the London area.* London: Batsford, Ltd.

Nash, R.F. 1989. *The rights of nature.* Madison, Wisc.: The University of Wisconsin Press.

National Academy of Sciences. 1991. *Animals as sentinels of environmental health hazards.* Washington, D.C.: National Academy Press.

Norton, B.G. 1987. *Why preserve natural variety?* Princeton, N.J.: Princeton University Press.

Novak, M. 1987. Beaver. In *Wild furbearer management and conservation in North America,* eds., M. Novak, J.A. Baker, M.E. Obbard, and B. Malloch. Ontario, Canada: Ministry of Natural Resources.

Noyes, J.H., and D.R. Progulske, eds. 1974. *Wildlife in an urbanizing environment,* Planning and Resource Development Series, No. 28. Amherst: University of Massachusetts.

O'Donnell, M.A., and L.W. VanDruff. 1983. Wildlife conflicts in an urban area: Occurrence of problems and attitudes toward wildlife. In Proceedings of the First Eastern Wildlife Damage Control Conference, ed. D.J. Decker. Ithaca, N.Y.: Cornell University Cooperative Extension.

Ordish, G. 1981. *The living American house.* New York: William Morrow and Company, Inc.

————. 1959. *The living house.* New York: Lippincott.

Page, R.J.C. 1981. Dispersal and population density of the fox *(Vulpes vulpes)* in an area of London. *Journal of Zoology, London* 194: 485–91.

Platt, R.H., R.A. Rowntree, and P.C. Muick. 1994. *The ecological city.* Amherst: The University of Massachusetts Press.

Pulliam, H.R. 1988. Sources, sinks, and population regulation. *American Naturalist* 132: 652–61.

Rees, W. 1996. Ecological footprints. *People and the planet* 5(2).

Regan, T. 1983. *The case for animal rights.* Berkeley: University of California Press.

Reiter, D.K., M.W. Brunson, and R.H. Schmidt. 1999. Public attitudes toward wildlife damage management policy. *Wildlife Society Bulletin* 27: 746–58.

Richardson, J.H., R.F. Shore, and J.R. Treweek. 1997. Are major roads a barrier to small mammals? *Journal of Zoology,* London 243: 840–846.

Riley, S.R., J. Hadidian, and D.A. Manski. 1998. Population density, survival, and rabies in raccoons in an urban national park. *Canadian Journal of Zoology* 76: 1153–64.

Robinson, W.L., and E.G. Bolen. 1984. *Wildlife ecology and management.* New York: Macmillan Publishing Company.

Rolston, H. 1986. *Philosophy gone wild: Essays in environmental ethics.* New York: Prometheus Books.

Rublowsky, J. 1967. *Nature in the city.* New York: Basic Books, Inc.

Ryder, R.D. 1989. *Animal revolution.* Oxford: Basil Blackwell.

San Julien, G. 1987. The future of wildlife damage control in an urban environment. In Proceedings of the Third Eastern Wildlife Damage Control Conference, ed. N.R. Holler. Gulf Shores, Ala.: Auburn University.

Scheffey, A.J.W. 1967. Farm and urban resources: Remarks of the chairman. In Transactions of the Thirty-second North American Fish and Wildlife Conference.

Schmidt, R.H. 1989a. Animal welfare and animal management. In Transactions of the Fifty-fourth North American Wildlife and Natural Resources Conference.

—————. 1989b. Vertebrate pest control and animal welfare. In *Vertebrate pest control and management materials,* eds. K.A Fagerstone, and R.D. Curnow. ASTM STP.

Shaw, W.W., and W.R. Mangun. 1984. Nonconsumptive use of wildlife in the United States. Fish and Wildlife Service Research Publication 154. Washington, D.C.: U.S. Department of the Interior.

Shenstone, J.C. 1912. The flora of London building sites. *Journal of Botany* 50: 117–24.

Shirley, P. 1996. *Urban wildlife.* London: Whittet Books, Ltd.

Singer, P. 1975. *Animal liberation.* New York: A New York Review Book.

Slate, D., R. Owens, G. Connolly, and G. Simmons. 1992. Decision making for wildlife damage management. In Transactions of the Fifty-seventh North American Wildlife and Natural Resources Conference.

Stenberg, K., and W.W. Shaw, eds. 1986. *Wildlife conservation and new residential developments.* Tucson: University of Arizona.

South Carolina Wildlife Federation (SCWF). 1997. *Working for wildlife: ways cities and counties can help wildlife.* SCWF.

Stearns, F. 1967. Wildlife habitat in urban and suburban environments. In Transactions of the Thirty-second North American Fish and Wildlife Conference.

Sudia, T.W. 1971. *Man, nature, city.* Urban Ecology Series. Washington, D.C.: U.S. Government Printing Office.

—————. 1978. *Wildlife and the city.* Urban Ecology Series. Washington, D.C.: U.S. Government Printing Office.

Sukopp, H., M. Numata, and A. Huber. 1995. Urban ecology as the basis of urban planning. In *Urban wildlife and human well-being,* eds. L.W. VanDruff, D.L. Leedy, and F.W. Sterns. Amsterdam: SPB Academic Publishing bv.

Szot, T.R. 1975. Perception of urban wildlife by selected Tucson residents. Masters thesis, University of Arizona.

Temple, S.A. 1986. Ecological principles of wildlife management. In *Management of nongame wildlife in the midwest: A developing art,* eds. J.B. Hale, L.B. Best, and R.L. Clawson. Chelsea, Mich.: North Central Section of the Wildlife Society.

Thomas, K. 1983. *Man and the natural world: A history of modern sensibility.* New York: Pantheon Books.

Trefil, J. 1994. *A scientist in the city.* New York: Doubleday.

Twiss, R.H. 1967. Wildlife in the metropolitan landscape. In Transactions of the Thirty-second North American Fish and Wildlife Conference.

United Nations. 1987. The prospect of world urbanization. United Nations Population Studies, ST/ESA/SER/101.

U.S. Department of Agriculture (USDA). 1994. *Animal Damage Control Program: Final environmental impact statement.* Washington, D.C.: USDA, Animal and Plant Health Inspection Services, Wildlife Services.

U.S. Government. 1979. Presidential Memorandum: August 2, 1979. *The President's 1979 message on the environment,* Washington, D.C.: The White House.

Van der Ryn, S., and S. Cowan. 1996. *Ecological design.* Washington, D.C.: Island Press.

VanDruff, L.W., D.L. Leedy, and F.W. Sterns. 1995. Urban wildlife and human well-being. In *Urban ecology as the basis of urban planning.* Eds. H. Sukopp., M. Numata, and A. Huber. Amsterdam: SPB Academic Publishing bv.

Vessel, M.F., and H.H. Wong. 1987. *Natural history of vacant lots.* Berkeley: University of California Press.

Villard, P. 1975. *Wild animals around your home.* New York: Winchester Press.

Vitousek, P.M., H.A. Mooney, J. Lubchenco, and J.M. Melilo. 1997. Human domination of earth's ecosystems. *Science* 277(5325): 494–99.

Wacker, J.L. 1987. Land use planning and urban wildlife. In *Integrating man and nature in the metropolitan environment,* eds. L.W. Adams and D.L. Leedy. Columbia, Md.: The National Institute for Urban Wildlife.

Warren, M.A. 1997. *Moral status: Obligations to persons and other living things.* Oxford: Clarendon Press.

Whitham, J.H., and J.M. Jones. 1990. White-tailed deer abundance on metropolitan forest preserves during winter in northeastern Illinois. *Wildlife Society Bulletin* 18: 13–16.

Witter, D.J., D.L. Tylka, and J.E. Werner. 1981. Values of urban wildlife in Missouri. In Transactions of the Forty-sixth North American Wildlife and Natural Resources Conference.

Zawistowski, S.L. 1998. Henry Bergh. In *Encyclopedia of animal rights and animal welfare,* ed. M. Bekoff. Westport, Conn.: Greenwood Press.

Fertility Control in Animals

Jay F. Kirkpatrick and Allen T. Rutberg

From Mortality Control to Fertility Control

For most of the twentieth century, government agencies charged by law with managing wildlife were dedicated to building the size and productivity of populations of game species. Under a utilitarian philosophy of wildlife conservation, this dedication made sense and, in its time, was arguably a highly progressive view of wildlife (Dunlap 1988).

In the United States, state game management went far to reverse the wildlife catastrophe of the nineteenth century. In the 1800s hunting and trapping for commercial markets drove Carolina parakeets and passenger pigeons extinct and nearly extirpated bison, elk, deer, beavers, egrets, waterfowl, songbirds, and any other furred or feathered creature that could make a meal or adorn a hat (Tober 1981). Predatory birds and mammals were shot on sight because of the threat they posed to domestic livestock and poultry and because they were believed by some to be genuinely evil (Dunlap 1988).[1]

Through an aggressive program of reintroduction, habitat management, and restrictions on killing, state wildlife agencies succeeded in restoring populations of deer, elk, beavers, otters, waterfowl, and other game and fur-bearing species (Gilbert and Dodds 1992). The linchpin of this effort was recreational hunting and trapping, which furnished funding (through license sales and Pittman-Robertson grants), volunteer labor, and a dedicated political constituency.

At the beginning of the twenty-first century, this neat system is unraveling. Demographic changes are producing a shrinking and aging population of hunters and trappers (hunters, for example, now represent only 7 percent of the total U.S. population) (U.S. Fish and Wildlife Service 1997); a growing public appreciation of "nongame" species that have been neglected, and even harmed, by management of game species; and changes in public values, from utilitarian views to moral views of wildlife (Kellert 1985; Dunlap 1988). The biggest challenge to the system may arise from the failure of state agencies to respond effectively to the problems associated with dense populations of deer, geese, and other species, especially in urban and suburban communities.

How could a system founded on hunting and trapping—killing—find itself unable to control wildlife populations and solve problems associated with abundant wildlife? There are several reasons. Reflecting cultural attitudes—and regulations—that discourage the killing of females, public hunting has focused on removing male deer and other big-game animals, leaving populations streamlined for reproduction. Many of the most severe wildlife conflicts arise in locations that are effectively unhuntable, such as parks, research campuses, and suburban neighborhoods. Killing of some species, such as wild horses, is simply unacceptable to the public. The public's tolerance of invasions of their parks and backyards by armed strangers is declining just as its sympathy for wild animals and its interest in nonlethal solutions to wildlife problems are rising.

While the public is searching for new, humane approaches to solving conflicts with wildlife, state wildlife agencies persist in recommending hunting and its variations. Wildlife agencies in some states, such as New York, are required by law to promote recreational hunting (Marion 1987). But, more pervasively, most state agency personnel have strong cultural and political links to the hunting and trapping community. This community is (somewhat irrationally) hostile to the concept of nonlethal management of wildlife (Kirkpatrick and Turner 1995; Hagood 1997). Wildlife agencies' advocacy of hunting and trapping is coupled with a reluctance to pursue or encourage research into other approaches. As a result, the public is turning elsewhere for solutions.

There are, effectively, only two choices for actively managing the size of animal populations: reducing the birth rate and increasing the death rate. (Local population size may also be controlled by movement of individuals in and out; but when the size of animal populations concerns us, movement of individuals merely relocates the concerns. We are not absolved of our responsibility for animals simply because they go somewhere else.) Killing certainly can reduce and even destroy wildlife populations if enough animals of the right description are removed from the population. Until the last decade of the twentieth century, however, fertility control for wildlife was not seen as a feasible option.

Everything changed between 1988 and 1989. The successful use of a remotely deliverable immunocontraceptive on free-ranging wild horses at Assateague Island National Seashore, in Maryland, opened a new universe of possibilities for the humane, nonlethal control of wildlife populations.

The History of Wildlife Fertility Control

The history of wildlife fertility control and its application to the management of free-roaming and captive wildlife populations is relatively short, perhaps no more than fifty years. Until the late 1980s, wildlife contraception was a "boutique" subject among scientists and wildlife managers. This lack of interest is a bit surprising, because the technology developed for contraception in humans has been impressive and its application to wildlife is fundamentally sound, at least in a pharmacological context. Various compounds developed for use in humans were first tested in animal models. The resistance to new approaches in wildlife management, which played a significant role in the slow pace of development and interest in wildlife contraception, stem not from science but from a variety of social, cultural, and economic factors.

That said, the history of wildlife contraception can be traced broadly by examining the technological approaches and, more specifically, the nature of the chemicals, hormones, and other compounds that have been applied to various species. Chronologically, these approaches can be classified as (1) nonhormonal chemicals, (2) steroid hormones, (3) nonsteroidal hormones, (4) barrier methods, and (5) immunocontraceptives.

This oversimplification is compounded by the various permutations of chemical agent, delivery system, and specific species. For example, a contraceptive can be delivered (1) orally, (2) by surgically placed implant, (3) by hand-injection, or (4) by remotely delivered dart.[2] The historical development of wildlife contraceptives had to take into account whether the animal was (1) small and easily live-trapped, (2) usually wary and unapproachable, (3) living in a captive setting, (4) capable of being induced to take baits, or (5) classified as a food animal by the U.S. Food and Drug Administration (FDA).

Nonhormonal Compounds

Nonhormonal compounds have been used most extensively in birds. Some of the compounds used were classified as fungicides and seed disinfectants (Arasan®, DuPont Co.) (Elder 1964), others as anticholesterol agents (22,25-diacholesterol dihydrochloride, later marketed as Ornitrol®, G. D. Searle and Co.) (Wofford and Elder 1967). In both cases, fertility was inhibited but toxic effects made the compounds unacceptable. Most of the other compounds used for birds (thiotepta and triethylene melamine) had similar shortcomings (Davis 1959, 1962). In general, nonhormonal compounds were abandoned because of their accompanying toxic effects. While some degree of contraception, and in a few cases sterilization, could be achieved, the administered dose had to be very precise. This was not possible with oral delivery in wildlife. In addition, the mechanisms of action were poorly understood, and it is unlikely that any of these compounds could have

passed the rigorous regulatory requirements of today's FDA or Environmental Protection Agency (EPA).

Some nonhormonal compounds were derived from plant products and based on historical evidence that Native Americans used certain plants for contraceptive purposes. A comprehensive review (Farnsworth and Waller 1982) listed fifty plant families with documented antifertility effects in males and females. Despite some controlled tests with laboratory animals (Cranston 1945; Barfnect and Peng 1968) and a few wild species of rodents (Berger et al. 1977) and reports of occasional interference with fertility in humans (Shao 1987), few investigators have attempted to exploit these naturally occurring substances to control reproduction in wildlife. This area remains a fertile subject for interested scientists.

Steroid Hormones

Research into the use of steroid hormones for wildlife fertility control became common in the 1960s and '70s and was based on the research originally directed at human fertility control (Pincus et al. 1958). In general, steroid hormones work as contraceptives by feeding back upon the hypothalamus and/or pituitary glands and depressing gonadotropic hormones, thereby reducing or eliminating ovulation or spermatogenesis, or by changing the speed with which the ovum moves through the oviducts. Diethylstilbestrol (DES, a synthetic estrogen) was introduced into bait and fed to foxes (Vulpes vulpes) (Linhart and Enders 1964; Cheatum 1967; Oleyar and McGinnes 1974; Allen 1982), coyotes (Canis latrans) (Balser 1964; Brushman et al. 1967), whitetailed deer (Odocoileus virginianus) (Harder 1971; Harder and Peterle 1974), and black-tailed prairie dogs (Cynomys ludovicianus) (Garrott and Franklin 1983) with significant contraceptive effects. Another steroid, mestranol, which is closely related to DES, was fed to red foxes (Storm and Sanderson 1969), small rodents (voles, rats, and mice) (Marsh and Howard 1969; Howard and Marsh 1969; Storm and Sanderson 1970), and cats (Burke 1977) with some contraceptive success, but bait acceptance decreased quickly. At about the same time, oral medroxyprogesterone acetate (MPA) was tested in red foxes (Storm and Sanderson 1969). Shortly thereafter, other investigators explored the use of oral progestins for controlling fertility in domestic canids. Oral melengestrol acetate (MGA) was highly effective in inhibiting fertility in dogs (Sokolowski and Van Ravenswaay 1976) and a related compound, megestrol acetate (MA), was approved for commercial use in dogs (Ovaban®, Schering Corporation) (Wildt and Seager 1977).

The use of these and similar oral steroid hormones in wildlife was restricted by problems with bait acceptance and dosage and by environmental concerns, especially effects on nontarget species (all these steroids pass through the food chain). These problems changed the focus of wildlife contraceptive research to more narrowly targeted delivery systems. Steroid hormones were administered via injection or surgically placed implants in wapiti (*Cervus elaphus*) (Greer et al. 1968), large exotic species of cats (Seal et al. 1976), deer (Bell and Peterle 1975; Levenson 1984), and wild horses (*Equus caballus*) (Kirkpatrick et al. 1982; Plotka and Vevea 1990). Significant contraceptive effects were achieved in these species, but several new problems arose. Application of these steroids to free-roaming wildlife required relatively large doses of the compounds, negating the use of remote delivery via darts. This meant that each animal had to be captured before it could be hand-injected or given a surgical implant. This was impractical with most species, because of the stresses associated with capture, the frequency with which the steroid had to be administered, and the large doses that had to be administered. Unknown at the time but evident in later years were various pathologies that resulted from long-term use of these steroids, particularly among (but not restricted to) felids

(Buergelt and Kollias 1987). These molecules were also shown to have profound effects upon the behavior of treated animals, something that would be undesirable in valued wildlife species.

Norplant® implants containing levonorgestrol were effective in striped skunks (*Mephitis mephitis*) (Bickle et al. 1991), and raccoons (*Procyon lotor*) (Kirkpatrick, unpublished data), which could be easily captured in live traps in urban settings, but these two species were clearly an exception to the practical application of injectable or implant steroids to larger species.

Nonsteroidal Hormones

Wildlife contraceptive research with nonsteroidal hormones has been largely confined to agonists and antagonists of gonadotropin releasing hormone (GnRH) (Becker and Katz 1997). Normally GnRH signals the pituitary to secrete the gonadotropin luteinizing hormone (LH) or follicle stimulating hormone (FSH), both necessary for normal function in the ovaries and testes. The agonists and antagonists of GnRH block the effects of GnRH on the pituitary by one of several mechanisms. These compounds have been used successfully to inhibit fertility in dogs (Vickery et al. 1984, 1985; Inaba et al. 1996), monkeys (*Macaca* spp.) (Fraser et al. 1987), and a variety of other species. To date, however, these compounds have been short-lived in their effects and require large doses for extended effectiveness.

Barrier Methods

Mechanical birth control devices have been tested in white-tailed deer (unsuccessfully), horses (successfully), and a variety of zoo animals (mixed results), but the logistics of application to free-roaming wildlife are prohibitory in most species. These methods have included IUD-like barriers for the deer (Matschke 1980) and horses (Daels and Hughes 1995) and silastic vas deferens plugs in the zoo animals (Porton et al. 1990). More comprehensive reviews of the history

of wildlife contraception exist (Kirkpatrick and Turner, 1985, 1991).

Immunocontraception

More recently, immunocontraception, or vaccine-based fertility control, became a reality for use in wildlife. Immunocontraception is based on the same principles as is disease prevention through vaccination. Humans and other animals are vaccinated against diseases by injections of dead or attenuated disease bacteria or viruses or of molecules that are harmless but similar to toxins the disease organisms produce. The stimulated immune systems then produce antibodies against some essential event or structure in the reproductive process.

A variety of immunocontraceptive vaccines are under development, including vaccines against brain reproductive hormones such as GnRH (Hassan et al. 1985; Ladd et al. 1988, 1989; Bell et al. 1997) and LH (Al-Kafawi et al. 1974) and vaccines against sperm (Primikoff et al. 1988; Herr et al. 1989) and egg (Florman and Wassarman 1985), which prevent fertilization. One of the first immunological approaches was a vaccine against the zona pellucida of the mammalian egg, which was patented as an antifertility agent in 1976 by R. B. L. Gwatkin for Merck and Company (Skinner et al. 1996). In 1988 this vaccine was applied to wild horses with great success. Success with the porcine zona pellucida vaccine (PZP) has opened the door to a practical approach to wildlife fertility control; since then other experiments with anti-sperm vaccines have been initiated.

The biology of the PZP vaccine, which is derived from pig eggs, is both simple and complex. An extracellular matrix known as the zona pellucida (ZP) surrounds all mammalian eggs. The ZP consists of three major glycoprotein families, one of which, ZP3, is thought to be the principal sperm receptor in most species (Prasad et al. 2000). When the vaccine is injected into the muscle of the target female animal, it stimulates her immune system to produce antibodies against the vaccine. These antibodies attach themselves to the sperm receptors on the ZP of the target's eggs and distort their shape, thereby blocking fertilization (Florman and Wasserman 1985).

The Art and Science of Wildlife Immunocontraception

In the late 1980s, the failure to achieve practical results and the dangers associated with steroid hormones had led to a reexamination of the problems associated with wildlife contraception. Research had been proceeding without an idealized standard by which to evaluate each new approach. Kirkpatrick and Turner (1991) created such a standard, which included the following goals:

1. Contraceptive effectiveness of at least 90 percent
2. The capacity for remote delivery with no (or minimal) handling of animals
3. Reversibility of contraceptive effects (more important for some species than for others)
4. Safety for use in pregnant animals
5. Absence of significant health side effects, short or long term
6. No passage of the contraceptive agent through the food chain
7. Minimal effects upon individual and social behaviors
8. Low cost

While some of these goals are more or less arbitrary, they at least provided reasonable guidelines for discussion and planning. They were built exclusively around wild-horse contraception and did not address all problems associated with diverse species and settings.

In the development of the PZP vaccine for certain species, some of these problems became clear. The challenge of deer contraception, for example, even in urban areas, was and is

to develop a single-dose form of the vaccine that would provide at least one, and perhaps several, years of contraception from one application. (The use of the raw, native form of the PZP vaccine requires two inoculations the first year, which can be very difficult with wary species like deer.) The challenge of elephant contraception, where doses of vaccine must be ten times larger than standard wild-horse or deer doses, raised the need for the development of a synthetic form of the vaccine. The process of producing the native PZP vaccine is laborious, and the number of doses that can be produced in a year is limited at this time by the production process. A synthetic form of the vaccine would expand the application of wildlife contraception beyond present logistical restrictions and eliminate some of the regulatory concerns raised by the use of natural products.

The mere availability of a good physiological immunocontraceptive does not insure its effective application to wildlife. The first step in the development of a wildlife contraceptive is to test its efficacy in captive animals or domestic counterparts, but once this has been done and physiological efficacy has been determined, strategies for application to free-roaming species must be developed. It is a large leap from inoculating a deer in a pen to inoculating a wild free-roaming deer; it's yet another leap from administering the vaccine in the field to controlling a wildlife population.

Actual application to free-roaming species requires a variety of delivery and access strategies. Immunocontraceptives can currently be delivered by intramuscular injection: an animal must be given the vaccine either by hand injection or by a dart. Two delivery systems require at least two access strategies. Hand injection requires physical capture of the target animal; it increases the stress for the target animal, danger to the person(s) doing the work, and expense. Although in some settings, such as zoos, access is not so great a problem, it is not always possible to hand-inject animals without causing some degree

of capture-related stress. In other situations, such as with wild horses in the West, hundreds of animals at a time are rounded up for entry into adoption programs, and it is relatively easy to hand-inject animals as they pass through a chute.

For most species of wildlife, the only delivery option is by dart. It has advantages and disadvantages. The most obvious advantage is that it eliminates the need for stressful capture of animals. The small volume of vaccine necessary to immunize an animal (1.0 cc) permits the use of very small and light darts. This increases the effective range of darting and decreases the chances of injury to the target animal. The disadvantages include the need to approach the animal to within fifty meters, the need to separate the animals that have been inoculated from those that haven't, and the labor-intensive nature of the endeavor.

Despite the fact that inoculation of free-roaming wildlife with a contraceptive vaccine is at best difficult, a significant degree of success has been achieved under field conditions.

Wild Horses

Liu et al. (1989) first discovered that the PZP vaccine would inhibit fertility in domestic mares. Soon after, wild horses were treated with the PZP vaccine on Assateague Island National Seashore, in Maryland; studies have continued for twelve years. The vaccine was delivered remotely, with small darts. Contraceptive efficacy was greater than 95 percent (Kirkpatrick et al. 1990). The vaccine was safe to administer to pregnant animals and did not interfere either with pregnancies in progress or the health of the foals born to inoculated mothers. A single annual booster inoculation was sufficient to maintain the contraceptive effects (Kirkpatrick et al. 1991), and contraception was reversible after three and four years of treatment (Kirkpatrick et al. 1992, 1995a, 1996a). No changes occurred in the social organization or behaviors of the treated animals. In 1994 the National Park Service began the management of the Assateague wild horses via the PZP vaccine and, after only three years, the herd reached zero population growth (Kirkpatrick 1995; Kirkpatrick et al. 1997). This approach as of 2000 was being applied to large wild-horse herds in Nevada (Turner et al. 1996a), and trials with feral donkeys (*E. asinus*) in Virgin Islands National Park have been successful (Turner et al. 1996b).

White-Tailed and Black-Tailed Deer

Populations of white-tailed deer and, to a lesser extent, black-tailed deer (*O. hemionus*) exploded in North America during the last two to three decades of the twentieth century. The causes of the population explosion are undoubtedly complex. It is generally attributed to the use of high-yield crops; the spread of deer-friendly suburbs, which offer a diverse menu of heavily fertilized ornamental shrubs and grasses intermingled with disturbed "natural areas" such as small parks and woodlots; increasingly mild winters; the absence of natural predators; and recreational hunting practices ill-suited to controlling deer populations in suburbs.

With burgeoning deer populations and suburban sprawl has come a rapid rise in conflicts between deer and people. These have centered on an increase in deer-vehicle collisions, damage to crops and ornamental plants, undesirable impacts on some forest ecosystems, and tick-borne zoonotic diseases, particularly Lyme disease (Conover 1997; Rutberg 1997). There is now enormous interest in finding new tools that will allow people and deer to coexist, and much public attention has focused on immunocontraception. In autumn 1997 alone, for example, The Humane Society of the United States (HSUS) received requests for information on deer immunocontraception from people in more than sixty communities across the United States.

The 1988–89 field demonstration on wild horses at Assateague spurred preliminary testing of PZP on captive deer. Effects on captive deer resembled those in wild horses; the two-shot vaccine protocol was highly effective, the vaccine could be delivered remotely, its effects were reversible after at least two years of treatment, and no health side effects were apparent (Turner et al. 1992, 1996c, 1997; Kirkpatrick et al. 1997; see also Miller et al. 1999). A subsequent trial with semi–free-roaming deer at the Smithsonian Institution's Conservation and Research Center, in Front Royal, Virginia, provided evidence that the vaccine could be delivered remotely under field conditions; although there was evidence that PZP treatments extended the mating season, treated females gained more weight than untreated females, presumably because they were spared the energetic costs of pregnancy and lactation (McShea et al. 1997). A study begun in 1993 at Fire Island National Seashore, New York, launched a series of field studies that explored the effectiveness and costs of different field techniques, vaccination schedules, and vaccine preparations, as well as investigated effects of PZP on behavior and survival (Kirkpatrick et al. 1997; Thiele 1999; Walter 2000; Rudolf et al. 2000). The Fire Island study was the first to show that biologically significant numbers of females could be efficiently and effectively treated in the field; approximately 200 females a year were under treatment by 1996. However, vaccine effectiveness in this study was lower than in previous deer studies, especially in the first year following treatment, probably due to incomplete or misdelivered initial vaccinations (Kirkpatrick et al. 1997; Thiele 1999, HSUS unpublished data).

The first demonstration that immunocontraception reduced an unconfined deer population was accomplished at the National Institute of Standards and Technology (NIST). NIST, a 574-acre federal research facility within the city of Gaithersburg, Maryland, supported a deer population of approximately 180 animals in 1993. By the time PZP treatments began in autumn 1996, the popula-

tion had risen to approximately 250, and it peaked at approximately 300 in autumn 1997 (Thiele 1999). By autumn 1998, however, more than 90 percent of the NIST females were receiving PZP treatments, and the population had declined about 20 percent below peak levels by spring 2000 (HSUS, unpublished data). Good access to deer for treatment, high population mortality (the majority due to vehicle collisions), and relatively low reproductive rate all contributed to success in controlling this population.

Zoo Animals

A third application of the concept of wildlife immunocontraception is the control of the production of "surplus" animals in zoos. Despite often-heard discussions of the challenges of breeding endangered species in captivity, most zoo species breed quite successfully, and the production—and disposition—of surplus animals is perhaps the largest single problem facing zoos worldwide. Beginning in 1990 the PZP vaccine was applied to various exotic species in zoos, beginning with Przewalski's horses (*E. przewalskii*) and banteng (*Bos javanicus*) at the Cologne Zoo (Kirkpatrick et al. 1995b), and five species of deer at the Bronx Zoo (now the Wildlife Conservation Center) (Kirkpatrick et al. 1996b). The PZP vaccine has been tested in more than ninety species in more than seventy zoos worldwide (Frisbie and Kirkpatrick 1998). Today it is reducing zoo births and providing some relief to the problem of surplus animals.

African Elephants

A fourth major application is under way in Africa. Devastated by the lucrative trade in elephant ivory, populations of African elephants (*Loxodonta africana*) were reduced to dangerously low numbers during the 1970s and 1980s. Elephants basically retreated to the sanctuary of national parks. In the meantime, much former elephant habitat outside of these parks has come under intensive agricultural use. In a sense Africa's elephant populations are now trapped in the national parks. As poaching has diminished, their numbers are increasing by as much as 5 percent per year. Ironically in some areas elephants are now threatening both the ecosystems of national parks and their own health. In recent years this problem has been managed through "culling," a euphemism for shooting. Four African nations currently kill elephants in order to keep populations within the carrying capacity of their parks. (Kruger National Park, in South Africa, killed 300 to 700 elephants annually for thirty years but suspended culling in 1995.) This is tragic, particularly for a species that is believed to understand the concept of death.

In 1995 preliminary experiments provided evidence that the PZP vaccine would work in elephants. Several zoo elephants were treated with the vaccine and, while these were not breeding animals, we determined that they produced antibodies against the vaccine. In October 1996 twenty-one elephants in Kruger National Park were captured, radio-collared, and treated with the PZP vaccine in order to determine its contraceptive efficacy. In November 1996 and again in June 1997, each treated elephant was given a single booster inoculation by means of a dart fired by a shooter in a helicopter. None of the animals was captured for these booster inoculations, proving that elephants need not be captured to be vaccinated (Fayrer-Hosken et al. 1997). In this trial pregnancy rates in elephants were reduced from 90 percent in untreated control animals to approximately 37.5 percent in treated animals. Based on the successful preliminary results, there may be a nonlethal solution to the wise management of park elephants. Additional studies designed to increase the efficacy of the vaccine in elephants were carried out in 1998. In this latest round of trials, fertility was reduced by 75 percent. There were no changes in behavior among the treated animals, the contraceptive effects were reversible, and the reproductive sys-

tem of the treated animals (uteri and ovaries) remained normal.

Other Species

In May 1997 ZooMontana, under contract to the U.S. Navy, began treating thirty water buffalo (*Bubalis bubalis*) on the island of Guam with the PZP vaccine. Preliminary results indicate that the experiment significantly reduced pregnancies in these animals. These results have led to a new, five-year project by the U.S. Navy and the U.S. Fish and Wildlife Service using PZP to control water buffalo on the U.S. naval base at Guam. This project will set the important precedent of nonlethal control of wildlife by the Department of Defense.

On Point Reyes National Seashore in California, Tule elk (*C. elaphus nannodes*) are being treated with PZP as part of a series of tests to determine whether the herd can be managed with contraception. Preliminary evidence shows that elk can be successfully contracepted with PZP (Kirkpatrick et al. 1996b; Heilmann et al. 1998; Shideler, personal communication).

Research in Progress

The PZP vaccine appears to come close to the optimum contraceptive agent when measured against the "ideal" wildlife contraceptive. So far, at least, its physiological actions appear to be sound and safe; it does not appear to pass through the food chain; and it is not associated with immune responses to somatic tissues (Turner et al. 1997; Barber and Fayrer-Hosken 2000). However, the ideal wildlife contraceptive vaccine would require only a single inoculation in order to achieve several years of contraception. It would use adjuvants that have already been federally licensed for use in food animals, instead of the experimental or nonapproved adjuvants currently in use, or use no adjuvants at all. The remote delivery system would in some man-

ner mark the animal as well as inoculate it, so that it could be distinguished from untreated animals. The ZP antigen itself would be readily available in large and inexpensive quantities, which suggests the need for genetically-engineered or synthetic forms. Current research addressing these goals is described below.

A One-Inoculation Vaccine

The current vaccine requires animals to be treated twice before full effectiveness is achieved, with the second vaccination being administered a few weeks before the onset of the breeding season. However, it is quite difficult to treat individual wild animals twice, and the time just prior to the breeding season is not always the most practical time for administering treatments. Consequently, research is focusing on the development and testing of a longer-acting one-inoculation vaccine.

The first approach to a one-inoculation vaccine used microspheres formed from a lactide-glycolide polymer that is biodegradable after injection and nontoxic as it breaks down (Kreeger 1997; Turner et al. 1997). These microspheres can be engineered to release the incorporated vaccine at varying rates by means of altering the size of the spheres and the ratio of lactide to glycolide (Eldridge et al. 1989). In the first experiment with these microspheres, in wild horses in Nevada, a single inoculation achieved the same degree of contraception as two inoculations of the raw vaccine. However, the spheres clogged syringes, needles, and darts, and delivery was impractical (Turner et al. 2001). This led to experiments with small pellets, made of the same material but shaped to fit into the needle of a dart. When the pellets are injected into the muscle of the animal, along with a bolus of raw vaccine and adjuvant, they begin to erode, releasing the vaccine at one and three months. In an initial study with the pellets, antibody titers in domestic mares remained at contraceptive levels for close to a year, and in a small pilot study with wild mares, significant contraception was achieved (Liu and Turner, personal communication). Additional research is being carried out in an attempt to develop pellets that will release at nine months, thereby permitting two years of contraception from a single inoculation.

A second approach involves the packaging of the PZP vaccine in liposomes, which are formed from phospholipids and cholesterol in saline (Brown et al. 1997a). This preparation, which is being tested under the name SpayVac™ (NuTech, Halifax, Canada), has shown especially promising results for gray seals (*Halichoerus grypus*), some of which remained infertile for at least six years after a single dose (Brown et al. 1996, 1997b). Published data concerning the effects of SpayVac in other species are limited at this time, but there is considerable interest in further testing, which is under way.

PZP, Adjuvants, and the Immune System

The PZP vaccine works in most mammalian species because the ZP molecule is similar, but not identical, among many species. The drawback to this similarity across species is that PZP is not very good at causing antibodies to be formed. Thus, it must be given with a general immunostimulant known as an adjuvant. The adjuvant, when given with a specific vaccine, causes the body to make greater concentrations of antibodies against the vaccine, which results in better contraception. The most effective available adjuvant, and the one employed in most previous PZP tests, is known as Freund's Complete Adjuvant (FCA). In many species, however, FCA also causes localized inflammation and tissue damage and may trigger false-positive tuberculosis tests after injection (Hanly et al. 1997). Thus, the FDA and other regulators, as well as those concerned with animal welfare, discourage its widespread use. Several new adjuvants are under study for use with the PZP vac-

cine, and success may lead to more-relaxed regulation of the vaccine by the FDA.

Different adjuvants may target different immune pathways, which has important implications for both the mechanism and duration of action (Weeratna et al. 2000). PZP has been assumed to work through short-term activation of the humoral immune system. However, some adjuvants appear to activate the cellular immune system, which could lead to the destruction of target tissues, such as the ovaries. Preliminary experiments suggest that conjugation of PZP to other immunogenic molecules, such as keyhole limpet hemocyanin (KLH) or tetanus toxoid, may also activate the cellular immune system.

Activation of the cellular immune system against the ZP protein could lead to irreversible sterilants, as well as more effective contraceptives. The ability to cause sterilization rather than temporary contraception may represent a huge advantage with some species in some situations, such as white-tailed deer or companion animals.

Genetically Engineered or Synthetic ZP Vaccines

Currently the PZP vaccine must be made as a natural product; the actual glycoprotein antigen is extracted from the zona pellucida of pig eggs. Production of the vaccine is very labor intensive and must rely on an adequate supply of pig ovaries from slaughterhouses. It is unlikely that any given small laboratory operation can produce more than fifteen thousand 65 μg doses per year. That level of production can probably meet demands for wild horses, zoo animals, and deer, but use in elephants (which currently requires three 600 μg doses) and companion animals (which number in the hundreds of thousands or millions) will far exceed the ability to produce the native PZP (see also the discussion of ethics, below). Thus,

there is a significant need to produce a synthetic form of the vaccine.

A number of investigators have successfully cloned the protein backbone of the ZP molecules of several species (Harris et al. 1994; Prasad et al. 2000). Thus far, however, they have been unsuccessful at producing a recombinant ZP with contraceptive effects, probably because of difficulties in glycosylating this backbone. This step is essential in order to impart adequate antigenicity to the antigen. Even several large pharmaceutical companies have failed in their attempts to produce a genetically engineered form of the vaccine. Work on this project continues in several foreign companies and a number of research groups; among the most promising approaches is conjugating short sequences of the ZP antigen to tetanus toxin or other nonspecific immune-system booster (Patterson et al. 1999; but see Kaul et al. 1996).

Marking Darts, Oral Delivery, and Transmissible Vectors

The ability to treat free-roaming wildlife remotely with darts and know which animals have been treated is essential in the course of most applications in wildlife management. To this end, a dart has been developed by Pneu-dart® that inoculates the animal with vaccine and leaves a small paint or dye mark on the animal at the same time. While this would not allow long-term individual recognition, it would allow darters to discriminate between treated and untreated animals, which is all that is needed when success is measured by impact on the population. At the present time, this dart works in a fairly reliable manner but only at relatively short ranges; improvements are being pursued. The various dyes tested thus far have also fallen short of the mark. Deer in particular have a tendency to lick the dye off the injection site. More permanent, nontoxic dyes must be found that will survive attention by the target animal and persist over at least a three-to-four-week period.

Delivering contraceptives to wildlife orally, in baits, would be easier and more cost effective than darting. However, for safety and ethical reasons, both the public and regulatory agencies are likely to demand that any oral contraceptive must be species specific. This will be extremely difficult and expensive to accomplish, and little progress thus far has been made. A second problem is that the PZP vaccine (or any ZP vaccine) is protein in nature and easily destroyed by the digestive process of most animals. Needed is a delivery system that permits the undigested protein of the antigen to pass into the lymph of the target animal's gastrointestinal system. Several strategies to accomplish this are available. One is to insert a ZP vaccine into a nontransmissible bacterial or viral vector; this is the approach used for the oral rabies vaccine, which is incorporated into a *Vaccinia* (smallpox) vaccine (Bradley et al. 1997; Linhart et al. 1997; Miller 1997). Another method would be to incorporate the ZP vaccine into a microcapsule designed to be absorbed through the lymphoid tissue (or other route) in the digestive tract (Miller 1997). Until the species-specificity issue is resolved, however, solving the technical problems of oral delivery will not move the idea far toward management application.

Researchers working with the Australian government are seeking to engineer the genes for PZP and similar contraceptive molecules into transmissible, nonpathogenic viruses for use in controlling populations of introduced wildlife species such as European rabbits (*Oryctolagus cuniculus*) (Holland et al. 1997; Robinson et al. 1997). These viruses would be introduced into the wild populations, then transmitted from animal to animal without further human intervention. While the approach is scientifically feasible, controlling the spread of the vaccine would be a serious problem, and such a vaccine would raise serious safety and environmental concerns in the United States and around the world (see the discussion of ethics below).

Abortifacients

At least two research groups are seeking to administer compounds that will cause abortion in recipient animals. This has already been shown to be feasible in deer, with prostaglandin F2 delivered remotely via biobullet (DeNicola et al. 1997). By its nature, however, this method will require annual application, and a multi-year treatment will not be possible. Moreover, the social objections that will attend this method of wildlife control make it an unlikely solution to large-scale management efforts, especially if a safe and effective contraceptive is available.

Immuno-sterilization for Companion Animals

The invention of an immunosterilant for companion animals would be an extraordinary gift to the millions of dogs and cats worldwide who suffer and die each year for want of compassionate care and loving homes. In the United States alone, an estimated 6 to 8 million unwanted dogs and cats are euthanized in shelters each year, and countless other stray, feral, and abandoned animals live and die under the harshest conditions imaginable. Elsewhere the situation for cats and dogs is far, far, worse. There are many useful and important approaches to the problems faced by dogs and cats—most notably, educational outreach by animal shelters (in those communities that even *have* animal shelters). However, only effective population control will allow such problems to be solved through these efforts.

To be truly useful to animal shelters and others trying to control stray and feral populations, the ideal immunosterilant would require only one shot, be free of harmful or unpleasant side effects, and cause permanent sterility (although a multi-year, one-shot contraceptive vaccine might be somewhat helpful for controlling stray and

feral populations). Ideally, such a sterilant should also mimic the behavioral and health effects of surgical sterilization, including reduced aggression in males and reduced incidence of ovarian cancer in females.

As noted above, a number of hormonal methods have been used successfully for contraception of dogs and cats (see "History of Wildlife Fertility Control"). Some, including megestrol acetate (Ovaban®) and Mibolerone (the synthetic androgen "Cheque"), are licensed for use as oral contraceptives on dogs and/or cats. However, behavioral and health side effects are common, and they are of no use to animal shelters or for control of stray and feral populations, since effectiveness ends soon after treatment stops.

Thus, immunological approaches may prove more fruitful, and research efforts in these fields have been accelerating. In an attempt to immunize dogs against their own LH, injections of human chorionic gonadotropin (hCG) were administered (Al-Kafawi et al. 1974). This experiment failed because canine LH did not crossreact with anti-hCG antibodies. An immunological approach to fertility control was also attempted in cats (Chan et al. 1981). Feline ovaries were homogenized and used to raise rabbit antibodies against the protein fractions. The antibodies, when administered to pregnant cats, caused some fetal resorption, but the results were discouraging. As in dogs, nonspecificity of the antibody appeared to be the cause of failure.

In a different immunological approach, male dogs were immunized against their own GnRH (gonadotropin releasing hormone) with GnRH conjugated to human serum globulin or tetanus toxoid (Hassan et al. 1985; Ladd et al. 1994). Plasma testosterone, LH, and sperm counts were all depressed; however, the effect was reversed when antibody levels dropped. A GnRH vaccine would have several important advantages. First, it should work on both sexes. Second, it could convey the same benefits as surgical sterilization, including loss of libido and estrus, reduction of aggressive behavior, and reduced incidence of reproductive tract cancers.

Another promising approach to dog contraception/sterilization is immunization with the PZP vaccine (Mahi-Brown et al. 1985, 1988). Small and infrequent doses of the PZP vaccine appeared to cause cellular-mediated immune responses in bitches and led to a longer-term infertility. Long-term studies were not carried out, but in the short term this cellular immune response was associated with histologic alterations of the ovaries. Concerns about potential pathologies would have to be resolved before this approach could be considered safe (Mahi-Brown et al. 1988). Some of these concerns might be resolved by use of a more highly purified PZP preparation than was used in these studies. As mentioned above, careful selection of recombinant ZP peptides should allow a more targeted immune response and help resolve these concerns (Paterson et al. 1999; Prasad et al. 2000).

Culture, Regulations, and Politics

Immunocontraception faces a variety of technical, cultural, regulatory, and political obstacles before it will be used as a tool for management of free-ranging wildlife. The technical issues have already been discussed: what is needed is a safe, effective, one-shot, multi-year vaccine that can be delivered remotely to wildlife under field conditions. In some ways, however, the technical obstacles are the least significant.

In our view, the single most formidable barrier to the adoption of immunocontraception as a wildlife management tool is the entrenched culture of wildlife use. In the United States, this culture is most evident in the wildlife management establishment, which includes the state wildlife management agencies, much of the U.S. Fish and Wildlife Service, the hunting community, the arms and archery manufacturers, the trapping and fur industries, and the other commercial interests that profit directly or indirectly from the killing of wildlife (Gill and Miller 1997; Hagood 1997). In this paradigm wildlife has no value or significance apart from its use. This is evident in the jargon of the culture: deer are the "deer resource"; beavers and otters are "fur bearers"; wildlife is divided into "game" and "nongame" species; ending an animal's life is "harvesting."

In a culture of use, contraception of "game" animals is illogical: why prevent animal births when you can instead stimulate births and "harvest" a surplus for human use? A choice to contracept rather than kill also introduces into wildlife management a new moral dimension disconcerting to those who think in terms of exploitation: that each individual animal has a claim on the world and on us, a claim to its own life. Recognizing this claim collapses the jargon of "harvest" and "resource" and undermines the paradigm of use that it supports.

The moral challenge that wildlife immunocontraception poses to the culture of use is, in our view, the only possible explanation for the extraordinary antipathy wildlife immunocontraception has generated in state wildlife agencies and the hunting community. It is certainly not the threat that the technology itself poses to hunting; immunocontraception, at least the dart-delivered kind, is not and will not be an effective management tool in the environments in which most recreational hunting occurs (Kirkpatrick and Turner 1995).

But the antipathy is unmistakable. Almost every attempt to get a state permit to conduct an immunocontraception field study on deer has exploded into a titanic political battle, with the state agencies often leading (or goading) the opposition. One proposed study, in Amherst, New York, was blocked by a lawsuit by Safari Club International. Another was nearly blocked by the personal intervention of several pro-hunting members of Congress. The publications of the hunting industry regularly feature articles on how immunocontraception can't work—it is too cumbersome and/or expensive, it is failing in this way or that, and of course, it is inferior to hunting in every way. One more extreme hunting newsletter featured a letter that drew parallels between our research and that of the Nazis. In community deer meetings, angry hunters stand up one after another to denounce immunocontraception as a fraud, as a threat to wildlife management and a traditional way of life, as "playing God," and as an anti-hunting plot (Kirkpatrick and Turner 1997). A national bowhunting advocacy group recently began issuing action alerts notifying its members of our public speaking engagements.

In the United States the culture of wildlife use is waning, especially in the cities and suburbs, where most people now live (Kellert 1985, 1993). Interest in and support for wildlife immunocontraception on the part of the public, the media, and some state legislatures suggests that this obstacle will be overcome.

In much of the world, however, the culture of wildlife use remains dominant and is reflected in the multi-billion-dollar worldwide trade in wildlife and wildlife parts (Freese 1998). Among people struggling to support their families and maintain human life and dignity, such attitudes are understandable, if tragic. But no such "necessity defense" can be constructed for the profiteers, the entrepreneurs from wealthy nations who make fortunes trading in wild-caught birds, bear gall bladders, and rhinoceros horn. Although the international community frowns on smuggling, the entire premise of treaties such as the Convention on International Trade in Endangered Species of Fauna and Flora (CITES) is that wildlife use is good so long as it is "sustainable."

Wildlife contraception makes little sense in that context. Why contracept elephants when you could shoot them, eat the meat, and sell the hides and tusks for great profit? The answers to that question are not simple. They ultimately rest on the morality of shooting elephants and the long-term economic, social, and spiritual advantages of treating these and other wild creatures with respect and compassion. But the question will have to be answered, and answered convincingly, before immunocontraception can be widely applied to elephants and other locally overabundant wildlife throughout the world.

Regulatory and Practical Issues

Several specific regulatory and practical issues will have to be addressed and resolved before PZP or other immunocontraceptives become mainstream management tools.

Within the United States, the most important regulatory barrier is approval by the Center for Veterinary Medicine of the U.S. Food and Drug Administration (FDA). The FDA has little experience with animal vaccines. Most animal vaccines are regulated by the U.S. Department of Agriculture (USDA), but the USDA's authorizing legislation only permits it to regulate vaccines for disease prevention. Since pregnancy is not considered a disease, regulatory authority reverts to the FDA. Unfortunately, most of the FDA regulations and standards that apply to immunocontraception are tailored to approval of drugs, which are generally more stringently regulated and require more rigorous testing than do vaccines.

As of mid-2000, research on PZP is being carried out under the authority of Investigational New Animal Drug (INAD) files established with the FDA. (In our case, the INAD is held by The HSUS.) The INAD file is the heart of a process designed to control development and testing of new animal drugs and vaccines and guide acceptable products toward eventual FDA approval for marketing and commercial distribution. Fundamentally, the FDA asks this question when considering a product for approval: Is the specific product safe and effective for its intended purpose if used as directed? The question is asked comprehensively; it extends to manufacturing, storage, packaging, means and schedule of delivery, animals targeted, and labeling of the vaccine or drug. These will be high hurdles for PZP or any contraceptive vaccine (especially a recombinant form) or drug to overcome. But it can be done, and eventually it will be done for a safe, effective wildlife contraceptive.

Since management of wildlife in the United States is carried out under state authority (with some exceptions on federal land), applying immunocontraceptives to free-ranging wildlife will generally require permits from state wildlife agencies (Messmer et al. 1997). Many will yield such permits only slowly and grudgingly. However, as the novelty of the technique wears off, as its limitations and successes are demonstrated in field studies, as a safety record is accumulated, and as FDA concerns are met, state agencies will become more comfortable with immunocontraception techniques. Some progress has already been made, at least in the agencies' rhetoric. While in the early 1990s the response of state agencies to deer contraception was "no, not now, not ever," by the close of the decade many state agency personnel were conceding that PZP does at least stop deer from breeding, and they began to speak of contraception as an important tool for future management efforts. Given the scope and seriousness of public concerns over deer and other wildlife, it is inconceivable that state agencies could resist indefinitely public demands for a humane, nonlethal tool that could help solve at least some conflicts with deer.

The practical issues include determining who will pay for wildlife contraception and who will carry it out. State agencies are uniquely unsuited to pay for or conduct wildlife management through immunocontraception. They have neither the money nor the personnel (a situation that certainly aggravates agency worries over the potential spread of immunocontraception as a management tool). The resources they do have are generated principally by hunters, who repeatedly and loudly voice their objections to having their license fees spent on contraception. State legislatures have become accustomed to state wildlife agencies generating their own funds and depending on hunters to conduct management activities. They are extremely reluctant to start diverting general revenues to these otherwise self-supporting agencies. Although some immunocontraception studies have received state funding and support (notably in New York and Connecticut), the prospects for state wildlife agencies getting any money to conduct immunocontraception management programs in the field are very limited.

If state agencies do not fund and conduct these programs, who will? We believe the answers are already beginning to emerge. Generally, HSUS immunocontraception studies have been funded at least in part by land owners, land management agencies, and communities in which the studies occur. The wild-horse contraception projects at Assateague Island and Cape Lookout National Seashores are being funded and carried out by the National Park Service, which is also involved in supporting and carrying out the deer project at Fire Island National Seashore and the Tule elk project at Point Reyes National Seashore. Wild-horse contraception studies on western public lands have been cooperative efforts of The HSUS, the research team, and the Bureau of Land Management; over time, the BLM is increasing its responsibility for carrying out these programs. NIST, part of the U.S. Department of Commerce, is jointly undertaking a deer contraception study with The HSUS on the NIST campus in Maryland. The U.S. Navy is implementing fertility control of water buffalo on Guam. Local agencies, such as Columbus-Franklin County Metro Parks, in Ohio, and Morris County Parks, in New Jersey, have also taken lead roles in conducting deer immunocontraception studies on their own properties. At Fire Island and in Groton, Connecticut, funding has been provided by local communities and residents.

Deer management, in particular, is increasingly being carried out at the local level. Confronted with increasing numbers of deer-human conflicts, town councils, county governments, park commissions, and other municipal bodies have developed deer-management plans and employed city police, animal control officers, volunteer hunters, and private contractors to carry them out. This localization has been formally recognized in Maryland, where the state deer-management plan emphasizes local needs and preferences, and in New Jersey, where recently approved legislation establishes community-based deer management plans. These plans would be developed locally by county and municipal governments, submitted to the state divisions of fish, game, and wildlife for review and approval, and carried out by either government personnel or private contractors. While the emphasis of these plans clearly now rests on killing, fertility control is explicitly recognized in the New Jersey legislation as a local management alternative.

We envision that immunocontraception projects (indeed, all urban wildlife management) eventually will be funded locally, carried out by local government personnel or private contractors, and regulated by the states, which will establish policies, issue permits, oversee research, and certify private contractors and other practitioners.

The Ethics of Immuno-contraception

Ethical questions concerning the application of immunocontraception to wildlife have been raised by people expressing a wide spectrum of viewpoints, from sport hunters to hard-line animal rights advocates. We choose to take a pragmatic approach. When immunocontraception is considered, it will be considered as one of several management alternatives, and so to each of the questions posed below must be added the implicit question, "compared to what?" (Oojges 1997; Singer 1997).

Is it right to manipulate a wild animal's reproductive system, and potentially its behavior, for human purposes? All other things being equal, our ethical and esthetic preference would be simply to leave wildlife alone. We recognize the intrinsic right of all wild creatures to live out their lives unmanipulated by humans, and we personally take great pleasure in observing and participating in the continuing and ever-surprising story of life on earth. But the lives of many wild creatures—especially those close to human habitation—are already subject to human manipulation, much of it deliberately or incidentally destructive. We shape the terms of animal existence by our settlement patterns; engineering of land and water; discharging of the byproducts of human life into the rivers, oceans, and atmosphere; and invasion of almost every corner of the planet.

And as a practical matter, leaving them alone is not always a choice we have. The public demands that action be taken when public health, safety, or subsistence are threatened by wildlife. Not only is this view ethically defensible, but (more to the point) it is also widespread, and we do not see this consensus changing in our lifetimes. The action taken need not be manipulation of wildlife populations; but at very high population densities, "passive" management techniques (e.g., exclusion and traffic manipulation) may be insufficient to resolve public concerns. Alternatives typically considered include some form of public hunting, sharpshooting, capture and relocation or slaughter, or other actions that are lethal, cruel, or both. In comparison to those alternatives, immunocontraception appears to be a fairly gentle population manipulation.

Isn't immunocontraception unnatural? Many sport hunters feel that they fill the ecological niche vacated by the natural predators that have been eliminated from the landscape and that hunting is therefore a natural activity. (Some take this further,

asserting that humans are hunters by nature and that hunting fulfills some biological imperative.) To this role they contrast immunocontraception, which they dub "unnatural" and "playing God."

A strong case can be made that sport hunting is not natural. The use of all-terrain vehicles, laser sights, GPS units, and other twenty-first-century gadgets and gizmos is not natural, nor are the pervasive population, behavioral, even genetic effects of American sport hunting: the focus on trophy animals, the likely disruption of normal social organization, the distortion of normal population age and sex structures. Sport hunter (or predator) populations are not regulated by game (or prey) populations, as they would be in nature. Although the population, behavioral, and genetic effects of immunocontraception are not yet fully known, they are unlikely ever to achieve the profound and unnatural impacts of sport hunting.

Is it right to kill pigs (to make PZP) to save deer and horses? No. PZP is produced from the ovaries of pigs purchased from slaughterhouses. If we believed that more pigs were dying because we were making PZP, we would stop. More than 100 million pigs are killed in slaughterhouses each year, and we cannot believe that PZP research has any impact on that total. Nevertheless, this consideration adds urgency to the search for a synthetic form of the vaccine, especially if a form of ZP should ever prove applicable to companion animals. In that case, the commercial production of millions of doses per year might actually affect the market for dead pigs, and extraction of PZP from pigs on that scale would be ethically unacceptable to us.

Would it ever be appropriate to use oral contraceptives or transmissible contraceptives on free-ranging wildlife? Oral contraceptives for wildlife, packaged in attractive baits, would certainly make vaccine delivery easier and cheaper. Consequently, they would broaden the range of potential applications. This could be good or bad. We would consider it desirable if contraceptives could replace noxious lethal controls with minimal behavioral and ecological effects. Like poison baits and pesticides, however, oral contraceptives offer many opportunities for abuse. Rather than the careful and limited application that dart delivery forces on our current use of immunocontraceptives, oral contraceptives could be scattered incautiously and indiscriminately, leading to unpredictable biological effects on a large scale. These risks are amplified if the immunocontraceptives are not species specific.

The subject of transmissible contraceptives is even more complex. In his 1985 novel *Galapagos*, Kurt Vonnegut describes a world in which the human population is driven nearly to extinction by a virus that sweeps across the planet rendering its human hosts infertile (except for a small group isolated on the Galapagos Islands, where the plot then unfolds). This is the deepest fear engendered by the concept of transmissible contraceptives—that once released, such an agent could not be controlled and its unanticipated effects could be catastrophic for the target species, for nontarget species, and even for our own species. We believe that there would be absolutely no support in the United States for release of such an agent: no wildlife overabundance problem with which we are presently coping could justify even considering assuming that level of risk.

In Australia, where much of the research on transmissible immunocontraceptives is being conducted, a different story line is unfolding. The introduction and phenomenal prosperity of European rabbits, red foxes, domestic cats, and house mice has devastated dozens of native marsupial species in a true ecological catastrophe. Australia's response has been to kill these once-welcomed invaders by the millions with poison, traps, guns, blasting, gas, disease, and every other cruel, destructive device imaginable. That animal welfare catastrophe, in conjunction with the ecological catastrophe, has led animal protection groups in Australia to support (with

conditions) the ongoing research into transmissible immunocontraceptives (Oojges 1997). But because the risks of releasing such agents would extend beyond Australia, a clash between Australians and the rest of the world might be anticipated, even among animal protectionists.

Conclusion

In spite of the frustrations and obstacles—personal, political, and bureaucratic—we remain optimistic about the future of wildlife contraception. It may be that we are simply optimistic people, but our optimism draws support from our experience. One of us (JFK) has been working on wildlife fertility control for almost thirty years and the other (ATR), for just under a decade; we have seen progress. Operationally, we've progressed in thirty years from capture, field surgery, and implantation with gobs of physiologically and environmentally suspect steroids to darting animals in the field at a distance of twenty-five to fifty yards with one-fifth of a teaspoon of biodegradable vaccine. In the public's eyes, wildlife contraception has gone from a joke to a pretty darned good idea, "if you can make it work." Even in the deer meetings we've survived (Kirkpatrick and Turner 1997; Rutberg 1997), after all the shouting, blustering, posturing, and accusing is over, there's usually someone who takes us aside and says, "You know, these animals really are a problem, but it's not right to kill them, so if you could find another way to control them it would make people really, really, happy."

For the animals—the old mares on Assateague, the old does on Fire Island, and the rest—and for those people in the back of the room, we should all be working to find that other way.

Notes

[1]These attitudes still linger, and many of these species, such as gray wolves and grizzly bears, still confront them in their path to recovery.
[2]Dart delivery systems have changed dramatically in the past twenty-five years and have improved significantly the ability to treat free-

roaming animals at greater ranges; thus, dart-delivered drugs were not an early priority for scientists looking into this field.

Literature Cited

Al-Kafawi, A.A., M.L. Hopwood, M.H. Pineda, and L.C. Faulkner. 1974. Immunization of dogs against human chorionic gonadotropin. *American Journal of Veterinary Research* 35: 261–64.

Allen, S.H. 1982. Bait consumption and diethylstilbestrol influence on North Dakota red fox reproductive performance. *Wildlife Society Bulletin* 10: 370–74.

Balser, D.C. 1964. Management of predator populations with antifertility agents. *Journal of Wildlife Management* 28: 352–58.

Barber, M.R., and R.A. Fayrer-Hosken. 2000. Evaluation of somatic and reproductive immunotoxic effects of the porcine zona pellucida vaccination. *Journal of Experimental Zoology* 286: 641–46.

Barfnect, C.F., and H.C. Peng. 1968. Antifertility factors from plants. I. Preliminary extraction and screening. *Journal of Pharmaceutical Sciences* 57: 1607–08.

Becker, S.E., and L.S. Katz. 1997. Gonadatropin-releasing hormone (GnRH) analogs or active immunization against GnRH to control fertility in wildlife. Pp. 11–19 in *Contraception in wildlife management*, ed. T. J. Kreeger. USDA/APHIS Technical Bulletin No. 1853.

Bell, R.L., and T.J. Peterle. 1975. Hormone implants control reproduction in white–tailed deer. *Wildlife Society Bulletin* 3: 152–56.

Bell, M., C. A. Daley, S. L. Berry, and T. E. Adams. 1997. Pregnancy status and feedlot performance of beef heifers actively immunized against gonadatropin-releasing hormone. *Journal of Animal Science* 75: 1185–89.

Berger, P.J., E.H. Sanders, P.D. Gardner, and N.C. Negus. 1977. Phenolic plant compounds functioning as reproductive inhibitors in *Microtus montanus*. *Science* 195: 575–77.

Bickle, C.A., J.F. Kirkpatrick, and J.W. Turner Jr. 1991. Contraception in striped skunks with Norplant® implants. *Wildlife Society Bulletin* 19: 334–38.

Bradley, M.P., L.A. Hinds, and P.H. Bird. 1997. A bait-delivered immunocontraceptive for the European red fox *(Vulpes vulpes)* by the year 2002? *Reproduction, Fertility, and Development* 9: 111–16.

Brown, R.G., W.D. Bowen, J.D. Eddington, W.C. Kimmins, M. Mezei, J.L. Parsons, and B. Pohajdak. 1997a. Temporal trends in antibody production in captive grey, harp, and hooded seals to a single administration immunocontraception vaccine. *Journal of Reproductive Immunology* 35: 53–64.

————. 1997b. Evidence for a long-lasting single administration contraceptive vaccine in wild grey seals. *Journal of Reproductive Immunology* 35: 43–51.

Brown, R.G., W.C. Kimmins, M. Mezei, J.L. Parsons, B. Pohajdak, and W.D. Bowen. 1996. Birth control for grey seals. *Nature* 379: 30–31.

Brushman, H.H., S.B. Linhart, D.S. Balser, and L.W. Sparks. 1967. A technique for producing anti-fertility tallow baits for predator mammals. *Journal of Wildlife Management* 32: 183–84.

Buergelt, C.P., and G.V. Kollias. 1987. Proliferative disease in the uterus of two large Felidae receiving melengestrol acetate. Proceedings of the Thirty-fourth Annual Meeting of the Amerocan College of Veterinary Pathology, Monterey, California (Abstract).

Burke, T. 1977. Fertility control in the cat. *Veterinary Clinics of North America* 7: 699–703.

Chan, S.W.Y., D.E. Wildt, and P.K. Chakraborty. 1981. Development and characterization of feline ovarian antiserum. *American Journal of Veterinary Research* 42: 1322–27.

Cheatum, E.L. 1967. Rabies control by inhibition of fox reproduction. Doctoral dissertation. Ithaca, N.Y.: Cornell University.

Conover, M.R. 1997. Monetary and intangible valuation of deer in the United States. *Wildlife Society Bulletin* 25: 298–305.

Cranston, L. 1945. The effect of Lithospermum ruderale on the estrus cycle in mice. *Journal of Pharmacology and Experimental Therapeutics* 83: 130–42.

Daels, P.F., and J.P. Hughes. 1995. Fertility control using intrauterine devices: An alternative for population control in horses. *Theriogenology* 44: 629–39.

Davis, D.E. 1959. Effects of triethylenemelamine on testes of starlings. *Anatomical Record* 134: 549–53.

————. 1962. Gross effects of triethylenemelamine on gonads of starlings. *Anatomical Record* 142: 353–57.

DeNicola, A.J., D.J. Kessler, and R.K. Swihart. 1997. Remotely delivered prostaglandin F2 implants terminate pregnancy in white-tailed deer. *Wildlife Society Bulletin* 23: 527–31.

Dunlap, T.R. 1988. *Saving America's wildlife.* Princeton, N.J.: Princeton University Press.

Elder, W.H. 1964. Chemical inhibition of ovulation in the pigeon. *Journal of Wildlife Management* 28: 556–75.

Eldridge, J.H., R.M. Gilly, J.K. Stass, Z. Moldozeanu, J.K. Muelbroek, and T.R. Tice. 1989. Biodegradable microcapsules: vaccine delivery systems for oral immunization. *Current Topics in Microbiology and Immunology* 146: 59–66.

Farnsworth, N.R., and D.P. Waller. 1982. Current status of plant products reported to inhibit sperm. *Research Frontiers in Fertility Regulation* 2: 1–16.

Fayrer-Hosken, R.A., P. Brooks, H. Bertschinger, J.F. Kirkpatrick, J.W. Turner Jr., and I.K.M. Liu. 1997. Management of African elephant populations by immunocontraception. *Wildlife Society Bulletin* 25: 18–21.

Florman, P.M., and H.M. Wassarman. 1985. Olinked oligosaccharides of mouse egg ZP3 account for its sperm receptor activity. *Cell* 41: 313–24.

Fraser, H.M., J. Sandow, H. Seidel, and W. von Rechenberg. 1987. An implant of a gonadotropin releasing hormone agonist (buserelin) which suppresses ovarian function in the macaque for 3–5 months. *ACTA Endocrinologica* 115: 521–27.

Freese, C.H. 1998. *Wild species as commodities.* Washington, D.C.: Island Press.

Frisbie, K., and J.F. Kirkpatrick. 1998. Immunocontraception of captive species. A new approach to population management. *Animal Keeper's Forum* 25: 346–50.

Garrett, M.G., and W.L. Franklin. 1983. Diethylstilbestrol as a temporary chemosterilent to control black-tailed prairie dog populations. *Journal of Range Management* 36: 753–56.

Gilbert, F.F., and D.G. Dodds. 1992. *The philosophy and practice of wildlife management.* 2nd edition. Malabar, Fla.: Krieger Publishing Co.

Gill, R.B., and M.W. Miller. 1997. Thunder in the distance: The emerging policy debate over wildlife contraception. Pp. 257–67 in *Contraception in wildlife management,* ed. T.J. Kreeger. USDA/APHIS Technical Bulletin No. 1853.

Greer, K.R., W.H. Hawkins, and J.E. Catlin. 1968. Experimental studies of controlled reproduction in elk (Wapiti). *Journal of Wildlife Management* 32: 368–76.

Hagood, S. 1997. State wildlife management: The pervasive influence of hunters, hunting, culture, and money. Washington, D.C.: The Humane Society of the United States.

Hanly, W.C., B.T. Bennett, and J.E. Artwohl. 1997. Overview of adjuvants. Pp. 1–8 in *Information resources for adjuvants and antibody production: Comparisons and alternative technologies 1990-97,* ed. C.P. Smith. Beltsville, Md.: National Agricultural Library, USDA/ARS.

Harder, J.D. 1971. The application of an antifertility agent in the control of a white-tailed deer population. Doctoral dissertation. Ann Arbor: University of Michigan.

Harder, J.D., and T.J. Peterle. 1974. Effects of diethylstilbestrol on reproductive performance in white-tailed deer. *Journal of Wildlife Management* 38: 183–96.

Harris, J.D., D.W. Hibler, G.K. Fontenot, K.T. Hsu, E.C. Yurewicz, and A.G. Sacco. 1994. [sic] Cloning and characterization of zona pellucida genes and cDNA's from a variety of mammalian species: The ZPA, ZPB, and ZPC gene families. *DNA Sequencing* 4: 361–93.

Hassan, T., R.E. Falvo, V. Chandrashekar, B.D. Schanbacher, and C. Awoniyi. 1985. Active immunization against LHRH in the male mongrel dog. *Biology of Reproduction* 32 (Suppl. 1): 222.

Heilmann, T.J., R.A. Garrott, L.L. Cadwell, and B.L. Tiller. 1998. Behavioral response of free-ranging elk treated with an immunocontraceptive vaccine. *Journal of Wildlife Management* 62: 243–50.

Herr, J., D.J. Conklin, and R.S. McGee. 1989. Purification of low molecular weight forms of seminal vesicle antigen by immunoaffinity chromatography on bound monoclonal antibody MHS 5. *Journal of Reproductive Immunology* 16: 99–113.

Holland, M.K., J. Andrews, H. Clarke, C. Walton, and L.A. Hinds. 1997. Selection of antigens for use in a virus vectored immunocontraceptive vaccine: PH-20 as a case study. *Reproduction, Fertility, and Development* 9: 117–24.

Howard, W.E., and R.E. Marsh. 1969. Mestranol as a reproductive inhibitor in rats and voles. *Journal of Wildlife Management* 33: 403–08.

Inaba, T., T. Umehara, J. Mori, R. Torii, H. Tamada, and T. Sawada. 1996. Reversible suppression of pituitary-testicular function by a sustained release formulation of a GnRH agonist (leuprolide acetate) in dogs. *Theriogenology* 46: 671–77.

Kaul, R., A. Afzalpurkar, and S.K. Gupta. 1996. Strategies for designing an immunocontraceptive vaccine based on zona pellucida synthetic peptides and recombinant antigen. *Journal of Reproduction and Fertility* (Supplements 50): 127–34.

Kellert, S.R. 1985. Historical trends in perceptions and uses of animals in twentieth-century America. *Environmental Review* 9: 19–33.

———. 1993. Public view of deer management. Pp. 8–11 in *Deer management in an urbanizing region,* ed. R.L. Donald. Washington, D.C.: The Humane Society of the United States.

Kirkpatrick, J.F. 1995. Management of wild horses by fertility control: The Assateague experience. National Park Service (NPS) Scientific Monograph. Denver, Co.: NPS.

Kirkpatrick, J.F., and J.W. Turner Jr. 1985. Chemical fertility control and wildlife management. *Bioscience* 35: 485–91.

———. 1987. Chemical fertility control and the management of the Assateague feral ponies. Final Report, NPS contract CA 1600-30005, Assateague Island National Seashore, Berlin, MD.

———. 1991. Reversible fertility control in nondomestic animals. *Journal of Zoo and Wildlife Medicine* 22: 392–408.

———. 1995. Urban deer fertility control: Scientific, social, and political issues. *Northeast Wildlife* 52: 103–16.

———. 1997. Urban deer contraception: The seven stages of grief. *Wildlife Society Bulletin* 25: 515–19.

Kirkpatrick, J.F., J.W. Turner Jr., and A. Perkins. 1982. Reversible fertility control in feral horses. *Journal of Equine Veterinary Science* 2: 114–18.

Kirkpatrick, J.F., I.K.M. Liu, and J.W. Turner Jr. 1990. Remotely-delivered immunocontraception in feral horses. *Wildlife Society Bulletin* 18: 326–30.

Kirkpatrick, J.F., I.K.M. Liu, J.W. Turner Jr., and M. Bernoco. 1991. Antigen recognition in feral mares previously immunized with porcine zonae pellucidae. *Journal of Reproduction and Fertility* (Supplements 44): 321–25.

Kirkpatrick, J.F., I.K.M. Liu, J.W. Turner Jr., R. Naugle, and R. Keiper. 1992. Long-term effects of porcine zonae pellucidae immunocontraception on ovarian function of feral horses (Equus caballus). *Journal of Reproduction and Fertility* 94: 437–44.

Kirkpatrick, J.F., R.Naugle, I.K.M. Liu, J.W. Turner Jr. 1995a. Effects of seven consecutive years of porcine zona pellucida contraception on ovarian function in feral mares. *Biology of Reproduction* Monograph Series 1: Equine Reproduction VI. 411–18.

Kirkpatrick, J.F., W. Zimmermann, L. Kolter, I.K.M. Liu, and J.W. Turner Jr. 1995b. Immunocontraception of captive exotic species. I. Przewalski's horse (Equus przewalski) and banteng (Bos javanicus). *Zoo Biology* 14: 403–16.

Kirkpatrick, J.F., I.K.M. Liu, and J.W. Turner Jr. 1996a. Contraception of wild and feral equids. Pp. 161–69 in *Contraception in wildlife management,* ed. T.J. Kreeger. Washington, D.C.: U.S. Government Printing Office.

Kirkpatrick, J.F., P.P. Calle, P. Kalk, I.K.M. Liu, and J.W. Turner Jr. 1996b. Immunocontraception of captive exotic species. II. Formosa sika deer (Cervus nippon taiouanus), Axis deer (Cervus axis), Himalayan tahr (Hemitragus jemlahicus), Roosevelt elk (Cervus elaphus roosevelti), Reeve's Muntjac (Muntiacus reevesi), and sambar deer (Cervus unicolor). *Journal of Zoo and Wildlife Medicine* 27: 482–95.

Kirkpatrick, J.F., J.W. Turner Jr., I.K.M. Liu, R.A. Fayrer-Hosken, and A. Rutberg. 1997. Case studies in wildlife immunocontraception: Wild and feral equids and white-tailed deer. *Reproduction, Fertility, and Development* 9: 105–10.

Kreeger, T.J. 1997. Overview of delivery systems for the administration of contraceptives to wildlife. Pp. 29–48 in *Contraception in wildlife management,* ed. T.J. Kreeger. USDA/APHIS Technical Bulletin No. 1853.

Ladd, A., G. Prabhu, Y.Y. Tsong, T. Probst, W. Chung, and R.B. Thau. 1988. Active immunization against gonadotropin-releasing hormone combined with androgen supplementation is a promising antifertility vaccine for males. *American Journal of Reproductive Immunology and Microbiology* 17: 121–27.

Ladd, A., Y.Y. Tsong, G. Prabhu, and R. Thau. 1989. Effects of long-term immunization against LHRH and androgen treatment on gonadal function. *Journal of Reproductive Immunology* 15: 85–101.

Ladd, A., Y.Y. Tsong, A.M. Walfield, and R. Thau. 1994. Development of an antifertility vaccine for pets based on active immunization against luteinizing hormone-releasing hormone. *Biology of Reproduction* 51: 1076–83.

Levenson, T. 1984. Family planning for deer. *Discover* Dec.:35–38.

Linhart, S.B., and R.K. Enders. 1964. Some effects of diethylstilbestrol in captive red foxes. *Journal of Wildlife Management* 28: 358–63.

Linhart, S.B., A. Kappeler, and L.A. Windberg. 1997. A review of baits and bait delivery systems for free-ranging carnivores and ungulates. Pp. 69–132 in *Contraception in wildlife management*, ed. T.J. Kreeger. USDA/APHIS Technical Bulletin No. 1853.

Liu, I.K.M., M. Bernoco, and M. Feldman. 1989. Contraception in mares heteroimmunized with porcine zona pellucida. *Journal of Reproduction and Fertility* 85: 19–29.

McShea, W.J., S.L. Monfort, S. Hakim, J. Kirkpatrick, I. Liu, J.W. Turner Jr., L. Chassy, and L. Munson. 1997. The effect of immunocontraception on the behavior and reproduction of white-tailed deer. *Journal of Wildlife Management* 61: 560–69.

Mahi-Brown, C.A., R. Yanagimachi, J.C. Hoffman, and T.T.F. Huang. 1985. Fertility control in the bitch by active immunization with porcine zonae pellucidae: Use of different adjuvants and patterns of estradiol and progesterone levels in estrous cycles. *Biology of Reproduction* 32: 761–72.

Mahi-Brown, C.A., R. Yanagimachi, M.L. Nelson, H. Yanagimachi, and N. Palumbo. 1988. Ovarian histopathology of bitches immunized with porcine zonae pellucidae. *American Journal of Reproductive Immunology and Microbiology* 18: 94–103.

Marion, J.R. 1987. Whose wildlife is it anyway? How New York's fish and game statutes, regulations, and policies endanger the environment and have disenfranchised the majority of the electorate. *Pace Environmental Law Review* 4: 401–38.

Marsh, R.E., and W.E. Howard. 1969. Evaluation of mestranol as a reproductive inhibitor of Norway rats in garbage dumps. *Journal of Wildlife Management* 33: 133–38.

Matschke, G.H. 1980. Efficacy of steroid implants in preventing pregnancy in white-tailed deer. *Journal of Wildlife Management* 44: 756–58.

Messmer, T.A., S.M. George, and L. Cornicelli. 1997. Legal considerations regarding lethal and non-lethal approaches to managing urban deer. *Wildlife Society Bulletin* 25: 424–29.

Miller, L.A. 1997. Delivery of immunocontraceptive vaccines for wildlife management. Pp. 49–58 in *Contraception in wildlife management*, ed. T.J. Kreeger. USDA/APHIS Technical Bulletin No. 1853.

Miller, L.A., B.E. Johns, and G.J. Killian. 1999. Long-term effects of PZP immunization on reproduction in white-tailed deer. *Vaccine* 18: 568–74.

Oleyar, C.M., and B.S. McGinnes. 1974. Field evaluation of diethylstilbestrol for suppressing reproduction in foxes. *Journal of Wildlife Management* 38: 101–06.

Oojges, G. 1997. Ethical aspects and dilemmas of fertility control of unwanted wildlife: An animal welfarist's perspective. *Reproduction, Fertility, and Development* 9: 163–67.

Patterson, M., M.R. Wilson, Z.A. Jennings, M. van Duin, and R.J. Aitken. 1999. Design and evaluation of a ZP3 peptide vaccine in a homologous primate model. *Molecular Human Reproduction* 5: 342–52.

Pincus, G., J. Rock, C.R. Garcia, E. Riceway, M. Paniangua, and I. Rodriguez. 1958. Fertility control with oral medication. *American Journal of Obstetrics and Gynecology* 75: 1333–46.

Plotka, E.D., and D.N. Vevea. 1990. Serum ethinylestradiol (EE2) concentrations in feral mares following hormonal contraception with homogenous silastic implants. *Biology of Reproduction* 42 (Supplement 1): 43.

Porton, I., C. Asa, and A. Baker. 1990. Survey results on the use of birth control methods in primates and carnivores in North American Zoos. Pp. 489–97 in Proceedings of the An. A.A.Z.P.A. Conference.

Prasad, S.V., S.M. Skinner, C. Carino, N. Wang, J. Cartwright, and B.S. Dunbar. 2000. Structure and function of the proteins of the mammalian zona pellucida. *Cells Tissues Organs* 166: 148–64.

Primakoff, P., W. Lathrop, L. Woolman, A. Cowan, and D. Myles. 1988. Fully effective contraception in the male and female guinea pigs immunized with the sperm protein PH20. *Nature* 335: 543–46.

Robinson, A.J., R. Jackson, P. Kerr, J. Merchant, I. Parer, and R. Pech. 1997. Progress towards using the recombinant myoma virus as a vector for fertility control in rabbits. *Reproduction, Fertility, and Development* 9: 77–84.

Rudolph, B.A., W.F. Porter, and H.B. Underwood. 2000. Evaluating immunocontraception for managing suburban white-tailed deer in Irondequoit, New York. *Journal of Wildlife Management* 64: 463–73.

Rutberg, A.T. 1997. Lessons from the urban deer battlefront: A plea for tolerance. *Wildlife Society Bulletin* 25: 520–23.

Seal, U.S., R. Barton, L. Mather, K. Oberding, E.D. Plotka, and C.W. Gray. 1976. Hormonal contraception in captive female lions (Panthera leo). *Journal of Zoo Animal Medicine* 7: 1–17.

Shao, Z.Q. 1987. Tripterygium wilfordii, a Chinese herb effective in male fertility regulation. *Contraception* 36: 335–45.

Singer, P. 1997. Neither human nor natural: Ethics and feral animals. *Reproduction, Fertility, and Development* 9:157–62.

Skinner, S.M., S.V. Prasad, T.M. Ndolo, and B.S. Dunbar. 1996. Zona pellucida antigens: Targets for contraceptive vaccines. *American Journal of Reproductive Immunology* 35: 163–74.

Sokolowski, J.H., and F. Van Ravenswaay. 1976. Effects of melengestrol acetate on reproduction in the beagle bitch. *American Journal of Veterinary Research* 37: 943–45.

Storm, G.L., and G.C. Sanderson. 1969. Effect of medroxyprogesterone acetate (Provera) on productivity in captive foxes. *Journal of Mammology.* 50: 147–49.

—————————. 1970. Effect of mestranol and diethystilbestrol on captive voles. *Journal of Wildlife Management* 34: 835–43.

Thiele, L.A. 1999. A field study of immunocontraception in a white-tailed deer population. Master's thesis. College Park: University of Maryland.

Tober, J.A. 1981. *Who owns the wildlife?* The political economy of conservation in nineteenth-century America. Westport, Conn.: Greenwood Press.

Turner, J.W., Jr., I.K.M. Liu, and J.F. Kirkpatrick. 1992. Remotely delivered immunocontraception in captive white-tailed deer. *Journal of Wildlife Management* 56: 154–57.

Turner, J.W. Jr., I.K.M. Liu, A.T. Rutberg, and J.F. Kirkpatrick. 1996a. Immunocontraception limits foal production in free-roaming feral horses in Nevada. *Journal of Wildlife Management* 61: 873–80.

Turner, J.W. Jr. , I.K.M. Liu, and J.F. Kirkpatrick. 1996b. Remotely delivered immunocontraception in free-roaming feral burros. *Journal of Reproduction and Fertility* 107: 31–35.

Turner, J.W. Jr., J.F. Kirkpatrick, and I.K.M. Liu. 1996c. Effectiveness, reversibility, and serum antibody titers associated with immunocontraception in captive white-tailed deer. *Journal of Wildlife Management* 60: 45–51.

Turner, J.W. Jr., J.F. Kirkpatrick, and I.K.M. Liu. 1997. Immunocontraception in white-tailed deer. Pp. 147–59 in *Contraception in wildlife management,* ed. T.J. Kreeger. USDA/APHIS Technical Bulletin No. 1853.

Turner, J.W. Jr., I.K.M. Liu, D.R. Flanagan Jr., A.T. Rutberg, and J.F. Kirkpatrick. 2001. Immunocontraception in feral horses: One inoculation provides one year of infertility. *Journal of Wildlife Management,* in press.

U.S. Fish and Wildlife Service. 1997. 1996 National survey of fishing, hunting, and wildlife-associated recreation.

Vickery, B.H., G.I. McRae, W. Briones, A. Worden, R. Seidenberg, B.D. Shanbacher, and R. Falvo. 1984. Effects of an LHRH agonist analog upon sexual function in male dogs. *Journal of Andrology* 5: 28–42.

Vickery, B.H., G.I. McRae, B.B. Roberts, A.C. Worden, and A. Bajka. 1985. Estrus suppression in the bitch with potent LHRH agonist analogs: A new approach for pet contraception. *Biology of Reproduction* 32 (Supplement 1): 106.

Walter, W.D. 2000. A field test of the PZP immunocontraceptive vaccine on a population of white-tailed deer *(Odocoileus virginianus)* in suburban Connecticut. Master's thesis. Durham: University of New Hampshire.

Weeratna, R.D., M.J. McCluskie, Y. Xu, and H.L. Davis. 2000. CpG DNA induces stronger immune responses with less toxicity than other adjuvants. *Vaccine* 18: 1755–62.

Wildt, D.E., and S.W.J. Seager. 1977. Reproduction control in dogs. *Veterinary Clinics of North America* 7: 775–87.

Wofford, J.E., and W.H. Elder. 1967. Field trials of the chemosterilant SC12937 in feral pigeon control. *Journal of Wildlife Management* 507–14.

About the Contributors

Martha Armstrong is vice president of companion animals and equine protection for The HSUS.

Frank R. Ascione is a professor of psychology at Utah State University. His research currently focuses on developmental aspects of cruelty to animals. He is co-editor of *Cruelty to Animals and Interpersonal Violence,* published by Purdue University Press.

Richard Farinato is director of captive wildlife protection for The HSUS.

David Fraser is professor of animal welfare at the University of British Columbia, cross-appointed by the Faculty of Agricultural Sciences and the Centre for Applied Ethics. After studying ethology in Canada and the United Kingdom, he has pursued a career in the behavior, management, and welfare of animals. His research has ranged from designing better pig pens to reducing traffic accidents involving moose.

Alan M. Goldberg is director of the Johns Hopkins Center for Alternatives to Animal Testing and professor of toxicology in the Department of Environmental Health Sciences at the Johns Hopkins School of Public Health. He is a leading authority on the creation, development, and validation of alternative toxicological methods, and he currently serves as president of the In Vitro Specialty Section of the Society of Toxicology. He received The HSUS's first Russell and Burch Award in 1991 and the Society of Toxicology's Ambassador of Toxicology Award in 1998.

Temple Grandin is a designer of livestock-handling facilities and an assistant professor of animal science at Colorado State University. Dr. Grandin received her doctorate in animal science from the University of Illinois in 1989. She is the author of more than three hundred articles on animal handling, animal welfare, and animal facility design.

John Hadidian is the director of Urban Wildlife Programs for The HSUS and co-editor of *Wild Neighbors: The Humane Approach to Living with Wildlife.* Prior to joining The HSUS, he was a wildlife biologist with the National Park Service's National Capital Region.

David Hancocks is director of Victoria's Open Range Zoo in Werribee, Australia.

Harold Herzog is professor of psychology at Western Carolina University. His research includes studies of the cockfighting subculture of the Appalachian mountains, attitudes toward animal experimentation, moral dilemmas of veterinary students, and gender differences in human/animal interactions.

Christyna Hunter is editorial assistant of *Animal Sheltering* magazine, a publication of The HSUS.

Paul G. Irwin is president and chief executive officer of The HSUS, the nation's largest animal protection organization. An officer of The HSUS since 1976, he also serves as president of the World Society for the Protection of Animals. He is an ordained United Methodist minister and the author of *Losing Paradise,* published by Square One Publishers.

Leesteffy Jenkins has a private law practice specializing in international, environmental, and animal protection issues and trade and environment. She has been a legal advisor to The HSUS for nine years.

Jay F. Kirkpatrick is director of science and conservation biology and curator of animals at ZooMontana in Billings; an associate professor at the School of Veterinary Medicine, University of California, Davis; and an HSUS consultant. Since receiving his doctorate in reproductive physiology from Cornell University in 1971, Dr. Kirkpatrick has carried out research on wildlife fertility control and non-capture methods for studying reproduction in free-roaming wildlife. He is the author of *Into the Wind: North America's Wild Horses* and is probably best known for his contraceptive research on wild horses on Assateague Island, Maryland, for the study of reproduction in the bison of Yellowstone National Park, and for his work in African elephant contraception at Kruger National Park, Republic of South Africa.

Daniel E. Kossow has a master's degree in animals and public policy from Tufts University School of Veterinary Medicine.

Randall Lockwood is vice president for research and educational outreach of The HSUS and scientific director of Humane Society Press. He is co-editor of *Cruelty to Animals and Interpersonal Violence,* published by Purdue University Press.

Franklin M. Loew is president of Becker College in Worcester, Massachusetts, and former dean of the Tufts University School of Veterinary Medicine. He is the author of *Vet in the Saddle: John L. Poett, First Veterinary Surgeon of the North West Mounted Police* and coauthor of *The Animal Research Controversy: Protest, Process and Public Policy.*

Joy Mench is a professor of animal science and the director of the Center for Animal Welfare in the College of Agricultural and Environmental Sciences at the University of California, Davis. She received her doctorate in ethology from the University of Sussex in 1983 and now conducts research on the behavior and welfare of farm, com-

panion, and laboratory animals. She also teaches courses on animal welfare and the ethics of animal use.

Suzanne Millman is director of scientific programs in the Farm Animals and Sustainable Agriculture section of The HSUS. She received her doctorate in applied ethology from the Department of Animal and Poultry Science, University of Guelph, Canada, and has taught courses for veterinary and animal science students.

Andrew N. Rowan is senior vice president for research, education, and international issues at The HSUS. He is author of *Of Mice, Models, and Men* and coauthor of *The Animal Research Controversy: Protest, Process, and Public Policy.*

Allen Rutberg is senior scientist for wildlife and habitat protection for The HSUS and a clinical assistant professor at the Tufts University School of Veterinary Medicine. He received his doctorate in zoology in 1984 from the University of Washington, Seattle. Before coming to The HSUS in 1991, Dr. Rutberg held positions on the biology faculties of Vassar College and Shippensburg and Pennsylvania State Universities. At The HSUS Dr. Rutberg has overseen the wildlife immuno-contraception effort as well as HSUS programs on urban deer, wild horses, and national park management.

Sydney Smith is manager of business development and corporate relations for The HSUS. She is an urban wildlife specialist working toward her master's degree in community planning at the University of Maryland.

Martin Stephens is vice president for animal research issues at The HSUS, where he directs The HSUS's work on the use of animals in research, testing, and education. He received his doctorate in biology from the University of Chicago in 1984 and joined the staff of The HSUS in 1985.

Robert Stumberg is a professor of law at Georgetown University Law Center, where he is also clinical director of the Harrison Institute for Public Law.

Susan Tomasello is administrative assistant in the Companion Animals section of The HSUS.

Bernard Unti is a doctoral candidate at American University. His dissertation focuses on the history of organized animal protection in the United States before World War II.

Index

Page numbers appearing in italics refer to tables or figures

A

A-B-C model of societal attitudes, 57
Acute Toxic Class Method, 129
African Elephant Conservation Act, 156
Alachua County (FL) Animal Services, 76–77
Alternatives approach
    1960s: dormancy of the movement, 123–124
    1970s: animal protectionists heed the call, 125, 127
    1980s: government and industry begin to heed the call, 126–129
    1990s: alternatives begin to be validated and accepted for regulatory use, 129–131
    alternatives chronology: 1876–1959, *122*
    alternatives chronology: 1960–1969, *123*
    alternatives chronology: 1970–1979, *125*
    alternatives chronology: 1980–1989, *126–127*
    alternatives chronology: 1990–1999, *130–131*
    in the context of the animal research issue, 121–122
    Draize Test of eye irritancy, 128
    five principles for animal experimentation, 122
    genetic engineering and, 133
    hostility to, 133
    launching of the approach, 122–123
    origin of the concept, 116, 121
Alternatives Research and Development Foundation, 117
"Alternatives to Animal Use in Research, Testing and Education" report from the U.S. Office of Technology Assessment, 129
American Association of Zoological Parks and Aquariums (AZA), 142
American Dog Owners Association, 75
American Horse Council Foundation, survey of horse ownership, 9
American Humane Association (AHA)
    focus of, 22
    hypoxia euthanization, 79
    period between World War I and World War II, 21
    pound seizure issue, 73
    Standards of Excellence program, 73
    training for animal control officers, 72
American Kennel Club
    growth of registration, 78
    proof of spaying/neutering for pet-quality puppies, 83
    puppy mills and, 83
    registration of dogs and puppies, 75
American Meat Institute Guidelines for slaughter, 106
American Medical Association, animal rights poll, 58
American Pet Products Manufacturers Association (APPMA), survey of pet acquisition, 75
American Psychological Association (APA), animal research polls, 62, 63
American Society for the Prevention of Cruelty to Animals (ASPCA), 7, 71, 176
American Society of Landscape Architects, 170
American Veterinary Medical Association (AVMA)
    early-age sterilization, 83
    spay/neuter clinics, 74
    survey of pet acquisition, 75
Angell, George Thorndike, 71
Animal abuse
    balanced and restorative justice (BARJ) model, 48
    conduct disorder and, 42–45
    corporal punishment and, 43–44, 45–46
    definition of cruelty to animals, 39
    developmental aspects of, 40–41, 49
    domestic violence and, 46, 49–50
    ecology of, 48–49
    elder abuse and neglect and, 46–47
    future needs and directions, 48–51
    legislative and law enforcement responses, 47–48
    link to other forms of human violence, 16
    number of state felony cruelty laws, 47
    pet abuse, 2–3
    philosophical statements about, 39–40
    prevalence of, 41–42

prevention and intervention/treatment, 50

societal concerns and responses to, 47, 50

Animal Attitudes Scale, 56

Animal control laws, 7

Animal control officer certification, 72

Animal Damage Control program, 30

Animal Industry Foundation (AIF), survey on animal agriculture and animal rights, 65–66

Animal Legal Defense Fund, 7

Animal Liberation, 24, 97–98, 116

Animal Protection Institute, 7

Animal-related Trauma Inventory, 44

Animal research

animal-related hierarchy of concern, *61*

animal user categories, 112

approximate number of animals used in research in Great Britain, 1900–1998, *9, 112*

changes in oversight, 116–117

cosmetics testing, 63

decline in use, 113–114

genetically engineered animals, 114, 118

NIH extramural grants and research animal use in the United States, *113*

NIH mouse and total animal use, *114*

numbers of cats, dogs, primates, hamsters, guinea pigs, and rabbits reported used annually, *113*

opinions of APA members and psychology students concerning use of animals for specific research procedures, *62*

pain and distress issue, 117–118

personal-care and household product testing, 112

polls and surveys on, 55, 58–63

postwar demand for laboratory animals, 22

pound seizure and, 116

primates, 118

public attitude toward, 9–10, 115–116

public behavior regarding cosmetics testing, *63*

public opinion on the humane treatment of laboratory animals, *62*

public opinion on using nonhuman animals in painful and injurious research, *59*

public opinion on using nonhuman animals in research, *59*

public opinion on using nonhuman animals in research for specific illnesses, *60*

public opinion (United Kingdom) on using monkeys and mice in specific research, *61*

ratio between commercial, noncommercial, and government laboratories, 112

reducing animal numbers, 118–119

significant milestones in animal research oversight in the United States, *117*

Three Rs alternatives approach, 116, 121–134

three time periods, 111

trends in Great Britain and Europe, 112–113

trends in the United States to 1990, 113–114

trends in the United States since 1990, 114

Animal Research Survey, 56

Animal Rights International, 24

Animal Welfare Act (AWA), 7, 13, 22, 23, 25, 30, 83, 129

Animal Welfare Institute (AWI), 7, 22, 116, 123

Animal Welfare League of Arlington (VA), 73

Animals in Research booklet, 124

Anti-cruelty laws, 7, 13. See *also specific laws*

Anti-vivisection organizations, 7

Antibiotics as feed additives for farm animals, 92

Antisocial personality disorder, animal abuse and, 41

Article XX of the GATT

arbitrary or unjustifiable discrimination or a disguised restriction, 159–160

burden of proof requirement, 156

conserving exhaustible resources exemptions, 158

exceptions clause, 151

measures necessary to protect human, animal, or plant life or health, 152–153

protecting life or health exemption, 157–158

public morals protection, 158–159

scope of exceptions, 156–160

Assateague Island wild horses, fertility control measures, 187, 192

Associated Press, animal rights poll, 57

Audubon Society, 144

Australia, fertility control measures, 194

Austria, labeling of premium meat products, 96

Avanzino, Richard, 79–80

Avon Products, 128

B

Balanced and restorative justice (BARJ) model, 48

Bald Eagle Protection Act, 7

BARJ model for animal abuse, 48

Baylor University Center for Community Research and Development, poll of public attitudes toward animal research, 10

Beavers, in urban areas, 172

Beef cattle

factory farms and, 12

housing, 91–92

Bem Sex Role Inventory, 56

Bergh, Henry, 71, 176

Biocentrism concept, 177

Biophilia, 139, 178

Biotic right concept, 177

Bishop, Arthur Gary, 43

Breeding moratoriums, 78–79

Bristol-Myers Squibb, 128

Burch, Rex, 116, 121, 122–124, 132, 133–134

Bureau of Land Management, wild horse contraception, 192

C

California
  animal cruelty laws, 47
  pound seizure laws, 73
Canada
  insurance for pig producers, 96
  supply management system for egg production, 96
Canada geese, in urban areas, 173, 177
Caravan Opinion Research Corporation, animal rights
  survey, 66
Cargill, 11
Carson, Rachel, 177
Carter, Mike, 43
Catholic Society for Animal Welfare, 7, 22
Cats. *See also* Companion animals; Dogs
  acquisition methods, 75
  clothing and novelties made of dog and cat fur, 3, 7
  feral cats, 81
  increase in number of owned animals, 2
  increase in population, 78–79
  licensing of, 73–74, 81
  pet abuse concerns, 2–3
  rates of sterilization, 2
  shelter euthanasia of owned animals, 2
  status of, 81–82
Cattle. *See also* Beef cattle; Dairy cattle
  captive bolt stunning, 101
  changes in the U.S. inventories of livestock,
    1950–1998, *10*
  elimination of face branding, 29
  genetic selection, 96
CD. *See* Conduct disorder
Centers for Disease Control and Prevention, salmonella
  increase in young children, 84
Charlotte/Mecklenburg County (NC), cat licensing
  program, 73–74, 81
Chickens. *See* Poultry
Child Behavior Checklist (CBCL), 42–43
Children, animal abuse and, 40–45
China
  changes in animal agriculture, 93
  demand for pork, 11
  pork production, 88
Chorio-Allantoic Membrane (CAM) test, 128
Circus animals, 29
Cockfighting, 7, 47
Colgate-Palmolive, funding of research into the
  Chorio-Allantoic Membrane (CAM) test, 128
College students, as subjects for opinion polls and
  surveys, 56–57
Colorado
  animal cruelty laws, 47
  regulation of large-scale hog confinement facilities, 97
Columbus-Franklin County Metro Parks (OH), deer
  fertility measures, 192
Community studies of animal protection campaigns, 27–28

Companion animals
  advances in medical care, 74
  behavior assistance programs, 82
  early-age sterilization, 82–83
  euthanasia issues, 79–80
  feminization of the veterinary profession and, 78
  fertility control measures, 190–191
  nonsurgical alternatives to sterilization, 78
  pet overpopulation issues, 75
  property status, 80–81
  relations between humane and veterinary
    communities and, 74–75
  sterilization programs and breeding moratoriums,
    78–79
ConAgra, 11
Conduct disorder, animal abuse and, 42–45
Conetics Corporation, 128
Consumer Price Index, increase in retail costs to
  consumers for meat and poultry products, 92
Continental Grain, 11
Convention on International Trade in Endangered and
  Threatened Species of Wild Fauna and Flora (CITES),
  154, 191
Conway, William, 143, 144
Corporal punishment, animal abuse and, 43–44, 45–46
Cosmetic, Toiletry, and Fragrance Association, 128
Cosmetics testing, 63, 128, 129–131
Council for Livestock Protection, 103
Council of Environmental Ministers of the European
  Communities, 127
Council of Europe, Resolution 621 on alternatives to
  animal research, 125
Cruelty to animals. *See* Animal abuse

D

Dairy cattle
  factory farms and, 12
  housing, 91
  pasture systems, 95
  robotic milking systems, 95
  transport to slaughter problems, 107
Dassmann, Raymond, 178
Davey, Stuart, role of wildlife in an urban environment,
  166
Deer
  deer-vehicle collisions, 169, 187
  fertility control, 185, 187, 190, 192–193
  in urban areas, 173
Delinquent animal abuse, 45
Design with Nature, 169
Developing countries
  animal product consumption, 88
  changes in animal agriculture, 93
  farm animals used for draft power, 87
Diet. *See* Vegetarianism
Diet for a New America, 97–98

Dogs. *See also* Cats; Companion animals
   breed-specific ban legislation, 76
   clothing and novelties made of dog and cat fur, 3, 7
   dangerous or vicious dogs, 76
   increase in number of owned animals, *2*
   leash and licensing laws, 71
   pet abuse concerns, 2–3
   puppy mills, 3, 75, 83
   rates of sterilization, *2*
   shelter euthanasia of owned animals, *2*
   stray dogs, 71, 72
Dolphins, 14–15
Domestic violence, animal abuse and, 46, 49–50
Doris Day Animal League (DDAL), Spay Day USA
   program, 78
Dorney, Robert, framework for environmental
   management, 176
Dowdichuk, Alexa, 82
Draize Test of eye irritancy, 128
Duffield, David, 80
Dumb Friends League (DFL), 77

E

Earthwatch, 144
Elder abuse and neglect, animal abuse and, 46–47
Elephants, fertility control measures, 187–188
Endangered Species Act, 7, 23
Ethology, 23
European Centre for the Validation of Alternative
   Methods (ECVAM), 129
European Community
   cages for laying hens, 95
   directives on farm animal welfare standards, 97
   standard definitions for alternative production
      methods, 96
European Union
   alternative testing approaches, 129
   ban on marketing of cosmetics tested on animals, 131
   hormone ban, 160
   Leghold Regulation and Cosmetics Testing Directive,
      156
   regulation banning the sale of pelts caught by using
      steel-jaw leghold traps, 150, 155
Exotic animals, in shelters and pounds, 84
Exploratory/curiousity-based animal abuse, 45
Extinction rates, 13
Eyberg Child Behavior Inventory, 42

F

Factory farms, 10–13, 31
Farm animals. *See also specific animals*
   animal byproducts, 87
   animal numbers and distribution, 87–88
   animal welfare issues, 93–94
   antibiotics as feed additives, 92
   aquaculture and mariculture growth, 87
   changes in the U.S. inventories of chickens, 1950-
      1998, *10*
   changes in the U.S. inventories of livestock, 1950-
      1998, *10*
   changes in worldwide inventory of chickens kept for
      all purposes 1961–1999, *88*
   changes in worldwide inventory of common farm
      animals kept for all purposes 1961–1999, *88*
   concrete flooring and, 93
   confinement housing, 88, 93, 95
   cultural factors and technology and, 94–95
   debate over animal agriculture, 97–98
   economic incentives and policies, 96
   factory farms and, 10–13
   genetic selection, 92, 94, 95–96
   growth hormones, 92
   housing and handling methods, 88–92
   increase in consumption of, 87–88
   issues in the next ten years, 31
   legal protection of, 96–97
   legislative protection, 13
   marketing changes and economic pressures and, 94
   per capita consumption of red meat, poultry, and fish
      in the United States, 1970–1998, *89*
   polls and surveys on, 65–66
   pork industry changes, 11
   price competition and, 94–95
   productivity enhancing methods, 92
   protection measures, 95–97
   public opinion on farm animal treatment, *65*
   public opinion on the humane treatment of specific
      farm animals, *65*
   regional concentration of animal production, 11–12
   replacement of traditional family-owned farms by
      large corporations, 92–93
   use of electronics to solve animal management
      problems, 95
Federal and state legislation, 7–8
Federation of American Societies of Experimental
   Biology, 118
Fertility control, 16. *See also* Immunocontraception
   abortifacients, 190
   African elephants, 187–188
   barrier methods, 185
   for companion animals, 190–191
   cultural, technical, and political obstacles, 191–192
   ethics issues, 193–194
   genetically engineered or synthetic ZP vaccines, 189
   immunocontraception, 185–186
   marking darts, oral delivery, and transmissible vectors,
      189–190
   from mortality control to fertility control, 183–184
   nonhormonal compounds, 184
   nonsteroidal hormones, 185
   one-inoculation vaccines, 188–189
   PZP, adjuvants, and the immune system, 189
   regulatory and practical issues, 192–193

steroid hormones, 184–185

white-tailed and black-tailed deer, 187

wild horses, 186–187

zoo animals, 187

Fire Island National Seashore (NY), fertility control of animals, 187, 192

Fire setting, animal abuse and, 44–45

First Strike initiative, 17

Fish and Wildlife Conservation Act, 173

Fitter, Richard S.R., 166

Fixed Dose Procedure, 129

Florida, pound seizure laws, 73

Food Marketing Institute, survey of attitudes toward ethical treatment of animals, 57

Foreman, Richard, phases of ecological landscape planning and design, 170

Foster, Todd, 80

Foundation for Biomedical Research, 119

Fox farms, 5

FRAME (Fund for the Replacement of Animals in Medical Experiments), 124

ATLA Abstracts, 125

challenges to the routine use of animals in toxicity testing, 128

Freedom Foods program in the United Kingdom, 96

French, Richard, 111

Freund's Complete Adjuvant (FCA), 189

Friends of Animals, 7, 22, 78

Friends of the Earth, 144

Fund for Animals, 7, 22, 29, 176

Fur industry

cruelty-free fur use in the fashion industry, 29

farmed foxes, 5

fur ranching, 5

mink facilities, 5

polls and surveys on attitudes toward wearing fur, 63–64

public opinion on wearing fur, *4, 64*

survival of, 30

U.S. caged-fur statistics, 6

U.S. caged mink facilities, 5

U.S. fur apparel imports, 5

U.S. retail fur sales, *4*

wild-caught fur, 5

Fur Seal Act, 7

Future strategies

developing new approaches to interactions with wildlife, 18

developing partners and alliances, 17

developing programs to enhance human-animal bonds, 18

eliminating animal terms of verbal abuse, 18

working with academe, 17–18

G

Gallup Organization, 56

animal research poll, 63

diet choice survey, 66–67

public attitudes toward animal research poll, 9–10

sport hunting poll, 64

GATT. See General Agreement on Tariffs and Trade

General Agreement on Tariffs and Trade

Article XX, 151, 152–153, 155–160

Beef Hormone case, 160

Belgian Family Allowances decision, 150

comparative advantage theory, 150–151

exceptions clause, 151

framework for balancing trade and noneconomic interests, 151–152

multilateral environmental agreements, 153–155, 160

"National Treatment" clause, 152

national treatment on internal taxation and regulations, 155–156

original framework of, 151

Preamble to the Agreement Establishing the WTO, 151

Preamble to the Agreement on the Application of Sanitary and Phytosanitary Measures, 151

Reformulated Gasoline decision, 153, 159

Sanitary and Phytosanitary Measures Agreement (SPS Agreement), 151, 160

Shrimp-Turtle AB decision, 153, 159

Technical Barriers to Trade (TBT) Agreement, 151

Tuna-Dolphin cases, 155–156

General Social Survey (GSS), 56–57, 64

Genetic selection of farm animals, 92, 94, 95–96, 108

Genetically engineered animals, 114, 118, 133

Germany

Center for the Documentation and Evaluation of Alternative Methods to Animal Experiments, 127–128

Goats, housing of, 91–92

Gottman, Jean, 166

Gray squirrels, in urban areas, 173, 175

Great Britain. *See* United Kingdom

Green consumerism, 29

Greenpeace, 7, 144

Growth hormones, 92

Guam, water buffalo fertility control measures, 188, 192

Gwatkin, B.L., 185

H

Hall, Marshall, 122

Harp seals, 14

Harris, Stephen, urban fox population of Bristol, England, 167

Hawaiian Humane Society (HHS), 82

Health Research Extension Act, 128

Hediger, Heini, 139–140

High Pressure Liquid Chromatography (HPLC) techniques, 131
High Seas Driftnet Enforcement Act, 156
Hoffman-La Roche, animal use, 113, 132
Hogs. *See* Pigs
Horse Protection Act, 7
Horses
    fertility control, 185, 186–187, 192
    horse-racing industry, 8–9
    horse rescue organizations and/or equine sanctuaries, 9
    number of horses and participants by industry, 1999, 8
    Premarin® production, 9
    television series and, 8
    wild horse as symbol of American freedom, 8
Human Society of Washington County (MD), 77
Humane Slaughter Act, 7, 13, 22, 23, 101, 102, 156
Humane Society of the United States (HSUS)
    Animal Control Academy, 72
    animal research focus, 116
    Animals in Research booklet, 124
    Be A P.A.L.—Prevent A Litter month, 78
    behavior problem focus groups, 77, 82, 83
    breeding moratoriums, 79
    committee of experts on alternatives, 125
    deer immunocontraception, 187
    elimination of pain and distress in laboratory animals initiative, 118
    focus of, 22
    formation of, 22
    guidelines for regulating dangerous dogs, 76
    hypoxia euthanization opposition, 79
    immunocontraception study funding, 192
    membership expansion during the 1980s and 1990s, 67
    mission, 1
    National ProPets, 73
    Pets for Life program, 77, 82
    process of problem evaluation and response for urban wildlife control, 175
    professionalism of staff members, 25
    programs on wildlife issues, 176
    statewide public referenda to curb animal use and abuse, 29
    training for mental-health providers in recognizing cruelty to animals, 48
    urban wildlife poll, 175, 176–177
    wild horse contraception study funding, 192
Humane Transport of Equines to Slaughter Act, 7
Hume, Major Charles, 122, 124, 133–134
Hunting. *See* Sport hunting

I

ICCVAM Authorization Act, 131
ICR Survey Research Group, 56

Iguanas, increased incidence of salmonella in children and, 84
Immunocontraception, 16, 18, 185–186
Improvements in the state of animals
    animals as research subjects, 9–10
    decline in sport hunting, 3–4
    decline in trapping and fur sales, 4–6
    dogs and cats, 2–3
    horses, 8–9
    increase in federal and state legislation, 7–8
In Vitro International, 128
Ingersoll, Ernest, 166
Institute for Laboratory Animal Resources (ILAR), surveys of animal use, 113, 114
Institutional Animal Care and Use Committees (IACUCs), 116, 133
Intensive Population Management of zoos, 142
Interagency Coordinating Committee on the Validation of Alternative Methods (ICCVAM), 129
International Agreement on the Conservation of Polar Bears, 15
International Committee for Laboratory Animal Science, survey of animal use, 113
International Convention for the Abolition of Import and Export Prohibitions and Restrictions, 151
International Fund for Animal Welfare, 7
International Society for Animal Rights, 7, 22
International Trade Organization, 151
Internet, horse rescue organizations and/or equine sanctuaries, 9
Interview for Antisocial Behavior (IAB), 43
ITO. *See* International Trade Organization

J

Japan, whaling practices, 14
Jasper, James, 27
Johns Hopkins University, Center for Alternatives to Animal Testing (CAAT), 128
Johnson, Velma B. "Wild Horse Annie," 8
Jones, Grant, 141
Journal of the American Medical Association, editorial criticizing FRAME, 124
Journal of Wildlife Management, urban wildlife articles, 167

K

Kant, Immanuel, 39–40
Kellert, Stephen, American attitude toward wildlife poll, 58, 67, 172
Kieran, John, 166
Kleiman, Devra, 143
Kruger National Park, fertility control of elephants, 188

L

Laboratory Animal Welfare Act, 7, 55, 116
Laboratory animals. *See* Animal research

Lacey Act, 7
The Lancet, comments on the alternatives approach, 123
Land O'Lakes, diet choice survey, 67
Landscape immersion, 141–142
Lane-Petter, William, 122
Lawson Tait Trust, 124
League of Nations, Economic Committee, 152, 157
Leigh Brown Trust, 122
Leopold, Aldo, concept of a land ethic, 177
Lieberman, Dr. Leo, 82
Littlewood Committee, 124, 131
Local Lymph Node Assay, 129
Lord Dowding Fund, 124
Lorenz, Konrad, 23
Los Angeles Times, animal rights poll, 57–58
Louis Harris and Associates, 56
    wildlife organization membership poll, 67
Louisiana, spay/neuter clinics, 74
Lyme disease, 187

M

Maddie's Fund, 80
Maple, Terry, 138, 140
March for the Animals, 30, 58
Marine Mammal Protection Act, 7, 14, 15, 23, 156
Marine mammals, 14–15. *See also specific mammals*
Massachusetts Society for the Prevention of Cruelty to
  Animals (MSPCA), 7, 71
    pound seizure laws, 72
    programs on wildlife issues, 176
    training for executives and law enforcement officials,
      72
McHarg, Ian, 169
Medawar, Sir Peter, 122, 124, 131
Medical Research Council, Laboratory Animals Bureau,
  123
Megalopolis, 166
Mental Research Institute (MRI), 48
"Metaphysical Principles of the Doctrine of Virtue,"
  39–40
Mice, genetically engineered for animal research,
  114–115, 118, 133
Michigan, spay/neuter clinics, 74
Migratory Bird Treaty Act, 7, 169
Mink ranches, 5
Mobilization for Animals, 30
Morris, Desmond, 141
Morris County Parks (NJ), deer fertility measures, 192
Mrazek, Rep. Bob, 73
Multilateral environmental agreements (MEAs),
  153–155, 160

N

The Naked Ape, 141
National Academy of Sciences (NAS), meeting on
  alternatives, 127

National Cancer Institute, laboratory animal use, 114,
  132–133
National Consumer's League, animal research poll, 63
National Council on Pet Population Study and Policy
  (NCPPSP), 3, 75
    behavior issues study, 82
    homeless pet study, 79
    pet relinquishment study, 77
National Institute for Urban Wildlife, 167
National Institute of Environmental Health Sciences
  (NIEHS), criteria for the validation and regulatory
  acceptance of alternative testing, 129
National Institute of Standards and Technology (NIST),
  fertility control of deer population, 187, 192
National Institutes of Health (NIH)
    alternatives program, 128
    decline in in-house use of mice, 133
    growth in budget, 111
    increase in funding of extramural research, 113
    NIH mouse and total animal use, *114*
National Opinion Research Center
    animal research poll, 58
    diet choice survey, 66
    sport hunting poll, 64
National Park Service
    fertility control of wild horses, 186–187, 192
    urban wildlife research facility, 167
National ProPets, 73
National Restaurant Association, diet choice survey, 67
National Science Board (NSB)
survey of public attitudes toward animal research, 60,
  115
National Shooting Sports Foundation, sport hunting
  survey, 55–56, 64
National Society for Medical Research (NSMR), 72
    animal research poll, 60, 115
National Testing Corporation, 128
National Toxicology Program Interagency Center for the
  Evaluation of Alternative Toxicological Methods
  (NICEATM), 129
The Natural History of London, 166
A Natural History of New York City, 166
Nature Conservancy, 144
Nature magazine, comments on the alternatives
  approach, 123
Netherlands
    Animal Protection Law, 125
    animal research trends, 113
    number of monkeys used in the production and
      testing of polio vaccine, 131
Neutersol nonsurgical sterilization method, 78
Nevada, wild horse fertility control measures, 187, 188
New Mexico, animal cruelty laws, 47–48
New Scientist, animal research poll, 62–63
New York City Center for Animal Care and Control, 77
    early-age sterilization, 83
NIH Revitalization Act, 129, 131

No-kill shelters, 77, 79–80
Nonhormonal compounds for fertility control, 184
Nonsteroidal hormones for fertility control, 185
Norplant®, 185
Norway
    animal housing system regulations, 97
    price subsidies for small farms, 96
    whaling practices, 14

O

Omaha Zoo's Lied Jungle, 138
Organization for Economic Cooperation and
  Development (OECD)
    as authority on the acceptance of alternative methods,
      129
    guidelines for toxicity testing, 128

P

Palm Beach County (FL) Animal Regulation, 76
Parents magazine
    animal research survey, 55, 63
    sport hunting poll, 64
Pathognomonic animal abuse, 45
People for the Ethical Treatment of Animals, 7, 25, 176
Personal-care and household product testing, 112
Pet Protection Act, 73
Pets for Life National Training Center, 77
Pets for Life program, 82
Pigs
    annual per capita consumption of pork for selected
      regions, 12
    carbon dioxide or electrical stunning, 101
    changes in farm size in the U.S. hog industry,
      1993-1998, 93
    changes in farm size of the U.S. pork industry, 11
    changes in hog inventory in selected countries,
      1961-1999, 89
    changes in the U.S. inventories of livestock,
      1950-1998, 10
    confinement housing, 90–91, 94
    decline in number of pig farms, 93
    factory farms and, 12
    genetic selection, 94, 96, 108
    gestation crates, 90–91
    outdoor farrowing systems, 95
    pork industry changes, 11
    state moratoriums blocking the development of
      factory hog farms, 13
    tail docking, 94
    top five U.S. pork-producing companies during 1999,
      11
    top five U.S. states for pork production, 1998, 12
Pittman-Roberston Act, 167, 173, 183
Pneu-dart®, 189
Point Reyes National Seashore (CA), Tule elk fertility
  control measures, 188, 192

Polar bears, 15
Porcine zona pellucida (PZP) vaccine, 16, 78, 185–188, 191
Postwar animal protection
    1950–1975: revival, 21–23, 31
    1975–1990: mobilization and transformation, 23–26,
      31–32
    1990–2000: consolidation, 28–30, 32
    animal cognition and, 23
    animal-interest caucuses, 25
    campaign against dissection, 30
    circus animals, 29
    civil disobedience, 24
    community studies, 27–28
    current context, 30–31
    demographics of animal advocates, 26–27
    ethology and, 23
    female participation in humane work, 26
    grassroots activism, 24, 32
    "green consumerism" and, 29
    media visibility and, 25
    milestones chart, 34–37
    next ten years, 31
    period between World War I and World War II, 21
    "pound seizure" and, 21–22
    professionalism within the ranks of animal protection
      groups, 25
    Reagan administration and, 25–26, 83
    relations with the veterinary community, 31
    resource mobilization theory, 27
    rise of ecology and, 22–23
    scholarly analysis, 26
    science of animal welfare, 25
    social-psychological identity formation of activists, 27
    understanding animal protection, 26–28
Poultry
    beak trimming and toe trimming, 90, 94
    changes in the U.S. inventories of chickens,
      1950–1998, 10
    changes in worldwide inventory of chickens kept for
      all purposes 1961–1999, 88
    confinement housing, 89, 93–94
    factory farms and, 12
    forced molting, 89–90
    free-range systems, 95
    genetic selection, 94, 95–96
    increase in consumption of, 87–88
    large corporation control of the market, 92–93
    percentage of laying hens on farms of different sizes
      in the United States during 1987, and in Canada
      during 1986, 97
Pound seizure, 21–22, 72–73, 116
Premarin®production, 9
Primates, used for animal research, 118
Princeton Survey Research Associates, animal rights
  survey, 57
Princeton Survey Research Associates, sport hunting
  poll, 56

The Principles of Humane Experimental Technique, 122–124, 134
Procter and Gamble, 128
Progressive Animal Welfare Society, 176
Puppy mills, 3, 75, 83

R

Rabb, George, 143
Rainforest exhibits in zoos, 138
Ralls, Katherine, 142
Reader's Digest
    animal research survey, 55
    no-kill shelters investigation, 80
Red fox, as an urban animal, 167
Regan, Tom, 24
Research animals. *See* Animal research
Research Modernization Act, 29, 127
Resource mobilization theory, 27
Revlon, 128
Robbins, John, 97–98
Rockefeller University, laboratory for toxicological
    assay development, 128
Rolling Stone magazine, animal rights poll, 58
Russell, William, 116, 121, 122–124, 132, 133–134

S

Safari Club International, immunocontraception
    opposition, 191
Saint Augustine, 39
Salt Lake Area Juvenile Firesetter/Arson Control and
    Prevention Program, 44–45
San Diego Zoo, 142
San Francisco Animal Care and Control, 79–80
San Francisco Society for the Prevention of Cruelty to
    Animals, no-kill policy, 77
San Mateo County (CA), feral cat pact, 81–82
Sanitary and Phytosanitary Measures Agreement (SPS
    Agreement), 151, 160
Santa Cruz (CA) SPCA, 73
Scale of Attitudes toward the Treatment of Animals,
    56
Schmidt, Oscar, 102
Seals, 14
Seattle (WA) Woodland Park Zoo, 140, 141
Secretariat, 8
Seiling, Eleanor, 124, 127
Self magazine, animal research poll, 63
Senior citizens. *See* Elder abuse and neglect
Sheep
    changes in the U.S. inventories of livestock,
        1950–1998, *10*
    housing, 91–92
Shelters and pounds
    British roots, 71
    differential licensing, 73
    early-age sterilization, 82–83

euthanasia issues, 79–80
exotic animals, 84
new facilities, 73–74
no-kill shelters, 77, 79–80
post World War II, 72
pound seizure, 21–22, 72–73
present state of, 76–77
property status controversy, 81
shelter euthanasia of owned animals, *2*
shelters at the turn of the twentieth century, 71–72
spay/neuter clinics, 73, 74–75
sterilization at adoption, 83
urban wildlife issues, 174
Silent Spring, 177
Silver Spring monkeys case, 25
Singer, Peter, 24, 97–98, 116, 128
Skinner, B.F., 141
Slaughter techniques
    ASPCA pen, 102, 103
    behavioral principles, 103–104
    captive bolt stunning, 101
    carbon dioxide stunning, 101
    center track (double rail) conveyor restrainer for
        handling cattle, *104*
    current problems, 105–106
    curved chute system, 103
    dairy and pig industry problems, 107–108
    employee psychology and, 106
    good stockmanship and, 108
    head-holding device mounted on the end of the
        conveyor restrainer for kosher slaughter, *105*
    improvements in vocalization percentages in a cow
        slaughter plant when practices and equipment were
        changed, *107*
    kosher slaughter in the 1970s, 102–103
    kosher slaughter in the 1990s, 104–105
    side view of the ASPCA pen for holding cattle in an
        upright position during ritual slaughter, *102*
    stress of slaughter, 105
    upright restraint devices, 102–103
    V conveyor system, 102, 103
    vocalization scoring, 106–107
Smithfields Foods, 11
Smoot-Hawley Tariff Act, 7
Social-psychological identity formation of activists, 27
Societal attitudes and animals
    A-B-C model, 57
    advantages and disadvantages of professional polling
        organizations, 56
    attitudes toward animal research, 59–63
    consistency of attitudes, 57–58
    diet choice, 66–67
    farm animal issues, 65–66
    hunting, 64–65
    membership of U.S. adults in animal and
        environmental organizations; 1976, *67*
    "non-attitudes," 58

public opinion on eating specific food items, 66
public support of animal protection philosophy, 67
sample surveyed, 56–57
wearing fur, 63–64
wording of questions, 55–56
Society for Animal Protective Legislation, 7
Spaying and neutering. *See also* Fertility control
early-age sterilization, 82–83
legislation for, 7
spay/neuter clinics, 73, 74–75
SpayVac™, 189
Species Survival Plan (SSP), 142–143
Spencer Foods, 102
Spira, Henry, 24, 104, 128
Sport hunting
fertility control and, 183
hunters, by census division: 1955–1985, *3*
"outdoors woman" workshops, 4
paid hunting license holders, 1989–1999, *3*
polls and surveys on, 55–56, 64–65
programs aimed at retaining current hunters and recruiting new ones, 3–4
Star Tribune/WCCO-TV survey on animal rights, 65–66
Stearns, Forest, wildlife habitat paper, 166
Steroid hormones for fertility control, 184–185
Stevens, Christopher, 123
Summa Contra Gentiles, 39
Surveys. *See* Societal attitudes and animals; specific surveys and organizations
Sweden
animal housing system regulations, 97
Central Committee on Experimental Animals, 125
dairy cow protection laws, 96
Swift Fresh Meats, 101–102
Swine. *See* Pigs
Switzerland
alternatives legislation, 127
animal housing system regulations, 97

T

Technical Barriers to Trade (TBT) Agreement, 151
Tennessee Walking Horses, 9
Thirty-second North American Fish and Wildlife Conference, 166
Three Rs alternatives approach to animal research. *See* Alternatives approach
3T3 Neutral Red Uptake Phototoxicity Test, 129
Tinbergen, Niko, 23
Transepithelial Electrical Resistance Test and Episkin, 129
Transmissible contraceptives, 190, 194
Tule elk, fertility control measures, 188
Tuna industry, 14
Turkeys. *See* Poultry
Turner, James, 111
Twenty-Eight Hour Law, 7, 13

Twiss, Robert, paper on wildlife in the metropolitan environment, 166
Tyson Foods, 92–93

U

United Action for Animals, 7, 124, 127
United Kingdom
animal housing system regulations, 97
animal research poll, 60
animal research trends, 112–113
Animals (Scientific Procedures) Act, 127, 133
approximate number of animals used in research in Great Britain, 1900–1998, *9, 112*
Committee of Inquiry into the workings of the 1876 Cruelty to Animals Act, 124
decline in the number of animals used in research, 118, 132
Freedom Foods program, 96
personal-care and household product testing, 112
ratio between commercial, noncommercial, and government laboratories, 112
support for the alternatives approach, 123–124
symposium on the place of nature in cities and towns, 166
Three Rs concept, 122
use of genetically modified mice, 133
veal calf protection, 96–97
Universities, centers for animal welfare or the human-animal bond, 17–18
Universities Federation for Animal Welfare (UFAW)
handbook on the care and management of laboratory animals, 122
origin of the alternatives approach, 121, 122–123
Up and Down Method, 129
Urban wildlife, 15
aggregate-with-outliers concept, 170–171
animal welfare and protection concerns, 176–177
attitudes about control practices, 172–173
attitudes toward, 172–173
biocentrism concept, 177
biotic right concept, 177
cities as wildlife habitat, 167–168
cluster zoning and, 171
conservation subdivisions and, 171
ecological landscape planning and design and, 170
ecological perspective of urbanization, 165
ecology of, 168
edge habitat, 169
historical background, 166–167
human-wildlife interactions, 171–172
integrated pest management strategies, 175
land development and, 168–171
linking design and environment, 169
loss of habitat and habitat fragmentation, 169
management of, 173–176
nongame management, 173–174

nonlethal control approaches, 175–176
nuisance-wildlife control industry, 174
open-space management and, 170
physical characteristics of urbanization, 165
planned unit development and, 171
problem-oriented management, 174
prognosis, 178
reasons why urban wildlife should be valued and better understood, 165–166
regulatory authority and programmatic responsibility for, 175
social consequences of urbanization, 165
timing of land clearing and, 169–170
wildlife rehabilitators, 174–175
U.S. Department of Agriculture (USDA)
Animal and Plant Health Inspection Service, 83
animal vaccine regulation, 192
Annual Reports, 113–114
commercial and noncommercial animal use, 112
development of a workable definition of animal distress, 118
diet choice survey, 66
elimination of face branding of cattle, 29
Integrated Wildlife Damage Management concept, 175
keeping of large exotic cats, 84
legal challenges to research animal oversight, 117
oversight of animal use in biomedical research, 129
slaughter employee survey, 106
violations of dog and cat acquisition for sale to research laboratories, 117
U.S. Department of Defense
laboratory animal use, 114
water buffalo fertility control measures, 188
U.S. Department of Justice
firesetter/arson control program, 44–45
report linking animal abuse to other criminal activity, 45
U.S. Fish and Wildlife Service
"Man and Nature in the City" conference, 166
water buffalo fertility control measures, 188
U.S. Food and Drug Administration (FDA), animal vaccine regulation, 192
U.S. Office of Technology Assessment, "Alternatives to Animal Use in Research, Testing and Education" report, 129
Utica Veal, 103

V

Vaccine-based fertility control.
    See Immunocontraception
"Validation and Regulatory Acceptance of Toxicological Test Methods," 129
Vanity-license plate programs, 7
Veal Calf Protection Act, 29
Vegetarian Resource Group, diet choice survey, 66
Vegetarian Times, diet choice survey, 66

Vegetarianism, polls and surveys on attitudes toward, 66–67
Verbal abuse using animal terms, 18
Vermont, limit to the sale or use of chemicals that deplete the ozone layer, 153
Veterinary Record, comments on the alternatives approach, 123
Virginia, spay/neuter clinics, 74

W

Wall Street Journal, sport hunting poll, 64
Water buffalo, fertility control measures, 188, 192
Waxman, Rep. Henry, 131
Wenstrup, John, 82
Whales, 14–15
White, Caroline Earle, 71
Whittel, George, 73
Wild Animals in Captivity, 140
Wild Bird Conservation Act, 156
Wild Free-Roaming Horse and Burro Act, 7, 8, 23
Wild Neighbors, 166
Wildlife Services, 30
Willems, Don, 102
Wilson, E.O., 138, 139
Women
    battered women and animal abuse, 46, 49–50
    feminization of the veterinary profession and, 78
    as primary animal advocates, 26–27
    sport hunting and, 4, 57
Women's SPCA of Pennsylvania, 7, 71
World Congress on Alternatives and Animal Use in the Life Sciences, 129, 131, 132
World Trade Organization. See also General Agreement on Tariffs and Trade
    Biosafety Protocol, 154
    decisions that undercut measures for animals, 152–155
    dolphin protection and, 17
    establishment of, 151
    future needs, 155–160
    multilateral environmental agreements and, 154
    prohibition against government-initiated, market-based remedies, 149
    Third Ministerial in Seattle, WA, 149, 150, 161
    Trade-Related Intellectual Property Rights (TRIPS) Agreement, 154–155
    vision of, 160
    "winner take all" strategy, 150
Worsening of the state of animals
    animals raised for food, 10–13
    extinction rate, 13
Wright, Phyllis, 75, 78
WTO. *See* World Trade Organization

Z

Zoo Atlanta, gorilla habitat, 138, 140

ZooMontana, water buffalo fertility control measures, 188

Zoos

amusement-park attitude, 140
animals displayed as jewels, 138–139
biophilia, 139
breeding programs, 142–143
euthanasia as a management tool, 142–143
fertility control of animals, 187
food service at, 141
Hediger's philosophies, 139–140
improvements in, 137
Intensive Population Management, 142
landscape immersion, 141–142
the new institutions, 143–144
night cages, 137
public display areas, 137–138
rainforest exhibits, 138
species of animals represented, 138
Species Survival Plan, 142–143
standards of care, 15
using nature as the norm, 140
Wildscreen approach, 144
zoo horticulture, 142
zookeepers, 138